THE RIGHT OF COMMUNICATION TO THE PUBLIC IN EU COPYRIGHT LAW

This monograph conducts a comprehensive analysis of the EU right of communication to the public, one of the exclusive rights under EU copyright law, and provides an alternative framework for its interpretation and application. The present state of the law is unsatisfactory; there is uncertainty in the *acquis communautaire* and courts at the EU and domestic levels have struggled to apply the right. Therefore, the book identifies the problems with the existing right of communication to the public and proposes recommendations for reform.

In addition to reforming the scope of the right of communication to the public, the jurisdiction and applicable law in relation to the right are analysed and changes are recommended. Thus, the book covers both the scope and practicalities of a coherent and effective reform of the right. In light of the continuing development and accompanying tribulations with this right at the EU level, this book provides a topical and timely analysis that will be of interest to academics and practitioners working on EU copyright law.

The Right of Communication to the Public in EU Copyright Law

Justin Koo

•HART•
OXFORD • LONDON • NEW YORK • NEW DELHI • SYDNEY

HART PUBLISHING

Bloomsbury Publishing Plc

Kemp House, Chawley Park, Cumnor Hill, Oxford, OX2 9PH, UK

HART PUBLISHING, the Hart/Stag logo, BLOOMSBURY and the Diana logo are trademarks of Bloomsbury Publishing Plc

First published in Great Britain 2019

A catalogue record for this book is available from the British Library.

Library of Congress Cataloging-in-Publication data

Names: Koo, Justin, editor.

Title: The right of communication to the public in EU copyright law / Justin Koo.

Description: Oxford, UK ; Chicago, Illinois : Hart Publishing, 2019. | Based on author's thesis (doctoral – King's College London, 2016) issued under title: The proper scope of the communication to the public right in EU copyright law. | Includes bibliographical references and index.

Identifiers: LCCN 2018059515 (print) | LCCN 2018060064 (ebook) | ISBN 9781509920679 (EPub) | ISBN 9781509920655 (hardback)

Subjects: LCSH: Copyright—European Union countries. | Freedom of expression—European Union countries. | BISAC: LAW / Intellectual Property / General.

Classification: LCC KJE2655 (ebook) | LCC KJE2655 .K66 2019 (print) | DDC 346.2404/82—dc23

LC record available at https://lccn.loc.gov/2018059515

ISBN: HB: 978-1-50992-065-5
ePDF: 978-1-50992-066-2
ePub: 978-1-50992-067-9

Typeset by Compuscript Ltd, Shannon
Printed and bound in Great Britain by CPI Group (UK) Ltd, Croydon CR0 4YY

MIX
Paper from responsible sources
FSC® C013604

To find out more about our authors and books visit www.hartpublishing.co.uk. Here you will find extracts, author information, details of forthcoming events and the option to sign up for our newsletters.

PREFACE

The beginnings of this book were born in the academic year 2011/2012 when I was first introduced to the concept of communication to the public during my LLM at King's College London. A thematic copyright class delivered by Dr Makeen of SOAS (University of London) ignited a spark in my brain that developed into an ongoing copyright obsession.

The right of communication to the public under EU copyright law has become one of the most controversial and debated issues within the field. Between December 2006 and August 2018, the Court of Justice of the European Union delivered 23 decisions directly pertaining to the right. These disputes concerned acts of traditional broadcasting and retransmission by cable and satellite; acts of reception in public; and more modern incidents involving the Internet. The controversy surrounding the right has emerged due to the absence of clear definitions of what is 'communication to the public' at both the international and regional levels and moreover, rapid advancements in technology that have stretched the right to breaking point.

Consequently, the aim of this book is to explore the development and application of the communication to the public right under EU copyright law and in so doing, propose a reformed right that is coherent and effective. Particular emphasis is placed on analysing the scope and application of the right, culminating in the proposal for a reformed right that is underlined by the norms of legal certainty and proportionality. The reforms proposed in the book are comprehensive and call for a holistic reformation of the framework in which the communication to the public right is used. Thus, reforms are proposed in respect of: the scope of the right; the relationship of the communication to the public right with the other exclusive rights under EU copyright law; the method by which an act of communication to the public is located; and the determination of jurisdiction and applicable law in copyright cases.

While the approach adopted in the book is ambitious, it should be noted that the issues posed by the incoherence of the existing EU right of communication to the public are pervasive and threaten to undermine the dissemination and use of copyright works. Thus, an overhaul of the interpretation and application of the communication to the public right is warranted. In fact, at the close of writing this book, the problem continues to grow with more references for preliminary rulings being made to the Court of Justice of the European Union.

The time is indeed ripe for a comprehensive evaluation of the right of communication to the public, which is offered in this book.

ACKNOWLEDGEMENTS

This book is dedicated to my parents, Chris and Lisa, who sacrificed so much to ensure the completion of my PhD from which this book was born.

The book would not have been possible without the guidance of my doctoral supervisor, Professor Tanya Aplin, who was a brilliant role model and academic mother to me during my thesis. Thanks must also be given to my secondary supervisor, Dr Barbara Lauriat, for all her help and assistance. In addition, I thank Dr Makeen for introducing me to the life-changing topic of communication to the public.

I would also like to thank my partner, Emma, for accommodating me during the summer of 2018 when the bulk of the work on this book was done.

Finally, thank you to Hart Publishing, particularly Dr Roberta Bassi, for all the pre-production work that went into the book and most of all for publishing my work.

CONTENTS

TABLE OF CASES

European Union (CJEU)

European Union (AG Opinion)

European Court of Human Rights

Australia

Austria

Canada

Germany

Italy

Netherlands

Singapore

United Kingdom

United States

TABLE OF LEGISLATION

International Treaties and Conventions

EU Treaties

EU Secondary Legislation

Dutch Legislation

French Legislation

German Legislation

UK Legislation

Documents

International

European Union

Introduction

I. Subject-Matter

The rights of reproduction and communication to the public are the cornerstones of copyright.[1] With advances in technology the 'communication to the public' right is coming to the fore in place of the reproduction right. The communication to the public right was initially designed to address acts of terrestrial broadcasting. The scope of the right was soon expanded to cover acts of retransmission, including rebroadcasting, cable retransmission and satellite retransmission as seen under Article 11bis of the Berne Convention.[2] However, technological advancements in the twenty-first century have led to on demand content and increasingly efficient means of disseminating content, notably via the Internet. As a result, the law was updated so that on demand technologies such as the Internet would come within the scope of the communication to the public right. This was achieved via the introduction of the 'making available' aspect of Article 8 of the WIPO Copyright Treaty 1996, which has been dubbed the most significant innovation of that Treaty.[3] This trend of digital technological development has rapidly continued. While the use of the Internet may not be novel, the availability of faster Internet speeds and larger stores of bandwidth, together with more advanced computing equipment and software, have resulted in the increased digital dissemination of works. This digital sharing has been encouraged and promulgated by technological developments such as: hyperlinking, internet streaming, peer-to-peer (P2P) file sharing and cloud computing. These technologies are worth singling out because their use can engage the communication to the public right.

Despite communicative technologies rapidly developing, the development of the communication to the public right has not kept apace. The right of communication to the public under EU copyright law is in fact subject to a number of problems that have significant consequences for the way that users and intermediaries interact with copyright works. From a preliminary stand-point it is worth

[1] F Brison and S Depreeuw, 'The right of 'communication to the public' in the European Union' in P Torremans (ed), *Research Handbook on Copyright Law*, 2nd edn (Edward Elgar Publishing Ltd, 2017) 96.

[2] Berne Convention for the Protection of Literary and Artistic Works, as amended 24 July 1971: http://www.wipo.int/treaties/en/text.jsp?file_id=283698.

[3] The importance of the making available aspect has led to claims that communication to the public has replaced reproduction as the core right of copyright – G Dimita, 'The WIPO right of making available' in P Torremans (ed), *Research Handbook on Copyright Law*, 2nd edn (Edward Elgar Publishing Ltd, 2017) 136.

noting that the EU communication to the public right can be found under four different Directives.[4] The consequence of this has been inconsistent and unclear decision-making concerning the application of the right. Furthermore, the framework and scope of the right as developed by the CJEU can be criticised. Analysing the case law from *Rafael Hoteles*[5] to the most recent case, *Renckhoff*,[6] demonstrates the difficulties encountered by the CJEU in applying the communication to the public right. Moreover, the problems with the communication to the public right become particularly apparent in relation to Internet usage. When the changes in technology are combined with the maximalist protection approach employed by the CJEU, the result has been the unjustified extension of the communication to the public right beyond its intended scope, culminating in an unbalanced right and overregulation.[7] The consequence of this is a chilling effect on the development of new technologies and accompanying business models and, ultimately, the prejudicing of end users and intermediaries.

This book sets out to explore the existing right of communication to the public, analyse its problems and propose a reformed right for EU copyright law. Thus, the primary aim is to establish a reformed communication to the public right that is certain and proportionate by balancing all the competing pressures and interests that influence the scope and application of the right. To this end, the book addresses: the framework upon which EU copyright law should be constructed; the problems with the existing communication to the public right; the proposal for a reformed communication to the public right; the reconciliation of the proposed right with the existing EU copyright law framework; and the application and enforcement of that reformed communication to the public right. Reforming the communication to the public right is imperative because the scope of the existing EU right has negative implications for the way that copyright works are used and the development and operation of new communicative technologies and business models.

[4] Article 2 of Council Directive 93/83/EEC of 27 September 1993 on the coordination of certain rules concerning copyright and rights related to copyright applicable to satellite broadcasting and cable retransmission [Satellite and Cable Retransmission Directive], [1993] OJ L248/15, 6.10.1993, Article 5(d) of Directive 96/9/EC of the European Parliament and of the Council of 11 March 1996 on the legal protection of databases [Database Directive], [1996] OJ L77/20, 27.3.1996, Article 8 of Directive 2006/11/EC of the European Parliament and of the Council of 12 December 2006 on rental right and lending right and on certain rights related to copyright in the field of intellectual property [Rental and Lending Right Directive] [2006] OJ L372/12, 27.12.2006, and Article 3(1) of Directive 2001/29/EC of the European Parliament and of the Council of 22 May 2001 on the harmonisation of certain aspects of copyright and related rights in the information society [Information Society Directive], [2001] OJ L167/10, 22.6.2001.

[5] Case C-306/05 *Sociedad General de Autores y Editores de España (SGAE) v Rafael Hoteles SA* [2006] ECLI:EU:C:2006:764.

[6] Case C-161/17 *Land Nordrhein-Westfalen v Dirk Renckhoff* [2018] ECLI:EU:C:2018:634.

[7] PB Hugenholtz and M Kretschmer, 'Reconstructing Rights: Project Synthesis and Recommendations' in PB Hugenholtz (ed), *Copyright Reconstructed: Rethinking Copyright's Economic Rights in a Time of Highly Dynamic and Technological and Economic Change* (Kluwer Law International BV, 2018) 1–2.

II. Significance and Contribution

This book is significant for two main reasons. Firstly, it comprehensively addresses the development of the EU communication to the public right from its inception to the most recent case law. Secondly, and more importantly, it analyses the manner in which the EU right of communication to the public should be developed, inclusive of recommendations for the reform of the right. In the course of this book, it will be argued that all aspects of EU copyright law must balance the relevant competing pressures and interests, guided by the principles of proportionality and certainty. This approach is similar to the one put forward by Ramalho,[8] but is constructed in the context of a specific problem, namely, the development of a more coherent and effective communication to the public right in EU copyright law. Thus, one notable contribution of the book is the recommendation on how EU copyright law should be (re)developed from its conceptualisation to its legislation, application and enforcement.

More importantly, an original contribution is also made with regard to the right of communication to the public under EU copyright law, which has been subject to a number of problems concerning its scope, structure and application. This is because there are few publications that comprehensively analyse the right.[9] Of importance in this regard is Makeen's *Copyright in a Global Information Society*.[10] Makeen's book is of central importance because it was ground-breaking and continues to offer the most comprehensive analysis of the historic development of the communication to the public right in the existing literature. However, since the publication of Makeen's book in 2000,[11] there have been many developments in technology and subsequently in the case law, which require analysis. In particular, there is a gap in the existing literature pertaining to comprehensive analysis of the communication to the public right and its development through

[8] A Ramalho, *The Competence of the European Union in Copyright Lawmaking: A Normative Perspective of EU Powers for Copyright Harmonisation* (Springer International Publishing Switzerland, 2016).

[9] Most publications address specific aspects of the communication to the public right, such as: specific cases, specific technologies or specific issues with the right. For example, see: A Tsoutsanis, 'Why copyright and linking can tango' (2014) 9(6) *Journal of Intellectual Property Law & Practice* 495, E Arezzo, 'Hyperlinks and making available right in the European Union: What future for the Internet after *Svensson*?' (2014) 45(5) *International Review of Intellectual Property and Competition Law (IIC)* 524 and Association Littéraire et Artistique Internationale (ALAI), *Opinion Proposed to the Executive Committee and adopted at its meeting, 17 September 2014 on the criterion 'New Public', developed by the Court of Justice of the European Union (CJEU), put in the context of making available and communication to the public* (2014): http://www.alai.org/en/assets/files/resolutions/2014-opinion-new-public.pdf.

[10] M Makeen, *Copyright in a Global Information Society: The Scope of Copyright Protection Under International, US, UK and French Law* (Kluwer Law International, 2000).

[11] Makeen's cut-off point for his research was October 1998. Note, Makeen has subsequently published an article on the *Rafael Hoteles* case in M Makeen, 'The Controversy of Simultaneous Cable Retransmission to Hotel Rooms Under International and European Copyright Laws' (2010) 57 *Journal of the Copyright Society of the USA* 59.

the case law of the CJEU. As such, this book builds on the work of Makeen by continuing the mapping and analysis of the communication to the public right, albeit in the context of EU copyright law.

While Makeen's book comprehensively examined the development of the communication to the public right up to the year 2000, this book goes beyond, to engage with contemporary problems (some of which were presaged by Makeen) that have resulted from the growth of widespread digital culture and use, as well as the new types of technologies present. Thus, this work differs from Makeen's book because the emphasis is not on the statutory development or the history of the right, but rather the problems with the application of the EU right in the twenty-first century. Additionally, recommendations to solve the problems of the existing EU communication to the public right are made. These recommendations are subsequently applied to existing technologies that have proven problematic for courts. Therefore, this book builds on Makeen's contribution by analysing jurisprudence that has developed since 2000.[12]

Another book worthy of individual discussion is Depreeuw's *The variable scope of the exclusive economic rights in copyright*,[13] which offers an historical account of the development of the EU communication to the public right up to the *Svensson* ruling.[14] However, the book at hand goes beyond Depreeuw's work, given that it addresses the EU right of communication to the public with holistic reform and, moreover, accounts for the post-*Svensson* developments. In addition to Makeen and Depreeuw's books, there are a few articles that interrogate the development of the communication to the public right at the pre-*Svensson* stage, such as: Rizzuto,[15] Ross and Livingstone,[16] Mysoor[17] and Aplin.[18] However, the relevance of these articles is now limited because they comprise shorter analyses and have been superseded by recent case law of the CJEU. Subsequent to this, the issues surrounding the right of communication to the public have come to the forefront of EU copyright law and consequently, there is now a plethora of journal articles discussing post-*Svensson* developments with great emphasis on the notion of hyperlinking.

[12] It should be noted that several of Makeen's recommendations are followed in this book.

[13] S Depreeuw, *The variable scope of the exclusive economic rights in copyright* (Kluwer Law International, 2014).

[14] Case C-466/12 *Svensson and others v Retriever Sverige AB* [2014] ECLI:EU:C:2014:76.

[15] F Rizzuto, 'The European Union law concept of communication to the public and the protection of copyright in electronic transmissions' (2012) 18 *Computer and Telecommunications Law Review* 179.

[16] A Ross and C Livingstone, 'Communication to the public: Part 1' (2012) 23(6) *Entertainment Law Review (Ent L Rev)* 169 and A Ross and C Livingstone, 'Communication to the public: Part 2' (2012) 23(7) *Ent L Rev* 209.

[17] P Mysoor, 'Unpacking the right of communication to the public: a closer look at international and EU copyright law' [2013] *Intellectual Property Quarterly* 166.

[18] T Aplin, '"Reproduction" and "Communication to the Public" Rights in EU Copyright Law: *FAPL v QC Leisure*' (2011) 22(1) *King's Law Journal* 209.

With that in mind, this book contributes to the existing literature by comprehensively addressing all the CJEU case law pertaining to the EU communication to the public right and analysing the resultant problems, inclusive of its: conceptualisation, scope, structure, application and enforcement. The book culminates with recommendations for a more coherent and effective EU right of communication to the public.

III. Structure

The book begins with a structural analysis of EU copyright law. Chapter one analyses the framework on which EU copyright law, and consequently the right of communication to the public, should be constructed. It will be argued that the principles of proportionality and certainty should guide the development of all copyright laws from inception to application. Within this discussion, the relevant pressures and interests, including the constitutional considerations affecting EU copyright law, will be addressed and balanced. Furthermore, the challenges facing the development of the communication to the public right will be analysed. The findings established in Chapter one will inform the analysis and recommendations made in the remainder of the book.

The ensuing chapters of the book focus on developing the reformed communication to the public right and reconciling the existing EU copyright law framework to accommodate the proposed reformed right. As such, Chapter two evaluates the background and development of the existing right of communication to the public, highlighting the issues with the right that are then specifically interrogated in Chapter three. The problems include: the broad interpretation of the right attributed by the CJEU; the definition of the term 'communication'; the role of the 'making available' aspect; acts of reception in public; the 'new public' criterion and the 'for profit' and 'knowledge' criteria with their consequential overlap with secondary liability. Following the analysis of the problems with the existing right, the reformed right is expressed in Chapter four. Chapter four also examines how the reformed right of communication to the public will fit within the existing EU copyright framework. This analysis includes the relationship of the reformed right with the existing exclusive rights and the exceptions and limitations provided under the Information Society Directive (ISD); how the proposed changes should be adopted and the mechanisms for completing the harmonisation of the communication to the public right.

Chapter five then progresses the discussion to address where the act of communication to the public occurs and who is responsible for the act. In this chapter a new 'Completion theory' is proposed that aids the determination of jurisdiction and of applicable law, which are discussed in Chapters six and seven respectively. Subsequently, Chapters six and seven propose copyright-specific rules that account for the nuances of digital copyright law in the EU context and, furthermore, accommodate the ubiquity of acts of communication to the public. The final chapter then applies the proposed reformed rule on communication to the public to a number of case studies in order to demonstrate how the reformed right will operate.

IV. Scope

The primary purpose of the book is to propose a reformed communication to the public right that is coherent and effective, and moreover, compatible with the EU copyright law framework. With this in mind, it is necessary to articulate several parameters.

Firstly, it is not suggested that the structure of copyright law be overhauled. Thus, the abolition of copyright law or replacing copyright law with an access right, creative commons, compulsory licensing, 'copyleft' or other alternative concepts are not advocated. This means that the core understanding of copyright law and its exclusive rights is maintained. Furthermore, the underlying framework of EU copyright law is largely maintained with respect to the pressures and interests that it must account for.

Secondly, focus is limited to EU copyright law. Therefore, the case law of the CJEU is most significant. The laws and decisions of the various Member States and other non-EU countries are only discussed where relevant to the argument being made.

Thirdly, the recommendations made are solely concerned with primary liability. Matters that may have ordinarily come within the exclusive right of communication to the public on the basis of the existing CJEU case law, but are subsequently excluded, will be justified accordingly. Where primary liability under the reformed communication to the public right cannot be established, it will be briefly discussed whether secondary liability has a role to play.[19]

Fourthly, the implications of the proposals made for the contracting and licensing of works are not discussed.

Finally, the law that is analysed is accurate as at 9 August 2018.

[19] Note, a substantive discussion on secondary liability exceeds the scope of this book. See C Angelopoulos, *European Intermediary Liability in Copyright: A Tort-Based Analysis* (Kluwer Law International BV, 2017) and J Riordan, *The Liability of Internet Intermediaries* (Oxford University Press, 2016).

1

Justifying EU Copyright Law: Constructing a Normative Framework for the Right of Communication to the Public

I. Introduction

The development of EU copyright law has been influenced by several pressures and interests, some attributable to general EU law and others unique to copyright law. These considerations include: the international copyright treaties; the domestic *droit d'auteur* and copyright traditions of the Member States; the Directives on copyright; EU law and policy; economic perspectives on copyright; and stakeholders' interests. With this in mind, all aspects of EU copyright law must account for these considerations in order to create laws that are proportionate and certain.

These two norms – proportionality and certainty – provide the normative backbone for producing effective copyright law. Therefore, the analysis and reform of the communication to the public right in this book will be conducted using the norms of proportionality and certainty, as the measure to determine the shortcomings of the law. This chapter will argue that it is not enough to introduce the norms of proportionality and certainty only while interpreting copyright law at the litigation stage. Rather, they must also be prominently used during the conceptualisation and enactment of copyright legislation. Thus, this chapter will outline how the norms of proportionality and certainty are to be construed and the challenges associated with developing copyright law.

II. Constructing a Normative Framework for the EU Right of Communication to the Public

In order for EU copyright law to be effective, it must balance all the competing interests that are present. Additionally, the expression of the law must be clear, precise and consistent. Consequently, the norms of proportionality and certainty are essential to the production of effective law and must be applied from the conceptualisation of the law through to its interpretation and application.

With this purpose in mind, the two norms of proportionality and certainty form the normative framework against which the right of communication to the public will be analysed and reformed.

By way of a general introduction to proportionality and certainty, these two norms are derived from the general principles of EU law.[1] The general principles of EU law have been described as basic, unwritten ideas that underlie the EU system.[2] Due to the fact that the principles are unwritten and there is no widespread agreement about their genesis, justification or function, they are considered a controversial source of law.[3] For example, Sieburgh explains that principles can be used for a number of different functions such as: generating concrete rules, interpretation tools, gap-filling[4] and a means of derogation.[5] Alternatively, Morvan suggests that principles exist to set aside concrete legal provisions that have inopportune effects in a specific case.[6] What this means is that the general principles have the potential to influence the development and interpretation of EU copyright law. In particular, the general principles are often used where there is uncertainty about how a particular case should be resolved.[7]

The use of these two principles together is not new, given that they operate in tandem in a number of Directives relevant to copyright law – Information Society Directive (ISD),[8] E-Commerce Directive[9] and Enforcement Directive.[10]

[1] The general principles of EU law include: proportionality, legal certainty, equality, subsidiarity and fundamental rights.

[2] The general principles of the EU are often inferred from the decisions of the CJEU. For example, the proportionality principle was developed in Case C-11/70 *Internationale Handelgesellschaft mbH v Einfuhr- und Vorratsstelle für Getreide und Futtermittel* [1970] ECLI:EU:C:1970:114 and Case C-331/88 *The Queen v Minister for Agriculture, Fisheries and Food and Secretary of State for Health, ex parte Fedesa et al* [1990] ECLI:EU:C:1990:391.

[3] C Semmelmann, 'General Principles of EU Law: The Ghost in the Platonic Heaven in Need of Conceptual Clarificaton' (2013) 2 *Pittsburgh Papers on the European Union* 1, 4–5. Also see P Morvan, 'What's a Principle?' (2012) 20(2) *European Review of Private Law* 313, 322, who states that there is no one size fit all approach in regards to principles. Thus, different aspects of law may have different conceptions about principles and their roles.

[4] Also see T Tridimas, *The General Principles of EU Law*, 2nd edn (Oxford University Press 2006) and N de Boer, L Dijkman and S van Kampen, 'The Changing Role of Principles in the European Multilayered Legal Order: Conference Report of the Symposium "Principles and the Law"', Utrecht University, 25 May 2011' (2012) 20(2) *European Review of Private Law* 425, 428–29.

[5] C Sieburgh, 'Principles in Private Law: From Luxury to Necessity – Multi-Layered Legal Systems and the Generative Force of Principles' (2012) 20(2) *European Review of Private Law* 295, 301.

[6] Morvan (2012) 319 and de Boer, Dijkman and van Kampen (2012) 428–29.

[7] de Boer, Dijkman and van Kampen (2012) 426.

[8] Recitals 4, 21, 25, 48, 58 and Article 8(1) of Directive 2001/29/EC of the European Parliament and of the Council of 22 May 2001 on the harmonisation of certain aspects of copyright and related rights in the information society [Information Society Directive] [2001] OJ L167/10, 22.6.2001. Also see, Commission, *Copyright and Related Rights in the Information Society* (Green Paper COM(95) 382 final, 1995) 33, para 88.

[9] Recitals 7, 10, 22 and Articles 3(4)(a)(iii) and 20 of Directive 2000/31/EC of the European Parliament and of the Council of 8 June 2000 on certain legal aspects of information society services, in particular electronic commerce in the Internal Market [E-Commerce Directive], [2000] OJ 178/1, 17.7.2000.

[10] Recitals 22, 25, 31 and Articles 3(2), 8(1), 10(3), 12 and 14 of Directive 2004/48/EC of the European Parliament and of the Council of 29 April 2004 on the enforcement of intellectual property rights [Enforcement Directive], [2004] OJ L157/1, 30.4.2004.

Consequently, for the purposes of this book, the norms of proportionality and certainty will be clearly defined in terms of their meaning, usage and justification.

III. Proportionality

The concept of proportionality in EU law can be derived from two sources. Firstly, there is the concept of proportionality under the general principles of EU law, which can be argued to be one of the central elements of EU law, given that it has the status of a constitutional principle by virtue of its inclusion under Article 5 of the TEU. It has the specific meaning of: 'Union action shall not exceed what is necessary to achieve the objectives of the Treaties' (Article 5(4)).[11] This allows the CJEU to measure the intensity of actions taken by the EU.[12] Therefore, proportionality transcends the definition of what a general principle is by virtue of being accepted and explained. Alternatively, there is also a principle of proportionality arising out of the fundamental rights literature.[13] While there is some overlap with how proportionality is used in balancing competing fundamental or human rights and the general EU principle of proportionality, care should be taken to avoid conflation. This is important because proportionality can be used in both contexts in a single case.[14]

Notably, the CJEU has relied on the proportionality principle in its determination of the suitability of court orders and remedies.[15] For example, *Scarlet Extended v SABAM* demonstrates this because the court order requiring Scarlet Extended to block its Internet users from accessing particular websites was dismissed, given that it was in conflict with Article 15(1) of the E-Commerce Directive 2000, Article 3 of the Enforcement Directive 2004 and Article 16 of the Charter of Fundamental Rights.[16] The blocking order in this case was dismissed because it would have been disproportionate to require the Internet service provider (ISP) to

[11] Compare with proportionality used in human rights and fundamental rights – J Christoffersen, 'Human rights and balancing: The principle of proportionality' in C Geiger (ed), *Research Handbook on Human Rights and Intellectual Property* (Edward Elgar Publishing Ltd, 2015).

[12] N Emiliou, *The principle of proportionality in European Law – a comparative study* (Kluwer Law International, 1996) 140 and M van Eechoud et al, *Harmonizing European Copyright Law: The Challenges of Better Law Making* (Kluwer Law International, 2009) 20.

[13] For more discussion on the proportionality principle see S Halpern and P Johnson, *Harmonising Copyright Law and Dealing with Dissonance* (Edward Elgar Publishing Ltd, 2014) 131–32 and O Afori, 'Proportionality: a new mega standard in European copyright law' (2014) 45(8) *International Review of Intellectual Property and Competition Law (IIC)* 889, 895–904 and 908–11.

[14] See Case C-70/10 *Scarlet Extended SA v Société belge auteurs, compositeurs et éditeurs SCRL (SABAM)* [2011] ECLI:EU:C:2011:771 and Case C-314/12 *UPC Telekabel Wien GmbH v Constantin Film Verleih GmbH* [2014] ECLI:EU:C:2014:192.

[15] Case C-275/06 *Prodctores de Música de España (Promusicae) v Telefónica de España SAU* [2008] ECLI:EU:C:2008:54, paras 68 and 70, *Scarlet Extended v SABAM* [2011] para 48, Case C-461/10 *Bonnier Audio AB v Perfect Communication Sweden AB* [2012] ECLI:EU:C:2012:219, para 59 and *UPC Telekabel* [2014] para 46. Also see Case C-355/12 *Nintendo Co Ltd and others v PC Box Srl and another* [2014] ECLI:EU:C:2014:25, para 30.

[16] Charter of Fundamental Rights of the European Union (2012).

actively monitor all of its customers for an unlimited period of time.[17] By contrast, in *UPC Telekabel* the CJEU upheld the injunction granted by the domestic court where it permitted the defendant to choose the means to restrict its customers' access to the infringing websites.[18] Similarly, in *Bonnier Audio* the CJEU allowed an order requiring an ISP to provide the names and addresses of copyright infringers. It is also worth noting that the proportionality principle has been employed for the determination of infringement. In *Nintendo v PC Box*, the CJEU in following Advocate General (AG) Sharpston's Opinion,[19] agreed that finding infringement for the circumvention of technological protection measures (TPMs) must not negatively affect devices that have commercially significant purposes other than to circumvent TPMs.[20] As such, the Court must consider whether the finding of infringement will produce unwarranted negative externalities to the detriment of desirable activities, for example the development of technology.

Alternatively, in the case of *Promusicae* the proportionality principle was considered in relation to the transposition and interpretation of various Directives, requiring Member States to strike a fair balance between competing fundamental rights, as well as ensure consistency with the other constitutional considerations, in particular, the internal market consideration.[21] Therefore, the balance that is struck between the various competing constitutional considerations must be proportionate so as to ensure that the objectives of the Treaties are not prejudiced. These cases illustrate that the principle of proportionality has been primarily used as an external balancing tool to ensure that the transposition and interpretation of Directives, or the finding of copyright infringement and its consequences do not produce unjustified or undesirable results that are unduly unfair to defendants or compromise the achievement of the objectives set out in the Treaties.

The proportionality principle has importance for the development of EU copyright law, given that it can influence the decisions made by the CJEU.[22] However, the general EU principle of proportionality should play a greater role than it does currently. Proportionality should have a greater role to play at the legislative level where it can contribute to determining how the balance between various competing interests should be struck.[23] This will provide for a more proactive copyright

[17] *Scarlet Extended v SABAM* [2011] paras 46–53 – The CJEU held that allowing the blocking order would not respect the requirement of striking a fair balance between the competing interests. Striking a fair balance would necessarily include a proportionate outcome.

[18] *UPC Telekabel* [2014] paras 51–53 and 64.

[19] Case C-355/12 *Nintendo Co Ltd and others v PC Box Srl and another* [2013], Opinion of AG Sharpston, ECLI:EU:C:2013:581, paras 53–63.

[20] *Nintendo v PC Box* [2014] paras 30–37.

[21] *Promusicae* [2008] paras 68 and 70. Also see Case C-112/00 *Eugen Schmidberger, Internationale Transporte Planzüge v Republik Österreich* [2003] ECLI:EU:C:2003:333 for balancing the fundamental rights with the fundamental freedoms of the internal market.

[22] A Ramalho, *The Competence of the European Union in Copyright Lawmaking: A Normative Perspective of EU Powers for Copyright Harmonisation* (Springer International Publishing Switzerland, 2016) 79.

[23] De Boer, Dijkman and van Kampen (2012) 427 and Sieburgh (2012) 302.

framework, thus reducing the burden on the courts to balance conflicting or competing interests because the balancing act would have already been conducted at the legislative stage.[24]

Therefore, it is proposed that the proportionality norm should be defined and applied in terms of the following three criteria: suitability, necessity and proportionality *sensu stricto*.[25] Although these criteria come from CJEU case law, it has been noted that the CJEU does not always follow the three steps listed. Instead, the CJEU has tended to focus on the suitability and necessity criteria.[26] Notwithstanding this, Ramalho suggests the use of all three criteria for the drafting of copyright legislation because it can produce better results.[27] In this regard, Ramalho argues that the EU legislator should: 'evaluate the adequateness of the legislation harmonising copyright in relation to the objectives it wishes to attain', consider alternative options that are equally effective and less restrictive, and balance the different interests at stake.[28] While Ramalho's suggestion is acceptable, the use of the proportionality norm should not be limited to the creation of copyright legislation. It should be equally applied to the analysis, interpretation and reform of the law.

The use of the three-step approach in defining the proportionality norm is justifiable because of the comprehensive coverage provided by each of the steps in relation to what the proportionality norm proposes to do. That is, balance the scope of copyright law from its conceptualisation to its interpretation and application. The first criterion of suitability requires that the measure adopted should be appropriate to achieve the objective stated.[29] In the context of the right of communication to the public, this means that the provision must be capable of achieving its primary objective of controlling the non-material dissemination of works. This aspect of the three-step approach will be addressed in Chapter two, where the communication to the public right will be analysed in terms of what it sets out to achieve and what actually occurs.

The second criterion, necessity, presupposes that the least restrictive option will be utilised.[30] This should be interpreted to mean the option that is chosen is

[24] Rosati argues that legislators cannot leave the task of shaping EU copyright law and policy solely to the CJEU – E Rosati, 'Towards an EU-wide copyright? (Judicial) pride and (legislative) prejudice' [2013] *Intellectual Property Quarterly (IPQ)* 47, 68. According to Halpern and Johnson, the CJEU's judicial activism has overtaken the Commission's initiative for copyright harmonisation in recent years – Halpern and Johnson (2014) 102.

[25] See, *The Queen v Minister for Agriculture* [1990] para 13. Also see J Jans, 'Proportionality Revisited' (2000) 27(3) *Legal Issues of Economic Integration* 239.

[26] X Groussot, *General Principles of Community Law* (Europa Law Publishing, 2006) 152–56 – It is arguable that the reason for omitting the proportionality *sensu stricto* criterion, is to avoid any contravention of the separation of powers. This is because the policy choices of the EU legislator may come under scrutiny.

[27] Ramalho (2016) 113.

[28] ibid.

[29] ibid 112–13 and Jans (2000) 243–45.

[30] Ramalho (2016) 113 and Jans (2000) 245–47.

procedurally and/or substantively less onerous. For the purposes of the communication to the public right, this relates to the scope of the right. The right should not be so broad that it overreaches its primary objective. This has relevance for the 'Transmission' versus 'Access' approach and the relationship of the communication to the public right with the other exclusive rights. In other words, the second step deals with the scope of the communication to the public right that is addressed in Chapters two, three and four.

Lastly, the third criterion, proportionality *sensu stricto*, relates to the balancing of competing interests affecting copyright law. Unlike the current approach, whereby copyright law is subjected to a balancing exercise by courts, a more rigorous balancing exercise should begin at the stage of conceptualising and legislating for the law. In this way, the burden on the CJEU and domestic courts is reduced, as the right of communication to the public ought already to reflect a balanced approach. For this purpose it is necessary to account for the following: the constitutional considerations, the international copyright treaties; the domestic *droit d'auteur* and copyright traditions of the Member States; the Directives on copyright; EU law and policy; economic perspectives on copyright; and stakeholders' interests.

A. Constitutional Considerations of EU Law

At the forefront of the EU law considerations are the constitutional considerations that underpin the development of all EU laws. The constitutional considerations include: the internal market; fundamental rights and the general principles of EU law.

(i) Internal Market

The aim of achieving a functioning internal market is one of the central goals for the EU.[31] This ideal originated with the inception of the European Economic Community (EEC) in 1957 via the Treaty of Rome.[32] Article 2 of the Treaty of Rome set out to establish a common market between the signatories for the purpose of approximating economic activities to promote harmonious economic development and expansion.[33] However, the Treaty of Rome was not limited to the removal of trade barriers, as it included the wider implication of

[31] Ramalho (2016) 92–95.

[32] Treaty establishing the European Economic Community (1957) (Treaty of Rome).

[33] The internal market is now found under Article 26 of the Consolidated Version of the Treaty on the Functioning of the European Union (TFEU) [2012] OJ C 326/47. Also see Article 3(3) of the Consolidated Version of the Treaty on European Union (TEU) [2012] OJ C 326/13.

establishing the fundamental freedoms – free movement of goods,[34] services,[35] persons[36] and capital.[37] Notwithstanding this, Article 36 of the Treaty of Rome held that the establishment of the common market did not preclude prohibitions or restrictions on the protection of industrial or commercial property. Thus, intellectual property (IP) at the legislative level remained largely unaffected by the development of the common market in the initial stages.[38] It was not until the 1985 White Paper on 'Completing the Internal Market' that IP was directly addressed for the purpose of the internal market.[39] Here it was noted that differences in IP laws of the various Member States had a 'direct and negative impact on intra-community trade and on the ability of enterprises to treat the common market as a single environment for their economic activities'.[40] As such it was proposed that a consultative document be produced addressing the issues relating to IP, including copyright.[41]

Following this recommendation, a Green Paper on 'Copyright and the Challenge of Technology' was produced in 1988 where it was stated by the Commission that the first general concern for the Community in relation to copyright was to ensure the proper functioning of the common market.[42] In particular, it was stated that a Directive on the legal protection of computer programs was necessary for the completion of the internal market.[43] From that point onwards, the internal market has repeatedly been cited as a major reason, if not the primary reason for the harmonisation of copyright law.[44] The *travaux préparatoires* concerning EU copyright law validate this claim, in particular, the Green Papers leading to the ISD.[45]

[34] Articles 28–29 TFEU.

[35] Articles 56–62 TFEU.

[36] Articles 45–55 TFEU.

[37] Articles 63–66 TFEU.

[38] Although there was no real discussion of copyright or IP law until 1985, it is necessary to note that there was case law pertaining to the exhaustion of IP rights within the European Community (as it was then). See Case C-78/70 *Deutsche Grammophon Gesellschaft mbH v Metro-B-Grossmärkte GmbH & Co KG* [1971] ECLI:EU:1971:59, Cases C-15/74 and C-16/74 *Centrafarm BV et Adriaan de Peijper v Sterling Drug Inc and Centrafarm BV et Adriaan de Peijper v Winthrop BV* [1974] ECLI:EU:C:1974:114 and Case C-144/81 *Keurkoop BV v Nancy Kean Gifts BV* [1982] ECLI:EU:C:1982:289.

[39] Commission, *White Paper on Completing the Internal Market* (White Paper COM(85) 310 final, 14.6.1985) [White Paper on Completing the Internal Market].

[40] ibid 36, para 144.

[41] ibid 37, para 149.

[42] Commission, *Copyright and the Challenge of Technology – Copyright Issues Requiring Immediate Action* (Green Paper COM(88) 172 final, 7.6.1988) [Green Paper on Copyright and the Challenge of Technology] 3, para 1.3.2.

[43] ibid 180, para 5.4.1. Also see Annex to the White Paper on Completing the Internal Market (1985) – Time Table for Completing the Internal Market by 1992, Period 1987–92.

[44] Ramalho (2016) 28.

[45] Commission, *Copyright and Related Rights in the Information Society* (Green Paper COM(95) 382 final, 19.7.1995) [Green Paper for the ISD] 10, para 10 and Commission, *Follow-Up to the Green Paper on Copyright and Related Rights in the Information Society* (COM(96) 586 final, 20.11.1996) [Follow-Up to the 1995 Green Paper] 2 (Summary), paras 1 and 4.

This internal market reasoning is also mirrored in the Directives concerning copyright law.[46] The reason for the internal market consideration being the driving force behind the pursuit of the harmonisation agenda in EU copyright law is the financial and cultural value attributed to copyright works and the wider development of the information society. It is argued that failing to harmonise copyright law across the Member States would culminate in restrictions to the free movement of goods and services and furthermore, would create a disincentive to invest in the production of copyright works, thus inhibiting the development of the information society.[47] In other words, failing to harmonise copyright law would undermine the completion and operation of the internal market.[48] Such is the importance of the information society to the EU and its internal market, the Commission has touted the idea of the free movement of knowledge and innovation as a 'fifth freedom' in the single market.[49]

With this background to the internal market in mind, it is important to discuss its relationship with EU copyright law in more detail. Given that the internal market is one of the central tenets of the EU, by virtue of being included under the TFEU, it has inevitably contributed to the shaping and development of EU copyright law. The role of the internal market is to approximate the domestic copyright laws of the Member States so as to ensure the consistent application and interpretation of the law. The primary importance attributed to the internal market has led to the consequent harmonisation agenda being a domineering force in the development of EU copyright law. Both the Union legislature and the CJEU have repeatedly relied on the internal market as the justification for the manner in which they have developed EU copyright law.[50] This is to the extent that the

[46] Council Directive 91/250/EEC of 14 May 1991 on the legal protection of computer programs, codified under: Directive 2009/24/EC of the European Parliament and of the Council of 23 April 2009 on the legal protection of computer programs [Computer Programs Directive] [2009] OJ L111/16, 5.5.2009, Recitals 4–5, Council Directive 92/100/EEC of 19 November 1992 on rental right and lending right and on certain rights related to copyright in the field of intellectual property, codified under: Directive 2006/11/EC of the European Parliament and of the Council of 12 December 2006 on rental right and lending right and on certain rights related to copyright in the field of intellectual property [Rental and Lending Right Directive] [1992] OJ L346/61, 27.11.1992, Recital 1, Directive 96/9/EC of the European Parliament and of the Council of 11 March 1996 on the legal protection of databases [Database Directive] [1996] OJ L77/20, 27.3.1996, Recitals 2–4, Information Society Directive Recitals 1, 3 and 7, Enforcement Directive Recitals 1 and 3, Council Directive 93/98/EEC of 29 October 1993 harmonizing the term of protection of copyright and certain related rights, codified under: Directive 2006/116/EC of the European Parliament and of the Council of 12 December 2006 on the term of protection of copyright and certain related rights (codified version) [Term Directive] [2006] OJ L372/12, 27.12.2006, Recitals 3 and 12 and E-Commerce Directive, see recitals generally.

[47] Green Paper for the ISD COM(1995) 382, 11, paras 16 and 29, para 74 and Follow-Up to the 1995 Green Paper 7 COM(96) 586.

[48] This claim was reiterated by the Wittem Group in 2011. See Wittem Group, 'European Copyright Code' (2011) 33(2) *European Intellectual Property Review (EIPR)* 76, 77.

[49] Commission, *Copyright in the Knowledge Economy* (COM(2008) 466 final, 2008) 3 para 1.2.

[50] PB Hugenholtz, 'Harmonisation or Unification of European Union Copyright Law' (2012) 38(1) *Monash University Law Review* 4, 4 and A Ramalho, 'Copyright law-making in the EU: what lies under the 'internal market' mask?' (2014) 9(3) *Journal of Intellectual Property Law & Practice (JIPLP)* 208, 208. Also see R Hilty, 'Copyright in the internal market' (2004) 7 *IIC* 760, 770–71, T Georgopoulos,

harmonisation agenda, with its internal market focus, currently shrouds EU copyright decision-making.[51] Despite this recurring trend, Hugenholtz asserts that the beneficial effects of harmonisation for the purpose of the internal market remain largely unproven.[52] Furthermore, the overarching reliance on the internal market reasoning is dangerous because it does not offer any real guidance as to what the substance or scope of EU copyright law should be. It merely suggests the adoption of a consistent approach across Member States.[53]

Although the internal market is an important consideration for the development of EU copyright law, it is one of a number of essential interests to bear in mind. Therefore, its domineering status in EU copyright law is disconcerting. The internal market consideration must be balanced with a number of other competing interests: fundamental rights, the general principles of EU law and the copyright specific interests. This is a difficult task because there is the potential for conflict between these elements. As a result, EU copyright law faces the complicated process of striking the right balance among these pressures and interests, while developing a coherent copyright framework. However, there is no consistent approach to balancing these competing interests.[54] Instead, the balance is currently drawn on a case-by-case basis.[55]

While the internal market interest has been of fundamental importance in the development of harmonised EU copyright law it must be remembered that it is not absolute. As a result, the development of EU copyright law should not be solely driven by the harmonisation agenda pursued through the guise of the internal market requirement. What is required is a far more nuanced and balanced process incorporating all the relevant competing interests.[56] Therefore, the internal market is not an absolute consideration, given that it can be set aside if upholding it would mean conflict with one of the other constitutional pressures such as the general principles of the EU.

'The Legal Foundations of European Copyright Law' in T Synodinou (ed), *Codification of European Copyright Law: Challenges and Perspectives* (Kluwer Law International, 2012) 33 and J Griffiths, 'Constitutionalising or harmonizing? The Court of Justice, the right to property and European copyright law' (2013) *European Law Review* 65.

[51] Burrell and Hudson argue that the EU judiciary like the Commission is likely to remain 'more concerned with harmonisation than with making IP law fit for purpose' – R Burrell and E Hudson, 'Property Concepts in European Law: The Case for Abandonment' in H Howe and J Griffiths (eds), *Concepts of Property in Intellectual Property Law* (Cambridge University Press, 2013) 231.

[52] Hugenholtz (2012) 8. Also see Hilty (2004) 761 – Hilty argues that the factual justifications in the recitals of the directives that support the harmonisation agenda often appear weak.

[53] Hugenholtz (2012) 8. Also see Burrell and Hudson in Howe and Griffiths (2013) 231.

[54] S de Vries, 'Balancing Fundamental Rights with Economic Freedoms According to the European Court of Justice' (2013) 9(1) *Utrecht Law Review* 169, 191.

[55] Compare Case C-265/95 *Commission of the European Communities v French Republic* [1997] ECLI:EU:C:1997:595 and *Schmidberger* [2003]. For more examples see: Case C-36/02 *Omega Spielhallen- und Automatenaufstellungs-GmbH v Oberbürgermeisterin der Bundesstadt Bonn* [2004] ECLI:EU:C:2004:614, Case C-341/05 *Laval un Partneri Ltd v Svenska Byggnadsarbetareförbundet* [2007] ECLI:EU:C:2007:809 and Case C-438/05 *International Transport Workers' Federation, Finnish Seamen's Union v Viking Line ABP, OÜ Viking Line Eesti* [2007] ECLI:EU:C:2007:772.

[56] de Vries (2013) 191.

(ii) Fundamental Rights

Before the Treaty of Lisbon 2009, human rights and fundamental rights arising from the European Convention on Human Rights (ECHR)[57] and Charter of Fundamental Rights (Charter), respectively, had no binding force in the EU. But, it was largely accepted that human rights were part of the general principles that should be accounted for in the decision-making of Member States, given that they were all individually parties to the ECHR. Following the Lisbon Treaty the status of fundamental rights and human rights was clarified and elevated.[58] The new Article 6(2) and (3) of the TEU established the EU's accession to the ECHR and made it expressly clear that human rights under the ECHR constitute general principles of EU law. Similarly, the Charter of Fundamental Rights was elevated to the status of a constitutional consideration by virtue of being bestowed the same legal value as the foundational Treaties, under Article 6(1) of the TEU. The result of this is that fundamental rights comprise one of the constitutional considerations that must be taken into account by EU copyright law.[59] However, it must be reconciled with the internal market consideration, given the difference in subject focus. Whereas, the internal market consideration is solely concerned with ensuring free trade, fundamental rights are focused more broadly on protecting substantive rights.

Thus, it is necessary to explore the impact that fundamental rights have had on the development of EU copyright law.[60] From a preliminary perspective it is worth noting that the relationship of fundamental rights to EU copyright law is both internal and external. This is because fundamental rights are taken into account in the creation of copyright legislation, as well as during its application and interpretation. Hence, it has been suggested that fundamental/human rights is IP's new frontier,[61] given the increasingly interwoven relationship of the two areas.[62] The result of this has been literature pertaining to the development of a human/fundamental rights framework for IP and copyright law.[63] With the Charter

[57] Convention for the Protection of Human Rights and Fundamental Freedoms 1950 (as amended).

[58] Ramalho (2016) 96–101.

[59] Halpern and Johnson (2014) 133.

[60] It should be noted that Article 52(3) of the Charter guarantees that rights which exist under the ECHR will be given the same meaning and scope under the Charter. Therefore, there is some overlap in taking into account the rights under the Charter and the ECHR respectively.

[61] L Helfer, 'The New Innovation Frontier? Intellectual Property and the European Court of Human Rights' (2008) 49 *Harvard International Law Journal* 1, 1.

[62] L Helfer, 'Human Rights and Intellectual Property: Conflict or Coexistence' (2003) 5 *Minnesota Intellectual Property Review* 47, 47 and L Helfer, 'Toward a Human Rights Framework for Intellectual Property' (2007) 40 *University of California, Davis Law Review (UC Davis L Rev)* 971, 1020.

[63] See: Helfer (2007), P Yu, 'Reconceptualizing Intellectual Property Interests in a Human Rights Framework' (2007) 40 *UC Davis L Rev* 1039, C Geiger, '"Constitutionalising" intellectual property law? The influence of fundamental rights on intellectual property in the European Union' (2006) 37(4) *IIC* 371 and P Torremans (ed), *Intellectual Property and Human Rights: Enhanced Edition of Copyright and Human Rights* (Kluwer Law International, 2008).

being bestowed equal standing to the foundational treaties, the issue whether fundamental rights and IP conflict or coexist has become a non-issue. Instead, the question is now how do we reconcile the two?[64] Following the express inclusion of IP under the right to property in Article 17(2) of the Charter, it is reasonable to say that the coexistence view has prevailed because it is mandatory that EU copyright law is compatible with fundamental rights.[65]

Bearing that in mind, the application of fundamental rights in relation to EU copyright law can be interpreted from three different viewpoints. Firstly, fundamental rights can be seen as a justification for copyright law, in particular, the right to property.[66] This is because the inclusion of IP under the right to property adds legitimacy to the proprietary nature of IP rights. Secondly, it can be viewed as an interpretation tool that assists the development of copyright law, especially in situations where copyright law seems to exceed its boundaries.[67] In other words, fundamental rights can act as a check and balance on the development of copyright law to prevent overregulation or unwarranted expansion. A third possibility also exists where copyright law and fundamental rights conflict, giving rise to the need for concessions within the scope of copyright law. This may occur in situations where, for example, the rights to property and freedom of expression, or freedom to conduct a business, conflict. Unlike the second possibility that involves an external account of fundamental rights, this third scenario involves the internal conflict of fundamental rights within the scope of copyright law. Nonetheless, the latter two possibilities can be linked to the second limb of the proportionality norm concerning necessity because they address what the scope of the law should be.

In looking at fundamental rights as a justification for copyright law, Geiger makes the argument that adopting a fundamental rights framework to support copyright law would abolish the need to expressly invoke natural law theories in support of the system of copyright, given that fundamental rights offer a synthesis

[64] The conflict view posits that copyright and fundamental rights are incompatible. As such, one has to win over the other, for example, in the form of adopting fundamental rights primacy or upholding copyright as a strong property right. On the other hand, the coexistence view holds that copyright and fundamental rights are compatible because they pursue the same aim, albeit from different starting points. See: Helfer (2003) 48, Helfer (2007) 1018, P Yu, 'Ten Common Questions About Intellectual Property and Human Rights' (2007) 23 *Georgia State University Law Review* 709, 709–10 [Yu2], D Gervais, 'Intellectual Property and Human Rights: Learning to Live Together' in P Torremans (ed), *Intellectual Property and Human Rights: Enhanced Edition of Copyright and Human Rights*, 2nd edn (Kluwer Law International, 2008) 3 and E Derclaye, 'Intellectual Property Rights and Human Rights: Coinciding and Cooperating' in P Torremans (ed), *Intellectual Property and Human Rights: Enhanced Edition of Copyright and Human Rights* (Kluwer Law International, 2008) 133–34.

[65] Even though EU copyright law must account for fundamental rights, this does not remove the fact that there are conflicts and tensions between the two.

[66] Helfer (2008) 5 and Geiger (2006) 382, 386.

[67] Helfer (2008) 4–5, Helfer (2007) 1015 and 1017, Geiger (2006) 389, C Geiger, 'Fundamental rights, a safeguard for the coherence of intellectual property law?' (2004) 35(3) *IIC* 268, 268, 278 and 280 and Gervais in Torremans (2008) 15.

of natural law and utilitarian reasoning.[68] For Geiger this means that fundamental rights can be used as a substitute for the traditional justificatory theories that are often invoked in support of copyright law because the values that copyright law have traditionally been constructed on are inherent to fundamental rights. In order for this approach to be successful, a fair balancing of the various fundamental rights is essential. In the case of copyright law, the rights of property and freedom of expression are particularly important.[69] The value in Geiger's argument is that the disagreement over the foundation or justification of copyright law is avoided, given that fundamental rights embody principles that are generally accepted.[70] Therefore, basing the protection of copyright law on those accepted principles adds validity to the concept of copyright law itself.[71]

However, in justifying copyright law on the basis of fundamental rights, care must be taken to prevent the development of an incoherent copyright framework. There is the concern that overreliance should not be placed on the fact that IP is included under the Article 17(2) right to property.[72] Copyright should not be protected simply because it is considered property under the Charter, since this could lead to arguments that copyright is being protected as an end in itself. Furthermore, this sort of property rhetoric runs the risk that the 'right to property' justification may be used to augment existing copyright protection,[73] the likely consequence of this being the development of a more maximalist approach to copyright protection.[74] This will be unjustified in terms of the public interest/access aspect of copyright. It must be remembered that the right to property is not inviolable or absolute, as it is only one of a number of equally important rights.[75] This is a legitimate fear given the tendency of the EU to uphold a property logic that idealises copyright as 'a completely positive, self-sufficient measure required by fundamental rights'.[76]

Therefore, it is essential to achieve an effective balance for the various fundamental rights relevant to copyright law. The aim of achieving balance among the fundamental rights also plays an important role for the other intersections of

[68] Geiger (2006) 382 and 386 and C Geiger, 'Copyright's fundamental rights dimension at EU level' in E Derclaye (ed), *Research Handbook on the Future of EU Copyright* (Edward Elgar Publishing Ltd, 2009) 34, 37.

[69] Geiger (2006) 386.

[70] The dilemma concerning the acceptance of natural rights justifications as opposed to economic justifications is avoided.

[71] Geiger (2006) 388.

[72] See Griffiths (2013) for discussion on balancing the right to property with other competing interests.

[73] Helfer (2008) 1015.

[74] Yu (2007) 1125 and C Geiger, 'Intellectual property shall be protected!? Article 17(2) of the Charter of Fundamental Rights of the European Union: a mysterious provision with an unclear scope' (2009) 31(3) *EIPR* 113, 114.

[75] Geiger (2009) 116 and S Ricketson, 'Intellectual Property and Human Rights' in S Bottomley and D Kinley (eds) *Commercial Law and Human Rights* (Ashgate Publishing Ltd, 2001) 194.

[76] A Peukert, 'Intellectual property as an end in itself' (2011) 33 *EIPR* 67, 71.

fundamental rights and EU copyright law. These intersections include the use of fundamental rights internal to copyright law as a legislative tool or, alternatively, as an external interpretation tool. It is argued that using fundamental rights in relation to copyright law can lead to the development of a more balanced framework.[77] The reason for this is that fundamental rights account for a wide array of interests that would not ordinarily come within the scope of copyright law. In particular, this includes the non-property and non-economic interests that are for the benefit of users, such as access to works, the development of new technology and business models that may involve copyright works and the cultural and educational development of society.

From the internal perspective, this is an important point to make because the development of EU copyright law in the Directives has been largely pursued from the perspective of ensuring a high level of protection for right holders. However, the scope of EU copyright law should not be solely based on this singular goal given that the recitals of the Directives expressly take account of other considerations, including fundamental rights. Therefore, the EU legislature has a duty to prevent the development of excessive exclusive rights, exclusive rights that unjustifiably conflict with other fundamental rights, and more generally to prevent copyright law from becoming too one-sided in favour of right holders.[78] Thus, fundamental rights can provide a means for the internal regulation of copyright law to prevent unjustified or undesirable results. This often takes the form of carve-outs in the law, including curbing the scope of the right provided or the provision of exceptions and limitations so as to ensure that the competing fundamental rights are adequately addressed. This provides the legislature with the opportunity to ensure that the law is balanced and flexible in its protection of copyright works without the need for courts to restrict the law.[79]

As for the external role of fundamental rights, it can be used to regulate the interpretation of EU copyright law. Unlike the internal perspective that relates to the shaping of the express provisions set out in the Directives by the legislature, the external role addresses the interpretation of the exclusive rights by courts. Geiger describes the use of fundamental rights by the CJEU as a creative force in its development of EU copyright law.[80] In particular, the external role has importance where copyright law exceeds its bounds despite the efforts, or lack thereof, of the legislature. For example, copyright overstepping its bounds is likely to occur in relation to new forms of exploitation or circumstances that were not accounted for during the legislation process.[81] In such situations, the court should limit the

[77] Yu (2007) 1123 and Helfer (2003) 58.

[78] Helfer (2007) 1017 and Geiger (2006) 398.

[79] Geiger (2006) 397 and 399.

[80] C Geiger, 'The Role of the Court of Justice of the European Union: Harmonizing, Creating and sometimes Disrupting Copyright Law in the European Union' in I Stamatoudi (ed), *New Developments in EU and International Copyright Law* (Kluwer Law International, 2016) 441.

[81] For example, Midelieva argued that the challenge of balancing competing fundamental rights is acute in relation to hyperlinking where an array of rights are at stake, notably, freedom of expression,

application of copyright law as a means of ensuring any competing fundamental rights are balanced. In this way, specific fundamental rights can be invoked to limit the scope of copyright law in accordance with the necessity limb of the proportionality norm.

However, invoking specific fundamental rights may lead to arguments that some fundamental rights are more important than others, such as the right to life compared to the right to property. It is established that all the fundamental rights are of equal value given that a 'fair balance' must be established between competing rights.[82] But, there is disagreement on this issue with some commentators arguing that certain fundamental rights are really just 'high ranking policy objectives rather than individual entitlements'.[83] This is problematic because the potential exists that a hierarchy of fundamental rights will eventually develop,[84] leading to the depreciation in value of some rights.[85] Presently, this fear does not seem to have materialised. Nevertheless, the CJEU's method of balancing the rights remains questionable. In the first place, balancing the competing fundamental rights has been done on a case-by-case basis that is not desirable or helpful as a matter of legal certainty.[86] Secondly, the concept of 'fair balance' does not really provide any substantive guidance, given that the term is not defined.[87] Therefore, where the balance between competing fundamental rights is struck is at the discretion of the particular court involved.

This is made evident in comparing the blocking order cases of *Scarlet Extended* and *UPC Telekabel*, where the Article 17(2) right to property conflicted with the Article 16 right of freedom to conduct a business, among other fundamental rights included under the Charter.[88] Although both cases involved blocking orders, the extent of the orders was quite different in each, which resulted in the CJEU reaching opposite conclusions in the cases. In *Scarlet Extended*, the blocking order in question concerned the installation of an Internet filter to prevent the sharing

freedom to conduct a business and right to property – L Midelieva, 'Rethinking hyperlinking: addressing hyperlinks to unauthorized content in copyright law and policy' (2017) 39(8) *EIPR* 479, 479.

[82] *Promusicae* [2008] para 68, followed in *Scarlet Extended v SABAM* [2011] paras 44–45, *Bonnier Audio* [2012] para 56 and *UPC Telekabel* [2014] para 46. Also see: Geiger (2009) 116, Geiger (2006) 386, Geiger (2004) 278, Yu2 (2007) 712 and Griffiths (2013) 71.

[83] J Cornides, 'Human Rights and Intellectual Property: Conflict or Convergence?' (2004) 7(2) *Journal of World Intellectual Property* 135, 139, P Ducoulombier, 'Interaction between human rights: Are all human rights equal?' in C Geiger (ed), *Research Handbook on Human Rights and Intellectual Property* (Edward Elgar Publishing Ltd, 2015), T Koji, 'Emerging Hierarchy in International Human Rights and Beyond: From the Perspective of Non-derogable Rights' (2001) 12(5) *European Journal of International Law* 917.

[84] The idea of a hierarchy of human/fundamental rights is one of the most debated topics in that area of law.

[85] Cornides (2004) 138.

[86] For an alternative approach see Afori (2014) 891–92 and 908–09, who argues that balancing competing interests requires broad discretion for the court.

[87] Griffiths (2013) 73–74.

[88] In *Scarlet Extended v SABAM* and *UPC Telekabel*, Article 8 on the protection of personal data and Article 11 on the right to freedom of expression and information were also invoked.

of music files.[89] However, this would have been costly, complicated and time-consuming to the ISP, given that it would have to install the filter at its own cost, as well as actively monitor it. Thus, the CJEU held that the blocking order must be precluded because it would result in a serious infringement of the freedom of the ISP to conduct its business in addition to potentially undermining the right to protection of personal data and the freedom to receive or impart information, given the blanket nature of the filter in question. Furthermore, the monitoring aspect of the filter would be in contravention of Article 3(1) of the Enforcement Directive.[90] In making this decision the CJEU reiterated that the right to property is not absolute and a fair balance must be struck between competing fundamental rights.[91]

Conversely, in *UPC Telekabel* the contested blocking order concerned the prohibition of access to a particular website. However, the method of blocking the website was left open to the ISP and only required them to adopt a reasonable measure. Similar to *Scarlet Extended*, the CJEU emphasised the need to strike a fair balance between competing fundamental rights, in this case between the same Articles 8, 11, 16 and 17(2) of the Charter. However, the blocking order was less restrictive and did not require active monitoring; therefore, the CJEU held that the blocking order was not precluded despite the fundamental rights concerns that were raised.[92] The point to note is that the balancing of the fundamental rights is dependent on the factual scenario at hand. The diverging decisions in *Scarlet Extended* and *UPC Telekabel* can be attributed to the differences in the blocking orders sought. Although this may be positive in ensuring the flexibility of the system, it is not desirable for the purpose of establishing legal certainty. This is because there is no guarantee of consistency in the balancing of the competing fundamental rights.[93]

In order to establish a more consistent and predictable balancing mechanism, a more in-depth analysis of the competing fundamental rights needs to be undertaken.[94] As such, the approach used by the European Court of Human Rights (ECtHR) should be adopted. The approach of the ECtHR is desirable because there is appreciation for the role and purpose of the human rights both outside and within the context of the case at hand. In other words, the individual values of the rights are taken account of in the decision-making process of the ECtHR.

[89] Using the filter would mean monitoring all Internet traffic and stepping in to block traffic involving the transfer of music files that are illegal. See *Scarlet Extended v SABAM* [2011] para 38 for the steps involved.

[90] ibid paras 43–53.

[91] See Case C-201/13 *Johan Deckmyn and Vrijheidsfonds VZW v Helena Vandersteen and others* [2014] ECLI:EU:C:2014:2132, para 27.

[92] *UPC Telekabel* [2014] para 64.

[93] For other cases of conflicting fundamental rights in copyright cases see: *Promusicae* [2008] and *Bonnier Audio* [2012]. Also see de Vries (2013) 191.

[94] Griffiths supports this viewpoint by suggesting that the CJEU's fair balance concept is vague and calls it little more than 'window-dressing' – Griffiths (2013) 74, 76–78.

While the factual scenario remains important, it is equally important to understand the value of the fundamental rights with respect to each other and for the larger public interest.[95] In pursuing this approach, greater understanding about the rights is attained, which in turn will allow for more predictable and consistent decision-making in the long run. By contrast, the current approach of the CJEU is limited to understanding the relevant rights only within the context of the factual case at hand. This is because the CJEU too hastily glosses over the value of each right individually, in the pursuit of reaching a decision.[96] Therefore, any precedent established by the CJEU is of limited value for future cases because the interpretation of the fundamental rights is highly contextualised.

In addition to establishing a more comprehensive mechanism for reconciling competing fundamental rights, it is also important to remember that other considerations must be taken into account, namely, the internal market, the general principles of the EU and the copyright specific interests.[97] Thus, it is necessary to proportionately balance the individual fundamental rights with each other,[98] as well as to balance the fundamental rights against the other competing pressures.[99] Failing to strike a fair balance could result in abuse of the fundamental rights framework to achieve unjustified ends.[100] In other words, the application of the fundamental rights is subject to restrictions. Yet, it would seem that balancing fundamental rights is a matter for case-by-case determination, thus creating potential problems of unpredictability or inconsistency in decisions where there is conflict concerning fundamental rights.

This is undesirable because parties cannot reasonably anticipate the consequences of their actions, thus compromising the certainty norm. As a result, it would also be desirable to adopt a similar approach to that of the ECtHR in reconciling the competing constitutional interests. In this way, the individual value of the fundamental right(s) is appraised alongside the value of the competing consideration(s). Such an approach will ensure that the conflicting interests are

[95] See for example: *Anheuser-Busch Inc v Portugal* (2007) 45 EHRR 36, *MGN Ltd v United Kingdom* (2011) 53 EHRR 5 and *Mosley v United Kingdom* (2011) 53 EHRR 30.

[96] For example, compare the CJEU judgment in *Scarlet Extended v SABAM* [2011] with the ECtHR judgment in *Anheuser-Busch Inc v Portugal* (Application no 73049/01), 11th January 2007, 44 EHRR 42, where the ECtHR gave a significantly more detailed explanation of the protection of IP under the right to property.

[97] The European Copyright Code produced by the Wittem Group reminds us of the importance of taking into account all the competing considerations – see Wittem Group (2011) 77.

[98] The concept of proportionality used here, though similar to the general EU principle of proportionality, is not exactly the same. Proportionality in this sense refers to the individual weighting of the competing interests against the factual context at hand; whereas, the general EU principle of proportionality has the specific meaning that 'Union action shall not exceed what is necessary to achieve the objectives of the Treaties' – Article 5(4) TEU. Also see *The Queen v Minister for Agriculture* [1990] para 13.

[99] Yu2 (2007) 711, Cornides (2004) 167 and de Vries (2013) 172–77.

[100] Yu2 (2007) 738.

properly weighed, not just in terms of the factual scenario, but their wider value. From this, parties can better gauge the potential liability of their future actions in the interest of ensuring certainty.

The discussion of fundamental rights has focused on its three primary roles: as a justification for copyright law, a legislative tool and an interpretation tool. From the existing literature and the case law it would seem that it has been primarily used as an interpretation tool to ensure that copyright law remains within its legislated scope and, moreover, balances all the competing fundamental rights present. Therefore, applying fundamental rights to EU copyright law can be valuable because it can facilitate a more balanced interpretation of the law in accordance with the necessity limb of the proportionality norm.[101] However, to achieve this, a more detailed balancing mechanism is required because the current approach is too superficial. It may be helpful in this regard to follow the approach of the ECtHR, which is more comprehensive in its analysis of the individual competing human rights. Furthermore, fundamental rights should be subject to greater inclusion in the scope of protection at the legislative level. While this may already be the case for the exceptions and limitations such as, parody, educational and scientific use, and quotation, there is the need for fundamental rights to be a greater part of the conceptualisation of and legislation for the exclusive rights. This will provide for a more balanced right from the outset and would reduce the need for courts to engage in case-by-case balancing activities in accordance with the third limb of the proportionality norm, proportionality *sensu stricto*.

In terms of the role of fundamental rights as a justification, it does have value because it avoids the disagreement over the theoretical underpinnings of copyright law. It provides a justification based on generally accepted principles, thus increasing certainty in the law. Moreover, fundamental rights as a justification has value because it introduces a range of non-property and non-economic interests that would not ordinarily be present in substantive copyright law. This is increasingly becoming the case, as evidenced by the post-*GS Media* case law concerning communication to the public where fundamental rights were expressly discussed.[102] Therefore, in order to develop a more balanced and coherent copyright framework for the EU, it is necessary to adequately account for and reconcile fundamental rights.

[101] This claim can be evidenced by the CJEU's increased use of fundamental rights in its copyright decisions – Geiger in Stamatoudi (2016) 441–42.

[102] See Case C-160/15 *GS Media BV v Sanoma Media Netherlands BV and others* [2016] ECLI:EU:C:2016:644, paras 31 and 44–45, Case C-161/17 *Land Nordrhein-Westfalen v Dirk Renckhoff* [2018], Opinion of AG Sánchez Bordona ECLI:EU:C:2018:279, paras 31, 40 and 79 and Case C-161/17 *Land Nordrhein-Westfalen v Dirk Renckhoff* [2018], 7 August 2018, ECLI:EU:C:2018:634, para 41. Also see B Clark and J Dickenson, 'Theseus and the labyrinth? An overview of "communication to the public" under EU copyright law: after Reha Training and GS Media: Where are we now and where do we go from here?' (2017) 39(5) *EIPR* 265, 270.

(iii) *General Principles of EU law*

The concept of the general principles of EU law was previously discussed. However, it is worth reiterating that they include: proportionality, certainty, subsidiarity,[103] equality[104] and fundamental rights.[105] For the purposes of this book, emphasis is placed on proportionality and certainty, which form the normative framework for the analysis of the communication to the public right. Additionally, fundamental rights were addressed separately in the previous sub-section.

B. International Copyright Treaties

The relevant international treaties for the development of copyright law include the Berne Convention 1971,[106] the TRIPS Agreement 1994[107] and the WIPO Copyright Treaty (WCT) 1996. In addition to the copyright treaties, there are also international treaties concerning the rights of performers, phonogram producers and broadcasting organisations.[108] It is important to consider these international treaties because they are binding on the Member States of the EU. The first international copyright treaty to become binding on the EU was the TRIPS Agreement.[109] The implication of this was that Articles 1 to 21 of the Berne Convention, with the exception of Article 6bis, became indirectly binding on EU Member States by virtue of Article 9 of the TRIPS Agreement.[110] Furthermore, the exclusive rights pertaining to the protection of performers, phonogram producers and broadcasting organisations derived from the Rome Convention are also binding on the EU under Article 14 of the TRIPS Agreement. This was then followed by the EU becoming signatory to the WCT and WIPO Performances and Phonograms Treaty, making these two treaties binding on Member States.[111]

[103] The principle of subsidiarity is not further discussed in this chapter because it does not prominently feature in the EU copyright law literature. Furthermore, it is not really relevant, given that the EU has general competence to act in matters related to the development and harmonisation of copyright laws under the remit of the internal market that falls within the shared competencies of Article 4 of the TFEU. For more on the principle of subsidiarity see Halpern and Johnson (2014) 130–31.

[104] The principle of equality is not further discussed in this chapter because it does not prominently feature in the EU copyright law literature.

[105] K Davies, *Understanding European Union Law*, 3rd edn (Routledge-Cavendish, 2007) 58. Fundamental rights by virtue of Article 6(3) of the TEU is established as a general principle of EU law.

[106] Berne Convention for the Protection of Literary and Artistic Works 1971.

[107] Agreement on Trade-Related Aspects of Intellectual Property Rights (TRIPS Agreement) 1994.

[108] International Convention for the Protection of Performers, Producers of Phonograms and Broadcasting Organisations 1961 [Rome Convention] and WIPO Performances and Phonograms Treaty 1996.

[109] Council Decision 94/800/EC of 22 December 1994 concerning the conclusion on behalf of the European Community, as regards matters within its competence, of the agreements reached in the Uruguay Round multilateral negotiations (1986–94).

[110] Note, all Member States were already signatory to, or acknowledged, the Berne Convention by the time of the EU's signing of the TRIPS Agreement.

[111] Council Decision 2000/278/EC of 16 March 2000 on the approval, on behalf of the European Community, of the WIPO Copyright Treaty and the WIPO Performances and Phonograms Treaty, [2000] OJ L89/6, 11.4.2000.

The consequence of the EU becoming signatory to the TRIPS Agreement and the WIPO treaties was that EU copyright law must be internationally compliant. Thus, the international treaties have a direct impact on the development of the law. For example, Recital 15 of the ISD describes part of that Directive's role as implementing new international obligations from the WIPO treaties. But, it should be borne in mind that the international treaties only prescribe minimum rights.[112] Therefore, the EU is not prevented from introducing additional rights or adopting stronger levels of protection. Different aspects of EU copyright law have adopted varying levels of protection relating to the international requirements. For example, some aspects are directly transposed, such as the Article 3 communication to the public right, including the making available aspect that is a direct transposition of Article 8 of the WCT. Other areas of EU copyright law, such as the duration of copyright protection, adopt a higher level of protection (70 years *post mortem auctoris* – Article 1(1) of the Term Directive 2006) than that required at the international level (50 years *post mortem auctoris* – Article 7(1) of the Berne Convention). Alternatively, the EU has pursued its own approach to the exceptions and limitations of copyright law under Article 5 of the ISD, though this is in keeping with the requirement of Article 13 of the TRIPS Agreement that employs the three-step test. Similarly, the EU has chosen not to adopt compulsory licensing mechanisms in relation to copyright works, though they are utilised for related rights under Article 8 of the Rental and Lending Right Directive.

With this understanding in mind, EU copyright law must account for the rights and obligations that are provided under the international treaties. However, the manner in which they are implemented and the scope of protection afforded at the EU level are subject to the discretion of the EU. Therefore, they can adopt exclusive rights that are stronger in protection or wider in scope, so long as they do not conflict with the prescribed rights. Furthermore, the EU has competence freely to legislate in areas that are left unaddressed by the international treaties to which it is a signatory.

C. Domestic Traditions

In addition to the rights and obligations at the international level, EU copyright law must also account for the traditions[113] of the *droit d'auteur* and copyright regimes[114] at the Member State level because EU copyright law was

[112] Article 5 of the Berne Convention, Article 1 of the TRIPS Agreement and Article 3 of the WIPO Copyright Treaty.

[113] Ramalho argues that it is also necessary to account for the cultural traditions of the Member States – Ramalho (2016) 131–35. However, only the *droit d'auteur* and copyright legal traditions are discussed given the limitations on the scope of this thesis.

[114] 'Copyright law' is used descriptively to include copyright in the common law countries and *droit d'auteur* in the civil law countries.

not independently created.[115] It was stated in the ISD that: 'no new concepts for the protection of IP are needed, the current law on copyright and related rights should be adapted and supplemented to respond adequately to economic realities such as new forms of exploitation'.[116] In adopting this approach, the EU legislature chose to pursue a harmonisation agenda for copyright law instead of providing a substantively new framework or set of laws to replace the existing laws of Member States. EU copyright law supplements the existing domestic laws of Member States to ensure certain objectives are achieved. This harmonisation approach was accompanied by the justification that failing to harmonise the existing laws of Member States would lead to significant differences in protection that would restrict the free movement of goods and services and in doing so re-fragment the internal market.[117] It is thus the case that the traditions of the various Member States remain largely intact and are moreover, a relevant consideration for EU copyright law.

The justifications underlying the domestic *droit d'auteur* and copyright systems are important because law proposed at the EU level must be reconcilable with the domestic traditions and justifications of the respective Member States. Otherwise, there is the risk that the proposed law would not be accepted if it is incompatible with domestic laws. There is concern about this because the *droit d'auteur* approach is very different from that of the common law copyright systems.[118] Consequently, the EU legislature is faced with the task of reconciling competing traditions and justifications for the production of laws that can be adopted in diverse Member States. Therefore, the *droit d'auteur* and copyright traditions of the Member States affect what is included in the copyright Directives, how they are included and ultimately, whether EU copyright law will be implemented and applied at the domestic level.

The justifications for *droit d'auteur* and copyright law at the Member State level vary from country to country. Similarly to the copyright landscape at the international level, countries can be broadly divided into two distinct schools of thought. On the one hand, there are the civil law countries, such as France, which subscribe to natural rights justifications like the Lockean labour theory[119]

[115] Georgopoulos in Synodinou (2012) 32–33.

[116] Recital 5 of the ISD.

[117] Recital 7 of the ISD.

[118] See P Jougleux, 'The Plurality of Legal Systems in Copyright Law: An Obstacle to a European Codification' in T Synodinou, *Codification of European Copyright Law: Challenges and Perspectives* (Wolters Kluwer, 2012).

[119] J Locke, *Two Treatises of Government* (Peter Laslett (ed), Cambridge University Press 2010) The Second Treatise, Chapter 5 (Property) 285–302. For discussion on the Lockean labour theory in relation to intellectual property see: W Dibble, 'Justifying intellectual property' (1994) 1 *UCL Jurisprudence Review* 74, H Spector, 'An outline of a theory justifying intellectual and industrial property rights' (1989) 11(8) *EIPR* 270, L Zemer, 'On the value of copyright theory' [2006] *IPQ* 55, J Hughes, 'The Philosophy of Intellectual Property' (1989) 77 *Georgetown Law Journal* 287, S Shiffrin, 'Lockean Arguments for Private Property' in S Munzer (ed), *New Essays in the Legal and Political Theory of Property* (Cambridge University Press, 2001), G Alexander and E Peñalver, *An Introduction to Property*

and the Hegelian[120] personality theory.[121] On the other hand, there are the common law countries, such as the United Kingdom (UK), that rely on traditional utilitarianism[122] or economic utilitarian type justifications.[123] The justification relied on for a country's copyright laws has important implications for the scope and structure of the rights provided. This includes what rights are protected and the extent of protection. For example, countries relying on natural rights justifications

Theory (Cambridge University Press, 2012), D Attas, 'Lockean Justifications of Intellectual Property' in A Gosseries, A Marcano and A Strowel (eds), *Intellectual Property and Theories of Justice* (Palgrave Macmillan, 2008), A Rand, 'Patents and Copyrights' in A Rand (ed) *Capitalism: The Unknown Ideal* (Signet, 1967), E Hettinger, 'Justifying Intellectual Property' (1989) 18(1) *Philosophy & Public Affairs* 31, R Nozick, *Anarchy, State and Utopia* (Basic Books Inc, 1974) and M du Bois, 'Justificatory Theories for Intellectual Property Viewed through the Constitutional Prism' (2018) 21 *Potchefstroom Economic Law Journal/Potchefstroom Elektroniese Regsblad* 1. For an alternative perspective see W Fisher, 'Theories of Intellectual Property' in S Munzer (ed), *New Essays in the Legal and Political Theory of Property* (Cambridge University Press, 2001), who expresses doubt about the applicability of the Lockean labour theory to copyright law.

[120] For an alternative/relational theory to Hegel see Kant's personhood theory.

[121] GWF Hegel, *Elements of the Philosophy of Right*, A Wood (ed) (Cambridge University Press 2012) §41–69. Also see: P Drahos, A Philosophy of Intellectual Property (Dartmouth Publishing Company 1996) and M Radin, 'Property and Personhood' (1982) 34 *Stanford Law Review* 957. For more discussion on the Hegelian personality theory in relation to IP see: Hughes (1989), D Reznik, 'A Pluralistic Account of Intellectual Property' (2003) 46 *Journal of Business Ethics* (4) 319, J Schroeder, 'Unnatural Rights: Hegel and Intellectual Property' (2006) 60 *University of Miami Law Review* 453, Fisher in Munzer (2001), B Friedman, 'From Deontology To Dialogue: The Cultural Consequences Of Copyright' (1995) 13 *Cardozo Arts & Entertainment Law Journal* 157, L Lacey, 'Of Bread and Roses and Copyrights' (1989) *Duke Law Journal* 1532, T Palmer, 'Are Patents and Copyrights Morally Justified? The Philosophy of Property Rights and Ideal Objects' (1990) 13 *Harvard Journal of Law & Public Policy (Harv J L & Pub Pol'y)* 817 and du Bois (2018).

[122] For traditional utilitarianism see: J Bentham, *An Introduction to the Principles of Morals and Legislation* (White Dog Publishing, 2010) Chapter 1, J Mill, *Utilitarianism*, 7th edn (Longmans, Green and Co, 1879), J Mill, *Utilitarianism, On Liberty, Considerations On Representative Government*, G Williams (ed) (Everyman's Library, 1996), H Sidgwick, 'Utilitarianism' (2000) 12 *Utilitas* 253, J Driver, 'The History of Utilitarianism', *The Stanford Encyclopedia of Philosophy*, E Zalta (ed) (Summer Edition, 2009) <http://plato.stanford.edu/archives/sum2009/entries/utilitarianism-history/> accessed 18 March 2014, JJC Smart and B Williams, *Utilitarianism: for and against* (Cambridge University Press 1973), R Frey (ed), *Utility and Rights* (Basil Blackwell Ltd, 1985). For more discussion on traditional utilitarianism in relation to IP see: Fisher in Munzer (2001), Dibble (1994), Zemer (2006), S Sterk, 'Rhetoric and Reality in Copyright Law' (1996) 94 *Michigan Law Review* 1197, Reznik (2003), K Sykes, 'Towards a Public Justification of Copyright' (2003) 61 *U Toronto Faculty of Law Review* 1, Friedman (1995), G Lunney Jr, 'Reexamining Copyright's Incentives–Access Paradigm' (1996) 49 *Vanderbilt Law Review* 483, Hettinger (1989) and J Boyle, *Shamans, Software and Spleens* (Harvard University Press, 1996).

[123] For economic utilitarian justification see: P Menell, 'Intellectual Property: General Theories' in B Bouckaert and G De Geest (eds), *Encyclopedia of Law and Economics Volume II* (Edward Elgar Publishing Ltd, 2000) 148–49 for a list of authors discussing economic analysis of copyright. For more discussion on economic utilitarianism in relation to IP see: Sykes (2003), A Yen, 'Restoring the Natural Law: Copyright as Labor and Possession' (1990) 51 *Ohio State Law Journal* 517, Dibble (1994) 84, Fisher in Munzer (2001) 177, J Griffin, 'Copyright evolution – creation, regulation and the decline of substantively rational copyright law' [2013] *Intellectual Property Quarterly (IPQ)* 234, M Landes and R Posner, 'An Economic Analysis of Copyright Law' (1989) 18 *Journal of Legal Studies* 325, R Van den Bergh, 'The role and social justification of copyright: a "law and economics" approach' [1998] *IPQ* 17, P Samuelson, 'Should Economics Play a Role in Copyright Law and Policy?' (2004) 1 U Ottawa L & Tech J 3 and R Hurt and R Schuchman, 'The Economic Rationale of Copyright' (1966) 56 *The American Economic Review* 421.

tend to place greater emphasis on moral rights. This is evidenced by comparing the limited moral rights provisions provided by the UK under the Copyright, Designs and Patents Act (CDPA) 1988,[124] as opposed to the more extensive and perpetual French moral rights under its Intellectual Property Code.[125] Similarly, the scope of the economic rights under the different systems is also reflective of the different legal traditions. The French economic rights are subject to a restricted number of exceptions and limitations,[126] whereas, the UK is far more expansive in its approach to exceptions and limitations.[127] Consequently, the scope of the economic rights under UK copyright law can be argued to be weaker, given that it is subject to more exceptions, influenced by economic/utilitarian justifications that are more concerned with achieving efficient outcomes than protecting the natural rights of the author.[128]

Prima facie the copyright and *droit d'auteur* systems seem irreconcilable given their divergent underlying justifications, ideologies and goals; the primary difference being that *droit d'auteur* systems and their natural rights justifications focus on the protection of the author and his/her entitlement to protection of their works. Whereas, the economic/utilitarian influenced copyright systems are concerned with the value of protecting copyright.[129] These different perspectives mean that legislating for EU copyright laws involves a complicated process of negotiation. As such, the development of EU copyright law can be seen as a concession of ideas and positions for each side (common law versus civil law).[130] However, this issue is not unique to EU copyright law; rather it is symptomatic of any international or regional copyright legislation. The same problem was experienced at the Berne Convention where the civil law 'universalists' wanted stronger levels of protection based on the natural rights of the author than the common law 'pragmatists'.[131] The consequence of this conflict was that every law created at the Berne Convention was a compromise between the conflicting factions.

Therefore, the difficulty faced by the EU relates to the balancing and reconciling of the various competing pressures and interests. On the one hand, the EU has

[124] See ss 77–81 and ss 84–85 of the Copyright, Designs and Patents Act 1988.

[125] See Articles L 121-1, L 121-2 and L 121-4.

[126] See Articles L 122-5 and L 122-6.

[127] See ss 28A–76A CDPA 1988.

[128] Ramalho (2016) 7.

[129] Notwithstanding the differences in approach between the copyright and *droit d'auteur* systems, it can be argued that the underlying purpose of copyright law is to incentivise the creation of copyright works – S Bechtold, 'Deconstructing Copyright' in PB Hugenholtz (ed), *Copyright Reconstructed: Rethinking Copyright's Economic Rights in a Time of Highly Dynamic and Technological and Economic Change* (Kluwer Law International BV, 2018) 73. However, there is no universal agreement about what the proper function of copyright is – A Ohly, 'A Fairness-Based Approach to Economic Rights' in PB Hugenholtz (ed), *Copyright Reconstructed: Rethinking Copyright's Economic Rights in a Time of Highly Dynamic and Technological and Economic Change* (Kluwer Law International BV, 2018) 109.

[130] Jougleux in Synodinou (2012) 55–56.

[131] S Ricketson and J Ginsburg, *International Copyright and Neighbouring Rights: The Berne Convention and Beyond* (Oxford University Press 2006) paras 2.02–2.04 and M Makeen, *Copyright in a Global Information Society: The Scope of Copyright Protection Under International, US, UK and French Law* (Kluwer Law International, 2000) 24.

to account for its general law-making considerations, such as its constitutional considerations and policies. On the other hand, the copyright-specific considerations must also be accounted for. In particular, there is conflict between the attainment of a high level of protection – established as a key goal by the EU – and the inevitable compromise created by the diverging traditions of the Member States. Thus, any compromise reached between the competing traditions and justifications of the Member States must be counterbalanced with the need to establish a high level of protection for right holders. Consequently, the domestic copyright and *droit d'auteur* traditions feature prominently in the pre-legislative negotiations between the divergent Member States. The impact of this affects the inclusion of specific rights and the general scope of protection.[132] Additionally, the conflict in ideology also filters into the transposition, implementation and application of the law at the domestic level because the domestic traditions and justifications affect the way copyright law operates, even though EU copyright law is meant to be interpreted autonomously.

An example of the difficulty with reconciling conflicting legal traditions is evidenced by the absence of any harmonised rules for moral rights at the EU level. Although Article 6bis of the Berne Convention requires moral rights, which have been adopted by most EU Member States albeit in different forms, there are no moral rights in EU copyright law, given the controversial nature of the concept in the common law countries.[133] The absence of moral rights at the EU level may be interpreted in one of two ways. Firstly, it may be too difficult to legislate for harmonised moral rights given the diverse nature of the copyright systems of the Member States. This is compounded by the fact that EU copyright law lacks a clear philosophy in contrast to the individual Member States which have established copyright traditions. Alternatively, it may be that moral rights have no salience for the purpose of the functioning of the internal market and as such, have been omitted thus far.[134]

Another example that emphasises the importance of taking account of the varying traditions of the Member States is the exceptions and limitations provided under Article 5 of the ISD. The provision of an exhaustive list rather than a mandatory list is indicative of the compromise at the EU level to facilitate the diverse traditions of the Member States.[135] Recitals 31 and 32 confirm this by stating: 'this list [of exceptions] takes due account of the different legal traditions in Member States, while, at the same time, aiming to ensure a functioning internal market'. Furthermore, the fact that the list of exceptions and limitations is optional contributes to the argument of a compromise at the EU level. This is because Member

[132] A Lucas-Schloetter, 'Is there a concept of European copyright law? History, evolution, policies and politics and the *acquis* communautaire' in I Stamatoudi and P Torremans (eds), *EU Copyright Law: A Commentary* (Edward Elgar Publishing Ltd, 2014) 15–16, paras 1.20–1.21.

[133] This is reflective of the situation at the international level with the TRIPS Agreement where Article 6bis of the Berne Convention is excluded under the copyright protection afforded by TRIPS.

[134] Ramalho (2016) 178.

[135] Hugenholtz (2012) 7.

States can pick and choose which exceptions and limitations they want to implement. However, it should be noted that this does not allow Member States to interpret the exceptions and limitations in their own way. The CJEU in *Deckmyn* expressly dismissed this possibility.[136]

Nonetheless, the CJEU has consistently repeated that EU copyright law is to be interpreted autonomously. This means that the traditions of the various Member States should not be factored into the decision-making of courts when applying EU copyright law. As a result, the traditions and justifications of the Member States are limited to the pre-legislation stage when EU copyright laws are being negotiated. Despite this, the domestic traditions retain importance because they contribute to the substance of EU copyright laws, largely through forcing the EU legislature to compromise on the laws it proposes. Therefore, any reforms to the communication to the public right that will be proposed in this book must account for the domestic traditions of both the *droit d'auteur* and copyright law Member States. Otherwise, there is the risk that the proposed changes will be rejected or deemed unacceptable despite whatever merits they may comprise.[137]

D. Copyright Directives

EU copyright law reflects the key policy goals established within the *travaux préparatoires* and the recitals of the copyright Directives, which form an important part of the *acquis communitaire* for EU copyright law.[138] The starting point for the discussion of these goals is the Green Paper on Copyright and the Challenge of Technology. This Green Paper stated that the development of EU copyright law was important for the purposes of protecting the economic interests of authors, promoting ready access to information and pursuing cultural goals.[139] Thus, the focus of the EU from the outset was simultaneously economic, informational, cultural and technological. In addition to this, four fundamental concerns were also established, including: ensuring the proper functioning of the internal market, promoting the competitiveness of the media and information economy, preventing the misappropriation of creative effort and investment by non-EU persons without fair return, and balancing the interests of the right holder with those of third parties and the public.[140]

Despite the wide array of interests stated by the EU in order to justify the need for harmonised EU copyright protection, it can be argued that EU copyright law was primarily motivated by economic considerations in its initial stages. This is evidenced by the fact that all the issues mentioned above, if not directly economic

[136] *Deckmyn* [2014] para 15.
[137] Ramalho (2016) 176–78.
[138] See ibid, Chapter 2, for an account of the individual interests contained in the copyright Directives.
[139] Green Paper on Copyright and the Challenge of Technology (1988) 1.
[140] ibid 3–5.

in nature, involve some form of economic implication. For example, it was stated that the economic interests are 'inextricably interwoven with cultural interests and cultural needs'.[141] Furthermore, it was suggested that: 'intellectual and artistic creativity is a precious asset … it is a vital source of economic wealth … this creativity needs to be protected….'[142]

This economic focus was mirrored in the early copyright Directives that predated the ISD – the Computer Programs Directive, Rental and Lending Right Directive, Term Directive and Database Directive.[143] These Directives[144] illustrated a predominantly economic utilitarian approach, for example, it was explained that the investments made in copyright works must be protected as a result of the ease with which copying works takes place.[145] Otherwise, failing to provide stable legal protection for investments would dissuade investors from contributing to the creation of copyright works because they would not be able to easily recoup their expenditure.[146] Similarly, the protection of copyright works is also justified in the Rental and Lending Right Directive on the grounds that copyright works necessitate 'an adequate income basis for further creation'.[147] Furthermore, the recitals of these Directives state that the creation of copyright works is of fundamental importance to the economic development of the EU.[148] In addition to these justifications, the Directives are all underpinned by the goal of achieving the smooth functioning of the internal market.[149] This gives further support to Hugenholtz and Ramalho's claim that the legislative action of EU copyright law has been primarily based on the establishment and functioning of the internal market.[150] Hence, the pre-ISD copyright legislation was primarily economic/utilitarian in focus.

However, the introduction of the ISD heralded significant changes to EU copyright law. Not only was it the first attempt at harmonising copyright law generally, it also introduced new considerations that were not to be found in the previous copyright Directives. This has resulted in great significance being attributed to the ISD because it illustrates the direction in which modern EU copyright law is

[141] ibid 5.

[142] ibid 6.

[143] Also see Council Directive 93/83/EEC of 27 September 1993 on the coordination of certain rules concerning copyright and rights related to copyright applicable to satellite broadcasting and cable retransmission [Satellite and Cable Directive] [1993] OJ L248/15, 6.10.1993.

[144] Codified version of Directives referred to where possible – Computer Programs Directive 2009, Rental and Lending Right Directive 2006 and Term Directive 2006. The recitals of the codified versions of the Directives for the most part are consistent with the earlier Directives that they replaced.

[145] Recital 2 of the Computer Programs Directive and Recital 7 of the Database Directive.

[146] Recital 12 of the Database Directive.

[147] Recital 5 of the Rental and Lending Right Directive.

[148] Recital 3 of the Computer Programs Directive, Recital 3 of the Rental and Lending Right Directive. and Recital 9 of the Database Directive.

[149] Recital 4 of the Computer Programs Directive, Recitals 3 and 12 of the Term Directive, Recitals 3 and 4 of the Database Directive and Recitals 1 and 3 of the Rental and Lending Right Directive 1992 (note there is no recital concerning the functioning of the internal market under the Rental and Lending Right Directive 2006).

[150] Hugenholtz (2012) 4 and Ramalho (2014) 208.

proceeding.[151] It is also important to note that the ISD is the primary piece of EU legislation addressed in this book because it contains the Article 3 communication to the public right that is the focal point of discussion for the proposals made.

In terms of goals, the ISD restated the economic aims of the previous copyright Directives with the addition of new non-economic goals, in particular, the need to take into account the fundamental principles of EU law:

- Establishing an internal market including implementing/upholding the four freedoms – Recital 1;
- Ensuring competition – Recital 1;
- Foster the development of the information society – Recital 2;
- Copyright law must comply with the fundamental principles of EU law namely the right to property, freedom of speech and the public interest – Recital 3;
- The Directive aims to provide a high level of protection for the purpose of fostering substantial investment in innovation and creativity – Recitals 4 and 9;
- Copyright law should be adapted and supplemented for economic realities such as new forms of exploitation (deriving from new technologies) – Recital 5;
- If authors are to continue their creative work, they need to be rewarded – Recitals 10 and 11;
- Adequate protection of copyright works is important from a cultural standpoint – Recital 12;
- The Directive should seek to promote learning and culture by protecting works, while permitting exceptions and limitations in the public interest for the purpose of education and teaching – Recital 14; and
- A fair balance of rights and interests between right holders and users – Recital 31.

Looking at the goals in these recitals of the ISD reiterates the importance of the constitutional considerations that were previously discussed and highlights the plurality of considerations that EU copyright law must accommodate. The main goals of the ISD as highlighted above can be separated into three groups of considerations. Firstly, the economic considerations involving the development of the internal market and the information society; secondly, the encouragement and protection of authors and right holders' interests; and lastly, balancing the competing interests that include fundamental rights, development of technology and the promotion of learning and culture – the so-called users' interests.

The economic considerations under EU copyright law exist to further the internal market and develop the information society. These considerations have directly influenced the harmonisation agenda of the EU, as they require a greater level of

[151] Jütte suugests that the ISD introduced momentum to the development of the EU's copyright jurisprudence – B Jütte, 'The beginning of a (happy?) relationship: copyright and freedom of expression in Europe' (2016) *EIPR* 11, 16.

harmonisation between the laws of the various Member States. As such, the impact of these considerations has been the encouragement of increased harmonisation and even the pursuit of maximal harmonisation in some areas, for example the communication to the public right.[152] Alternatively, the goals concerning authors and right holders relate to the development of a high level of protection that will encourage authors to continue creating and ensure right holders are able to effectively exploit their works. The influence of this goal has been the adoption of broad interpretations of exclusive rights such as reproduction and communication to the public, under Articles 2 and 3 of the ISD respectively.[153] However, the term 'high level of protection' has not been defined. With the range of pressures and interests that are relevant to copyright law, it is unlikely that the term 'high level of protection' mandates that the interests of the author or right holder are elevated above the other competing considerations. As such, the term 'high level of protection' should be understood to mean that a sufficient or adequate level of protection is provided, to ensure that the interests of right holders are protected in an effective manner.[154]

Aside from the economic considerations and the pro-author and right holder considerations, the addition of fundamental rights and the other non-economic considerations has led to a rebalancing of copyright law. This is because courts, in interpreting EU copyright law, were prompted to consider the competing interests that intersect with copyright law for the purpose of achieving a more balanced copyright framework. The consequence of this is a more balanced approach whereby copyright laws, their interpretation and enforcement must be compatible with other interests such as business practices, development of technology, promotion of learning and culture and any other fundamental rights concerns, and moreover, the general EU principle of proportionality. As such, EU copyright law can no longer operate in a purely author-centric fashion. This claim is evidenced in the decisions of *Scarlet Extended*, *UPC Telekabel* and *Nintendo v PC*, where the non-economic and non-property interests were balanced with the right holders' interests, to provide a fair and justified result. Therefore, the development of EU copyright law must proportionately balance the interests of right holders with those of service providers and end users.[155]

[152] Case C-466/12 *Nils Svensson and others v Retriever Sverige AB* [2014] ECLI:EU:C:2014:76, para 36.

[153] The broad interpretation of the communication to the public right will be dismissed in Chapters two and three.

[154] Recital 4 of Directive 2001/84/EC of the European Parliament and of the Council of 27 September 2001 on the resale right for the benefit of the author of an original work of art uses the phrase: 'the imposition of such a right in all Member States meets the need for providing creators with an adequate and standard level of protection'. Alternatively, in Case C-456/06 *Peek & Cloppenburg KG v Cassina SpA* [2008] ECLI:EU:C:2008:232, para 37 and Case C-462/09 *Stichting de Thuiskopie v Opus Supplies Deutschland GmbH and others* [2011] ECLI:EU:C:2011:397, para 32, the CJEU interpreted 'a high level of protection' to mean that the right holder was entitled to an appropriate reward.

[155] D Kallinikou, 'CJEU Policy and Practice in the Field of European Copyright Law' in T Synodinou (ed), *Codification of European Copyright Law: Challenges and Perspectives* (Kluwer Law International, 2012) 90 and Commission, *Proposal for a European Parliament and Council Directive on harmonization*

E. Economic Perspective

Copyright law has a necessary connection with economics due to the fact that the intangible works, which are protected, are public goods.[156] As such, copyright law is a natural field for economic analysis and, moreover, the economic perspective should be an influential consideration.[157] The public good issue with respect to copyright law means that copyright works suffer from the effects of being non-excludable and non-rivalrous;[158] that is, use of a copyright work will not diminish the number available to other users[159] and two or more persons can use the same work simultaneously, respectively. As a consequence, this creates market failure, whereby in the absence of copyright regulation it is less likely that persons will want to create new works or increase investment because they cannot recoup their initial outlay.[160] The reason for this is that consumers can free ride in their consumption of copyright works where there are no measures to limit use, thus resulting in underproduction of works.[161] Therefore, copyright law, from the economic perspective, exists to prevent free riding.[162]

In order to solve the public good problem and the consequential free riding, it is imperative to strike the right balance between incentives to create works and

of certain aspects of copyright and related rights in the Information Society (COM(97) 628 final, 1998) 9 and *GS Media* [2016] para 31.

[156] Landes and Posner (1989) 326, Van den Bergh (1998) 20, P Samuelson, 'Should Economics Play a Role in Copyright Law and Policy?' (2004) 1 *University of Ottawa Law & Technology Journal* 1, 3, A Stojkov, G Naumovski and V Naumovski, 'Economics of Copyright: Challenges and Perspectives' (2013) 7(1) *Mizan Law Review* 126, 132, D Brennan, 'Fair price and public goods: a theory of value applied to retransmission' (2002) 22 *International Review of Law and Economics* 347, 349–51, P Samuelson, 'The Pure Theory of Public Expenditure' (1954) 36 *Review of Economics & Statistics (Rev Econ & Stat)* 387 and JP Conley and CS Yoo, 'Nonrivalry and Price Discrimination in Copyright Economics' (2009) 157 *University of Pennsylvania Law Review (U Pa L Rev)* 1801. For a nuanced discussion on copyright as a public good, see Brennan (2002) 351–61.

[157] Landes and Posner (1989) 325 and R Posner, *Economic Analysis of Law*, 9th edn (Wolters Kluwer Law & Business, 2014) Chapter 11.

[158] CS Yoo, 'Copyright and Public Good Economics: A Misunderstood Relation' (2007) 155 *U Pa L Rev* 635, 637, Conley and Yoo (2009) 1805–06 and E Mackaay, 'Economic Incentives in Markets for Information and Innovation' (1990) 13 *Harv JL & Pub Pol'y* 867, 880. For an alternative perspective arguing that digital copyright works are not public goods because persons can be excluded from their use see: F Lima and P Akester, 'The economic dimension of the digital challenge: a copyright perspective' [2005] 1 *IPQ* 69, 74. However, Samuelson and Brennan counter this argument by noting that there are variations of public goods. If a good is non-excludable or non-rivalrous, it is a mixed good, but still classifiable as a public good (as opposed to a pure public good – non-excludable and non-rivalrous) – P Samuelson, 'Aspects of Public Expenditure Theories' (1958) 40 *Rev Econ & Stat* 332, 335, Brennan (2002) 350 citing S Shmanske, *Public Goods, Mixed Goods and Monopolistic Competition* (Texas A&M University Press, 1991) 226–27, JG Head, 'Public Goods and Public Policy' (1962) 17 *Public Finance* 197 and DL Burk, 'The Market for Digital Piracy' in B Kahin and C Nesson (eds), *Cyberspace: Information Policy and the Global Information Infrastructure* (MIT Press, 1997) 205.

[159] This is also referred to as 'undepletable' given that the marginal cost of an additional consumer is zero – Brennan (2002) 351.

[160] Hurt and Schuchman (1966) 429 and Stojkov, Naumovski and Naumovski (2013) 132.

[161] Yoo (2007) 637–38.

[162] G Karnell, 'The Berne Convention between authors' rights and copyright economics – an international dilemma' (1995) 26(2) *IIC* 193, 193 and Van den Bergh (1998) 20.

access to those works.[163] Thus, the scope of copyright protection must be delicately balanced so that right holders are encouraged to create without unreasonable burdens being placed on users.[164] This effectively becomes a question of how far the exclusivity of copyright protection should go.[165] Karnell suggests that the intended purpose of copyright law is to 'create incentives that will cause a maximum difference between the value of the result of the creative efforts involved and the social cost of its creation, with the cost of the administration of the system included.'[166] However, copyright law is an inadequate response to the market failure issue, especially in the digital context.[167] There is no way to prevent free riding, it can only be contained.[168] Consequently, the best approach is to maximise net benefits and minimise costs and externalities.[169]

Although there is no way to solve the public good/market failure problem, this is not to say that the economic perspective is unimportant. On the contrary, the economic perspective *is* of importance and it is arguable that courts do not apply enough thought to the economic rationales and consequences of copyright law. Yen argues that it is often the case that courts decide controversial copyright cases with no consideration to the economic consequences that may result.[170] In order to establish a coherent communication to the public right, it is necessary that the economic background and perspective of copyright law be taken account of in determining the scope of protection. This is given impetus when one considers that intellectual property is of great economic importance[171] and provides a major contribution to the international economy;[172] as such, the scope of protection is of financial significance. This increased awareness about the relevance of economics for copyright law is visible, for example, in the recitals of the Information Society Directive.[173] However, this development has been slow because of the romantic notion of copyright born from the close connection of the creative industries to the policy- and law-makers.[174] Furthermore, lawyers have traditionally lacked the

[163] Karnell (1995) 194, Landes and Posner (1989) 326, Van den Bergh (1998) 21, P Letai, 'Don't think twice, it's all right: toward a new copyright protection system' (2014) 5(7) *Journal of Business and Economics* 1012, 1013 and Lima and Akester (2005) 75 and 80.

[164] Lima and Akester (2005) 69.

[165] Yoo argues that there is no 'invisible hand' (market forces of demand and supply) to guide the most efficient outcome – Yoo (2007) 642.

[166] Karnell (1995) 193.

[167] This is because of the ease of digital copying and the negligible cost attached to it – Lima and Akester (2005) 74.

[168] The possible results for copyright law range from complete market failure to efficient production given that copyright works can be argued to be an impure public good – Yoo (2007) 642 and 675.

[169] Letai (2015) 766.

[170] Yen (1990) 520.

[171] Lima and Akester (2005) 69.

[172] D Gervais, *(Re)structuring Copyright: A Comprehensive Path to International Copyright Reform* (Edward Elgar Publishing Ltd, 2017) 279 and G Raemello and F Silva, 'New Directions in Copyright Law and Economics' (2007) 3(3) *Review of Law & Economics* 643, 643.

[173] See Recitals 5, 6, 33, 38, 39 and 44. These Recitals note that it is important to consider the economic impact of copyright law and its application.

[174] J Griffin, 'Copyright evolution – creation, regulation and the decline of substantively rational copyright law' [2013] 3 *IPQ* 234, 248 and Samuelson (2004) 7.

specific skills required to engage in detailed economic analysis, perpetuated by the inability of law and economics scholars to speak in a language accessible to persons involved in copyright law.[175]

Despite the slow development of economic reasoning, it can be said that economic arguments and justifications are gaining weight within the sphere of EU copyright with regard to the pursuit of specific economic-influenced goals.[176] Consequently, economics as a consideration is no longer limited to being an external tool of analysis. For example, Landes and Posner's use of economics was in the context of an economic analysis of law, whereby the existing law is subjected to critique for the purpose of developing more economically efficient law.[177] Instead, economics now also forms an internal copyright consideration to be taken into account in the interpretation and application of laws by judges.[178] For the purposes of the framework established in this chapter, both economic analysis of law and economic reasoning are taken account of. With this in mind, Griffin's approach is attractive because he covers both aspects under the guise of 'economic reasoning'. Griffin divides economic reasoning into three parts: encouraging creation of works, regulating exploitation of works and encouraging efficient allocation of resources.[179]

Griffin's approach to economic reasoning provides a comprehensive approach to copyright law as a whole. He emphasises that the development of effective copyright laws must focus on creation, regulation and a wider goal, in this case economic efficiency, all of which are linked. Consequently, legislators and the judiciary alike must consider the rationales for and consequences of their decisions in this broad economic manner.[180] However, this economic perspective must be weighed with the other competing considerations discussed in this chapter. While economic reasoning does provide valuable insight into how copyright laws should be structured, interpreted and applied, it is not definitive. Given the rapid development in technology and the way that copyright works are used, it is insufficient to rely on economic reasoning as the sole means to regulate copyright law.[181]

[175] Samuelson (2004) 7–8. It should also be noted that Samuelson raises the issue of disagreement among economists themselves in analysing copyright law – Samuelson (2004) 8–9.

[176] K Koelman, 'Copyright law and economics in the EU Copyright Directive: is the droit d'auteur passe?' (2004) 35(6) *IIC* 603, 604. Griffin argues that formalist economic reasoning is gradually replacing traditional property justifications for copyright law – Griffin (2013).

[177] Landes and Posner (1989).

[178] P Hubkova, 'Economic Reasoning in the Court of Justice of the EU: A Study on the Use of Economics in Competition Case-Law' (LLM Thesis, European University Institute, 2014) 15, citing E Stavang, 'Some Thoughts on Economic Reasoning in Appellate Courts and Legal Scholarship' in K Mathis (ed), *Law and economics in Europe: foundations and applications* (Springer, 2013) 126.

[179] Griffin (2013) 234–35.

[180] Samuelson also suggests a similar approach in that economic reasoning should play a part in the creation of legislation, its amendment and subsequent interpretation – Samuelson (2004) 13–15.

[181] Martin-Prat argues that policy shaping for copyright law is complex because developments in technology, user habits and cross-border infringement raise questions about whether copyright should be regulated using the traditional means/considerations – M Martin-Prat, 'An Introduction – The EU Copyright Agenda' in I Stamatoudi (ed), *New Developments in EU and International Copyright Law* (Kluwer Law International, 2016) 181–83.

This is because technology exacerbates the market failure/free riding problem that cannot be eradicated.[182] As such, it is necessary to weigh all the competing considerations to strike the right balance for copyright law.

F. Stakeholders' Interests

Thus far, several considerations have been elucidated for the purpose of proposing a framework for the reform of the communication to the public right. It has been demonstrated that copyright law has been designed to accommodate specific interests.[183] These interests range from EU constitutional concerns to copyright-specific issues involving the raison d'etre of copyright law and general economic reasoning. Equally, the industries and the players affected by copyright law must also be addressed, including the parties that create, distribute and consume copyright content. Broadly, the relevant groups of entities include: authors and right holders, content industries, intermediaries and end users. In order to develop a forward looking EU copyright policy it is necessary to take account of the interests of all these groups.[184] However, the existing laws on copyright have struggled to balance the interests of stakeholders, and as such it is important to expose the needs of the various parties.[185]

(i) Authors and Right Holders

The interests of authors[186] and right holders[187] have always been a primary, if not central, focus of copyright law. Whether discussed in the context of economic reasoning, or a romantic notion of copyright law, the author/right holder is always central to the discussion. In the absence of the author/right holder, there will be no content or an underproduction of content, and as such it is imperative that their interests are taken into account to encourage the creation of more works which is beneficial to society at large.[188] However, as Gervais notes, there are different types of authors, and thus the development of copyright law should not be driven by a one-size-fit-all, author-centric policy, given the different needs and concerns of the various types of authors.[189] Consequently, it would be naïve to solely focus

[182] Copying can now be done at high speeds with negligible costs – Van den Bergh (1998) 20.
[183] Ramalho (2016) 39.
[184] The European Copyright Society suggests that EU copyright law must reflect the economic needs of traditional right holders, the fostering of cultural production, access to culture and knowledge and technological process – European Copyright Society, *General Opinion on the EU Copyright Reform Package* (2017) <https://europeancopyrightsociety.org/opinions/> accessed 6 August 2018, 4–5.
[185] Bechtold in Hugenholtz (2017) 68.
[186] In the traditional sense, authors are: writers, artists and musicians.
[187] Right holders meaning the persons who own/control the copyright works.
[188] This view is supported by the recitals of the ISD – Recitals 9–12 and 14.
[189] Gervais (2017) 167–69.

on providing a high level of protection for authors where there are authors who simply want their works to be seen as opposed to authors who primarily seek financial gain. This issue will be resolved where all the competing considerations discussed in this chapter are balanced.

(ii) Content Industries

Similar to authors and right holders, the interests of the content industries must be considered because it is often they who make the financial contributions facilitating the creation of works and moreover, allow for the dissemination of content to the public.[190] Presently, the interests of specific content industries, notably, software and databases are manifested in the form of stand-alone Directives on Computer Programs and Databases. Prima facie the interests of the content industries are often similar to those of authors/right holders, who primarily seek financial gain because their motivation is to recoup their investment and earn profit.[191] This viewpoint is reflected in Recital 9 of the ISD where industry is considered alongside authors, performers and producers. Recital 4 of the ISD also states that EU copyright law exists to foster substantial investment in content provision.

However, it must be noted that content industries are often the biggest beneficiaries of copyright protection because they control the works of authors, assignment being the industry standard. In other words, they are often also the right holder. As such, it is important that the development of copyright law considers the nuances of the relationship between authors and the content industries. Again, the idea of an author-centric policy approach is naïve because it does not reflect the practical realities of how copyright law works, given that content industries often own and control the copyright works. Similarly, a broad right that only aims to allow content industries to maximise revenue will not work because the other competing non-monetary interests are ignored. Hence, it is only with a careful balancing act of all the competing considerations that EU copyright law and its specific exclusive rights, like the communication to the public right, can be coherently developed.

(iii) Intermediaries

Unlike authors, right holders and the content industries that are involved in the creation of content directly or indirectly, intermediaries were traditionally third parties that 'provide a service capable of being used by a third party to infringe.'[192]

[190] This includes, record companies, publishers, movie studios, software producers and database companies.

[191] Ramalho (2016) 45.

[192] Case C-494/15 *Tommy Hilfiger Licensing LLC and others v Delta Center a.s.* [2016] ECLI:EU:C:2016:528, para 25.

This includes facilitating transactions between third parties on the internet, including: hosting and storage, transmission and indexing content.[193] Hence, the intermediaries of concern for this book include: ISPs;[194] social networks;[195] auction platforms;[196] search engines;[197] providers of open wireless networks;[198] digital storage hosts including cloud providers;[199] broadcasters;[200] and other telecommunication providers. In other words, intermediaries can be seen as content carriers.[201] The general approach to intermediaries is to ensure that their actions do not amount to direct or indirect copyright infringement. This has been facilitated by the provision of exceptions and limitations designed as carve-outs from the exclusive rights of copyright law.[202] However, this approach has become increasingly problematic in the digital context, where intermediaries have become more directly involved with the content they disseminate. As such, the distinctions between content creator, disseminator and consumer have become increasingly blurred as is the case with YouTube and other websites that allow for user-generated content or alternatively, websites such as VCAST.[203] With this in mind, the critical question is how much help/assistance in facilitating users' interactions with works amounts to copyright infringement.

Given the technological developments, it is necessary that the rules reflect the changes in intermediary involvement. In the context of the communication to the public right it will be necessary to reform the scope of the right in a way that takes into account for the changing status of intermediaries in conjunction with the other competing considerations, rather than relying solely on exceptions and limitations.

(iv) End Users

End users traditionally represent the consumers of copyright content. Unlike authors and right holders, who are ascribed positive rights under copyright law

[193] K Perset, 'The Economic and Social Role of Internet Intermediaries' (OECD Study, DSTI/ICCP (2009)9/Final) 9.

[194] *Scarlet Extended v SABAM* [2011]. For the liability of ISPs see G Dinwoodie, *Secondary Liability of Internet Service Providers* (Springer, 2017).

[195] Case C-360/10 *SABAM v Netlog* [2012] ECLI:EU:C:2012:85.

[196] Case C-324/09 *L'Oréal and others v eBay International AG and others* [2011] ECLI:EU:C:2011:474.

[197] Case C-131/12 *Google Spain SL and Google Inc v Agencia Española de Protección de Datos (AEPD) and Mario Costeja González* [2014] ECLI:EU:C:2014:317.

[198] Case C-484/14 *Tobias McFaddden v Sony Music Entertainment Germany GmbH* [2016] ECLI:EU:C:2016:689.

[199] See ASY Cheung and RH Weber (eds), *Privacy and Legal Issues in Cloud Computing* (Edward Elgar Publishing Ltd, 2015).

[200] Note, broadcasters can be creators of copyright content where their broadcasts are subject to copyright protection. For example, see the rights ascribed under the Satellite and Cable Directive – Article 4 and the ISD – Articles 3–4.

[201] Ramalho (2016) 48.

[202] See Articles 12–15 of the E-Commerce Directive and Article 5(1) of the ISD.

[203] Case C-265/16 *VCAST Ltd v RTI SpA* [2017] ECLI:EU:C:2017:913.

by virtue of the exclusive rights, the 'rights' of users are dependent on the scope of those rights and any applicable exceptions or limitations. Traditionally, end users have not featured at the forefront of copyright policy-making. However, with the increased prominence of economic reasoning and the digital revolution, end users need to be considered in greater detail. In terms of economic reasoning, access to works must be balanced with the incentives for creation. In this context, emphasis is placed on promoting greater access in order to balance the broad exclusive rights of copyright law. This is of importance when one considers the different types of end user such as those in education or developing countries, where the potential for financial return is limited, but the need for access to works is considerable.

Access is also emphasised due to developments in technology.[204] Digital technology has resulted in more widespread use of works and moreover, the ability of users to seamlessly switch roles to being content creators.[205] Notably, social media has had an impact in the growth of this evolved user culture.[206] As such, access and use of works should be accommodated rather than the sole focus being on furthering the exclusivity of copyright. Thus, the way users interact with works through technology must be included in the discussion, or else the consequence could be overregulation of copyright works. Furthermore, it is potentially the case that any use of a digital copyright work involves the making of reproductions, be it permanent, temporary or transient. Consequently, a rethink of the exclusive rights is needed that better accounts for user interests and modern norms.

G. Summary of Considerations

The proportionality norm comprises three aspects – suitability, necessity, and proportionality *sensu stricto*. The suitability and necessity aspects will address whether the measure(s) adopted can achieve the stated objective and does so using the least restrictive approach, respectively. Thus, these two aspects will be applied to the interpretation and application stages of the communication to the public right. They form the standard of critique against which the scope and substance of the communication to the public right will be assessed. By contrast, the *sensu stricto* aspect will address the pre-legislation aspect of the communication to the public right.

Broadly, the interests that the *sensu stricto* aspect of the proportionality norm has to consider can be divided into the constitutional considerations of EU law

[204] Kallinikou in Synodinou (2012) 89.

[205] A Reindl, 'Choosing Law in Cyberspace: Copyright Conflicts on Global Networks' (1998) 19(3) *Michigan Journal of International Law* 799, 800. Also see, CHY Tan, 'Technological "nudges" and copyright on social media sites' [2015] 1 *IPQ* 62, 64–69.

[206] T Synodinou, 'The lawful user and a balancing of interests in European copyright law' (2010) 41(7) *IIC* 819, 821.

and copyright-specific interests. The constitutional pressures include the internal market, fundamental rights and the general principles of EU law. The copyright interests comprise the rights and obligations under the international copyright treaties, the domestic traditions of Member States and the goals designated for EU copyright law contained in the *acquis communitaire*, in particular, the copyright Directives and *travaux préparatoires*.

In the course of reforming the communication to the public right, the constitutional and copyright considerations will be applied to the conceptualisation, interpretation and application of the right. However, it is advocated that the most desirable outcome is for the legislator to take account of all of these considerations when designing the scope of the reformed communication to the public right, so that all the relevant considerations are embodied in the legislation. Thus, the burden on courts to conduct balancing exercises at the stage of interpretation and application will be greatly reduced. With this approach in mind, it is worth noting the importance and magnitude of the task given the inevitability of conflicting interests.

It is foreseeable that the internal market consideration will clash with fundamental rights, that fundamental rights will conflict with one another, and that the goals for EU copyright law will have to be compromised. In particular, the fundamental right to property will conflict with the rights of freedom of expression and access to information[207] and the freedom to conduct business, specifically where new forms of exploitation are involved. The aim of furthering the internal market will also be affected because an overbroad communication to the public right will impair the free movement of goods and services and, moreover, differences in the scope of the right in various Member States will cause the re-fragmentation of the market. Lastly, it is necessary to remember that EU copyright law has largely been developed with the aim of providing a high level of protection for right holders.[208] However, the interests of users have to be considered in greater detail.[209] Therefore, what is required is a delicate balancing of the competing pressures and interests. In particular, it is imperative that all stakeholders' interests are reconciled with the copyright-specific goals of the EU within the EU law framework.

Unlike the current use of the proportionality principle that has largely been restricted to an interpretation tool used by the CJEU, the *sensu stricto* aspect of the proportionality norm should play a greater role in determining the scope of the communication to the public right in the pre-legislation phase. If done correctly,

[207] For discussion on copyright versus freedom of expression see: *Ashby Donaldson and others v France* [2013] ECHR 287, *Fredrik Neij and Peter Sunde Kolmisoppi (The Pirate Bay) v Sweden* [2013] Application no 40397/12, 19.2.2013, Case C-145/10 *Eva-Maria Painer v Standard VerlagsGmbH and others* [2011] ECLI:EU:C:2011:798 and J Griffiths, 'Copyright law after *Ashdown* – time to deal fairly with the public' [2002] 3 *IPQ* 240.

[208] Jütte argues that the EU will have to come to terms with its right holder friendly position that privileges economic interests, so as to avoid prejudicing other competing interests such as freedom of expression in the future – Jütte (2016) 22. Also see Halpern and Johnson (2014) 109 and 129.

[209] Ramalho (2016) 51 and 139–43.

the proportionality norm will be able to produce a reformed communication to the public right that provides an adequate level of protection for right holders, while allowing users and developers of technology to still engage with copyright works in a useful manner. Moreover, the proposed communication to the public right must conform with the rights and obligations set out in the international copyright treaties and be compatible with the *droit d'auteur* and copyright traditions of the Member States, in order to follow the recommendations. Additional to the constitutional and copyright considerations, there are also practical issues to bear in mind. The scope of the proposed right should be technology-neutral to ensure its longevity. Similarly, overregulation that can lead to chilling effects on the development of technology and new business practices must be avoided. This is because an overly broad communication to the public right will have negative implications for the development of the information society and the dissemination of content that will be to the detriment of individuals' cultural and educational development and counterintuitive to the inherent economic element of copyright law.[210]

IV. Certainty

The legal certainty principle has been restricted to the recitals of the Directives relevant to copyright law.[211] Thus, it has been a consideration applied at the legislative level. For example, in the ISD, references to 'certainty' are made as justification for the provisions introduced under that Directive.[212] It is either the case that the pre-existing law was uncertain as in the case of on demand transmissions,[213] or that greater legal certainty was necessary or desirable for the achievement of other goals, such as the smooth functioning of the internal market or providing right holders with a high level of protection.[214] As a result, the certainty principle has mostly been used to justify the need for the provisions provided under the various copyright Directives.

From this, the principle of certainty exists to encourage the development and adoption of laws that are clear, coherent and consistent. The certainty principle was also employed in *UPC Telekabel* to ensure that the addressee of the injunction at hand was able to defend his actions regarding his compliance with the court order.[215] Thus, the certainty principle was used as a means of ensuring that

[210] This is because the access aspect of the economic equation will be compromised.

[211] The exception to this is in *UPC Telekabel* [2014] para 54, where the legal certainty principle was invoked to ensure that addressees of injunctions are able to defend their actions in implementing the requirements of the injunction.

[212] Recitals 4, 6, 7, 21 and 25 of the ISD.

[213] Recital 25 of the ISD.

[214] Recitals 4, 6 and 7 of the ISD.

[215] *UPC Telekabel* [2014] para 54.

the enforcement procedure is clear and consistent for defendants. Following from *UPC Telekabel*, it is suggested that the use of certainty in the normative framework proposed should be all-inclusive to cover the creation, interpretation and application of the legislation. In this way, the design of the law is clear, precise and coherent, but additionally, the interpretation and application of that law are equally certain as to the consequences resulting from a particular holding by the CJEU. Therefore, certainty is the standard against which decisions that are inconsistent as a matter of their precedential value can be criticised. To facilitate this, it is proposed that courts must bear in mind the various competing interests discussed under the context of the proportionality norm and, moreover, the court must consider the practical consequences of their decisions. In other words, the decisions of the CJEU concerning the communication to the public right must be consistent with the right's objectives and consistent as to precedent followed or set.

Therefore, the proportionality and certainty norms operate in tandem to ensure desirable results.

V. Conclusion – Developing the EU Right of Communication to the Public

This chapter established the normative framework against which the EU right of communication to the public will be scrutinised in the remaining chapters. The framework comprising the norms of proportionality and certainty proposes a comprehensive reform of the manner in which EU copyright law is legislated for, interpreted and applied. Under the norm of proportionality it is argued that all the competing interests affecting EU copyright law must be accounted for. This includes the constitutional considerations of EU law, notably, the internal market and fundamental rights; and the copyright considerations – the international copyright treaties; the domestic traditions of Member States, Directives on copyright, and EU policy considerations, including the inherent economic perspective and stakeholders' interests. In terms of reforming the communication to the public right, it is advocated that all the above interests must be balanced at the legislative, interpretation and application stages. Therefore, the recommendations for the reformed right will be guided by these various pressures and interests. This is not a simple task because of the inevitable conflict of the various competing elements.

However, this is only one aspect of the proportionality norm – proportionality *sensu stricto*. The other two aspects – suitability and necessity – must also be applied. These aspects address, respectively, whether the measure adopted can achieve the stated objective and whether it does so using the least restrictive approach. Thus, the very substance and scope of the communication to the public right will be criticised as to its viability and validity. The suitability and necessity of the communication to the public right are of particular importance, given the nexus of law and technology and its rapidly evolving dynamic. As such, the reforms proposed have to be delicately calculated to be technology neutral and 'future-proofed', while still maintaining their effectiveness.[216]

As for the certainty norm, beyond ensuring that the legislation is clear and precise, it will more importantly be used as the mode of critique to ensure that the decisions of the CJEU are coherent and consistent. Consequently, a comprehensive analysis of the right of communication to the public case law will be embarked upon in Chapters two and three.

[216] In other words, the proposal must avoid becoming outdated due to changes in technology.

2

Journey from *Rafael Hoteles* to *Renckhoff*: Exploring the EU Right of Communication to the Public

I. Introduction

The development of the communication to the public right under European Union (EU) copyright law has been fragmentary at the legislative level by virtue of comprising several subject-matter-specific rights. There is a communication to the public right for: satellite broadcasting under the Satellite and Cable Retransmission Directive,[1] related subject-matter under the Rental and Lending Right Directive,[2] databases under the Database Directive,[3] and copyright works under the Information Society Directive (ISD).[4] However, the concept of 'communication to the public' remains undefined in these Directives. Consequently, the development of the right has been achieved through the case law of the Court of Justice of the European Union (CJEU). Nevertheless, aspects of the communication to the public right's development are contentious and uncertain.[5] As such, this chapter will examine the development of the communication to the public right under EU copyright law.

Section II articulates the scope of the communication to the public right. Included in this discussion is a narrative of the development of the right, with

[1] Council Directive 93/83/EEC of 27 September 1993 on the coordination of certain rules concerning copyright and rights related to copyright applicable to satellite broadcasting and cable retransmission [Satellite and Cable Retransmission Directive] [1993] OJ L248/15, 6.10.1993.

[2] Council Directive 92/100/EEC of 19 November 1992 on rental right and lending right and on certain rights related to copyright in the field of intellectual property, codified in: Directive 2006/11/EC of the European Parliament and of the Council of 12 December 2006 on rental right and lending right and on certain rights related to copyright in the field of intellectual property [Rental and Lending Right Directive] [1992] OJ L346/61, 27.11.1992. The codified Directive will be referred to unless otherwise noted.

[3] Directive 96/9/EC of the European Parliament and of the Council of 11 March 1996 on the legal protection of databases [Database Directive] [1996] OJ L77/20, 27.3.1996.

[4] Directive 2001/29/EC of the European Parliament and of the Council of 22 May 2001 on the harmonisation of certain aspects of copyright and related rights in the information society [Information Society Directive] [2001] OJ L167/10, 22.6.2001.

[5] Commission, *Communication from the Commission to the European Parliament, the Council, the European Economic and Social Committee and the Committee of the Regions: Towards a modern, more European copyright framework* (COM(2015) 626 final, 2015) 9.

particular emphasis on the CJEU's rationale for that development and the criteria required to establish infringement. As such, the relevant Directives and the case law from *Rafael Hoteles*[6] to *Renckhoff*[7] will be examined. Section III then addresses the legal reasoning underlying the decision-making of the CJEU with regard to the right of communication to the public. It will be highlighted that three factors primarily guide the development of the CJEU's case law, the maximal protection approach, the harmonisation agenda and the economic influence.

II. Making Sense of the EU Communication to the Public Right

The concept of 'communication to the public' under EU copyright law can be found in four different Directives. Article 2 of the Satellite and Cable Retransmission Directive provides an exclusive right of communication to the public by satellite broadcast.[8] Article 8 of the Rental and Lending Right Directive has three subject-matter-specific rights. Performers are granted an exclusive right of communication to the public in their performances (Article 8(1)). Broadcasting organisations are afforded an exclusive right of communication to the public for the broadcasting and re-broadcasting of their broadcasts, but only where the broadcast is made accessible to the public for an entrance fee (Article 8(3)). By contrast, phonogram owners are provided with a compulsory licensing mechanism to remunerate the communication to the public of their phonograms, in lieu of an exclusive right (Article 8(2)).[9] Article 5(d) of the Database Directive grants a right of communication, display or performance to the public. Lastly, Article 3(1) of the ISD provides an exclusive right of communication to the public, including the making available of copyright works.[10] The 'making available' aspect is also extended to related subject-matter under Article 3(2).[11]

Despite these four sources, 'communication to the public' remains undefined. Although the recitals of these Directives provide limited guidance on the scope and operation of the rights provided, the burden has fallen on the CJEU to interpret and develop the right. As a result, the right of communication to the public has been developed in a piecemeal manner that leads to concerns about its

[6] Case C-306/05 *Sociedad General de Autores y Editores de España (SGAE) v Rafael Hoteles SA* [2006] ECLI:EU:C:2006:764.

[7] Case C-161/17 *Land Nordrhein-Westfalen v Dirk Renckhoff* [2018] ECLI:EU:C:2018:634.

[8] This provision conforms with the scope of protection provided in Article 11bis of the Berne Convention for the Protection of Literary and Artistic Works 1971.

[9] The provisions under Article 8 are based on Articles 7(1)(a), 12 and 13(d) of the International Convention for the Protection of Performers, Producers of Phonograms and Broadcasting Organizations 1961 [Rome Convention].

[10] Article 3(1) is based on Article 8 of the WIPO Copyright Treaty 1996.

[11] Article 3(2) is based on Articles 10 and 14 of the WIPO Performances and Phonograms Treaty.

coherence and, moreover, its state of harmonisation (or lack thereof). Furthermore, the lack of guidance and the complexity of the communication to the public right has resulted in numerous referrals to the CJEU from various Member States, concerning different aspects of the right. This has provided the CJEU with the opportunity to clarify the scope and operation of the right. Before highlighting the individual problems with the right, it is important to demonstrate how the right developed. The narrative will comprise discussion on the criteria of the communication to the public right, the consistency of the concept across Directives and the rationales for the development of the right.

A. The Criteria for Establishing Communication to the Public

The communication to the public right must be analysed in two phases.[12] The first phase concerns the initial interpretation of the right pre-*Svensson*,[13] characterised by traditional analogue thinking, given that the reasoning used in the cases focused on traditional modes of broadcasting and retransmission.[14] The second phase or the Internet phase began with *Svensson* and is distinguishable because of its Internet context. Post-*Svensson*, the criteria for finding infringement of the right of communication to the public underwent several significant changes. As such the movement from *Rafael Hoteles* to *Renckhoff* will be explored, with the development of the criteria for the communication to the public right central to the discussion.

(i) The First Phase – Rafael Hoteles *and the Pre-*Svensson *Broadcasting and Retransmission Cases*

The starting point for the communication to the public right's development must be attributed to *Rafael Hoteles*.[15] This was the first time[16] the CJEU

[12] The division of the two phases are not strictly chronological because there are some cases concerning traditional retransmission or reception in public interspersed with the 'making available' cases concerning the Internet.

[13] Case C-466/12 *Svensson and others v Retriever Sverige AB* [2014] ECLI:EU:C:2014:76.

[14] This is demonstrated in Case C-607/11 *ITV Broadcasting Ltd and others v TVCatchup Ltd* [2013] ECLI:EU:C:2013:147 where the Internet retransmission of television broadcasts was treated in a similar manner to traditional and satellite rebroadcasting.

[15] *Rafael Hoteles* has been described as the fundamental judgment on which the communication to the public right was constructed – F Brison and S Depreeuw, 'The right of 'communication to the public' in the European Union' in P Torremans (ed), *Research Handbook on Copyright Law*, 2nd edn (Edward Elgar Publishing Ltd, 2017) 119 and PB Hugenholtz and S Van Velze, 'Communication to a new public? Three reasons why EU copyright law can do without a "new public"' (2016) 47(7) *International Review of Intellectual Property and Competition Law (IIC)* 797, 804.

[16] F Rizzuto, 'The European Union law concept of communication to the public and the protection of copyright in electronic transmissions' (2012) 18(6) *Computer and Telecommunications Law Review* 179, 180.

substantively addressed the communication to the public right.[17] *Rafael Hoteles* was concerned with the cable retransmission of a centrally received broadcast to the private rooms of a hotel. The question for the Court was whether cable retransmission of a broadcast amounted to an act of communication to the public under Article 3(1) of the ISD. In looking at the concept of communication to the public, the CJEU stated that the right must be given an autonomous and uniform interpretation throughout the EU. This means that the right should be interpreted independently of the laws of the Member States and should be interpreted and applied consistently across Member States.[18] This reasoning is consistent with the EU's harmonisation agenda for copyright law. Additionally, the Court held that the right should be interpreted consistently with the international copyright treaties (in this case the Berne Convention)[19] and be construed broadly, so as to establish a high level of protection for copyright law.[20] These initial guidelines set the tone for how the CJEU thought the communication to the public right should be interpreted and applied; that is, in a broad manner, but consistent with international copyright obligations and in pursuit of a harmonised approach among Member States.[21] The viability of the broad interpretation will be discussed in Chapter three, section II.

Additional to the interpretive guidance, the CJEU in *Rafael Hoteles* provided the initial criteria for identifying an act of communication to the public. In order to establish communication to the public, there must be an act of 'communication' made to a 'public'. Furthermore, where the act is a retransmission or reception in public, there must be a 'new public'. The CJEU also noted that the profit-making nature of the communication is a relevant consideration. These criteria formed the initial approach for determining communication to the public infringement. With the exception of one addition in *ITV Broadcasting*, the initial criteria remained the same until *Svensson* and the beginning of the Internet cases that will be discussed in the second phase in section II.A.(ii).

The Court in *Rafael Hoteles* did not assess whether there was a 'communication', but instead assumed that the act of cable retransmission was an act of 'communication'.[22] Despite this, a definition for 'communication' can be inferred from two aspects of the *Rafael Hoteles* decision. The first inference of a definition can be drawn from the CJEU's approach to establishing a 'new public'. It was

[17] Prior to *Rafael Hoteles*, there was one other case which concerned the communication to the public right. However, that case was dismissed without any substantive discussion of the right because the Article 2 communication to the public right under the Satellite and Cable Retransmission Directive did not cover retransmissions of broadcasts to hotel rooms (only communication to the public by satellite was covered) – Case C-293/98 *Entidad de Gestión de Derechos de los Productores Audiovisuales (Egeda) v Hostelería Asturiana SA (Hoasa)* [2000] ECLI:EU:C:2000:66, paras 25–29.

[18] *SGAE v Rafael Hoteles* [2006] para 31.

[19] ibid para 35.

[20] ibid para 36. Also see Recital 23 of the ISD.

[21] These interpretive guidelines have been reiterated in all the CJEU's communication to the public cases.

[22] *SGAE v Rafael Hoteles* [2006] para 40.

stated that: 'the hotel is the organisation which intervenes, in full knowledge of the consequences of its action, to give access to the protected work to its customers.'[23] In other words, an act of communication to the public involves a knowing intervention to provide access to protected works to the 'public'.[24] However, this definition is problematic because the CJEU conflated the concept of 'communication' with the means of establishing a 'new public'.[25] The other possible definition found in *Rafael Hoteles* can be attributed to the statement: 'for there to be a communication to the public it is sufficient that the work is made available to the public in such a way that the persons forming the public may access it.'[26]

It was not until *FAPL v QC Leisure* that the CJEU expressly defined the term 'communication'. In this case, the showing of a broadcasted football match was held to be an act of 'communication', thus bringing acts of reception in public within the scope of the communication to the public right.[27] However, the CJEU, in making this finding, provided two definitions for 'communication'. It firstly stated that a 'communication' was 'any transmission of the protected works, irrespective of the technical means or process used'.[28] It then went on to state in the next paragraph that 'a hotel proprietor carries out an act of communication when he gives his customers access',[29] thus conflating the transmission and access approaches in the retransmission context. Subsequent to *FAPL v QC Leisure*, the CJEU has alternated between the use of the access and transmission approaches in defining 'communication'. For example, the CJEU in *Circul Globus Bucuresti* furthered the transmission approach by holding that the right of communication to the public 'does not cover any activity which does not involve a 'transmission' or a 'retransmission' of a work'.[30] Then in *SCF v Marco del Corso* the CJEU reverted to

[23] ibid para 42.

[24] This wording was expressly used to define 'communication' in Cases C-403/08 and C-429/08 *Football Association Premier League (FAPL) and others v QC Leisure and others and Karen Murphy v Media Protection Services Ltd* [2011] ECLI:EU:C:2011:631, para 194.

[25] The intervention approach has been followed in: Case C-135/10 *Societa Consortile Fonografici (SCF) v Marco del Corso* [2012] ECLI:EU:C:2012:140, para 82 and Case C-162/10 *Phonographic Performance (Ireland) Ltd (PPL) v Ireland* [2012] ECLI:EU:C:2012:141, para 31.

[26] *SGAE v Rafael Hoteles* [2006] para 43. This approach was cited and followed in *Svensson* [2014] para 19. Given the language used, it has been cited as evidence that the CJEU intended to apply the access approach to interpret communication to the public. This will be addressed where the access approach is discussed in defining the term 'communication' in Chapter 3, section III.

[27] *FAPL v QC Leisure* [2011] paras 191–96.

[28] ibid para 193.

[29] ibid para 194.

[30] Case C-283/10 *Circul Globus București (Circ & Variete Globus București) v Uniunea Compozitorilor și Muzicologilor din România – Asociația pentru Drepturi de Autor (UCMR – ADA)* [2011] ECLI:EU:C:2011:772, para 40. The transmission approach was also followed in: *ITV v TVCatchup* [2013] para 23, Case C-351/12 *Ochranný svaz autorský pro práva k dílům hudebním o.s (OSA) v Léčebné lázně Mariánské Lázně a.s* [2014] ECLI:EU:C:2014:110, para 25, Case C-151/15 *Portugese Society of Authors CRL (SPA) v Ministerio Público and others* [2015] ECLI:EU:C:2015:468, para 11, Case C-325/14 *SBS Belgium NV v Belgische Vereniging van Auteurs, Componisten en Uitgevers (SABAM)* [2016] ECLI:EU:C:2015:764, para 16, Case C-117/15 *Reha Training Gesellschaft für Sport- und Unfallrehabilitation mbH v Gesellschaft für musikalische Aufführungs- und mechanische Vervielfältigungsrechte eV (GEMA)* [2016] ECLI:EU:C:2016:379, para 38 and Case C-265/16 *VCAST Ltd v RTI SpA* [2017] ECLI:EU:C:2017:913, para 42.

the 'intervention to provide access' approach.[31] Therefore, it can be seen that the term 'communication' has been subjected to divergent definitions ranging from the narrow transmission approach to the wider intervention or access approaches. Thus, it is necessary that the concept of 'communication' is clarified and as such, the issue will be discussed in Chapter three, section III.

The other central criterion, 'public', was explored in *Rafael Hoteles*. The CJEU held that 'the term "public" refers to an indeterminate number of potential … viewers'.[32] With this definition in mind, the CJEU went on to establish that the determination of 'public' includes a cumulative account of potential viewers so that the private nature of hotel rooms did not prevent the finding of a 'public'.[33] This basic definition of 'public' was later expanded in *SCF v Marco del Corso* to read: 'the term "public" … refers to an indeterminate number of potential listeners, and, in addition, implies a fairly large number of persons'.[34] In addition, to fulfilling the 'public' requirement, the CJEU in *Rafael Hoteles* also required that the act of cable retransmission be made to a 'new public', given that it involved a communication made by a 'broadcasting organisation other than the original one'. This is because cable retransmission is not an act for simple reception; rather, it is an independent act for an audience larger than that intended by the initial broadcaster.[35] The 'new public' criterion was defined as a 'public different from the public at which the original act of communication of the work is directed'.[36] In the case of *Rafael Hoteles*, there was a 'new public' because the customers of the hotel would not have been able to enjoy the broadcasts without the intervention of the hotel. Therefore, all acts of retransmission must be made to a 'new public'. However, Chapter three, section VI will debate the appropriateness of the 'new public' criterion.

Notwithstanding the 'new public' criterion, the CJEU in *ITV v TVCatchup* developed an exception to the rule requiring a 'new public' where a retransmission is made. *ITV v TVCatchup* was the first case concerning the communication to the public right and the Internet. It involved the near simultaneous Internet retransmission of free-to-air broadcasts. However, instead of applying the 'new public' criterion as in the previous retransmission cases of *Rafael Hoteles*,[37] *Airfield v SABAM*[38] and *PPL v Ireland*,[39] the CJEU distinguished Internet

[31] *SCF v Marco del Corso* [2012] para 82.

[32] *SGAE v Rafael Hoteles* [2006] para 37 applying Case C-89/04 *Mediakabel BV v Commissariaat voor de Media* [2005] ECLI:EU:C:2005:348, para 30 and Case C-192/04 *Lagardere Active Broadcast v Societe pour la perception de la remuneration equitable (SPRE), Gesellschaft zur Verwerung von Leistungsschutrechten mbH (GVL)* [2005] ECLI:EU:C:2005:475, para 31.

[33] *SGAE v Rafael Hoteles* [2006] paras 38 and 54.

[34] *SCF v Marco del Corso* [2012] para 84.

[35] *SGAE v Rafael Hoteles* [2006] paras 40–41.

[36] ibid para 40.

[37] *SGAE v Rafael Hoteles* [2006] paras 40–42.

[38] Cases C-431/09 and C-432/09 *Airfield NV and another v Belgische Vereniging van Auteurs, Componisten en Uitgevers CVBA (SABAM) and Airfield NV v Agicoa Belgium BVBA* [2011] ECLI:EU:C:2011:648, paras 72–77.

[39] *PPL v Ireland* [2012] paras 49–51.

retransmission on the ground of being a 'specific technical means different from that of the original communication'.[40] Hence, Internet retransmission was treated as a separate act requiring fresh authorisation regardless of the fact that the retransmission contains content that is already freely available via ordinary broadcasts. Thus, *ITV v TVCatchup* made a significant addition to the initial criteria established in *Rafael Hoteles*.

Lastly, the CJEU stated that the profit-making nature of the act is a relevant consideration in establishing that there is a communication to the public, although not an essential requirement.[41] However, the CJEU did not elaborate on the 'for profit' requirement. Given the preceding discussion, to establish an act of communication to the public, it is now required that there is an act of 'communication' made to a 'public'. If the act is a retransmission or subsequent communication, the retransmission must be made to a 'new public' unless the retransmission is done through a different technical means to the initial communication.[42] If this is the case, fresh authorisation will be required because the subsequent act is treated as completely different to the original broadcast, rather than a mere retransmission.[43] Therefore, the unauthorised Internet retransmission of a free-to-air broadcast will require additional authorisation, separate from the permission granted concerning the initial broadcasting of the work regardless of the public reached by the Internet retransmission. By contrast, liability for an unauthorised act of satellite retransmission of a free-to-air broadcast will depend on the 'new public' criterion, because satellite broadcasting and ordinary terrestrial broadcasting are treated as the same technical means.[44] Therefore, separate authorisation will not be required if the terrestrial or satellite retransmission is made to the same public as the initial broadcast.

Regardless of the amendment introduced by *ITV v TVCatchup*, the initial criteria for the communication to the public right introduced in *Rafael Hoteles* largely remained unchanged until the dawn of the Internet cases concerning the communication to the public right, beginning with *Svensson*. Notwithstanding the developments in *Svensson* that will be discussed in the next subsection, the application of the criteria from *Rafael Hoteles* in relation to traditional broadcasting and retransmission cases remained largely the same.[45] However, it is uncertain in the aftermath of *GS Media*,[46] *Filmspeler*[47] and *Ziggo*[48] whether this will remain the case

[40] *ITV v TVCatchup* [2013] paras 26 and 39.

[41] *SGAE v Rafael Hoteles* [2006] para 44.

[42] The different technical means criterion will be analysed in part 3.5.

[43] See M Makeen, 'The Controversy of Simultaneous Cable Retransmission to Hotel Rooms Under International and European Copyright Laws' (2010) 57 *Journal of the Copyright Society of USA* 59, 67.

[44] *Airfield v SABAM* [2011].

[45] See: *SBS v SABAM* [2015], *PSA v Ministerio Público* [2015] and *Reha Training* [2016].

[46] Case C-160/15 *GS Media BV v Sanoma Media Netherlands BV and others* [2016] ECLI:EU:C:2016:644.

[47] Case C-527/15 *Stichting Brein v Jack Frederik Wullems (also trading under the name Filmspeler)* [2017] ECLI:EU:C:2017:300.

[48] Case C-610/15 *Stichting Brein v Ziggo BV and XS4All Internet BV* [2017] ECLI:EU:C:2017:456.

given that the two most recent retransmission cases did not substantively address the criteria of the communication to the public framework.[49]

(ii) The Second Phase – Svensson *and the Internet Cases*

The communication to the public cases addressing the Internet and its accompanying technologies have constantly pushed the boundaries of the communication to the public right. Beginning with the decision in *ITV v TVCatchup*, the scope, interpretation and application of the communication to the public right has had to adapt and evolve in order to accommodate the Internet. Whereas the introduction of 'specific technical means' in *ITV v TVCatchup* qualified the need to prove the 'new public' criterion,[50] the changes required in *Svensson* and beyond affect the core of the exclusive right. While the *ITV v TVCatchup* decision was important, its facts were still rooted in the traditional concept of retransmission. By contrast, the post-*Svensson* cases concerned the making available aspect of the communication to the public right under Article 3(1) of the Information Society Directive, which had not been previously addressed by the CJEU.

The new phase of communication to the public case law that began with *Svensson* was followed by the significant cases of: *Bestwater*,[51] *GS Media*, *Filmspeler*, *Ziggo*, *VCAST* and *Renckhoff*. In these cases, four significant issues were addressed: the perceived adoption of the access approach for the making available aspect, the maximal harmonisation of the communication to the public right, the operation of the 'new public' criterion on the Internet and the requirement of 'for profit' and/or 'knowledge'.[52] In looking at the CJEU's decision in *Svensson* and how it was followed in *Bestwater*, *GS Media*, *Filmspeler* and *Ziggo*, it can be said that the access approach was adopted as the means by which to interpret 'communication' for Internet technologies and the making available aspect. Moreover, from *Ziggo* it appears that the access approach has been widened to include any act that makes sharing works less complex.[53] However, the recent *VCAST* decision has cast doubt on this with the use of the transmission approach in relation to the streaming of data from the cloud.

[49] Case C-641/15 *Verwertungsgesellschaft Rundfunk GmbH v Hettegger Hotel Edelweiss GmbH* [2017] ECLI:EU:C:2017:131 and Case C-138/16 *Staatlich genehmigte Gesellschaft der Autoren, Komponisten und Musicverlegerregistrierte Genossenschaft mbH (AKM) v Zürs.net Betriebs GmbH* [2017] ECLI:EU:C:2017:218.

[50] This is supported by the language used in *GS Media* [2016] para 37.

[51] Case C-348/13 *BestWater International GmbH v Michael Mebes and Stefan Potsch* [2014] ECLI:EU:C:2014:2315.

[52] Peguera argued that *Svensson* opened the door to a re-conceptualisation of the communication to the public right – M Peguera, 'Hyperlinking under the lens of the revamped right of communication to the public' (2018) 34(5) *Computer Law & Security Review* 1099, 1100.

[53] *Ziggo* [2017] para 36. Also see G Dimita, 'The WIPO right of making available' in P Torremans (ed), *Research Handbook on Copyright Law*, 2nd edn (Edward Elgar Publishing Ltd, 2017) 160.

As for the maximal harmonisation of the right, the CJEU, in answering the fourth question in *Svensson*, concluded that the communication to the public right under Article 3(1) cannot be construed to include activities not referred to in the provision, so as to provide right holders with a wider scope of protection.[54] This effectively means that the scope of the communication to the public right is maximally harmonised so that Member States cannot create legislative differences with regards to the communication to the public right. The reason provided for this finding was to ensure the proper functioning of the internal market. However, this decision is undermined by the ever-expanding interpretation of 'communication' because courts, including the CJEU, have been able to widen the scope of the communication to the public right to include acts/technologies that should not come within the scope of the right. Thus, what does not constitute communication to the public is constantly shrinking.[55] This will be further discussed in Chapter three, section III.

With regard to the use of the 'new public' criterion on the Internet, the decision in *Svensson* exposed its shortcomings.[56] It was held that the ability to freely access the work on the Internet without the use of the hyperlink complained of meant that there was no 'new public'.[57] Consequently, it raised the possibility that where a work is made freely accessible online, the communication to the public right will be exhausted.[58] Furthermore, the CJEU in *Svensson* did not articulate whether the holding only applied to works made freely available with authorisation. Thus, the certainty of the communication to the public right was severely undermined. Although this latter issue was addressed in *GS Media*, the subsequent cases of *Ziggo* and *Renckhoff* have exposed inconsistencies in the determination of what constitutes a 'new public'.

A further conflict was also created between analogue and digital copyright works, where the right to communicate analogue works would not be subject to such exhaustion. To give a comparable example, the unauthorised retransmission/reception in public of a broadcasted work would amount to copyright infringement even if the initial broadcast was accessible. This is because in the absence of the act of retransmission, those users even though within the service zone of the initial broadcast, would not be able to enjoy the broadcast, but for the intervention of the re-broadcaster.[59] As such, there is no exhaustion of the

[54] *Svensson* [2014] paras 34–37.

[55] Dimita in Torremans (2017) 160.

[56] Rosén argued that *Svensson* was the trigger for the problems concerning the 'new public' criterion – J Rosén, 'How Much Communication to the Public is 'Communication to the Public'?' in I Stamatoudi (ed), *New Developments in EU and International Copyright Law* (Kluwer Law International BV, 2016) 331–32.

[57] *Svensson* [2014] paras 25–27.

[58] This was followed in *Bestwater* [2014] para 19. See Rosén in Stamatoudi (2016) 337, P Mezei, 'Enter the matrix: the effects of CJEU case law on linking and streaming technologies' (2016) 11(10) *Journal of Intellectual Property Law & Practice (JIPLP)* 778, 789 and U Furgal, 'Ancillary right for press publishers: an alternative answer to the linking conundrum?' (2018) 13(9) *JIPLP* 700, 703.

[59] See *SGAE v Rafael Hoteles* [2006] paras 40–42.

communication to the public right in relation to acts of broadcasting or retransmission. However, it must be noted that the use of the 'new public' criterion in any capacity is questionable and will be discussed in Chapter three, section VI.

Subsequent to the potential exhaustion of the communication to the public right on the Internet, the CJEU attempted to remedy the situation in *GS Media* by clarifying that only works made freely available online with the consent of the author would preclude a finding of communication to the public by virtue of having no 'new public'.[60] Therefore, the ruling in *Svensson* and the potential for exhaustion of the communication to the public right would not apply if the defendant made the work available on the Internet without authorisation, regardless of whether the work was freely available.[61] In simpler form, a 'new public' will arise where the right holder's permission does not extend to the subsequent act of communication.[62] The CJEU in *GS Media* also went a step further by introducing a more stringent *application* of the largely ignored 'for profit' criterion.[63] Prior to *GS Media*, the 'for profit' criterion was intermittently mentioned and, moreover, had little or no bearing on the decision-making of the CJEU.[64] The 'for profit' criterion was first mentioned in *Rafael Hoteles* where it was stated that the profitability of the communication was not a necessary condition for establishing an act of communication to the public.[65] However, in its next appearance, the CJEU adopted a different approach to the 'for profit' criterion, stating that the profit-making nature of a communication is not an irrelevant consideration.[66]

The uncertainty surrounding the role of the 'for profit' criterion was perpetuated by the CJEU's arbitrary use and definition of 'for profit'. In *Marco del Corso* – the only instance in which the 'for profit' criterion was afforded notable use prior to *GS Media* – the CJEU held that the retransmission of radio broadcasts in a waiting room was not a profit-making activity, as it did not affect the earnings of the dentist in question.[67] Consequent to this, a finding of no communication to the public was delivered.[68] It is important to note this decision because it was the first retransmission case where the CJEU held no communication to the public and interestingly the only case where the 'communication' was held to be not for profit.

[60] *GS Media* [2016] paras 41–42.

[61] ibid para 43.

[62] Hugenholtz and Van Velze (2016) 809–10.

[63] Given the radical changes introduced in *GS Media*, Dimita has argued that *GS Media* effectively overruled *Svensson* and the pre-existing communication to the public case law – Dimita in Torremans (2017) 156. Likewise, Peguera described *GS Media* as a significant departure from the established communication to the public framework – Peguera (2018) 9.

[64] *Rafael Hoteles* [2006] para 44, *FAPL v QC Leisure* [2011] para 204, *SCF v Marco del Corso* [2012] paras 88 and 97–99, *PPL v Ireland* [2012] para 36, *ITV v TVCatchup* [2013] paras 42–44 and *Reha Training* [2016] paras 49 and 63–64.

[65] *Rafael Hoteles* [2006] para 44.

[66] *FAPL v QC Leisure* [2011] para 204.

[67] *SCF v Marco del Corso* [2012] para 97.

[68] ibid paras 99–100.

This would suggest that there was a necessary connection between 'for profit' and the establishment of 'communication' and/or 'communication to the public'.[69]

Despite the holding in *Marco del Corso*, the CJEU continued its inconsistent approach to 'for profit', reverting to the notion that the 'for profit' criterion does not conclusively determine whether there is an act of communication to the public in *ITV v TVCatchup*.[70] Subsequent to this, the CJEU in *Reha Training* made an attempt to reconcile the conflict by stating in a non-committal and fence-sitting manner that 'for profit' is not conclusive, but also not irrelevant.[71] However, in *GS Media* the CJEU radically changed its approach by placing an increased emphasis on 'for profit' and moreover, linking it with the newly introduced 'knowledge' criterion.[72] In *GS Media*, the CJEU held that where a person shares a hyperlink without pursuing a profit, in the absence of actual knowledge that the work being hyperlinked to is unauthorised, it is presumed that the person 'does not know and cannot reasonably know, that the work has been published on the Internet without the consent of the copyright holder.'[73] By contrast, where a person shares a hyperlink to an unauthorised work for profit, it is presumed that they know or ought to have known that the hyperlink provides access to an unauthorised work.[74] In the absence of such actual or presumed knowledge, it cannot be said that the hyperlinker intervenes with full knowledge of the consequences of his actions to provide access to the work.[75] In other words, in the absence of knowledge, there is no act of 'communication' and consequently no communication to the public. The CJEU, by applying this logic in *GS Media*, effectively linked the determination of 'communication' with the 'for profit' and 'knowledge' criteria. The desirability of this annexation will be discussed in Chapter three, section VII.

More than the linking of 'communication' to the 'for profit' and 'knowledge' criteria, the introduction of a 'knowledge' criterion is questionable because primary copyright infringement has traditionally never had a knowledge requirement. Knowledge has been specifically reserved as an element of secondary liability.[76] Thus, the line between primary and secondary liability has been blurred by the CJEU.[77] Notwithstanding this, the 'knowledge' requirement was accepted and furthered in *Filmspeler*[78] and *Ziggo*.[79] From the structure of the judgments in

[69] ibid para 90.

[70] *ITV v TVCatchup* [2013] paras 42–44.

[71] *Reha Training* [2016] 49.

[72] *GS Media* [2016] paras 47–48 and 51.

[73] ibid para 47.

[74] ibid paras 49–51. Note, this presumption is rebuttable.

[75] ibid paras 47–48.

[76] Chapter 3, section VII will address the desirability of the 'knowledge' criterion.

[77] A Strowel, 'Reconstructing the Reproduction and Communication to the Public Rights: How to Align Copyright with Its Fundamentals' in PB Hugenholtz (ed), *Copyright Reconstructed: Rethinking Copyright's Economic Rights in a Time of Highly Dynamic and Technological and Economic Change* (Kluwer Law International BV, 2018) 239 and Peguera (2018) 2.

[78] *Filmspeler* [2017] paras 49–51.

[79] *Ziggo* [2017] paras 45–46.

GS Media, *Filmspeler* and *Ziggo*, the 'knowledge' criterion has, in effect, become the decisive criterion in determining whether there is an actionable communication to the public.[80] Thus, the 'for profit' and 'knowledge' criteria have not only been annexed to the determination of 'communication' but have become an integral aspect of the communication to the public framework.

In the aftermath of the communication to the public cases concerning the Internet, the criteria for establishing an infringement of the Article 3(1) right of communication to the public has markedly changed. The new emphasis on 'for profit' and the introduction of a 'knowledge' criterion were a significant departure from the pre-*Svensson* case law.

(iii) Communication to the Public at a Crossroad

With the development of the communication to the public right from *Rafael Hoteles* to *VCAST*, several notable problems have arisen, which will be addressed in Chapter three. In addition to these individual problems, there are some more holistic issues that need to be articulated, including: the impact of the post-*Svensson* cases on the overall communication to the public framework, the reconciliation of the communication to the public right across Directives and the legal reasoning underlying the CJEU's communication to the public decisions.

B. The Current Test to Establish 'Communication to the Public'

In the aftermath of the post-*Svensson* Internet cases, it is not certain what impact the introduction of the 'knowledge' criterion and the increased emphasis on 'for profit' will have on the traditional communication to the public right's framework. This is because none of the post-*GS Media* retransmission or 'reception in public' cases discussed the issue of 'for profit' or 'knowledge'. *Hettegger Hotel* was concerned with whether a cable retransmission to hotel rooms was an infringement of Article 8(3) of the Rental and Lending Right Directive, the emphasis being on whether the hotel room's rental fee was an entrance fee.[81] Similarly in *AKM*, the CJEU did not have to make a finding on whether there was an act of communication to the public, since it was accepted that there was no communication to the public.[82] Instead, the case focused on the applicability of an exception to the communication to the public right at the domestic level.[83]

[80] See *GS Media* [2016] para 51, *Filmspeler* [2017] paras 50–52 and *Ziggo* [2017] paras 45–47.
[81] *Hettegger Hotel* [2017] paras 21–25.
[82] *AKM* [2017] paras 28–30.
[83] ibid para 31.

In the absence of any guidance from the CJEU it can only be surmised that one of two possibilities will be followed. Option one would include the maintenance of the traditional *Rafael Hoteles* criteria as amended by *ITV v TVCatchup*; the consequence being that there are two different tests, one test for the retransmission and reception in public cases and a second test for communication to the public on the Internet by virtue of the making available aspect of the communication to the public right.[84] Such an approach may be defensible if it is argued that the making available aspect of the communication to the public right warrant its own nuanced framework for the determination of infringement.[85] However, this approach is undesirable because it segments the communication to the public right, creating conflict and uncertainty between analogue and digital works, and furthermore, would undermine the process of harmonising the communication to the public right.[86]

The second option, though not necessarily a preferable one, would be that the *Rafael Hoteles* criteria were updated to include the 'knowledge' criterion and an increased emphasis on the 'for profit' criterion. If this option is to be adopted, the test for the right of communication to the public would look as follows:

- Step 1 – There must be an act of 'communication' – defined as 'any transmission of the protected works, irrespective of the technical means or process used'[87] or where a user 'intervenes, in full knowledge of the consequences of his action, to give his customers access to a protected work.'[88]
- Step 2 – There must be a 'public' – defined as a large and fairly indeterminate number of persons.[89]
- Step 3 – If the act is a subsequent 'communication' then there must be a 'new public' unless it is done through a 'specific technical means different from those previously used' – 'new public' defined as an audience different from the one considered when authorising the initial 'communication'[90] and 'specific technical means' defined as the use of a different technological medium.
- Step 4 – If the alleged infringer has actual or presumed 'knowledge' that the work communicated is unauthorised, there will be an act of communication to the public. A presumption of 'knowledge' can be imputed where the act of

[84] It has been suggested that the post-*Svensson* Internet cases have created two lines of case law: the traditional cases addressing acts of transmission and retransmission, compared with the Internet cases which wholly rely on the access approach – B Clark and J Dickenson, 'Theseus and the labyrinth? An overview of "communication to the public" under EU copyright law: after Reha Training and GS Media: Where are we now and where do we go from here?' (2017) 39(5) *European Intellectual Property Review* 265, 268 and Dimita in Torremans (2017) 152.

[85] This issue will be addressed in Chapter three, section IV.

[86] Furgal (2018) 703.

[87] *AKM* [2017] para 23 and *VCAST* [2018] para 42.

[88] *Ziggo* [2017] para 26.

[89] ibid para 27.

[90] ibid para 28.

'communication' is done 'for profit'.[91] In the absence of such 'knowledge' there can be no act of 'communication to the public'.[92]

With that approach in mind, the test for communication to the public becomes dependent on the establishment of 'knowledge'.

C. Reconciling 'Communication to the Public' Across the Directives

It was previously noted that the concept of communication to the public can be found under four EU copyright Directives – the Satellite and Cable Retransmission Directive, the Rental and Lending Right Directive, the Database Directive and the ISD. However, there is no clear statutory guidance on whether the concept should be given a consistent interpretation across these Directives. If the Article 3(1) communication to the public right under the ISD is set as the starting point, because it was the first communication to the public right to be interpreted by the CJEU, the question is whether the communication to the public rights under Article 2 of the Satellite and Cable Retransmission Directive and Article 8 of the Rental and Lending Right Directive should be interpreted in the same manner.[93] Ultimately, this question asks whether the communication to the public right under the various Directives are subject to the criteria set out in *Rafael Hoteles* and beyond.

In the interest of a consistent and harmonised right, it is advocated that a single interpretation be adopted in terms of how 'communication to the public' is defined and applied. In the absence of such an approach, the decisions of the CJEU will be disproportionate and irreconcilable because the same concept will be interpreted in different ways. Furthermore, there will be an impact on the internal market because the use of copyright works and services will be affected through changes in pricing or availability, given the increased transaction costs of securing authorisation for the communication to the public of both copyright and related rights, which may not be subject to the same criteria. However, if a single approach to the communication to the public right is utilised, this will ensure a more efficient system because there will be no variables in relation to the type of work or the technology to be used. 'Communication to the public' will mean the same thing in all contexts. Hence, the application of the right to different media will be proportionate and certain. Finally, a consistent approach to the right will increase legal certainty.

[91] See *GS Media* [2016] paras 47–51 and *Filmspeler* [2017] para 49.

[92] *GS Media* [2016] paras 47–48.

[93] The communication to the public right under the Database Directive is not discussed in more detail because there is no CJEU case law on it.

The CJEU first dealt with the reconciliation issue in *Airfield v SABAM*, where the Court stated that the terms used in the Satellite and Cable Retransmission Directive should be interpreted 'in the light of the rules and principles established by other directives related to IP, such as, in particular, Directive 2001/29 [ISD]'.[94] Accordingly, the Article 2 communication to the public right under the Satellite and Cable Retransmission Directive was interpreted in a manner consistent with the Article 3(1) right under the ISD. Conversely, the CJEU in *Marco del Corso* departed from the harmonisation approach used in *Airfield v SABAM* by holding that the interpretation of the Article 8(2) communication to the public right under the Rental and Lending Right Directive should be given an individual interpretation independent of the Article 3(1) right under the ISD. The Court reasoned that Article 8(2) of the Rental and Lending Right Directive is similar to the right under the ISD, but nonetheless used in 'contexts which are not the same and pursue objectives … different to some extent.'[95] The CJEU in *OSA* reiterated the approach that the Article 3(1) right of communication to the public under the ISD should be interpreted independently of the namesake right under the Rental and Lending Right Directive.[96] However, this approach is troublesome because it leads to the interpretation of the same concept in different ways across Directives,[97] thus, compromising the EU's harmonisation agenda for copyright law.

Despite the finding in *Marco del Corso* and *OSA*, the CJEU in *Reha Training* made a *volte face* and stated that the concept of communication to the public under the Rental and Lending Right Directive and the ISD must have the same meaning unless the legislature expressed a different intention.[98] In the absence of such evidence, the communication to the public right should be interpreted consistently across Directives. Regardless of the differences in structure of the competing provisions, both rights provided have the same trigger, namely, the 'communication to the public' of the work. Consequently, they should be subject to the same criteria in order to avoid contradictory and incompatible interpretations and decisions.[99] This renewed position adopted in *Reha Training* was followed in *Hettegger Hotel*.[100] Therefore, it is expected that any future case concerning the right of communication to the public, irrespective of the Directive under which it is raised, will apply a consistent interpretation of the communication to the public right as developed by the CJEU.

[94] *Airfield v SABAM* [2011] para 44.

[95] *SCF v Marco del Corso* [2012] para 74.

[96] *OSA* [2014] para 35.

[97] Ross and Livingstone argue that the decision of the CJEU in *SCF v Marco del Corso* disrupted the understanding of the communication to the public right developed in the earlier case law – A Ross and C Livingstone, 'Communication to the public: Part 2' (2012) 23(7) *Entertainment Law Review* 209 [Ross and Livingstone Part 2] 209.

[98] Restating and reaffirming the position of the CJEU prior to *SCF v Marco del Corso* – see *FAPL v QC Leisure* [2011] para 188.

[99] *Reha Training* [2016] paras 29–34.

[100] *Hettegger Hotel* [2017] para 19.

III. Understanding the Legal Reasoning of the CJEU in the Communication to the Public Cases

In order to critique the right of communication to the public, it is necessary to understand the underlying legal reasoning that has informed the development of the right.[101] The CJEU, in framing its decisions, persistently outlined a number of motivations, objectives and beliefs that *supposedly* guide its decision-making.[102] Such interests include: the internal market, a harmonisation agenda, a high level of protection for right holders, the development of an independent and autonomous right, the creation of a broad right, and a right that respects international obligations. These interests can be grouped into three broad categories: the maximal protection approach, the harmonisation agenda, and the economic influence. With that in mind, it should be noted that this section does not question the capacity of the CJEU's decision-making ability, but only the premises used to support its decisions.[103]

Before looking at the specifics of the CJEU's legal reasoning with regard to the right of communication to the public, it is important to note some of the CJEU's general copyright traits identified by Favale, Kretschmer and Torremans. This will help place the discussion concerning the communication to the public right and the CJEU's legal reasoning into context. Favale *et al*, in their empirical analysis of the CJEU's copyright decisions up to *Svensson*, indicated that the CJEU has illustrated a sophisticated approach to copyright matters involving the balancing of rights and community interests.[104] In arriving at this conclusion, it was noted that

[101] For a more detailed view of the legal reasoning of the CJEU in copyright cases see M Favale, M Kretschmer and P Torremans, 'Is there an EU Copyright Jurisprudence? An Empirical Analysis of the Workings of the European Court of Justice' (2016) 79(1) *Modern Law Review* 31. For a general view on legal reasoning of the CJEU see: J Bengoetxea, *The legal reasoning of the European Court of Justice: towards a European jurisprudence* (Clarendon Press, 1993) and G Beck, *The Legal Reasoning of the Court of Justice of the EU* (Hart Publishing Ltd, 2012) Part II.

[102] The term 'supposedly' is used because the CJEU has often been criticised for its judicial activism, perceived lack of consistency and/or legal reasoning, overreaching its powers and controversial decisions – Favale, Kretschmer and Torremans (2016) 50–51, C Geiger, 'The Role of the court of Justice of the European Union: Harmonizing, Creating and sometimes Disrupting Copyright Law in the European Union' in I Stamatoudi (ed), *New Developments in EU and International Copyright Law* (Kluwer Law International, 2016) 440 and 443–45 and O Pollicino, 'Legal Reasoning of the Court of Justice in the Context of the Principle of Equality Between Judicial Activism and Self-restraint' (2004) 5(3) *German Law Journal* 283, 283.

[103] The question concerning the capacity of the CJEU and its 'true' judicial function exceeds the scope of this book. However, academics argue that the legitimate judicial function of the CJEU includes both the interpretation and creation of law, given the new legal order of the EU and the legislative gap-filling function of the CJEU. As such, the ability of the CJEU to adopt a judicial activist approach with regards to the right of communication to the public will not be debated. See: Pollicino (2004) 284 and 286–90, A Ramalho, *The Competence of the European Union in Copyright Lawmaking* (Springer International Publishing Switzerland, 2016) 59–60, Geiger in Stamatoudi (2016) 436 and Favale, Kretschmer and Torremans (2016) 36.

[104] Favale, Kretschmer and Torremans (2016) 67.

the CJEU's decision-making in the copyright cases revealed a prevalence of semantic and teleological approaches (with a preference for the teleological approach).[105] That is, analysis of the main texts and recitals in the copyright Directives (semantic approach) and reference to the objectives of the EU and its legislation (teleological approach), respectively.[106] This is in contrast to the systematic approach that relies on contextual factors to guide interpretive practices, such as: references to international legislation, legislative history, other EU legislation, legal philosophy, and economic factors.[107]

In looking specifically at the early CJEU case law on the right of communication to the public,[108] there was a more proportionate use of all three approaches – semantic, systematic and teleological. In addition to the semantic and teleological approaches discussed by Favale *et al*, the CJEU also directly referenced the Berne Convention and its explanatory guide,[109] the WIPO Copyright Treaty[110] and other EU Directives where necessary. Nonetheless, it is arguable that insufficient systematic/contextual analysis was conducted, illustrated by the controversy surrounding the use of the 'new public' criterion. Similarly, the absence of systematic analysis in the more recent communication to the public case law has facilitated the 'knowledge' criterion (post-*GS Media*) which is a novel requirement. Had a more thorough and consistent systematic/contextual approach been adopted, it is arguable that these missteps of the CJEU would not have occurred.[111]

The data analysed by Favale *et al* also suggested that two of the prominent factors guiding the CJEU's decision-making with regard to the right of communication to the public were a high level of protection for right holders and a broad approach. However, these two factors were not indicative guides of the CJEU's general copyright jurisprudence. Instead, Favale *et al* claimed that the CJEU has applied copyright law in a balanced way, accounting for the various facts of the cases.[112] Despite this claim of balance, a more detailed comparative analysis of the communication to the public case law would indicate a lack of consistency in the decision-making of the CJEU. Favale *et al* compared the cases of *OSA* and *Svensson*, both of which were decided by the Fourth Chamber of the CJEU some two weeks apart, using the same arguments and teleological approach, yet, opposite outcomes were produced.[113] The comparison of these two cases was not the best choice, given the differences in technology – cable retransmission/reception

[105] ibid 66.
[106] ibid 53–55.
[107] ibid 54.
[108] Case law up to *Svensson* [2014].
[109] See: *SGAE v Rafael Hoteles* [2006] paras 40–41, *FAPL v QC Leisure* [2011] paras 192 and 201, *Circul Globus București* [2011] para 35, *PPL v Ireland* [2012] para 34 and *Svensson* [2014] para 38.
[110] See: *SGAE v Rafael Hoteles* [2006] para 43.
[111] Note, Favale *et al* stated that the systematic approach was more prevalent in Advocate General opinions – Favale, Kretschemer and Torremans (2016) 54.
[112] ibid 58–60.
[113] ibid 68.

in public versus hyperlinking on the Internet, and moreover, due to the fact that the CJEU had never addressed the issue of the making available aspect of the communication to the public right before. Thus, *Svensson* was a novel case for the CJEU, unlike *OSA* that had the benefit of the case law since *Rafael Hoteles*. Nevertheless, the claim made by Favale *et al* was justified, in that the CJEU balances the facts of the individual cases. Therefore, it can be inferred that there are other factors affecting the decision-making of the CJEU.

Beyond the findings of Favale *et al* concerning the semantic, systematic and teleological approaches, the CJEU's communication to the public decisions are illustrative of three primary considerations: the maximal protection approach, the harmonisation agenda, and the economic influence. Favale *et al* did address aspects of these three considerations, but a more detailed nuanced analysis, specific to the communication to the public right, is required.

A. The Maximal Protection Approach

The express language and findings of the CJEU in relation to the communication to the public right illustrates that the Court has pursued the development of a very broad right in favour of right holders. From the beginning, in *Rafael Hoteles*, the CJEU emphasised that the right of communication to the public should be interpreted broadly in accordance with Recital 23 of the ISD. Moreover, a high level of protection for right holders should be established in line with Recitals 9 and 10 of the ISD.[114] In fact, the establishment of a high level of protection for right holders can be seen as the primary objective of the ISD.[115] In following this approach, the CJEU has pursued the development of maximal protection, whereby the aim has been to provide right holders with as much copyright protection as possible. This is evidenced in the communication to the public context by the CJEU constantly expanding the scope of 'communication'.

In addition to acts of broadcasting and retransmission, the CJEU expanded the scope of 'communication' in the traditional sense to include reception in public, which should come within the scope of a public performance right.[116] Similarly, the making available aspect of the communication to the public right has been given a very wide interpretation through the adoption of the access approach.[117] As such, the aggregation of hyperlinks[118] and torrent files[119] has been held to infringe even though these acts merely facilitate access as opposed to actually making the work available. The validity of the wide approach afforded to the interpretation

[114] *SGAE v Rafael Hoteles* [2006] para 36.
[115] See Recitals 4 and 9 of the ISD.
[116] See *SGAE v Rafael Hoteles* [2006] para 38 and *FAPL v QC Leisure* [2011] para 196.
[117] *Svensson* [2014] paras 19–20.
[118] See *Svensson* [2014], *GS Media* [2016] and *Filmspeler* [2017].
[119] See *Ziggo* [2017].

of 'communication' and the right as a whole will be discussed in Chapter three, sections II–IV.

What is clear is that the aim to establish a high level of protection for right holders has had a critical impact on the CJEU's interpretation of the key concept of 'communication'. Consequently, it has overstretched the communication to the public right, to the detriment of other legitimate competing interests.[120]

B. The Harmonisation Agenda

The development of the CJEU's communication to the public case law also reflects a clear harmonisation agenda. This agenda was influenced by a number of factors including the recitals of the ISD, the role the CJEU, the need to reconcile 'communication to the public' across the copyright Directives and the need to comply with international obligations. While these harmonising influences are diverse, the CJEU has taken account of all these considerations in its case law. Beginning with *Rafael Hoteles*, the CJEU outlined that the right of communication to the public must be given an autonomous and uniform interpretation. In other words, 'communication to the public' should be interpreted independently of any influence from the domestic laws of the Member States. The reason for this approach was to produce a harmonised right that will be consistently interpreted and applied across Member States for the benefit of furthering the internal market, in accordance with Recitals 1, 3 and 7 of the ISD, and moreover, in line with the EU's mandate to remove barriers to the proper functioning of the internal market.[121]

Another factor that must be taken into account in the growth of the harmonisation agenda is the CJEU's role in developing EU copyright law. Given that many concepts remain undefined under the EU copyright Directives, the CJEU has had no choice but to engage in judicial activism to help clarify, interpret and apply EU copyright law.[122] This includes the communication to the public right that is undefined, with little or no guidance to be found in the recitals. Consequently, the CJEU has had a marked impact on the development of the right, especially in terms of interpreting the right. This is evidenced by the CJEU's contributions to the communication to the public right, including: the wide interpretation of 'communication' and the introduction of the 'new public', 'for profit' and 'knowledge' requirements.[123] The significant level of interpretive intervention conducted by

[120] See Chapter one for the competing interests present in EU copyright law.

[121] K Koelman, 'Copyright law and economics in the EU Copyright Directive: is the droit d'auteur passe?' (2004) 35(6) *IIC* 603, 604.

[122] See P Torremans, 'When the Court of Justice of the European Union sets about defining exclusive rights: copyright *quo vadis*?' in P Torremans (ed), *Research Handbook on Copyright Law*, 2nd edn (Edward Elgar Publishing Ltd, 2017) 85 and S Bechtold, 'Deconstructing Copyright' in PB Hugenholtz (ed), *Copyright Reconstructed: Rethinking Copyright's Economic Rights in a Time of Highly Dynamic and Technological and Economic Change* (Kluwer Law International BV, 2018) 65.

[123] Rendas argues that the CJEU has had to go beyond the boundaries of the existing EU copyright framework in order to introduce flexibility into the law to achieve 'desirable' outcomes, especially

the CJEU, with its consequential harmonising impact, has led to accusations of a secret harmonisation agenda and, furthermore, of the unilateral creation of EU law given the activist approach adopted.[124] The CJEU's case law concerning the making available aspect of the communication to the public right is illustrative of this.[125] In particular, in the context of hyperlinking it can be said that the CJEU has exceeded its remit by harmonising secondary liability for acts of communication to the public via the implementation of the 'knowledge' requirement.[126]

The development of the communication to the public right has also been influenced by the need to establish consistency for the right, both at the international level and at the EU level. Therefore, the CJEU has referenced the international copyright treaties, including the Berne Convention and the WIPO Copyright Treaty, in order to gauge what the right should resemble.[127] However, the attempts at international harmonisation have not always been desirable, as the CJEU has made unfortunate missteps that have negatively impacted the development of the right. In particular, the accommodation of acts of reception in public and the inclusion of the 'new public' criterion are cause for concern. Similarly, the CJEU has also had to harmonise the communication to the public right across the different EU copyright Directives. The right can be found in four Directives and has been expressly synchronised under the ISD, Satellite and Cable Retransmission Directive and Rental and Lending Right Directive.

From the above discussion, it can be said that the development of the right of communication to the public has been directly influenced by a harmonisation agenda aimed at producing a clear and consistent right for a number of reasons. Whether the right is actually clear and consistent will be discussed in Chapter three.

C. The Economic Influence

The economic influence is not expressly manifested in the CJEU case law on the communication to the public right, though it can be increasingly inferred. At its core, the economic influence is derived from the internal market consideration

where digital technologies are involved – T Rendas, 'Copyright, technology and the CJEU: an empirical study' (2018) 49(2) *IIC* 153.

[124] Geiger in Stamatoudi (2016) 436–37 and 439–41.

[125] Dimita in Torremans (2017) 158.

[126] Peguera (2018) 12, J Ginsburg, 'The Court of Justice of the European Union Creates an EU Law of Liability for Facilitation of Copyright Infringement: Observations on *Brein v Filmspeler* [C-527/15] (2017) and *Brein v Ziggo* [C-610/15] (2017)' Columbia Law and Economics Working Paper No 572 (2017): <https://papers.ssrn.com/sol3/papers.cfm?abstract_id=3024302> accessed 3 August 2018 and A Ohly, 'The broad concept of "communication to the public" in recent CJEU judgments and the liability of intermediaries: primary, secondary or unitary liability' (2018) 13(8) *JIPLP* 664, 670.

[127] See for example: *SGAE v Rafael Hoteles* [2006] paras 40–41 and 43 and *FAPL v QC Leisure* [2011] para 192.

and the aim to achieve a high level of protection for right holders. The common theme for these two considerations is the furtherance of financial gain.[128] As such, to facilitate that gain, the CJEU has embarked on developing a harmonised and very wide scope for the communication to the public right. One of the consequences of this broad approach has been the reliance on the 'for profit' criterion in the post-*GS Media* cases. Strowel argued that placing focus on 'for profit' demonstrates the CJEU's economic vision for the right of communication to the public.[129] This argument is consistent with the CJEU's objective to ensure a high level of protection for right holders because the 'for profit' criterion, in effect, operates to prevent third parties from being unjustly enriched via unauthorised uses of right holders' works.

That aside, it can be said the CJEU's harmonisation of the right aims to increase cross-territory disseminations, as there should be no differences in the application of the communication to the public right and moreover, fewer transactional costs and greater efficiency involved. Therefore, trade should increase with fewer barriers to the internal market. On the flipside, the wide scope of the right also serves to incentivise right holders to invest more resources in creating new content. This is because, it is argued, high levels of protection will foster greater returns and offer greater security on creative and innovative investments.[130] The EU legislature is committed to this underlying raison d'etre, illustrated by their pro-right holder and pro-internal market focus, detailed in the recitals of the ISD. Similarly, the CJEU has followed suit with the communication to the public right, whereby, the most recent expansions of the scope of the right in *GS* Media, *Filmspeler* and *Ziggo* were aimed specifically at protecting right holders by any means possible. Therefore, it is fair to say that the pro-right holder approach and its underlying economic influence has had a large impact on the CJEU's communication to the public decisions.[131]

Taken together, the maximal protection approach, the harmonisation agenda and the economic influence illustrate that the CJEU's development of the communication to the public right has been focused on achieving specific aims and objectives, namely a high level of protection for right holders and the furtherance of the internal market. However, this has been to the detriment of other legitimate competing interests, which have been ignored or restricted. Therefore, it is proposed that the development of a more coherent and justifiable right of communication to the public requires a better balancing of the interests discussed

[128] Bechtold supports this view by arguing that an underlying economic motivation to reward authors can be inferred from the CJEU's case law. For example, he singles out the 'new public' criterion under the right of communication to the public as a means to ensure that authors are adequately remunerated in relation to how far their works are disseminated – Bechtold in Hugenholtz (2018) 65–66.

[129] Strowel in Hugenholtz (2018) 240.

[130] Koelman (2004) 606.

[131] D Kallinikou, 'CJEU Policy and Practice in the Field of European Copyright Law' in T Synodinou (ed), *Codification of European Copyright Law: Challenges and Perspectives* (Kluwer Law International, 2012) 71 and 88.

in Chapter one. Consequently, Chapter three will critically assess the shortcomings of the existing communication to the public right and the accompanying approaches adopted by the CJEU.

IV. Conclusion

This chapter set out to explore the development of the EU right of communication to the public. In doing so, the existing framework of the right and its constituent elements were illustrated. Moreover, the legal reasoning underlying the CJEU's development of the right was also exposed. However, in discussing the current status of the right, several problems were identified concerning its scope and operation. In particular, questions were raised about: the concept of 'communication' and its width, the validity of the 'new public' criterion; and the role of 'knowledge' and the 'for profit' criteria. The issues highlighted in this chapter will be analysed in Chapter three.

Given the problems with the right of communication to the public, it was expected that the Proposal for the Digital Single Market Directive[132] would have attempted to clarify the scope of the right.[133] However, the DSM Proposal failed to elucidate the communication to the public right, instead choosing to further complicate the situation by extending the making available aspect under Article 3(2) of the ISD to press publications via Article 11 of the DSM Proposal.[134] This piecemeal approach leaves the unclear and outdated copyright *acquis* intact.[135] Moreover, Article 11 of the DSM Proposal has been criticised for being unnecessary, undesirable and introducing further uncertainty.[136] As such it remains the case that the right of communication to the public is unclear and incoherent and moreover, the CJEU continues to control the reins over the interpretation and application of the right.

[132] Commission, *Proposal for a Directive of the European Parliament and of the Council on copyright in the Digital Single Market* (COM(2016) 593 final, 2016) [DSM Proposal].

[133] Furgal (2018) 700.

[134] ibid 710.

[135] European Copyright Society, 'General Opinion on the EU Copyright Reform Package' (2017) <https://europeancopyrightsociety.org/opinions/> accessed 6 August 2018, 3.

[136] L Bently *et al*, 'Calls For Views: Modernising the European Copyright Framework' (5 December 2016) 1: <https://www.cipil.law.cam.ac.uk/sites/www.law.cam.ac.uk/files/images/www.cipil.law.cam.ac.uk/documents/ipomodernisingipprofresponsepresspublishers.pdf> accessed 6 August 2018.

3

The Problems with the Right of Communication to the Public

I. Introduction

Chapter two explained the development of the EU communication to the public right from *Rafael Hoteles*[1] to *Renckhoff*.[2] It can be said that the CJEU has structured a right of communication to the public that conflicts with international copyright law, is inconsistent and reactionary.[3] Chapter two flagged several issues that require detailed analysis because they pose problems for the coherence, effectiveness and future development of the right. Consequently, these issues will be individually addressed for the purpose of understanding their significance and with a view to ultimately providing alternative solutions. The discussion includes: abandoning the broad interpretation of the right; defining the term 'communication' in terms of the transmission or provision of the work; understanding that the making available aspect is a subset of the general right; excluding acts of reception in public from the scope of the right; replacing the 'new public' criterion with the 'organisation other than the original one' criterion; abandoning the 'for profit' and knowledge criteria; and removing the overlap with secondary liability.

The recommendations produced in this chapter will then be complemented by suggestions targeted at more holistic aspects of the communication to the public right's framework in Chapters four and five. This includes: the reconciliation of the proposed reformed right of communication to the public with the other harmonised exclusive rights and exceptions and limitations; how to complete the harmonisation of the reformed right; who is responsible for an act of communication to the public; and where the act of communication to the public occurs.

[1] Case C-306/05 *Sociedad General de Autores y Editores de España (SGAE) v Rafael Hoteles SA* [2006] ECLI:EU:C:2006:764.

[2] Case C-161/17 *Land Nordrhein-Westfalen v Dirk Renckhoff* [2018] ECLI:EU:C:2018:634.

[3] F Brison and S Depreeuw, 'The right of "communication to the public" in the European Union' in P Torremans (ed), *Research Handbook on Copyright Law*, 2nd edn (Edward Elgar Publishing Ltd, 2017) 133.

II. Broad Interpretation

Recital 23 of the Information Society Directive (ISD)[4] states that the right of communication to the public should be understood in a broad sense. The broad interpretative approach was affirmed in *Rafael Hoteles* and subsequently repeated throughout the CJEU's communication to the public case law. This broad interpretation is a result of the EU's aim to ensure a high level of protection for right holders.[5] However, it will be argued that the communication to the public right should not be subject to a broad interpretation because it is unjustified and has facilitated the overbroad expansion of the right.

A. The Problem

The broad interpretation of the communication to the public right is unjustified because too much emphasis is placed on establishing a high level of protection for right holders. As discussed in Chapter one, achieving a high level of protection is only one of the interests that EU copyright law must take account of. Furthermore, it is not the case that a high level of protection should equate to overbroad exclusive rights. A 'high level of protection' can and should be interpreted as meaning that right holders can control the use of their works in a justified manner and receive an appropriate reward.[6] In this way, the interests of authors and right holders are held as important, but not to the extent that they are the sole guiding factor in determining the scope of exclusive rights under EU copyright law. Consequently, to produce a proportionately balanced right, the other competing interests discussed in Chapter one must be better accounted for; notably, fundamental rights and the interests of users and technology developers. In the absence of a proportional balance it is possible that there may be chilling effects on the development of communication technologies and the future dissemination of works, which will be to the detriment of the public interest.[7]

From the fundamental rights perspective, it may be the case that an overly broad communication to the public right prejudices individuals' right to freedom of expression and information and their freedom to conduct a business.[8] For instance, Litman has argued that we have always had the right to cite works.[9]

[4] Directive 2001/29/EC of the European Parliament and of the Council of 22 May 2001 on the harmonisation of certain aspects of copyright and related rights in the information society [Information Society Directive] [2001] OJ L167/10, 22.6.2001.

[5] *SGAE v Rafael Hoteles* [2006] para 36.

[6] S Depreeuw, *The variable scope of the exclusive economic rights in copyright* (Kluwer Law International, 2014) para 616.

[7] Z Efroni, *Access Right: The Future of Digital Copyright Law* (Oxford University Press, 2011) 285.

[8] Articles 10 and 16 of the Charter of Fundamental Rights of the European Union [2012] OJ C326/391–407, 26.10.2012.

[9] J Litman, *Digital Copyright* (Prometheus Books, 2001) 183.

Therefore, the act of hyperlinking should not be subject to the communication to the public right because the hyperlink merely references the work, as opposed to making it available or providing it.[10] Furthermore, excessive control over copyright works could prejudice access to educational and cultural works.[11] It must be remembered that the right to Intellectual Property under Article 17(2) of the Charter of Fundamental Rights of the EU is not absolute. Hence, the scope of exclusive rights under EU copyright law must be proportionately balanced in terms of protecting authors and allowing for access.[12]

From another perspective, the broad interpretation of the communication to the public right can be criticised because it facilitates the overreaching of the right. By adopting a broad approach, the CJEU has had the remit to create a very wide interpretation of the right, including the introduction of the access approach in interpreting the concept of 'communication'. The access approach means that any use of a work that allows an individual to interact with that work can amount to an act of 'communication'.[13] Therefore, there is no need for the work to be actually transmitted or even present, as is the case with hyperlinking and torrent files that merely take the user to the location where the work can be accessed.[14] As a result, the broad interpretation has allowed for the inclusion of acts within the scope of the communication to the public right that should be excluded.

Furthermore, it is arguable that the broad interpretation and the ensuing wide scope of the communication to the public right is inherently contradictory because

[10] S Dusollier, 'Realigning Economic Rights with Exploitation of Works: The Control of Authors over the Circulation of Works in the Public Sphere' in PB Hugenholtz (ed), *Copyright Reconstructed: Rethinking Copyright's Economic Rights in a Time of Highly Dynamic Technological and Economic Change* (Kluwer Law International BV, 2018) 196. This view of hyperlinks is not limited to communication to the public literature, but has been discussed by Sir Tim Berners-Lee (creator of the world wide web) – T Berners-Lee, 'Links and Law: Myths' (*Axioms of Web Architechture*, April 1997) <https://www.w3.org/DesignIssues/LinkMyths.html> accessed 1 August 2018. A similar approach was also used in the defamation case *Crookes v Wikimedia Foundation Inc*, 2011 SCC 47, paras 27 and 30 per Abella J. Also see C Lim Saw, 'Linking on the internet and copyright liability: a clarion call for doctrinal clarity and legal certainty' (2018) 49(5) *International Review of Intellectual Property and Competition Law (IIC)* 536, 559. For a different approach see Midelieva, who dismisses the comparison between hyperlinks and mere references or footnotes – L Midelieva, 'Rethinking Hyperlinking: Addressing Hyperlinks to Unauthorized Content in Copyright Law and Policy' (2017) 39(8) *European Intellectual Property Review (EIPR)* 479, 480–81.

[11] This fear was raised in Case C-161/17 *Land Nordrhein-Westfalen v Dirk Renckhoff* [2018] Opinion of AG Campos Sánchez-Bordona, ECLI:EU:C:2018:279, para 79.

[12] We must remember that the exclusive rights of copyright can be very broad, but they are not borderless – Efroni (2011) 277.

[13] The European Copyright Society argue that the broad interpretation of 'communication' can effectively establish an access right whereby any act providing access to a work can be actionable as a communication to the public – European Copyright Society, *Opinion on The Reference to the CJEU in Case C-461/12 Svensson* (2013): https://europeancopyrightsociety.org/opinion-on-the-reference-to-the-cjeu-in-case-c-46612-svensson/ 6.

[14] Dimita describes torrent files as containing the name and size of the file to be shared, the addresses of the trackers where the file is available and the information to divide, identify and reassemble the file. The torrent file does not contain any part of the work – G Dimita, 'Six characters in search of infringement: potential liability for creating, downloading, and disseminating.torrent files' (2012) 7(6) *Journal of Intellectual Property Law & Practice (JIPLP)* 466, 467.

the CJEU in *Svensson* held that Member States are not allowed to give wider interpretations to the concept of communication to the public under national law.[15] What this means is that the right was maximally harmonised, so that Article 3(1) provides the maximum scope of protection permitted for the communication to the public right under EU copyright law and the domestic laws of Member States. However, in adopting a broad interpretation of the right of communication to the public, this has allowed the CJEU to circumvent the maximal harmonisation of the right set out in *Svensson*, given that the Court is free to interpret the right in an excessively wide manner. This is illustrated by the unrestrained interpretation of 'communication' and the introduction of the new 'knowledge' requirement.

B. Proposed Solution

In order to remedy the problems discussed, it is advocated that the broad interpretation should be abandoned. Instead, a narrow interpretation should be adopted, together with a reformed communication to the public right that internally incorporates a flexible and balanced approach. This will require that the reformed right of communication to the public and its essential elements, 'communication' and 'public', are clearly defined. In adopting this approach, there will be no need for a broad interpretation because the substance of the right will already embody a proportional balance of the relevant interests and, moreover, will have built-in flexibility to accommodate new technologies. Similarly, the scope of the right will be expressly defined. Therefore, there will be no need for judges to engage in judicial activism to develop the communication to the public right.

III. 'Communication'

The term 'communication' is of fundamental importance to the communication to the public right because it is an essential part of the two basic criteria for establishing an act of communication to the public. Despite its importance, it has not been defined in the international copyright treaties, nor in any of the four Directives that include a right of communication to the public. It was left to the CJEU to define the term. Through the decision-making of the CJEU, the term 'communication' has been defined in two contrasting ways.

The first approach to the interpretation of 'communication' was provided in *Rafael Hoteles*. Though not an express definition for 'communication', the language used by the Court to describe the overall act of communication to the public does offer guidance as to how 'communication' should be perceived. It was first stated, albeit in the context of establishing a 'new public', that an act of 'communication to

[15] Case C-466/12 *Svensson and others v Retriever Sverige AB* [2014] ECLI:EU:C:2014:76, paras 33–37.

the public' involves an intervention in full knowledge of the consequences, to give access to protected works.[16] This was followed by the Court holding that for there to be a 'communication to the public' it is sufficient that the work is made available to the public in such a way that they may access it.[17] The common theme in both these statements was the provision of access to end users.

Subsequent to *Rafael Hoteles*, the CJEU, in *FAPL v QC Leisure*, gave a second, contrasting definition for 'communication'. It was stated that a 'communication' refers 'to any transmission of the protected works, irrespective of the technical means or process used'.[18] From this, the CJEU created two approaches to the interpretation of the term 'communication': the access approach, as in *Rafael Hoteles*, and the transmission approach, as stated in *FAPL v QC Leisure*. However, in *FAPL v QC Leisure*, the differences between the access and transmission approaches were avoided by the Court holding that the factual situation in *FAPL v QC Leisure* was comparable to that in *Rafael Hoteles*.[19] Similarly, the CJEU in *Reha Training* utilised both the transmission and access approaches in its decision. However, the Court failed to reconcile the divergent approaches by adopting the same logic in *FAPL v QC Leisure* that the situation was factually comparable to prior cases.[20]

Despite the uncertainty created by the two definitions, the issue was not problematic until *Svensson* because the technologies involved in the cases prior to *Svensson* all involved traditional broadcasting with retransmissions or reception in public. As such, there was always a transmission of the work involved. It was only in *Svensson* that the dilemma between the access and transmission approaches became apparent. This is because the act of hyperlinking concerned the making available aspect of the communication to the public right that had not been previously addressed. In the traditional context, acts of broadcasting and retransmission always involved the transmission of a work; whereas, acts of hyperlinking and other Internet facilities do not necessarily involve the transmission of a work. Instead, some Internet facilities merely provide access to the work. As such, the application of the access or transmission approach became centrally important to the determination of liability in *Svensson*.

The CJEU in *Svensson* applied the access approach by citing *Rafael Hoteles*[21] and in so doing held that acts of hyperlinking were 'communications' for the

[16] See P McBride, 'The "new public" criterion after Svensson: the (ir)relevance of website terms and conditions' [2017] 3 *Intellectual Property Quarterly (IPQ)* 262, 269–72. McBride argued that the CJEU in Cases C-403/08 and C-429/08 *Football Association Premier League (FAPL) and others v QC Leisure and others and Karen Murphy v Media Protection Services Ltd* [2011] ECLI:EU:C:2011:631 untangled the 'communication' and 'new public' criteria.

[17] *SGAE v Rafael Hoteles* [2006] paras 42–43.

[18] *FAPL v QC Leisure* [2011] para 193.

[19] ibid paras 194–95.

[20] Case C-117/15 *Reha Training Gesellschaft für Sport- und Unfallrehabilitation mbH v Gesellschaft für musikalische Aufführungs- und mechanische Vervielfältigungsrechte eV (GEMA)* [2016] ECLI:EU:C:2016:379, paras 38 and 46.

[21] *Svensson* [2014] paras 19–20.

purpose of the communication to the public right. Moreover, the *Svensson* decision also signalled that the making available aspect was to be interpreted in line with the access approach. This was followed in the subsequent cases of *GS Media*, *Filmspeler* and *Ziggo* to the extent that the aggregation of hyperlinks and torrent files amounted to acts of 'communication'. This situation is likely to further deteriorate given the CJEU's further expansion of 'communication' in *Ziggo* where the Court, in agreeing with the Advocate General, stated that 'communication' would include acts of sharing that make access less complex.[22]

Notwithstanding the ever-expansive approach of the CJEU in relation to 'communication', the recent case of *VCAST*[23] reintroduced the uncertainty concerning the definition of 'communication' by referencing the transmission approach. This has caused concern because the factual situation in *VCAST* involved the making available aspect, thus creating further copyright inconsistency with regard to the right of communication to the public.[24] In analysing *VCAST*, it appears that the CJEU wrongly interpreted the facts of the case to be about retransmission. This is supported by the fact that reference is made to *Reha Training*, a retransmission case. However, the act of recording a television programme in the 'cloud' for users to access at a later time does not amount to retransmission because it is not a near-simultaneous retransmission as was the case in *ITV v TVCatchup*. Consequently, the decision in *VCAST* directly illustrates the problems with the CJEU's approach to 'communication'. In the first place having two definitions leads to uncertainty, culminating in the inconsistent use of the divergent access and transmission approaches. Secondly, *VCAST* illustrated how volatile the line between analogue and digital technology is. As such, 'communication' should not be interpreted in accordance with the type of technology involved. Therefore, in order to establish a coherent communication to the public right, it is necessary that 'communication' is interpreted in a consistent manner that creates certainty. It is advocated that a nuanced form of the transmission approach should be the sole means of interpreting 'communication'.

A. Critiquing the Access Approach

The access approach is supported by a number of commentators, including the Association Littéraire et Artistique Internationale (ALAI), which argued that the act of making available includes not only transmission, but also the offering to

[22] Case C-610/15 *Stichting Brein v Ziggo BV and XS4All Internet BV* [2017] ECLI:EU:C:2017:456, para 36. ALAI agrees with this approach in stating that the 'indispensable role' of the communicator should not be interpreted strictly to mean the only means of access – ALAI, *Provisional Opinion of ALAI's Executive Committee On the Right of communication to the public; the Advocate General's Opinions in Filmspeler Case C-527/15 and Ziggo Case C-610/15* (2017) 3.

[23] Case C-256/16 *VCAST Ltd v RTI SpA* [2017] ECLI:EU:C:2017:913.

[24] AG Campos Sánchez-Bordona also refers to the transmission approach in relation to the act of making available in *Renckhoff* [2018] Opinion of AG Campos Sánchez-Bordona, paras 60 and 62.

the public of a work.[25] Ginsburg takes the argument for the access approach further by stating that the limitation of the making available aspect to actual transmissions will eviscerate the right.[26] Similarly, Tsoutsanis argued that the inclusion of the making available aspect evolved the communication to the public right beyond the concept of transmission, so that the mere offering of a work is sufficient.[27] However, support for the access approach in this regard is limited to the making available aspect of the communication to the public right. It is not clear whether the access approach should be expanded to cover the right as a whole. Certainly, it is possible that the access approach can govern the overall right, because 'access' is wide enough to include transmissions of works. But, it is debatable whether the access approach should be applied to the communication to the public right at all. This is because the access approach is subject to a number of criticisms.

In the first place, it can be argued that adopting the access approach is contradictory to the history and purpose of the communication to the public right. The Basic Proposal for the WIPO Copyright Treaty states: 'communication always involves transmission'.[28] Therefore, it makes sense to define the act of 'communication' in accordance with the transmission approach. Advocates for the access approach would criticise this argument on the basis that the inclusion of the making available aspect has led to the evolution of the right, so that it is not only about transmission. This criticism should be treated with caution because the replacement of the transmission aspect of communication to the public with the access approach would risk turning the communication to the public right into an access right.[29] If this were the case, the legislature would have made it expressly

[25] Association Littéraire et Artistique Internationale (ALAI), *Report and Opinion on the making available and communication to the public in the Internet environment – focus on linking techniques on the Internet* (2013) 3. ALAI in its later reports maintained its belief that acts of hyperlinking are 'communications' because they offer access to the protected works – ALAI, *Opinion Proposed to the Executive Committee and adopted at its meeting, 17 September 2014 on the criterion 'New Public', developed by the Court of Justice of the European Union (CJEU), put in the context of making available and communication to the public* (2014) 1 and ALAI, *ALAI Report and Opinion on a Berne-compatible reconciliation of hyperlinking and the communication to the public right on the Internet* (2015) 1, all available at: http://www.alai.org/en/resolutions-and-positions.html. Also see: T Dreier and PB Hugenholtz, *Concise European Copyright Law* (Kluwer Law International, 2006) 361, WIPO, *WIPO National Seminar on Copyright, Related Rights, and Collective Management* (2005) 13, para 56, S Ricketson and J Ginsburg, *International Copyright and Neighbouring Rights: The Berne Convention and Beyond* (Oxford University Press, 2006) para 12.58.

[26] J Ginsburg, 'Hyperlinking and "making available"' (2014) 36(3) *EIPR* 147, 147.

[27] A Tsoutsanis, 'Why copyright and linking can tango' (2014) 9(6) *JIPLP* 495, 498–501.

[28] WIPO, *Basic Proposal for the Substantive Provisions of the Treaty on Certain Questions Concerning the Protection of Literary and Artistic Works to be Considered by the Diplomatic Conference* (CRNR/DC/4) (1996) 46, para 10.15.

[29] For discussion on access right see: Efroni (2011), G Westkamp, 'Transient Copying and Public Communications: The Creeping Evolution of Use and Access Rights in European Copyright Law' (2004) 36 *George Washington International Law Review* 1057 and J Ginsburg, 'Essay: From Having Copies to Experiencing Works: The Development of an Access Right in US Copyright Law' (2003) 50 *Journal of the Copyright Society of USA (J Copyright Soc'y USA)* 113.

known under Article 8 of the WIPO Copyright Treaty (WCT) or an agreed statement, given the importance for the interpretation of the right.

Furthermore, Ginsburg's criticism that limiting the making available aspect to the transmission approach would eviscerate the right[30] can be dismissed because it unfairly rejects the transmission approach. This is because the transmission approach is capable of governing the making available aspect; however, not as broadly as the access approach. If the making available aspect is understood as the *potential transmission or provision of a work*, as opposed to the mere provision of access to the work, there is no issue with the evisceration of the making available aspect. This is because acts of making available involving a *provision of the work* will be subject to liability. For example, simple hyperlinks will be excluded on this basis because they do not involve the provision of a work; they simply redirect the user to where the work can potentially be found.[31] However, embedded hyperlinks such as framed[32] and inline links[33] can be argued to invoke the communication to the public right.[34]

Even if the above argument that communication to the public must involve a transmission or provision of the work rather than mere access is ignored, the access approach is still controversial because it will lead to an overbroad and unbalanced communication to the public right. The consequence will be detriment to the use and development of some Internet technologies, in particular, hyperlinking, P2P networks (including torrents) and cloud storage. Thus, end users will suffer because restrictions on the use and development of technology will negatively affect their use and dissemination of works. Therefore, the access approach should not be adopted because it is unlikely to be able to adequately balance the competing pressures and interests discussed in Chapter one.

The adoption of the access approach has led to an overbroad communication to the public right because it has allowed for acts such as simple hyperlinking and hyperlink and torrent file aggregation to be subject to the communication to the public right. In looking at the cases of *GS Media*, *Filsmpeler* and *Ziggo*, the hyperlinks and torrent files in question do not provide the works; they merely provide access to where the works can be found. Alternatively, it can be said that they make access to works less complex, given that they do not actually provide the works. In order for the scope of the right to be justified, only acts that involve the transmission or provision of the work should come within the scope of the right. Furthermore, the overbroad scope of the right is additionally compounded by the

[30] Ginsburg (2014) 147.

[31] European Copyright Society (2013) 2, 6.

[32] Framing hyperlinks make external websites visually perceptible on the host website, embedded in a 'frame' surrounded by the host website's information. It is similar to picture-in-picture formatting.

[33] Inline hyperlinks are similar to framed links, but differ because only an individual aspect of a webpage is portrayed. Inline links allow for the 'importation' of material from another website without the user knowing. For example, it can be an individual image found on an external website.

[34] Liability for the various types of hyperlinks will be discussed in the following subsection.

CJEU's failure to conduct an in-depth analysis of the technologies involved in the cases. In *Svensson*, *GS Media*, *Filmspeler* and *Ziggo*, the CJEU merely assumed that the acts in question were acts of 'communication'[35] or alternatively stated there was 'communication' because the act in question provided 'direct access'.[36] This is dangerous because the Court failed to distinguish that technology – notably hyperlinks, of which there are several types – can function in diverse ways;[37] the consequence being that any type of hyperlink could be an infringement.[38]

ALAI, though in support of the access approach, does concede that simple hyperlinks that merely take the user to a webpage should not be considered an act of communication to the public.[39] This logic should also be applied to hyperlink and torrent file aggregation. Simple hyperlinks and torrent files only provide the information as to where the work can already be found, as opposed to embodying the work when used. Therefore, continuing the CJEU's overbroad regulation of hyperlinks and torrent files is unjustified because it disproportionately benefits right holders at the expense of users.

While an overbroad communication to the public right does achieve a high level of protection for right holders, this comes at the expense of end users and technology developers, and therefore, negatively affects some of the copyright considerations, as well as the fundamental rights interests discussed in Chapter one. An overbroad communication to the public right fails to accommodate developments in technology and has the potential to limit future developments. This is because many Internet technologies may fall within the scope of the right under the access approach. Recital 5 of the ISD states that the law on copyright should be adapted and supplemented to respond *adequately* to new forms of exploitation. 'Adequately' should be interpreted to mean that right holders are afforded protection; however, that protection should not be to the detriment of the use or development of technology. The overbroad communication to the public right embodies the risk that technologies such as hyperlinking may be overregulated to the extent that they are no longer practical to use. This may have far reaching consequences given that hyperlinks make the internet functionally efficient. Similarly, developments in technologies such as P2P systems and torrent files may be reduced in response to decisions such as *Ziggo*. Furthermore, intermediaries can be held primarily liable for infringements by third party end users. Notwithstanding the above arguments, this does not mean that the operators of such activities

[35] *Svensson* [2014] paras 19–20.

[36] Case C-527/15 *Stichting Brein v Jack Frederik Wullems (also trading under the name Filmspeler)* [2017] ECLI:EU:C:2017:300, para 42 and *Ziggo* [2017] paras 32–34.

[37] For example, Tsoutsanis stresses that hyperlinks cannot be subjected to a 'one-size-fits-all' approach – Tsoutsanis (2014) 496–97.

[38] According to Arezzo, the CJEU's unquestioned assumption that hyperlinking is an act of 'communication' should have been given more consideration given that it is of 'crucial relevance.' See E Arezzo, 'Hyperlinks and making available right in the European Union: What future for the Internet after *Svensson*?' (2014) 45(5) *IIC* 524, 539.

[39] ALAI (2013) 9.

should be liability free; only that they should not face primary liability under the communication to the public right.[40]

In terms of fundamental rights, the overbroad communication to the public right can be seen as encroaching on the Article 11 right of freedom of expression and information under the Charter of Fundamental Rights. This is because right holders are given disproportionate power over end users, as the communication to the public right can be used to control acts that do not involve the transmission or provision of works.[41] The consequence of this can be unwarranted limits on end users sharing information and, moreover, restrictions on the promotion of learning and culture.[42] Taken together, these implications negatively affect the public interest.[43] Therefore, if the communication to the public right is subject to the access approach it will not be justifiable, given its overbroad scope and disproportionate balance of the competing interests that must be taken accounted of.

It can also be argued that the CJEU's adoption of the access approach and the resultant overbroad interpretation of 'communication' have created consequences for the 'public' element of the communication to the public right. It was stated that the CJEU has been careless in its determination of whether an act amounts to a 'communication'. The CJEU has compensated for this carelessness by using the 'new public' criterion to limit the reach of the communication to the public right. In *Svensson*, it was held that the act of hyperlinking to freely available newspaper articles was not an act of communication to the public because there was no 'new public', given that the works were available online to all Internet users.[44] This method of determining infringement is undesirable because the act in question is held to be a 'communication' made to a 'public'; however, it is not a 'communication to the public' because the works were freely available. Additionally, the use of the 'new public' criterion in *Svensson* effectively led to the exhaustion of the right for works made freely available online.[45] The availability of the work communicated should have no bearing on whether there is an act of communication to the public.[46] Instead of having to rely on the 'new public' criterion to prevent

[40] Such individuals may be liable under secondary liability or other similar grounds.

[41] Depreeuw (2014) para 657.

[42] See Recital 14 of the ISD.

[43] See Recital 3 of the ISD.

[44] *Svensson* [2014] paras 25–28.

[45] Arezzo (2014) 543, ALAI (2014) 2, PB Hugenholtz and S van Velze, 'Communication to a New Public? Three Reasons Why EU Copyright Law Can Do without a "New Public"' (2016) 47(7) *IIC* 797, 811, J Rosén, 'How Much Communication to the Public is "Communication to the Public"?' in I Stamatoudi (ed), *New Developments in EU and International Copyright Law* (Kluwer Law International, 2016) 331–50, P Savola, 'EU Copyright Liability for Internet Linking' (2017) 8 *Journal of Intellectual Property, Information Technology & Electronic Commerce Law (JIPITEC)* 139, 148, para 57 and V Benabou, 'Digital Exhaustion of Copyright in the EU or Shall We Cease Being so Schizophrenic?' in I Stamatoudi (ed), *New Developments in EU and International Copyright Law* (Kluwer Law International BV, 2016) 364.

[46] From *Svensson* it can be reasoned that hyperlinking to a work made available online without authorisation will constitute a communication to the public – *Svensson* [2014] para 31 and A Baker,

unwanted infringements, emphasis should be placed on limiting what counts as a 'communication'. This will provide for a more consistent and rational way of determining infringement. This recommendation has added importance because the 'new public' criterion will be refuted in this chapter.

Consequently, it is advocated that the access approach should be abandoned in lieu of a refined version of the transmission approach.

B. Adopting a Refined Transmission Approach

Given the arguments against the access approach, it is argued that a nuanced form of the transmission approach should be adopted because it will provide a more balanced and justifiable right of communication to the public. This is in line with the opinion of the European Copyright Society, which argues for the adoption of the transmission approach, primarily on the grounds of consistency and compatibility with the WCT[47] and the *travaux préparatoires* of the EU copyright Directives.[48] In addition to the historical compatibility argument, the nuanced transmission approach will provide for a more proportionate right because it provides an adequate level of protection for right holders while not prejudicing intermediaries, the development of technology or the burgeoning sharing norms of end users. Thus, the European Charter fundamental rights concerning freedom of expression and information (Article 11) and the freedom to conduct a business (Article 16) are sufficiently taken account of, together with the copyright considerations set out in the recitals of the ISD as discussed in Chapter one. Notwithstanding this, the aim to achieve a high level of protection is not compromised, as right holders will still have adequate control over the dissemination of their works.

Only acts that involve the *transmission or provision* of a work should fall within the scope of the communication to the public right. Therefore, acts that merely point users to where a work can be found – such as simple and deep hyperlinks and torrent files – should not be considered a 'communication'. This is because the work is not embodied in or provided from the communicative act and as such, the work is not 'made available' from that communication. Rather, it is the initial act

'EU Copyright Directive: can a hyperlink be a "communication to the public"?' (2014) 20(4) *Computer & Telecommunications Law Review* 100, 102. Furgal also argues that a single act of communication should not limit a right holder's ability to decide about future communications – U Furgal, 'Ancillary right for press publishers: an alternative answer to the linking conundrum?' (2018) 13(9) *JIPLP* 700, 703.

[47] WIPO, *Basic Proposal for the Substantive Provisions of the Treaty on Certain Questions Concerning the Protection of Literary and Artistic Works to be Considered by the Diplomatic Conference* (CRNR/DC/4) (1996) 46 para 10.15.

[48] European Copyright Society (2013) 2–6. See Commission, *Copyright and Related Rights in the Information Society* (Green Paper COM(95) 382 final, 1995) 56 [Green Paper for the ISD] and Commission, *Proposal for a European Parliament and Council Directive on the harmonisation of certain aspects of copyright and related rights in the Information Society* (COM(97) 628 final, 1998) 25–26 [Proposal for the ISD].

of uploading the file that makes available/provides the work to the user.[49] Simple hyperlinking and deep hyperlinks give indirect access to works that are already available. Torremans expressed a similar viewpoint in stating that focus should be placed on the act of transmission that provides access to the work, so that an act of 'communication' should only be established where the work is accessible without any further action being required of the user.[50] This is equivalent to the proposed concept of 'provision of the work'. To reiterate the point, 'communication' should only be established where the user has direct contact with the work during the course of the act in question, as opposed to a subsequent by-product of the act. Mere *access* after the initial provision of the work is made is not the pivotal concept for the making available aspect.[51]

AG Wathelet, in his Opinion on *GS Media*, also adopted a comparable approach in stating that hyperlinks, even those that lead directly to works, do not make those works available where the works are already available on another website.[52] AG Wathelet went on to state that an act of 'communication' should be a vital or indispensable intervention that allows users to benefit from or enjoy the works.[53] This statement can be interpreted to mean that there must be a nexus between the act and the obtaining of the work. However, AG Wathelet did not explain the concept of benefitting from or enjoying works, and as such it is unclear whether the benefit or enjoyment has to be direct. What AG Wathelet did focus on was the indispensable intervention element which resulted in a finding of no 'communication' because the works were already available. However, unfortunately, the CJEU did not follow AG Wathelet's Opinion.

With that in mind, the merit in AG Wathelet's Opinion relates to the nexus between the act and obtaining the work. If this underlying concept is applied with regards to the proposed nuanced transmission approach, a common theme emerges. An act should only be considered 'communication' if it embodies or provides the work. This is in contrast to acts that take the user to where the work

[49] Arezzo makes the argument that hyperlinks can be described as the wires that link the user to information/works already available on the Internet. Therefore, hyperlinks do not make the work available – Arezzo (2014) 526. Also see M Peguera, 'Hyperlinking under the lens of the revamped right of communication to the public' (2018) 34(5) *Computer Law & Security Review* 1099, 1104.

[50] P Torremans, 'When the Court of Justice of the European Union sets about defining exclusive rights: copyright *quo vadis*?' in P Torremans (ed), *Research Handbook on Copyright Law*, 2nd edn (Edward Elgar Publishing Ltd, 2017) 94. Also see: I Stamatoudi and P Torremans, *EU Copyright Law: A Commentary* (Edward Elgar Publishing Ltd, 2014) 412, para 11.24, M Walter and S von Lewinski, *European Copyright Law: A Commentary* (Oxford University Press, 2010) para 11.3.30 and Depreeuw (2014) 353–54 and 439.

[51] Ficsor argues that the upload of the work constitutes the moment of making available. In this sense it is the provision of the work that is important, rather than its accessibility. See M Ficsor, *The Law of Copyright and the Internet: The 1996 WIPO Treaties, their Interpretation and Implementation* (Oxford University Press, 2002) 499, para C8.08.

[52] Case C-160/15 *GS Media BV v Sanoma Media Netherlands BV and others* [2016] Opinion of AG Wathelet ECLI:EU:C:2016:221, para 54.

[53] ibid para 57.

can be found. In that case there is no nexus between the act and the work because the work is not made available by the hyperlink.

To best illustrate the practical application of the nuanced transmission approach, it is necessary to engage a discussion of the various types of hyperlinks. Failure to take into account the diversity of hyperlinks will lead to incorrect conclusions, given that simple and deep hyperlinks are very different to framed and inline hyperlinks.[54] From this, the European Copyright Society's blanket approach to hyperlinks should be distinguished.[55] While it is agreed that simple and deep hyperlinks should not come within the scope of the communication to the public right – because they do not transmit or provide the work, but instead merely offer a reference as to where the works can be found – the same is not true for other types of hyperlinks. Framed and inline hyperlinks may give rise to an act of 'communication' because they make the work directly perceptible to the user, in effect acting as a substitute for the original upload.[56]

Embedded hyperlinks operate by bringing the linked content to the user. Therefore, from the perspective of the user it appears as if the content is hosted on the website they are interacting with. However, this is not the case, as embedded hyperlinks effectively pull the content from the original page of upload to the webpage being viewed. Consequently, the user has direct contact with the work because of the hyperlink. This is in contrast to simple and deep hyperlinks that take the user to another location where the content is located. The primary practical difference with embedded hyperlinks is that the right holder loses control over the environment in which their works are 'made available' because the content, in whole or part, is pulled from the initial website to the latter website.[57]

Given that embedded hyperlinks can come within the scope of the proposed definition for 'communication', the practicality of such a finding must be discussed.

[54] The indiscriminate treatment of hyperlinks by the CJEU has meant that acts of embedding links to works made freely available online with authorisation cannot amount to acts of communication to the public even if the subsequent use is commercial or contrary to the right holder's wishes – M Leistner, 'Closing the Book on the Hyperlinks: Brief Outline of the CJEU's Case Law and Proposal for European Legislative Reform' (2017) 39(6) *EIPR* 327, 329–30. Also see P Mezei, 'Enter the matrix: the effects of CJEU case law on linking and streaming technologies' (2016) 11(10) *JIPLP* 778, 780.

[55] The European Copyright Society states that 'hyperlinks in general should be regarded as an activity that is not covered by the right to communicate the work to the public' – European Copyright Society (2013) 2. Lim Saw also shares this opinion, stating that framing and inline links should not amount to communication to the public because they still only make an indirect or secondary use of a work that has already been made available – Lim Saw (2018) 554–55.

[56] A Ohly, 'A Fairness-Based Approach to Economic Rights' in PB Hugenholtz (ed), *Copyright Reconstructed: Rethinking Copyright's Economic Rights in a Time of Highly Dynamic and Technological and Economic Change* (Kluwer Law International BV, 2018) 113, Dusollier in Hugenholtz (2018) 196 and Hugenholtz and Van Velze (2016) 814.

[57] J Poort, 'Borderlines of Copyright Protection: An Economic Analysis' in PB Hugenholtz (ed), *Copyright Reconstructed: Rethinking Copyright's Economic Rights in a Time of Highly Dynamic and Technological and Economic Change* (Kluwer Law International BV, 2018) 113 and Dusollier in Hugenholtz (2018) 319.

Simple and deep hyperlinks are an integral part of the internet's infrastructure.[58] The use of embedded hyperlinks has become common. As such, there is the question of whether hyperlinks in any form should be regulated by the right of communication to the public. The easy answer would be: 'Yes, for the purpose of ensuring a high level of protection for right holders'. The more nuanced answer should still be: 'Yes, because embedded hyperlinks have similar functionality to acts of traditional retransmission'. This is because they are subsequent communications that potentially widen the availability of the original upload without affecting the availability of the original communication. Therefore, it is justified that right holders should have control over subsequent uses of the works they upload on the internet, where there is the requisite nexus between the act and the transmission or provision of the work. Otherwise, the communication to the public right will be exhausted, contrary to Article 3(3) of the ISD.

As for the practicality of regulating acts of hyperlinking that come within the definition of 'communication', it should be indistinct from the traditional regulation of content that is uploaded online. That is, the procedures and remedies that apply to the regulation of content uploaded with or without authorisation should be equally applicable such as licensing, notice and takedown, website blocking orders and damages. Having said that, there are likely to be concerns by users and intermediaries about diminished access to creative content and increased transaction costs, which may jeopardise business models and consumption patterns.[59] Though these may be legitimate concerns, the scope of the right will be proportionately balanced across all of its elements to ensure that the interests of users are adequately upheld.

What the nuanced transmission approach as discussed demonstrates is that the concept of 'transmission' does not have to be interpreted as rigidly as its detractors, such as Ginsburg or Tsoutsanis, would suggest. If the term 'transmission' is expanded to include the *provision of the work*, the arguments concerning the lack of technological neutrality and the failure to embrace 'making available' are not as persuasive because the act of 'communication' is framed in a more neutral way that does not solely speak to the old concept of transmission.[60] Hence, 'communication' should be interpreted to mean any act that transmits or makes a provision of the work. This is wide enough to include some types of hyperlinks and other forms of making available that actually embody the work, but not so wide as to include items such as simple and deep hyperlinking, torrent files, or hyperlink and torrent file aggregation. Moreover, it will ensure that primary liability is attributed to the

[58] Mezei argues that hyperlinks are essential to the use of the Internet because they facilitate communication by speeding up access – Mezei (2016) 778–79. Also see *GS Media* [2017] Opinion of AG Wathelet paras 78–79.

[59] M Leistner, 'Copyright law on the internet in need of reform: hyperlinks, online platforms and aggregators' (2017) 12(2) *JIPLP* 136, 142.

[60] This dismisses the arguments of Tsoutsanis about why the transmission approach is not suitable – *Tsoutsanis* (2014) 498–501.

correct parties. In other words, intermediaries should not be held primarily liable for acts of communication to the public where they do not transmit or provide works. Where intermediaries have knowledge of the infringing actions of their third party end users, they are culpable. However, they should be held responsible under secondary liability. Therefore, a nuanced form of the transmission approach provides a proportionately well-balanced and flexible approach to interpreting the term 'communication'.

C. Proposed Solution

It is recommended that the access approach to the interpretation of 'communication' be abandoned and a single definition for 'communication' be adopted, influenced by the refined transmission approach – the transmission or provision of a work. 'Provision' should be taken to mean direct contact with the work from the act of 'communication'.

IV. The Making Available Aspect

The introduction of the making available aspect[61] was heralded as one of the major achievements of the WCT.[62] The making available aspect is seen as a success because it expanded the scope of copyright law to address on demand uses of copyright works, namely, for the Internet.[63] However, its relationship with the communication to the public right is unclear due to its legislative history and, more recently, the loose use of the term 'making available' by the CJEU. As such, this has implications for the scope and application of the communication to the public right under EU copyright law. Consequently, it is necessary to clarify that the making available aspect is a subset of the general communication to the public right and that the term 'making available' should not be used out of context.

The need for the making available aspect developed out of the uncertainty as to whether the communication to the public right under the Berne Convention

[61] The term 'making available' previously appeared under the Interpretive Declaration of the Berne Convention adopted at Paris in 1896 in relation to the definition of 'publication'. This was then included under Article 4(4) of the Rome Revision of the Berne Convention 1928. In addition to this, the term 'making available' was also included under Article 7(1) of the Stockholm Revision of the Berne Convention 1967. See Ficsor (2002) paras 4.34–4.36. However, the embryonic form of the modern making available right was proposed in 1982 at the WIPO/UNESCO Committee of Governmental Experts on Copyright Problems Arising from the Use of Computers for Access to or the Creation of Works – Ficsor (2002) para 4.56.

[62] Ricketson and Ginsburg (2006) 746, P Goldstein and PB Hugenholtz, *International Copyright: Principles, Law, and Practice*, 3rd edn (Oxford University Press, 2013) 335 and J Reinbothe, 'The new WIPO treaties: a first resume' (1997) 19 *EIPR* 171, 173.

[63] Ficsor (2002) paras 4.38 and 4.56.

could encompass acts such as on demand transmissions.[64] In other words, the question was whether 'pull' (on demand) technologies fell within the scope of the Berne Convention alongside the traditional 'push' technologies such as broadcasting and simultaneous retransmission by wire or wireless technology.[65] Dreier at the Harvard Symposium[66] argued that the communication to the public right under the Berne Convention was inadequate to address digital networks because its focus was on simultaneous, point-to-multipoint transmissions such as broadcasts,[67] whereas, on demand transmissions were non-simultaneous, point-to-point transmissions that could be accessed at a particular time or place chosen by the user. Consequently, part of Dreier's concern was that the 'public' element of the traditional communication to the public right would render acts of on demand transmission outside the scope of the communication to the public right. This is because the works would be accessible to individual persons in individual places and as a result the 'communication' would not be made to a 'public'.[68]

Following the discussions at the various WIPO symposiums, there was general agreement that the communication to the public right under the Berne Convention was in need of clarification and updating to address the new forms of digital transmission. The answer to this issue was the making available right.[69] However, there was uncertainty as to where this right should be located. Before its inclusion under the Article 8 communication to the public right of the WCT,[70] the right of reproduction, distribution, rental and even a completely new right were touted as possible solutions to harbour the new making available right.[71] However, what was opted for was the 'umbrella solution',[72] whereby national legislators could

[64] Ricketson and Ginsburg (2006) paras 12.48–12.49, 12.57, T Aplin, *Copyright Law in the Digital Society* (Hart Publishing, 2005) 127, Efroni (2011) 256, J Ginsburg, 'The (New?) Right of Making Available to the Public' in D Vaver and L Bently (eds), *Intellectual Property in the New Millennium, Essays in Honour of William R Cornish* (Cambridge University Press, 2004) 246, Depreeuw (2014) para 615 and Goldstein and Hugenholtz (2013) 335.

[65] Ricketson and Ginsburg argue that only the provisions that stated 'any communication to the public' could possibly address on demand technologies – Ricketson and Ginsburg (2006) para 12.49. Depreeuw argues that the Berne Convention was not suited to the interactive environment – Depreeuw (2014) para 501.

[66] One of the WIPO brainstorming meetings.

[67] T Dreier, 'Copyright Digitized: Philosophical Impacts and Practical Implications for Information Exchange in Digital Networks' in *WIPO Worldwide Symposium on the Impact of Digital Technology on Copyright and Neighbouring Rights* (1993) 193. Also see Green Paper for the ISD (1995) 56.

[68] Note, this fear was resolved by the notion of a cumulative 'public'.

[69] For the development of the making available right see Ficsor (2002) Chapter 4.

[70] The original plan was to leave it open to contracting parties to decide where the making available right was to be included. This was the so-called umbrella solution – Ficsor (2002) para C8.06.

[71] Aplin (2005) 128 and Walter and von Lewinski (2010) paras 11.3.4–11.3.5. The EU Commission was also faced with the same question of where the making available right should be placed and initially was in favour of placing it under the rental right. See the Green Paper for the ISD (1995) 57, Commission, *Follow-up to the Green Paper on copyright and related rights in the Information Society* (COM(96) 586 final, 1996) 13–14 and A Ohly, 'Economic rights' in E Derclaye (ed), *Research Handbook on the Future of EU Copyright* (Edward Elgar Publishing Ltd, 2009) 225.

[72] First introduced in M Ficsor, 'Digital Technology and Copyright' in *Copyright in the Asia-Pacific Region: Reprography and digital Copying* (Copyright Agency Limited, 1995) 147–52.

choose where the making available right was included.[73] Despite the suggestion of the umbrella solution, the making available right was ultimately included in the Article 8 communication to the public right because the majority of delegations were in favour of this approach; moreover, there were no objections.[74] The EU, under Article 3(1) of the ISD, followed the approach of the WCT and adopted the making available aspect as a subset of the general communication to the public right.[75] However, Article 3(2) introduced a stand-alone making available right for related rights.

A. The Uncertainty Problem

Under the ISD, the status of the making available aspect has been shrouded in some uncertainty due to its inclusion under the general communication to the public right. The uncertainty primarily relates to whether the right is a subset of the communication to the public right or a stand-alone right incorporated as a matter of convenience. This uncertainty can be seen in comparing the inclusion of the making available aspect under the general Article 3(1) communication to the public right against Recital 25 of the ISD which seems to suggest that it is a separate exclusive right.[76] The reason for this contradiction between Article 3(1) and Recital 25 may be because Article 3(2) provides an exclusive making available right for related subject-matter, separate to the general communication to the public right for authors. This is due to the fact that the general communication to the public right for related rights is found under Article 8 of the Rental and Lending Right Directive. In order to clarify this uncertainty, it is suggested that the communication to the public right be unified into one provision for both authorial works and related subject-matter, so as to provide a sense of legal certainty and to be in accordance with the EU's harmonisation agenda for copyright law.[77] Furthermore, the making available right should be expressly clarified as a subset of the general communication to the public right for both authorial works and related subject-matter.[78]

[73] Ficsor (2002) para C8.06 and C8.11, M Ficsor, 'International Harmonization of Copyright and Neighboring Rights' in *WIPO Worldwide Symposium on Copyright in the Global Information Infrastructure* (1995) 374–77 and P Geller, 'Conflicts of Law in the Cyberspace' in PB Hugenholtz (ed) *The Future of Copyright in a Digital Environment* (Kluwer Law International, 1996) 42.

[74] Ficsor (2002) paras C8.06–C8.07.

[75] Goldstein and Hugenholtz (2013) 336, Ficsor (2002) para C8.17 and Westkamp (2004) 1076.

[76] Ficsor (2002) para C8.18.

[77] This will be discussed in more detail under the harmonisation subsection of this chapter.

[78] This approach is supported by the fact that the Australian proposal to separate the making available right from the general communication to the public right was dismissed at the Diplomatic Conference for the WCT. See Ficsor (2002) para 4.148 and J Reinbothe and S von Lewinski, *The WIPO Treaties 1996: the WIPO Copyright Treaty and the WIPO Performances and Phonograms Treaty: commentary and legal analysis* (Butterworths LexisNexis, 2002) 103.

In addition to the legislative uncertainty concerning the place of the making available aspect,[79] the CJEU in *Rafael Hoteles*, *ITV v TVCatchup* and *Svensson* created further uncertainty about the relationship between making available and communication to the public. In *Rafael Hoteles* the CJEU, in answering the first comprehensive case on communication to the public, made the peculiar statement that:

> It follows from Article 3(1) of Directive 2001/29 and Article 8 of the WIPO Copyright Treaty that for there to be communication to the public it is sufficient that the work is made available to the public in such a way that the persons forming that public may access it.[80]

The use of the phrase 'made available to the public' here would seem to refer to the making available aspect. However, the issue in *Rafael Hoteles* was about the cable retransmission of a broadcast that did not concern making available. Therefore, the problem with the statement was that the CJEU mixed up the language of the making available aspect with that of the traditional communication to the public right. The issue here was that the Court's use of the language of making available might be misunderstood and misapplied by future courts, which did eventually happen in *ITV v TVCatchup*[81] and *Svensson*.[82] To give an analogous example, the error committed by the CJEU in *Rafael Hoteles* was akin to applying the broadcasting aspect of communication to the public to the uploading of a work on the Internet or vice versa. Therefore, as the first point of clarification, it is submitted that the making available right is a subset of communication to the public similar to broadcasting, rebroadcasting or cable retransmission. Thus, the language of making available should be reserved for on demand transmissions rather than being loosely used, as was the case in *Rafael Hoteles* and *ITV v TVCatchup*.[83]

The consequence of using the language of 'making available' in *Rafael Hoteles* was not discerned until *ITV v TVCatchup*. This case concerned the near-simultaneous Internet retransmission of television broadcasts. However, the CJEU erroneously applied the language of 'making available' because the Internet retransmission did not allow the user to access the work at a time individually chosen by them. Therefore, the language in *ITV v TVCatchup* was careless.[84] This

[79] Many consumers, end users and institutional users together with some Member States suggested that the scope of the making available right under the ISD is unclear – Commission, *Report on the responses to the Public Consultation on the Review of the EU Copyright Rules* (2014) 12, 14.

[80] *SGAE v Rafael Hoteles* [2006] para 43.

[81] Case C–607/11 *ITV Broadcasting Ltd and others v TVCatchup Ltd* [2013] ECLI:EU:C:2013:147, paras 26, 33 and 39.

[82] *Svensson* [2014] para 19.

[83] If the making available right is treated as a subset of communication to the public, the problem of mixing the language of the various types of communicative acts will be reduced in importance. However, it is still necessary for the purpose of legal certainty and clarity to resolve cases using the correct aspect of communication to the public.

[84] *ITV v TVCatchup* [2013] paras 26 and 39.

carelessness must be attributed to the general loose application of the phrase 'making available'. As a result, it is necessary to clarify what constitutes an act of making available and to reinforce that it is only to be applied to on demand acts. Thus, the CJEU should not use the terminology of 'making available' in its retransmission or other non-on demand cases.

In order to achieve this, it must be highlighted for the avoidance of doubt that the making available aspect is a specific type of communication to the public which *only* addresses on demand transmissions that allow the user to access the work at a time and place individually chosen by them. This is as opposed to a completely separate exclusive right or a general catchment provision. As a possible solution, it may be desirable to develop a hierarchical communication to the public system, whereby the making available aspect is applied first. If the making available aspect cannot apply, then the traditional broadcasting and retransmission aspects of the communication to the public right should be utilised.[85] Adopting this approach should prevent the loose use of the term 'making available' and ensure that the making available aspect is not misapplied to incompatible transmissions such as simultaneous Internet retransmissions.

The other correction that must be made in relation to the making available aspect is to clarify that it was incorrect for the CJEU in *Svensson* to reference paragraph 43 of *Rafael Hoteles* as the means for defining the making available aspect and consequently establishing an act of 'communication'.[86] This was the means by which future courts would misunderstand and misinterpret the loose use of the language of 'making available'. In this particular scenario, the problem was that *Rafael Hoteles* did not concern the making available aspect. As such, relying on *Rafael Hoteles* as the precedent for the application and scope of the making available aspect was both undesirable and incorrect. It can also be said that this problem was facilitated by the use of the access approach in defining 'communication' in *Rafael Hoteles*. Therefore, the CJEU should refrain from citing *Rafael Hoteles* in instances of on demand transmissions or as a precedent for the making available aspect, given the factual differences in the cases.

Secondly, it must be made clear that the uploading of a work to the Internet will amount to a separate act of making available requiring fresh authorisation, even if that work is already freely available on the Internet or was copied from the Internet. The AG's Opinion in *Renckhoff* mistakenly stated that copying a photo from one website and uploading it to another website is an act of subsequent communication rather than a completely new act requiring fresh authorisation.[87]

[85] Walter and von Lewinski (2010) para 11.3.32.

[86] *Svensson* [2014] para 19.

[87] *Renckhoff* [2018] Opinion of AG Campos Sánchez-Bordona and ALAI, *Opinion on Case C-161/17 (Land Nordrhein-Westfalen v Dirk Renckhoff)* (29.5.2018): http://www.alai.org/en/assets/files/resolutions/180529-opinion-land-nordrhein-westfalen-en.pdf, 2–3.

B. Proposed Solution

The EU legislature should expressly clarify that the making available aspect is a subset of the general communication to the public right as a matter of certainty. It must also be impressed upon the CJEU and national courts that more care should be taken to avoid misusing the language of 'making available'. Finally, *Rafael Hoteles* should not be the point of reference to aid the interpretation of the making available aspect, regardless of the fact that the access approach has been applied across the traditional aspects of 'communication' (broadcasting, retransmission and reception in public) in the pre-*Svensson* cases and more recently in relation to acts of making available on the Internet in the post-*GS Media* cases. This final suggestion is compounded by the fact that it was also proposed that the access approach should be abandoned. Therefore, the proposed interpretation of 'communication' under the reformed communication to the public right will be subject to a refined transmission approach. As such, what will constitute an act of making available under the reformed right may be different to the current understanding illustrated by the decisions of the CJEU.

V. Reception in Public

A. The Problem

The act of reception in public refers to the playing of a broadcasted work through a speaker or television or any other similar device in public.[88] The inclusion of this act under the EU communication to the public right is criticised because it is not an act of communication to the public; rather it is an act of public performance.[89] As such, it should not come within the scope of the EU communication to the public right.[90] It is proposed that the communication to the public right should exclude acts of reception in public from its scope, and instead, a harmonised public performance right should be adopted to address such acts.

[88] See Article 11bis(1)(iii) of the Berne Convention for the Protection of Literary and Artistic Works 1971 or Article 2(g) of the WIPO Performances and Phonograms Treaty (WPPT).

[89] M Makeen, *Copyright in a Global Information Society: The Scope of Copyright Protection Under International, US, UK and French Law* (Kluwer Law International, 2000) 78 and M Makeen, 'Rationalising performance "in public" under UK copyright law' [2016] *IPQ* 117, 122.

[90] Ricketson and Ginsburg (2006) para 12.41, Ficsor (2002) paras 4.22, C8.03, M van Eechoud *et al*, *Harmonizing European Copyright Law: The Challenges of Better Lawmaking* (Kluwer Law International, 2009) 82, T Aplin, '"Reproduction" and "Communication to the Public" Rights in EU Copyright Law: *FAPL v QC Leisure*' (2011) 22(2) *King's Law Journal* 209, 218, A Ross and C Livingstone, 'Communication to the public: Part 1' (2012) 23(6) *Entertainment Law Review* 169, 170, M Makeen, 'The Controversy of Simultaneous Cable Retransmission to Hotel Rooms Under International and European Copyright Laws' (2010) 57 *J Copyright Soc'y USA* 59, 78, Makeen (2000) 77, Reinbothe and von Lewinski (2002) 105, Depreeuw (2014) paras 373 and 434 and P Mysoor, 'Unpacking the right of communication to the public: a closer look at the international and EU copyright law' [2013] *IPQ* 166, 172–73.

The history behind the inclusion of reception in public under the communication to the public right began at the Berne Convention.[91] According to Ricketson and Ginsburg, the act of reception in public was included under Article 11bis, even though it was clearly similar to the public performance right under Article 11 given that 'the size of the potential audience was immensely increased'.[92] Surprisingly, there was no opposition to this reasoning.[93] Makeen also argued that the inclusion of reception in public under Article 11bis was a result of mis-drafting caused by the desire to keep 'all matters related to broadcasting under one article'.[94] However, none of these justifications are satisfactory. The consequence of this has been that the act of reception in public has been wrongly placed under the scope of the communication to the public right at the international and EU levels.[95] Apart from the express inclusion of reception in public under Article 11bis(1)(iii) of the Berne Convention and Article 2(g) of the WIPO Performances and Phonograms Treaty (WPPT), there are several arguments why the communication to the public right has continued to include acts of reception in public under EU copyright law.

In the first place, the proposal for the ISD stated that the act of publicly displaying works on screens was a communication to the public.[96] Secondly, it has been argued that the EU is a contracting party to the TRIPS Agreement and as such it is obligated to apply Articles 1–21 of the Berne Convention,[97] including Article 11bis(1)(iii), which protects reception in public as a specific act of communication to the public.[98] Thirdly, Walter and von Lewinski argue that the wording of Article 3(1) of the ISD does not make it expressly clear that reception in public or more generally public performance falls outside the scope of the communication to the public right.[99] This suggestion can also be applied to Article 8 of the Rental and Lending Right Directive, given that the act of reception in public is not expressly excluded in the recitals or the provisions of the Rental and Lending Right Directive. Furthermore, the public performance right has not been harmonised at the EU level; and as such, failing to include reception in public under the scope of the communication to the public right would mean that the playing of works in public would not be actionable under EU copyright law.

[91] See Makeen (2000) 75–76.

[92] Ricketson and Ginsburg (2006) para 12.41.

[93] ibid.

[94] Makeen (2000) 75–77 and Depreeuw (2014) para 373.

[95] Makeen (2000) 78.

[96] See Proposal for the ISD (1997) 25.

[97] Article 9(1) of the Agreement on Trade-Related Aspects of Intellectual Property Rights 1994 (TRIPS Agreement).

[98] Aplin (2011) 217.

[99] Walter and von Lewinski (2010) para 11.3.24. Mysoor builds on this interpretation by suggesting that the failure to repeat the 'without prejudice' wording of Article 8 of the WCT in Article 3(1) of the ISD has allowed the skewed interpretation of the CJEU to develop – Mysoor (2013) 172–73. Also see van Eechoud *et al* (2009) 82.

In addition to these EU-specific arguments, there are jurisdiction-neutral arguments that reception in public should be included under the scope of the communication to the public right. ALAI suggested that communication acts like performance or display might also constitute a communication to the public.[100] Moreover, the WIPO Glossary defined communication to the public as including public performance and the reception of broadcasts.[101] These arguments in favour of including reception in public under the communication to the public right were given impetus in *Rafael Hoteles* where the CJEU failed to make any distinction between the hotel's cable retransmission to its private rooms, and acts of reception in public in its public areas.[102] Consequently, cable retransmission and reception in public were afforded the same treatment under the EU communication to the public right.[103]

Despite the arguments supporting the inclusion of reception in public under the scope of the communication to the public right, it is maintained that acts of reception in public should not be considered a communication to the public. As already suggested, reception in public is an act of public performance right because it is a performance or communication made before a public that is physically gathered.[104] This is in contrast to the communication to the public right, which is subject to what Makeen terms the 'geographical aspect' criterion.[105] By 'geographical aspect', Makeen means that any 'communication' of a work to a 'public' that is geographically dispersed requires the author's consent because it is an act of communication to the public separate from the initial rendition or public performance of the work.[106] If this logic is followed, the act of reception in public should not fall within the scope of the communication to the public right because it is made to a physically gathered public. In other words, it does not meet the 'geographical aspect' criterion of the communication to the public right.

The same argument can also be made using Recital 23 of the ISD, where it is stated that for there to be a communication to the public: 'the public must not be present at the place where the communication originates'. The CJEU has interpreted Recital 23 to mean that the communication to the public right excludes the direct representation or performance of works.[107] In other words, acts of public

[100] ALAI (2013) 5.

[101] WIPO, *WIPO glossary of terms of the law of copyright and neighbouring rights* (1980) 42.

[102] *SGAE v Rafael Hoteles* [2006] para 38 and Makeen (2010) 97–98. Note, the referring Irish High Court in *PPL v Ireland* limited its questions to the broadcasts distributed to the private hotel rooms and not those to other areas of the hotel – Case C-162/10 *Phonographic Performance (Ireland) Ltd v Ireland* [2012] ECLI:EU:C:2012:141, para 18.

[103] Note, reception in public was not an express issue.

[104] Recital 23 of the Information Society Directive was only intended to harmonise the communication to the public right. Therefore, acts of reception in public that are more akin to an act of public performance should not fall within the scope of Article 3(1).

[105] Makeen (2000) 89 – Geographical aspect is discussed in the American context, but the principle is applicable to the communication to the public right generally.

[106] ibid 315.

[107] *FAPL v QC Leisure* [2011] para 201. Affirmed in Case C-283/10 *Circul Globus București (Circ & Variete Globus București) v Uniunea Compozitorilor și Muzicologilor din România – Asociația pentru Drepturi de Autor (UCMR – ADA)* [2011] ECLI:EU:C:2011:772, para 35.

performance are excluded from the scope of the communication to the public right.[108] Thus, Recital 23 achieves the same effect as Makeen's 'geographical aspect', so that the act of playing a television or radio or other analogous device should not constitute a communication to the public because the potential recipients will be physically gathered in front of the device. Therefore, the 'public' is present where the communication originates.[109] This gives further impetus to the claim that reception in public should fall under the scope of a public performance right. AG Kokott, in giving her opinion in *FAPL v QC Leisure*, adopted this view.[110] However, the CJEU in *FAPL v QC Leisure* disregarded AG Kokott's Opinion and held that there was a communication to the public because the 'public' was not gathered where the 'communication' originated. This finding incorrectly interpreted the meaning of Recital 23 as requiring 'direct physical contact' with the origin of the 'communication' and, moreover, assumed that the 'communication' took place where the broadcast originated rather than where the television was played.[111]

The correct interpretation should have been that the 'communication' originated where the television was played and as a result, the 'public' was present where the 'communication' originated.[112] This is because the act of 'communication' committed by the defendant is the displaying of the work via the television to a gathered 'public'. Hence, the communication to the public right under Article 3(1) should not have applied, as was the case in *Circul Globus București*, where the playing of music in a circus was not a communication to the public.[113] From the two inconsistent decisions of *FAPL v QC Leisure* and *Circul Globus București* it must be questioned how the playing of a television broadcast in a pub is different from the playing of music in a circus.[114] That criticism aside, interpreting Article 8 of the WCT and its relationship to Article 3(1) of the ISD would also indicate that reception in public should not come within the scope of Article 3(1). This is because Article 8 of the WCT fails to expressly mention

[108] *FAPL v QC Leisure* [2011] paras 201–03, Walter and von Lewinski (2010) para 11.3.23 and Ficsor (2002) para 4.18.

[109] Makeen (2010) 77 and *FAPL v QC Leisure* [2008] paras 259–60.

[110] Cases C-403/08 and C-429/08 *Football Association Premier League (FAPL) and others v QC Leisure and others and Karen Murphy v Media Protection Services Ltd* [2011], Opinion of AG Kokott, ECLI:EU:C:2011:43, paras 121–43. Also see: Ross and Livingstone (2012) 170, Aplin (2011) 216–17, Reinbothe and von Lewinski (2002) 102 and van Eechoud *et al* (2009) 82. Kitchin J also adopted this view that Article 11bis(1)(iii) was outside the scope of Article 3(1) of the ISD – *Football Association Premier League Ltd v QC Leisure* [2008] EWHC 1411 (Ch) para 259.

[111] *FAPL v QC Leisure* [2011] para 203.

[112] Mysoor argues that the 'communication' not only occurs where the subject-matter originates such as at the game, but also occurs where the communication is played by any technical means. Therefore, communication to the public should not be found where the 'public' is present at any of these places – Mysoor (2013) 171.

[113] *Circul Globus București* [2011] paras 37 and 41.

[114] Depreeuw uses a similar example in illustrating that the playing of a television broadcast in public would be a communication to a public; however, the playing of a DVD in public would be a public performance by the logic of the CJEU. Thus, the application of the communication to the public right in this case is dependent on the source of the work being played. See Depreeuw (2014) paras 625–26.

Article 11bis(1)(iii) as one of the Berne Convention provisions that it does not 'prejudice'. Therefore, on a literal interpretation of Article 8, reception in public does not come within the scope of the communication to the public right.[115] Thus, excluding acts of reception in public from the EU communication to the public right is justified if one considers that the primary purpose of Article 3(1) was to implement and harmonise Article 8 of the WCT.[116] With all these factors in mind, Article 3(1) of the ISD should not include acts of reception in public or more generally public performance, and therefore the decision in *FAPL v QC Leisure* was inconsistent with international copyright law.[117]

But, this only accounts for the communication to the public right under the ISD. The communication to the public right under Article 8 of the Rental and Lending Right Directive is based on the WPPT, where communication to the public expressly includes acts of reception in public under Article 2(g). Therefore, we are faced with the unfortunate situation where the scope of the communication to the public right in respect of related subject-matter is different to that of authorial works. In the interests of legal certainty and the harmonisation agenda of the EU, it would be desirable to have one harmonised right of communication to the public.[118] Therefore, it is suggested that in adopting a harmonised communication to the public right for copyright and related subject-matter, the act of reception in public should be expressly excluded from the scope of the communication to the public right for both authorial works and related rights. But in doing this, it will become necessary to harmonise the public performance right at the EU level; otherwise acts of reception in public would fall outside the scope of EU copyright law.[119] Establishing a harmonised public performance right at the EU level would ensure a high level of protection for right holders, as well as further the development of the internal market by ensuring a consistent approach across Member States for the public performance right.

It is important to consider the removal of reception in public from the scope of the communication to the public right and the adoption of a harmonised public performance right because the implications of the current framework include problems for licensing and the use of exceptions. In terms of licensing at the Member State level, it is unclear whether an act of reception in public would require a public performance licence or a communication to the public licence or

[115] Aplin (2011) 216–17, Makeen (2000) 75–77, Makeen (2010) 76 and 88 and Ficsor (2002) 494–95.

[116] See Recitals 15 and 23.

[117] Brison and Depreeuw in Torremans (2017) 133.

[118] It would then be a matter for collecting societies to determine how remuneration is to be divided between copyright and related rights holders. This should be unproblematic, as collecting societies already take care of these issues. For example, see the relationship between the Performing Right Society (PRS) for Music and Public Performance Licensing (PPL) in the UK – PRS for Music, <http://www.prsformusic.com/Pages/default.aspx> and <http://www.ppluk.com> accessed 12 June 2014.

[119] Ohly argues that there is no harmonised public performance right under the ISD because that right was already recognised in most countries and, moreover, was protected at the Berne Convention – Ohly in Derclaye (2009) 226.

alternatively, licences for both rights. The reason for this is that acts of reception in public could be interpreted as falling under both the public performance and communication to the public rights at the domestic level[120] and conversely, they would fall under the communication to the public right at the EU level. There are also concerns about the exceptions and limitations that are available at the domestic level. As a general point, determining whether an act of reception in public is a public performance or a communication to the public is important because it will determine which exceptions are applicable.[121] Finding an act of reception in public to be a communication to the public would restrict the range of applicable exceptions to those available under Article 5(3) of the ISD, given that the communication to the public right is subject to an exhaustive list of exceptions.[122]

Following the CJEU decision in *ACI Adam v Stichting*,[123] it can be inferred that the exceptions and limitations provided under Article 5 of the ISD are to be interpreted strictly, to the extent that there is not much leeway for Member States to expand their scope. This means that if reception in public is dealt with under the communication to the public right, Member States would only be able to apply the narrow exceptions found under Article 5(3).[124] However, if domestic courts find that reception in public falls under the public performance right it could be subject to a much wider range of exceptions and limitations, since the public performance right and its exceptions have not been harmonised at the EU level. The consequence of this would be conflicting law between the Member State level and the EU level, as was realised in *FAPL v QC Leisure* by the UK courts. For these reasons it is necessary to expressly clarify that the act of reception in public does not fall within the scope of the communication to the public right and that it is necessary to harmonise the public performance right at the EU level, including specific exceptions and limitations.[125]

Adopting this approach means that some of the previous references to the CJEU should have been differently decided. In *Rafael Hoteles* the CJEU should have separated the cable retransmission to the hotel rooms from the cable retransmission to the televisions in the public areas. Although the cable retransmission

[120] This was the case in *Football Association Premier League (FAPL) v QC Leisure and others* [2012] EWHC 108 (Ch) para 63.

[121] This was one of the important issues at stake in *FAPL v QC Leisure* [2012] paras 58–78. Kitchin J had to determine whether s 72 of the Copyright, Designs and Patents Act 1988 (CDPA 1988) was applicable to both the public performance right and the communication to the public right. This was in contrast to s 34 of the CDPA 1988, which was limited to acts of public performance.

[122] See Article 5(3) of the ISD.

[123] Case C-435/12 *ACI Adam BV and others v Stichting de Thuiskopie and another* [2014] ECLI:EU:C:2014:254.

[124] The UK Court of Appeal raised this concern in *Football Association Premier League (FAPL) v QC Leisure and others* [2012] EWCA Civ 1708, para 62 (Etherton LJ).

[125] The harmonisation of the public performance right was not discussed in the conceptualisation and development of the ISD, given that it is not mentioned in any of the *travaux préparatoires*. This is because the focus was primarily on 'on demand transmissions' and transposing the WCT into EU copyright law. The consequence of this was that the public performance right received no attention and as a result, is absent under harmonised EU copyright law.

of the signal to the hotel rooms would remain a communication to the public, the playing of the televisions in the public areas should have been considered separately, given that it did not constitute a communication to the public, but rather an act of reception in public, which should be dealt with by a harmonised public performance right. Similarly, the playing of broadcasts in a pub,[126] dentist office,[127] restaurant[128] or rehabilitation centre,[129] should also fall outside the scope of the communication to the public right, and should instead, be governed by a harmonised public performance right. Alternatively, in the case of *PPL v Ireland*, the provision of apparatus other than radios or televisions capable of playing phonograms, such as CD players, should not have amounted to an act of communication to the public. All of the above examples share the fact that the geographical aspect of the communication to the public right was not met, since the user was not geographically dispersed from the place of the communication. This is because the act of playing the work is the relevant 'communication' to consider, which took place in the same space where the user was situated. Therefore, these situations should be considered factually similar to that of *Circul Globus Bucureşti*, where the playing of music in a circus was held not to infringe the communication to the public right.

B. Proposed Solution

Despite the existence of Article 11bis(1)(iii) of the Berne Convention and Article 2(g) of the WPPT, it is necessary to harmonise the scope of the communication to the public right under EU copyright law so that acts of reception in public fall outside the scope of the communication to the public right and are instead addressed by a harmonised public performance right. This recommendation aims to create a coherent copyright framework and further the internal market, while balancing the goal of achieving a high level of protection for right holders with protecting the interests of users. Therefore, it is proposed that the EU make it expressly clear that reception in public does not constitute an act of communication to the public. This can be facilitated under a revised version of Recital 23 of the ISD and/or a refined description of 'public' to mean a fairly large and indeterminate number of users who are geographically dispersed from the place of 'communication'. It is also necessary that the communication to the public right be harmonised for both authorial works and related rights and, moreover,

[126] *FAPL v QC Leisure* [2011]. Note, Kitchin J adopted the preliminary view that there was no communication to the public in playing the football broadcasts in the pub – *FAPL v QC Leisure* [2008] para 262.

[127] Case C-135/10 *Societa Consortile Fonografici (SCF) v Marco del Corso* [2012] ECLI:EU:C:2012:140.

[128] Case C-151/15 *Portugese Society of Authors CRL (SPA) v Ministerio Público and others* [2015] ECLI:EU:C:2015:468.

[129] *Reha Training* [2016].

that a harmonised public performance right be adopted with relevant exceptions and limitations for all types of works under the ISD.[130]

VI. 'New Public'

The definition adopted by the CJEU that 'public' means a fairly large and indeterminate number of potential users is unproblematic and will not be disputed. However, the 'new public' criterion, which has had a dramatic impact on the shape of the communication to the public right,[131] and the 'specific technical means' carve-out will be refuted on the grounds that the CJEU was wrong to implement these criteria and that their continued use has contributed to the detrimental development of the communication to the public right.[132] It will be argued that the CJEU should have adopted the 'organisation other than the original one' criterion from Article 11bis(1)(ii) of the Berne Convention.

The CJEU defined the 'new public' criterion as 'a public different from the public at which the original act of communication of the work is directed, that is, to a new public'.[133] This definition is similar to the proposal forwarded by the Belgian delegation at the 1948 Brussels Revision of the Berne Convention, which suggested any retransmission of a work to a new audience or a fresh circle of listeners should be subject to the authorisation of the right holder.[134] However, the 'new public' criterion was expressly rejected at the Berne Convention because it was criticised as being too vague and unclear.[135] In particular, it has been argued that using the 'new public' criterion is problematic because it is difficult to draw a clear distinction between the original 'public' intended by the right holder and the 'new public'.[136] This has resulted in the fear that any act of retransmission or subsequent communication would be made to a 'new public'.[137] For these reasons the 'new public' criterion was rejected and instead the 'organisation other than the

[130] Brison and Depreeuw suggest that there is need for the EU communication to the public right to undergo a balancing exercise similar to the one conducted in designing Article 11bis of the Berne Convention. This includes an account of the types of modern communication, the existing technological framework and the conventional mode of exploitation – Brison and Depreeuw in Torremans (2017) 130.

[131] Rosén in Stamatoudi (2016) 331.

[132] ibid 347.

[133] *SGAE v Rafael Hoteles* [2006] para 40 – The CJEU has repeatedly followed the 'new public' criterion in the communication to the public cases concerning retransmission, reception in public and subsequent communication, with the exception of *ITV v TVCatchup* [2013].

[134] Ricketson and Ginsburg (2006) paras 12.26–12.27, Makeen (2000) 241 and Makeen (2010) 62–63.

[135] M Walter, 'Telediffusion and wired-distribution systems: Berne Convention and copyright legislation in Europe' (1974) 10 *Copyright* 302, 303–04, R Dittrich, 'On the interpretation of Article 11bis(1) and (2) of the Berne Convention' (1982) 18 *Copyright* 294, 295–98 and Makeen (2010) 63–64.

[136] Ricketson and Ginsburg (2006) para 12.27.

[137] Walter (1974) 303–04 and Makeen (2000) 241.

original one' was adopted as the governing criterion for the retransmission right under Article 11bis(1)(ii).[138]

However, this is not to say that the 'new public' criterion has no role in relation to the communication to the public right. Makeen argued that with the exception of Article 11bis(1)(ii), the other separate acts of communication to the public indicate that the legislature of the Berne Convention followed the 'new public' criterion. Makeen based his argument on what he terms the 'single rendition multiple prohibited act aspect'. In other words, 'every act of exploitation that communicates the rendition to a new potential audience is considered to be a separate and independent prohibited act'.[139] Thus, the Berne Convention separated acts of public performance, broadcasting, reception in public and the subject-specific rights of 'any communication to the public' because they amount to different technical uses of the work to different 'publics'.[140] Therefore, with the exception of Article 11bis(1)(ii), the 'new public' criterion can be argued as the basis on which the requirement of authorisation was based for acts of communication to the public. The old WIPO Guide to the Berne Convention adopted this point of view.[141] However, it is equally plausible to argue that the delineation between these rights was made on the basis of different technical uses[142] and in relation to different subject-matter.[143]

With this background in mind, it is necessary to discuss two issues. Firstly, why did the CJEU adopt the 'new public' criterion in its communication to the public case law?[144] And secondly, should the 'organisation other than the original one' criterion play a role in the decision-making of the CJEU? The CJEU first adopted the 'new public' criterion in *Rafael Hoteles*. Given that this case was about the cable retransmission of television broadcasts to hotel rooms, it was incorrect to apply the 'new public' criterion because the reasoning of Article 11bis(1)(ii) of the Berne Convention should have applied; that is, the 'organisation other than the original one'.[145] However, the CJEU in *Rafael Hoteles* relied on AG Sharpston's Opinion

[138] The ALAI report on the 'new public' criterion argues that the CJEU's use of the 'new public' criterion resulting from its misguided interpretation of the WIPO Guide to the Berne Convention (1978) is unfounded and in contradiction of the Berne Convention and consequently the WCT, because it has not been expressly mentioned in the treaties – ALAI (2014) 11 and 13–14.

[139] Makeen (2010) 62. Rosén also made a similar argument that the CJEU's use of 'new public' can be interpreted as a 'new act of communication to the public' – Rosén in Stamatoudi (2016) 342.

[140] Makeen (2010) 66–67. Also see ALAI (2014) 17.

[141] WIPO, *Guide to the Berne Convention* (1978) 68–69.

[142] See Makeen (2010) 67 and 71.

[143] This approach is the one the CJEU seems to adopt in *ITV v TVCatchup*, in distinguishing the 'new public' criterion and instead adopting the 'different technical means' approach – *ITV v TVCatchup* [2013] para 39.

[144] The use of the 'new public' criterion will be addressed in the various groups of communication to the public case law – retransmissions, reception in public and Internet cases.

[145] Makeen (2010) 99–100 and 103–04.

where she stated that the concept of 'new public' had the same essence as 'organisation other than the original one'.[146]

AG Sharpston's misguided Opinion was based on the old WIPO Guide to the Berne Convention,[147] as well as AG La Pergola's Opinion in *Egeda v Hoasa*.[148] The logic in these non-binding sources was that any new act of 'communication' made to a 'new public' would require the authorisation of the right holder.[149] This interpretation may be correct if we agree with Makeen's argument that the 'new public' criterion was the reason for the division of the individual aspects of the Article 11bis communication to the public right, with the exception of Article 11bis(1)(ii). However, in the context of a cable retransmission it was definitely the wrong finding because the governing criterion is expressly the 'organisation other than the original one' under Article 11bis(1)(ii) of the Berne Convention.[150] Thus, the decision in *Rafael Hoteles* conflicted with Article 11bis of the Berne Convention and is inconsistent with international copyright law.[151]

Consequently, the CJEU reached the correct decision in *Rafael Hoteles* in finding that the act of cable retransmission of a broadcast to hotel rooms was a communication to the public. However, using 'new public' to reach this conclusion was incorrect.[152] This error was subsequently repeated in the retransmission

[146] Case C-306/05 *Sociedad General Autores y Editores (SGAE) v Rafael Hoteles SA* [2006], Opinion of AG Sharpston, ECLI:EU:C:2006:479, para 50. This was followed by the CJEU – *SGAE v Rafael Hoteles* [2006] para 40.

[147] WIPO, *Guide to the Berne Convention* (1978) 68–69 – Where a 'communication' is made to an additional audience or a wider circle of listeners not contemplated by the author, the author has control over the 'new public' performance of that work. Rosén argued that this statement was made in the context of licensing and not infringement of/liability for breach of the right of communication to the public – Rosén in Stamatoudi (2016) 344–45. Ficsor also argued that the old WIPO Guide to the Berne Convention was not designed to provide thorough analysis – M Ficsor, '*Svensson* and the CJEU's "new public" theory: what the EU may learn from the US to avoid judicisal lapse' (23rd Annual Fordham Intellectual Property Law & Policy Conference, 2015) 2–3.

[148] Case C-293/98 *Entidad de Gestión de Derechos de los Productores Audiovisuales (Egeda) v Hostelería Asturiana SA (Hoasa)* [1999], Opinion of AG La Pergola, ECLI:EU:C:1999:403, paras 20–26 – AG La Pergola used the 'new public' criterion as the governing criterion to determine when a communication to the public would require authorisation from the right holder.

[149] ALAI argues that the CJEU's use of the 'new public' criterion seemed to misunderstand the idea that new acts of communication to the public should be subject to authorisation, to mean that there must be communication to a 'new public' for infringement to occur. The 'new public' aspect was only meant to justify why public communication by loudspeaker was an act of communication to the public under Article 11bis – ALAI (2014) 14 and 18.

[150] This is affirmed in: WIPO, *Guide to the Copyright and Related Rights Treaties Administered by WIPO and Glossary of Copyright and Related Rights Terms* (2003) [New WIPO Guide] 77–78. Also see ALAI (2014) 18 – it is argued that the inference of a 'new public' criterion from the old WIPO Guide to the Berne Convention (1978) 68–69, is out of context and misleading.

[151] Rosén in Stamatoudi (2016) 343–46 and M Ficsor, '*Svensson*: honest attempt at establishing due balance concerning the use of hyperlinks – spoiled by the erroneous "new public" theory' (2018), available at <http://www.copyrightseesaw.net/en/papers?page=3> accessed 8 August 2018.

[152] The CJEU supported its use of the 'new public' criterion by stating that in the absence of its intervention, the customers would not have been able to access the broadcasts despite being within the physical catchment area – *SGAE v Rafael Hoteles* [2006] para 42. Also see Makeen (2010) 100.

cases of *Airfield v SABAM*,[153] *PPL v Ireland*, *OSA* and *AKM*. By contrast, the CJEU committed a different error in *ITV v TVCatchup*, where it overlooked the 'new public' criterion. In this case, the CJEU stated that because the Internet retransmission was made 'under specific technical conditions, using a different means of transmission', it was no longer necessary to consider the 'new public' criterion.[154] Thus, the CJEU in *ITV v TVCatchup* created an exception to the 'new public' criterion where retransmissions are made by different technical means to the original communication. Yet again, the CJEU achieved the correct decision through the wrong means.

The application of the 'new public' criterion has been inconsistent across the range of EU communication to the public case law. In this regard, five particular decisions are of importance, *ITV v TVCatchup*, *AKM*, *Svensson*, *Ziggo* and *Renckhoff*. The first discrepancy to arise concerning the 'new public' criterion occurred in *ITV v TVCatchup*, where the CJEU qualified the criterion as being inapplicable to situations involving subsequent communications made by different technical means.[155] As such, where a subsequent communication is done through a specific technical means different from the initial communication fresh authorisation must be obtained from the right holder, regardless of who makes the subsequent communication and whether it was made to a 'new public'. However, the use of the 'specific technical means' is problematic because it was not legislated for under the EU copyright Directives or under international copyright law.[156] Furthermore, 'specific technical means' directly conflicts with the 'organisation other than the original one' criterion that was expressly adopted under Article 11bis(1)(ii) of the Berne Convention. This is because an act done through a different technical means by the initial communicator would amount to infringement under EU copyright law. This is contrary to Article 11bis(1)(ii), which only regulates subsequent communications by third parties.[157] Consequently, it is argued that the CJEU should have used the 'organisation other than the original one' criterion, since the near-simultaneous retransmission of a broadcast on the Internet is an act of webcasting and, as such, akin to an act of traditional retransmission.[158]

Another inconsistency with 'new public' relates to the *AKM* decision. *AKM* introduced further uncertainty regarding 'new public', when it stated that the cable retransmission of works by a third party to a public already taken into account

[153] Acts of satellite retransmission should be considered as coming within the scope of Article 11bis because satellite broadcasting is analogous to traditional terrestrial broadcasting and, as such, an act of communication to the public – Ricketson and Ginsburg (2006) paras 12.30, 12.33 and 12.35 and Ficsor (2002) para 4.42.

[154] *ITV v TVCatchup* [2012] paras 26 and 39.

[155] *ITV v TVCatchup* [2013] para 39.

[156] Rosén in Stamatoudi (2016) 338.

[157] ibid 340.

[158] Ricketson and Ginsburg (2006) para 12.40 – Webcasting falls under Article 11bis(1)(ii) because it amounts to a communication to the public by wire. Also see Walter and von Lewinski (2010) paras 11.3.31–11.3.32, Aplin (2005) 130 and Makeen (2010) 78.

by the initial broadcaster was not made to a 'new public'.[159] This finding is peculiar because the CJEU did not follow its approaches concerning 'new public' or specific technical means despite stating that cable retransmission was a different technical means to the original broadcast.[160] In light of that finding, the decision in *AKM* effectively distinguished *ITV v TVCatchup* because a finding of subsequent communication by a different technical means is supposed to require fresh authorisation regardless of whether it was made to a 'new public'.[161] However, the Court in *AKM* focused on the fact that the right holder was aware that the initial broadcasts could be received by all persons within the territory. As such, the finding in *AKM* is inconsistent with *ITV v TVCatchup* given that 'new public' was subsequently relied upon.

The decision in *AKM* also conflicts with the retransmission cases such as *Rafael Hoteles* and *OSA*. In the hotel and spa cases it was argued that the guests would not have been able to access the works but for the provision of televisions by the operators of the establishment; hence, there was a 'new public'. By contrast, in *AKM* it is seemingly suggested by the Court that the users could have already had access to the national broadcast independently of the cable retransmission and as such, there was no 'new public'. This decision is contestable because it seemingly draws an artificial distinction between retransmission for private residences and commercial places. In the context of *AKM*, the Court's finding appears to be that the individual users were in their own homes and as such, the users could have had access to the national broadcasts in any case. This is in contrast to the hotel and spa cases, where users are reliant on the commercial entity to receive the retransmissions. In the digital context, drawing a distinction between private and commercial establishments is tenuous because it is arguable that persons with Internet access can also already access some national broadcasts, both in their home or on the go in places such as hotel rooms.

Therefore, *AKM* sets a dangerous precedent on two fronts. Firstly, there was an act of 'communication' made to a 'public', but no act of communication to the public. This further exposed the unsuitability of using the 'new public' criterion because it unduly restricts the importance of the 'communication' element. Secondly, the rationale adopted in *AKM* would seem to be limited to the analogue sphere. As such, it illustrated the unsuitability of using 'new public' for the overall right of communication to the public.

The various forms of retransmission – rebroadcasting, cable, satellite and Internet, can be grouped together as they all require authorisation from the right holder by virtue of being made to a 'new public' or by a different technical means. In comparing *Rafael Hoteles* and the other cable retransmission cases with

[159] Case C-138/16 *Staatlich genehmigte Gesellschaft der Autoren, Komponisten und Musicverlegerregistrierte Genossenschaft mbH (AKM) v Zürs.net Betriebs GmbH* [2017] ECLI:EU:C:2017:218, paras 28–29.
[160] ibid para 26.
[161] *ITV v TVCatchup* [2013] para 26.

Airfield v SABAM, *ITV v TVCatchup* and *AKM*, it becomes clear that there is an inconsistent application of the 'new public' criterion and the 'specific technical means' criterion across the copyright Directives, subject-matter and technology. For the purpose of creating certainty it is necessary to harmonise the communication to the public right into one right for all types of subject-matter and technology. Furthermore, the 'organisation other than the original one' criterion should be adopted in lieu of the 'new public' and specific technical means criteria for the governance of near-simultaneous retransmissions. However, it is an open question as to what the governing criterion should be for the making available aspect. Thus far, the CJEU has applied the 'new public' criterion, as seen in the post-*Svensson* Internet cases.[162]

It is accepted that the making available aspect and the Internet are not bound by the Berne Convention, and hence, the 'new public' criterion can be applied without being subjected to the international copyright incompatibility arguments used in relation to the retransmission cases that were previously discussed. However, this does not absolve the 'new public' criterion from criticism because it is burdened by the free nature of the Internet. Notably, when a work is made freely accessible on the Internet with authorisation, it is available to all Internet users; that is, anyone with an Internet connection. Thus, any subsequent communication of that work online will not be to a 'new public' because it is already freely accessible by everyone.[163] Consequently, the communication to the public right can be de facto exhausted with regard to hyperlinks, contrary to Article 3(3) of the ISD, where 'new public' is the governing criterion.[164] This is because the CJEU in *Svensson* failed to consider the possibility that there are different categories of Internet users that can be divided into different markets according to factors such as language, geographic location, taste and preference (website interests).[165] Thus, the CJEU's finding in *Svensson* negatively affects right holders' ability to grant

[162] *Svensson* [2014] paras 24–28, Case C-348/13 *BestWater International GmbH v Michael Mebes and Stefan Potsch* [2014] ECLI:EU:C:2014:2315, para 18, *GS Media* [2016] paras 41–43, *Filmspeler* [2017] paras 47–48, *Ziggo* [2017] para 45.

[163] Peguera argued that the CJEU used the 'new public' criterion as a counterbalance for its expansive interpretation of 'communication'. This can be evidenced by the decision in *Svensson*. See Peguera (2018) 5.

[164] *Svensson* [2014] paras 25–28. See Rosén in Stamatoudi (2016) 343. For an alternative view see Quintais and Mysoor who argue that there was no act of 'communication to the public' in *Svensson* because the right holder, by making the work freely available online, impliedly consented to its subsequent sharing – J Quintais, 'Untangling the hyperlinking web: In search of the online right of communication to the public' (2018) *Journal of World Intellectual Property* 1 [advanced access], 16–17 and P Mysoor, 'Exhaustion, non-exhaustion and implied licence' (2018) 49(6) *IIC* 656, 680–81. This viewpoint is given impetus in *Renckhoff* [2018] para 29, where the CJEU states that authors have a right that is 'preventative in nature' allowing them to intervene to stop acts of communication to the public that may be contemplated. The language of the Court points in the direction of implied consent since the 'new public' criterion has been maintained despite the exhaustion concern created in *Svensson*.

[165] Note, the CJEU in *Renckhoff* segmented the 'public' in terms of the users of the initial website as different to those of the latter website where the work was uploaded without permission – *Renckhoff* [2018] para 35.

exclusive licences since they will be ineffective due to their inability to segment online markets.[166] Ultimately, this prejudices the high level of protection for right holders.[167]

Given the fundamental changes caused by the application of 'new public' in *Svensson*,[168] the CJEU in *GS Media* attempted to limit the impact of exhaustion by clarifying that the decision in *Svensson* was limited to situations where works were made freely available on the Internet with the consent of the right holder. Therefore, the communication to the public right would remain applicable to any unauthorised works on the Internet.[169] Regardless of the CJEU's limitation attempt in *GS Media*, the implication of potential exhaustion is that right holders will become more apprehensive about making their works freely accessible. This will be to the detriment of encouraging the dissemination of cultural works and as such, will prejudice the interests of users who would benefit from the making available of those works on the Internet. In this way, use of the 'new public' criterion does not proportionately balance the competing interests discussed in Chapter one. Consequently, it is submitted that the CJEU's adoption of the 'new public' criterion for acts of making available is ill-suited to the realities of the Internet. Given the potential for exhaustion, the risk exists that right holders will increasingly rely on technical protection measures to protect their works. This will undermine the free flow of information on the Internet.

Furthermore, the determination of a 'new public' in the online context has been subject to two distinct problems. Firstly, the CJEU has assessed 'new public' in scenarios where it was unnecessary to do so. Notably, in *GS Media*, *Filmspeler*, *Ziggo* and *Renckhoff*, there was no need to consider 'new public' because the communications in question were in relation to unauthorised works, and the case of *Renckhoff* was about an act of initial communication.[170] Therefore, there was no 'public' contemplated by the right holder at the time of the initial communication by the third party.[171] Only subsequent acts of communication that were initially authorised implicate the 'new public' criterion.[172] These cases illustrate a lack of certainty pertaining to the 'new public' criterion.

More than the uncertainty about when to invoke the 'new public' criterion, the CJEU has also been inconsistent in its determination of 'new public' on the Internet. In *GS Media* a 'new public' was established due to the unauthorised upload of the specific photographs that were being hyperlinked to; whereas, in *Ziggo*, 'new public' was established on the basis that the defendant could not be 'unaware that

[166] Rosén in Stamatoudi (2016) 340 and Brison and Depreeuw in Torremans (2017) 134.

[167] ALAI (2014) 15.

[168] Rosén in Stamatoudi (2016) 340.

[169] *GS Media* [2016] para 43.

[170] *Renckhoff* [2018] para 24.

[171] This approach was alluded to by AG Szpunar in his Opinion on *Ziggo* – Case C-610/15 *Stichting Brein v Ziggo BV and XS4ALL Internet BV* [2017] Opinion of AG Szpunar, ECLI:EU:C:2017:99, para 41.

[172] AG Campos Sánchez-Bordona also made the same mistake in the opinion on *Renckhoff* – *Renckhoff* [2018] Opinion of AG Campos Sánchez-Bordona, paras 99–108.

this platform [TPB] provides access to works published without the consent of the rightholders'.[173] The issue with this is that the CJEU has seemingly allowed claimants to establish acts of infringement without proving specific instances of infringement.[174] Furthermore, the CJEU in *Renckhoff* also introduced fresh uncertainty as to who constitutes the 'public' on the Internet. Unlike in *Svensson*, where it was held that the potential public for a freely accessible work on the Internet was 'all Internet users',[175] the Court in *Renckhoff* held that the 'public' can be segmented by users of the particular website so that the 'public' contemplated by the right holder will not include users of other websites.[176] This introduced a stark difference to the former approach which may have a long-reaching effect on the establishment of infringement.[177] Yet again, the use of the 'new public' criterion was illustrative of subjectivity.

Consequently, the application of the 'new public' criterion in relation to the EU right of communication to the public can be subjected to a number of criticisms. Hugenholtz and Van Velze argue that 'new public' is flawed historically, conceptually and economically, which is demonstrated via the arguments posed in this subsection.[178]

A. The 'Organisation other than the Original One' Approach

Notwithstanding the CJEU's current approach, it is advocated that the correct method of reasoning that should have been adopted in all the traditional retransmission cases was the 'organisation other than the original one' criterion from Article 11bis(1)(ii) of the Berne Convention. ALAI has suggested that adopting the 'new public' criterion has fundamentally changed the communication to the public right and potentially makes it incompatible with the Berne Convention.[179] Thus, to ensure that the EU communication to the public right is Berne-compatible and, moreover, certain, the 'organisation other than the original one' criterion should have been adopted. Had this been the case, the end result in the above cases would have been that there was a communication to the public by retransmitting the broadcasts, because the retransmission was done by a third party different from the initial broadcaster. Not only would this have been the correct reasoning for finding infringement, but it would also have been easier to

[173] *Ziggo* [2017] para 45.

[174] Peguera (2018) 10 and A Ohly, 'The broad concept of 'communication to the public' in recent CJEU judgements and the liability of intermediaries: primary, secondary or unitary liability' (2018) 13(8) *JIPLP* 664, 670.

[175] *Svensson* [2014] para 26.

[176] *Renckhoff* [2018] para 35.

[177] Segmenting internet markets is pro-right holder and makes it easier for them to establish infringement.

[178] Hugenholtz and Van Velze (2016) 811.

[179] ALAI (2014) 16.

use the 'organisation other than the original one' because it would have avoided the difficulties of the subjective and technical nature of the 'new public' criterion and, moreover, removed the room for inconsistency that developed in the CJEU's case law.[180]

Despite the 'organisation other than the original one' criterion being the correct method of reasoning for retransmission of broadcasts, it is not foolproof. Similarly to 'communication to the public' there is no definition of 'organisation other than the original one'. Therefore, there has been some uncertainty about what/who constitutes an 'organisation'.[181] Regardless of this uncertainty, most commentators agree that a hotel or satellite broadcaster would constitute an 'organisation' and therefore, the retransmission of broadcasts to hotel rooms or the satellite retransmission of broadcasts would be a communication to the public for the purposes of Article 11bis(1)(ii).[182]

In addition to the definitional concern, it has also been stated that the 'organisation other than the original one' criterion facilitates the possibility of double payment to authors. The reason for this is that a retransmission made in the same area as the initial broadcast by two separate entities would entitle the author to two separate payments. It has been argued that the author should only be entitled to one payment because he would have already taken into the consideration the recipients in that area when authorising the initial broadcast.[183] However, this criticism must be ignored, as it seeks to introduce the 'new public' criterion through the backdoor.[184] According to Walter, even using the 'new public' criterion as an 'auxiliary means of interpretation' would be in contradiction of Article 11bis(1)(ii).[185] Furthermore, the retransmission of broadcasts is included as a separate right under Article 11bis. Therefore, we must accept the 'organisation other than the original one' as the sole governing criterion for acts of retransmission involving broadcasts.

Despite these criticisms, the positive consequence of adopting the 'organisation other than the original one' criterion is that the demarcation between the initial broadcast and retransmissions of the broadcast is made clear.[186] This is in contrast to the subjective 'new public' criteria, where the emphasis and focus is

[180] Brison and Depreeuw in Torremans (2017) 132 and 134.

[181] Gaudel argues that the determination of 'organisation' should be based on a for profit basis – D Gaudel, 'Teledistribution' (1974) 81 *Revue Internationale du Droit d'Auteur (RIDA)* 119, 136. However, this has been criticised as being unsupported by the Berne Convention and, moreover, as being too vague. It remains the case that there is no concrete or accepted definition for 'organisation other than the original one' – Makeen (2010) 70–71.

[182] F Gotzen, 'Cable television and copyright in Belgium: A study of the Belgian law in relation to the Berne Convention and the Treaty of Rome' (1982) 18 *Copyright* 307, 312, H Desbois and A Francon, 'Copyright and the Dissemination by Wire of Radio and Television Programmes' (1975) 86 *RIDA* 3, 48–56, Gaudel (1974) 136 and Makeen (2010) 73.

[183] W Rumphorst, 'Cable distribution of broadcasts' (1983) 19 *Copyright* 301, 302, V Hazan, 'The body other than the original broadcaster in cable transmissions' (1984) 20 *Copyright* 228, 228, Makeen (2000) 243 and Makeen (2010) 65. Also, see Dittrich's service zone theory in Dittrich (1982).

[184] Makeen (2010) 66–67.

[185] Walter (1974) 304.

[186] Dittrich (1982) 298.

on a group of potential recipients that are uncertain in composition and number and, as a result, must be determined on a case-by-case basis.[187] That aside, Article 8 of the WCT chose to not prejudice Article 11bis(1)(ii) of the Berne Convention. Following this, Article 3(1) of the ISD ought to adhere to the 'organisation other than the original one' criterion, at least in cases concerning retransmissions of broadcasts.[188] However, with new developments in digital technology and subsequently new laws that were not contemplated at the time of the Berne Convention, there are questions concerning the role and suitability of the 'organisation other than the original one' criterion under modern copyright law. In particular, what is the role of the 'organisation other than the original one' under Article 8 of the WCT and subsequently, the EU communication to the public right under the Satellite and Cable Retransmission Directive, Rental and Lending Right Directive and ISD that have since been interpreted in a harmonised manner?[189]

Determining the role of the 'organisation other than the original one' criterion under EU copyright law is dependent on whether it is limited to acts of retransmission as defined under Article 11bis(1)(ii) of the Berne Convention. If we follow Makeen's argument that the separate acts of 'communication' under the Berne Convention are legislated for in that manner because they make the work accessible to different and/or 'new publics', then it is likely that the 'organisation other than the original one' criterion is limited to acts of cable retransmission and rebroadcasting. As such, 'new public' can be applied to other acts that do not come within the scope of Article 11bis(1)(ii). Alternatively, if we follow Walter's approach that the 'new public' criterion should not be considered at all, then 'new public' should not be applied to any aspect of the communication to the public right. However, the addition of the new making available aspect and developments in Internet technology pose a conundrum because these were not subject to consideration when Article 11bis was legislated for. Therefore, it is important to establish the governing criterion for acts of Internet retransmission and the new making available aspect.

B. Alternative Approaches

If it is found that the 'organisation other than the original one' criterion from Article 11bis(1)(ii) of the Berne Convention is restricted to traditional forms

[187] Hugenholtz and Van Velze argue that 'new public' lacks legal certainty and is unsound for the determination of infringement – Hugenholtz and Van Velze (2016) 810. Also see Furgal (2018) 703.

[188] As already noted, Article 3(1) follows the scope of Article 8 of the WCT. The question to be answered is whether 'organisation other than the original one' should be extended to all types of retransmissions and subsequent communications.

[189] Article 2 of the Satellite and Cable Retransmission Directive was harmonised with Article 3 of the ISD in Cases C-431/09 and C-432/09 *Airfield NV and another v Belgische Vereniging van Auteurs, Componisten en Uitgevers CVBA (SABAM) and Airfield NV v Agicoa Belgium BVBA* [2011] ECLI:EU:C:2011:648, para 44. Article 8 of the Rental and Lending Right Directive was harmonised with Article 3 of the ISD in *Reha Training* [2016] paras 28–34.

of retransmission designated under Berne, alternative approaches should be explored. The most obvious choice would be to extend the 'organisation other than the original one' from Article 11bis(1)(ii) of the Berne Convention to include the making available of works. This approach is desirable because it will lead to an internationally compliant and consistent communication to the public framework with one governing criterion for all acts of subsequent communication involving the initial communication of the work.[190] This means that all subsequent communications including rebroadcasting, cable, satellite and Internet retransmissions and hyperlinking or any other technology, whether near-simultaneous or not, will require authorisation if they are made by an organisation other than the original one responsible for the initial 'communication'. The term 'subsequent communication' is wider than 'retransmission' because it includes acts that are not executed on a near-simultaneous basis. However, the act must involve the further communication of the original transmission or provision of the work. This is automatically satisfied in cases of rebroadcasting or retransmission by cable, satellite and Internet. It also includes hyperlinks because the act of hyperlinking requires the existence of the initial provision of the work in order to operate: that is, if the initial provision on the work is removed, the hyperlink will no longer be subsequently communicating the work because there is nothing to communicate.

The 'organisation other than the original one' criterion will offer a balanced approach that accounts for the competing interests that are present in EU copyright law.[191] It will ensure that a high level of protection is afforded because right holders will retain control over subsequent uses of their works even where they are freely accessible on the Internet, provided the act of subsequent communication is a 'communication'. It is also the case that adopting a uniform approach to acts of retransmission and subsequent communication is in the best interest of the EU's harmonisation agenda in pursuit of furthering the internal market. This will be balanced with the interests of users, who will continue to enjoy the use of works that are made available. Furthermore, using the 'organisation other than the original one' approach has the added benefit that the criterion is already accepted at the international level, even though the CJEU chose to ignore it in favour of the 'new public' criterion.

However, there are three potential criticisms of adopting the 'organisation other than the original one' criterion. Firstly, the availability of works may be reduced if right holders refuse to allow third parties to retransmit works or, alternatively, they are bureaucratic or charge exorbitant fees for the licensing of their works. This concern should not undermine the 'organisation other than the original one' criterion because the market forces of demand and supply and the existing collective licensing mechanisms are likely to resolve this issue, unless the right

[190] 'Subsequent communication' means any act involving the further 'communication' of the initial transmission or provision of the work whether near-simultaneous or not.

[191] ALAI (2017) 5.

holder is irrational with his behaviour in choosing not to license any subsequent communications. Secondly, the concept of 'organisation other than the original one' is not defined. Therefore, for it to be certain and effective it should be clarified. The definition, in particular, has to make clear what constitutes an 'organisation'. It is advocated that 'organisation' should mean any party that engages with an act of retransmission or subsequent communication. It should not be limited to commercial entities. As for the 'other than the original one' aspect, its ordinary meaning should be adopted; that is, any party other than the initial communicator will require authorisation to make a retransmission or subsequent communication.

The third and perhaps most significant criticism is that the 'organisation other than the original one' criterion provides a disproportionate scope of protection for right holders, given that any act of subsequent communication by a third party will require authorisation. While it is true that 'organisation other than the original one' does provide a very wide scope of protection, it must be remembered that it is bounded by the overall scope of the right. In particular, it has been advocated that the scope of the communication to the public right should be interpreted narrowly and, moreover, 'communication' should be defined in terms of a refined version of the transmission approach. As such, the use of 'organisation other than the original one' in the context of a narrow communication to the public right can be proportionately balanced.

Notwithstanding the suggestion that 'organisation other than the original one' should be adopted, Coene puts forward a third possible criterion for governing the retransmission of works made available. He suggests that the retransmission of a work should only be considered a separate communication to the public where 'the perceptible act does not merely continue the same consumption chain … that was brought about by the initial communication … but on the contrary, gives rise to another consumption chain'.[192] Coene's idea of different consumption chains would seem to reflect a 'different use' approach. This is compatible with the Berne Convention and the WCT, given that the communication to the public right is divided into different types of 'communications' including broadcasting, retransmission, reception in public and making available. Coene argues that the criteria for establishing a different consumption chain are based on 'spatial and temporal limits'. By 'spatial' Coene means the area in which the work can be enjoyed, and in terms of 'temporal' he means the time in which the work can be enjoyed.[193] However, it would not be unreasonable to criticise this requirement as being a hybrid 'new public' in the sense that the governing criteria are not so much about people, but rather the space and time in which people can access the work. Nevertheless, the focus for Coene is more on the act of 'communication' and the time and space in which the work is accessible than on the 'public' who can potentially

[192] B Coene, 'What about the mirrored glass disco ball? Delimiting the right of communication to the public in copyright and related rights' (2014) *18/2014 ICRI Working Paper Series* 23.

[193] ibid 16.

receive the work. In illustrating his 'spatial' and 'temporal' criteria, Coene uses the examples of *Organismos v Divani Acropolis Hotel*,[194] *ITV v TVCatchup* and *Svensson*.

Addressing *Organismos v Divani Acropolis Hotel* first, Coene reached the conclusion that the cable retransmission of a broadcast to hotel rooms should not be a communication to the public because it did not alter the spatial or temporal limits of the initial broadcast. As such, it was merely a continuation of the original consumption chain.[195] Based on Coene's rationale there would have been no infringement in *Rafael Hoteles*, using the different consumption chain logic. Secondly, Coene's reinterpretation of *ITV v TVCatchup* led to the same result as reached by the CJEU, that the Internet retransmission of a broadcast was communication to the public. However, his reason for this was that Internet retransmission had the potential to extend the spatial and temporal limits of the initial broadcast and, as such, was a different consumption chain. He justified this claim by arguing that if the original broadcast was to become distorted for some viewers on their television, the Internet retransmission would likely be unaffected.[196] Lastly, Coene's reinterpretation of *Svensson* also produced the same result as the CJEU, that hyperlinking to a freely accessible work was not a communication to the public. Coene's reasoning here was the same as his reinterpretation of *Organismos v Divani Acropolis Hotel*. Given that the work was already available online, linking to that website did not alter the spatial or temporal limits of the work and as such, there was no new consumption chain.

Coene's idea of a different consumption chain produces a mixed bag of results because his finding that the cable retransmission of broadcasts to hotel rooms does not amount to a communication to the public is not consistent with the need to establish a high level of protection for authors[197] and, moreover, is inconsistent with Article 11bis(1)(ii) of the Berne Convention. In addition to this, Coene's different consumption chain may also erode the applicability of the public performance right, especially with regard to acts of reception in public. This is because reception of a work would not affect the spatial or temporal limits of the initial 'communication' and, as such, may not require authorisation under Coene's system. However, the value in Coene's idea is to be found in his emphasis on the act of 'communication' rather than the potential 'public'. The advantage of adopting this approach is that the finding of communication to the public becomes a more objective process because the volatile 'public' requirement becomes less important, if relevant at all. Despite this, Coene's idea is effectively a hybrid form of the 'new public' criterion

[194] The facts of this case were similar to those of *Rafael Hoteles*, as it also involved the cable retransmission of a broadcast to hotel rooms. The CJEU in this case also found that there was communication to the public, as the cable retransmission was to a 'new public'.

[195] Coene (2014) 24.

[196] ibid.

[197] Coene's finding that the retransmission of a broadcast to hotel rooms is not a communication to the public would prejudice a significant source of income for authors.

that shifts the focus from potential recipients to the space and time in which the 'communication' is perceptible to those same recipients.

In considering the three potential approaches to the governing criterion for acts of making available – 'new public', 'organisation other than the original one' and Coene's spatial and temporal limits approach – it is argued that the most suitable governing criterion would be the 'organisation other than the original one'. Therefore, the 'new public' criterion should be abandoned with respect to all aspects of the communication to the public right, given its incorrect adoption for acts of retransmission and its lack of suitability for the Internet.

C. Future Role for 'New Public'

The above discussion comprised arguments about why the 'new public' criterion should play no part in determining whether there is an act of communication to the public. Notably, it was argued that 'new public' is not in accordance with the international copyright treaties, it is unclear and imprecise, and unsuitable for the Internet. However, the concept of 'new public' does have potential to be developed into an exception or limitation to the communication to the public right under Article 5(3) of the ISD. This will be a better use for 'new public' as it can be properly justified and its scope proportionately balanced.

D. Proposed Solution

Given the issues with the 'new public' criterion for analogue and digital technologies, it is advocated that the criterion should be abandoned.[198] Instead, the 'organisation other than the original one' approach should be adopted for all aspects of the communication to the public right, including the making available aspect. In addition to this, the concept of 'organisation other than the original one' should be clearly defined to increase certainty.

VII. 'Knowledge' and 'for Profit'

The concept of 'knowledge' was expressly introduced as a separate criterion of the communication to the public framework in *GS Media*.[199] The reason for its introduction was to limit the precedent set in *Svensson* that hyperlinking to freely accessible works on the Internet would not invoke the communication to the public

[198] Hugenholtz and Van Velze agree that the communication to the public right can operate without the 'new public' criterion – Hugenholtz and Van Velze (2016) 811.

[199] *GS Media* [2016] paras 47–51.

right. Thus, to limit the exhaustion of the communication to the public right, the CJEU in *GS Media* used 'knowledge' as the mechanism to restrict the *Svensson* judgment to circumstances where there was express authorisation for the initial upload or where the communicator did not know that the work being shared was unauthorised. Therefore, the 'knowledge' criterion was the CJEU's remedy for its earlier missteps.[200]

The 'knowledge' requirement is divisible into two aspects, actual knowledge and presumed knowledge. Where the communicator has notice that the works being communicated are unauthorised it will be held to have actual knowledge.[201] Alternatively, 'knowledge' can be presumed where the act is done 'for profit'. The CJEU in *GS Media* stated that where an act is done 'for profit' there is a rebuttable presumption that the communicator has knowledge of the nature of the work, inclusive of any lack of authorisation.[202] By contrast, where a communicative act is not done 'for profit' it is presumed that the communicator does not know and cannot reasonably know whether the work was published on the Internet with consent.[203]

In looking at the use of 'knowledge' by the CJEU in *GS Media*, *Filmspeler* and *Ziggo*, it can be discerned that it is now a separate, key criterion for determining liability in relation to the making available aspect of the communication to the public right. This claim is evidenced by the structure of the cases whereby, the final point of analysis for the Court is whether the act in question was done with 'knowledge', be it actual or presumed.[204] As such, it can be inferred that in the absence of 'knowledge' there will be no communication to the public infringement. However, it should be noted that the use of the term 'knowledge' in the communication to the public framework is not new.

The idea of *knowledge* was used in the very first communication to the public case, *Rafael Hoteles*, albeit for a different purpose. In the cases that utilise the access approach in defining 'communication', it was stated that an act of 'communication' occurs where there is an intervention with full *knowledge* of the consequences of that action to provide access to a protected work.[205] However, in the pre-*GS Media* era, the Court paid no attention to the knowledge element; instead the focus was on the 'intervention' made.[206] In the absence of any clear reasoning for this approach, it can be inferred that 'full knowledge of the consequences' was equivalent to a purposeful or intentional act.[207] This inference is supported

[200] It is advocated that the CJEU should have reversed its position by declaring hyperlinks outside the scope of 'communication'.

[201] *GS Media* [2016] para 54, *Filmspeler* [2017] para 50 and *Ziggo* [2017] para 45.

[202] *GS Media* [2016] para 51.

[203] ibid para 47.

[204] ibid paras 51–54, *Filmspeler* [2017] paras 49–52 and *Ziggo* [2017] paras 45–47.

[205] See for example: *SGAE v Rafael Hoteles* [2006] para 42, *FAPL v QC Leisure* [2011] para 194, *Reha Training* [2016] para 46 and *GS Media* [2016] para 35.

[206] *FAPL v QC Leisure* [2011] paras 194–196, *SCF v Marco del Corso* [2012] para 94, *PPL v Ireland* [2012] para 40 and *Reha Training* [2016] paras 54–56.

[207] Peguera (2018) 9.

by AG Campos Sánchez-Bordona in *Renckhoff*.[208] Alternatively, another interpretation could be that the Court assumed there was knowledge because no permission was sought for the subsequent communication and, as such, it was unauthorised. This interpretation would fit better with the approach to 'knowledge' introduced post-*GS Media*.[209]

Nonetheless, the CJEU in *GS Media* linked the express criterion of 'knowledge' with the knowledge element of 'communication'. It was held that in the absence of knowledge the communicator 'does not as a general rule, intervene in full knowledge of the consequences of his conduct'.[210] Therefore, in the absence of 'knowledge', there can be no act of 'communication' and, as such, no 'communication to the public'. This approach to 'knowledge' is problematic because it conflates the concept of 'communication' with the newly introduced 'knowledge' criterion. The conflation creates uncertainty in relation to the structure of the communication to the public framework and its core elements.

Examining *GS Media*, *Filmspeler* and *Ziggo* evidences the conflation problem. In *GS Media*, the CJEU departed from its traditional approach of separately determining whether there was an act of 'communication', 'public' and 'new public'. Instead, the judgment reads as an amalgam of all the core issues into one undefined discussion.[211] By contrast, the subsequent cases of *Filmspeler* and *Ziggo* reverted to the traditional CJEU approach of addressing the core elements separately. In these two cases, the Court held that there were acts of 'communication' in the first place,[212] but then went on to discuss 'knowledge' separately before ultimately deciding there was an act of 'communication to the public'. The problem with the format in these three cases is the lack of certainty. If the 'knowledge' requirement is part of 'communication' it should be addressed under that heading and not in two separate aspects of the decision. Conversely, if the 'knowledge' requirement is a separate criterion then it should be clearly demarcated from 'communication', as opposed to the approach adopted in *GS Media*.

Similarly, the CJEU has also conflated the 'knowledge' requirement with the 'new public' criterion. In *GS Media* it was assumed that if there is 'knowledge' that the work in question is unauthorised, there will be a 'new public'.[213] Likewise, in *Ziggo* it was stated by the Court that there must be a communication to a 'new public' because the operators of The Pirate Bay could not be unaware that their platform provided access to unauthorised works.[214] It can be inferred from this statement that where the communicated work is unauthorised, this will lead to a finding of 'new public'.[215] If this is indeed the case, it raises the question of the

[208] *Renckhoff* [2018], Opinion of AG Campos Sánchez-Bordona, para 65.
[209] ibid para 70.
[210] *GS Media* [2016] para 48, read in conjunction with para 47.
[211] ibid paras 47–55.
[212] *Filmspeler* [2017] para 42 and *Ziggo* [2017] paras 30–34.
[213] *GS Media* [2016] para 52.
[214] *Ziggo* [2017] para 45.
[215] *GS Media* [2016] paras 42–43 and *Filmspeler* [2017] paras 47–48

purpose of the 'new public' criterion, given that it would seem to be superfluous where the 'knowledge' criterion is used and, moreover, allows claimants to establish liability without proving any specific acts of infringement.[216] Alternatively, it can be said that the 'knowledge' requirement is superfluous because it fulfils the same function as the 'new public' criterion in this scenario. Given that it has been advocated that the 'new public' criterion should be replaced by the 'organisation other than the original one' criterion, it is necessary to consider the usefulness of the 'knowledge' criterion.

Thus far, the introduction and use of the 'knowledge' criterion has been discussed. However, the validity and usefulness of the 'knowledge' criterion must be equally discussed given that it can be criticised on several grounds – the inconsistent use of 'for profit', the usefulness of 'knowledge', and the consequential overlap with secondary liability.

A. 'For Profit' Inconsistency

The 'for profit' criterion must be understood in its two phases. The post-*GS Media* use of 'for profit' as part of the 'knowledge' criterion has already been discussed. However, this use is inconsistent with its initial pre-*GS Media* conception. Prior to *GS Media*, 'for profit' was considered to be not irrelevant, but not essential for proving an act of communication to the public.[217] The only notable mention of 'for profit', pre-*GS Media*, occurred in *Marco del Corso* where the 'communication' made was *not* 'for profit' and, interestingly enough, was the only retransmission/reception in public case in which communication to the public was not found.[218] However, the CJEU in *GS Media* transformed 'for profit' into a key element of the communication to the public framework by linking it with the newly introduced 'knowledge' requirement. Therefore, it is necessary to analyse the 'for profit' criterion in the pre and post-*GS Media* stages because its validity and scope remain unclear.

In the pre-*GS Media* case law, the application of 'for profit' was unclear and inconsistent. In *FAPL v QC Leisure*, the CJEU stated that an act of 'communication' will be 'for profit' where it has an effect upon the number of people going to the establishment and ultimately on its financial results.[219] This definition was followed in *Marco del Corso*, where the Court held that the playing of music over speakers in a dentist office was not 'for profit'. This is because the music would neither attract more customers, nor affect the dental treatments and, as such, had no impact on the income of the dentist.[220] However, in a factually comparable

[216] Ohly (2018) 670.

[217] *Rafael Hoteles* [2006] para 44, *FAPL v QC Leisure* [2011] para 204 and *Reha Training* [2016] 49.

[218] *Marco del Corso* [2012] paras 97–99.

[219] *FAPL v QC Leisure* [2011] para 205.

[220] *SCF v Marco del Corso* [2012] paras 97–98.

situation in *Reha Training*, the CJEU held that the playing of television broadcasts in the waiting and training rooms of a rehab centre was 'for profit' because it was an additional service which, despite having no medical benefit, made the rehab centre more attractive and gave it a competitive advantage.[221] The CJEU came to this conclusion on the basis that 'for profit' includes any act that has an impact on an establishment's attractiveness, giving it a competitive advantage. From these three cases it is difficult to discern any consistency with regard to the application or definition of 'for profit'.

In addition to lacking certainty, the use of 'for profit' prior to *GS Media* can also be criticised for being too wide, with no clear threshold. In looking at the most recent definition from *Reha Training* it can be argued that any playing of copyright works at a venue can make the place more attractive and thus give it a competitive advantage. However, this does not necessarily translate into *profitability*. As such, there is a need for some clarity and consistency between the definitions provided in *FAPL v QC Leisure* where there is the financial result aspect, and *Reha Training* that talks about competitive advantage. Moreover, there is need for further guidance as to quantifying 'for profit'. In the absence of such clarity, it will remain difficult to reconcile *Marco del Corso* with *Reha Training*, given the competing definitions present, because it is arguable that the playing of music in a dentist office does lead to it being more attractive than an office with no entertainment. Therefore, it is suggested that 'for profit' must be expressly defined and quantified if its use is to be continued. Quantification can be achieved by expressly defining 'for profit' in line with accounting principles such as 'net profit' or 'gross profit'.

Additionally, it is necessary to reconcile the pre and post-*GS Media* use of 'for profit'. Firstly, it is unclear whether 'for profit' as part of the 'knowledge' requirement will extend to the traditional cases on retransmission and reception in public or will remain limited to the making available aspect in relation to the Internet cases. In the interest of establishing certainty for the right of communication to the public, there needs to be consistency of concepts. As such, 'for profit' should only have one meaning or use if it is to be perpetuated. Secondly, it remains the case that the threshold of 'for profit' remains undefined.[222]

From the case law, the CJEU has adopted a broad approach to 'for profit', including direct and indirect profit of varying degrees.[223] Hence, it is necessary to clarify the threshold for establishing a 'for profit' act because there continues to be speculation about the standard of care imputed to users via the 'knowledge' requirement.[224] From the existing CJEU decisions there has been no discussion on

[221] *Reha Training* [2016] para 63.

[222] Ohly argued that it is unclear whether the determination of an act 'for profit' is rooted in economic analysis or reflects the intuition of judges – Ohly in Hugenholtz (2018) 103.

[223] Savola (2017) 145 para 40 and B Clark and J Dickenson, 'Theseus and the Labyrinth? An Overview of 'Communication to the Public' under EU Copyright Law: after Reha Training and GS Media. Where Are We now and Where Do We Go from Here?' (2017) 39(5) *EIPR* 265, 269–70.

[224] Savola suggests that 'it seems likely that the standard may have been intended to be set somewhat higher, for example in actively seeking and obtaining financial gain.' As opposed to instances where the

the balancing of the 'for profit' criterion and the subsequent duty of care imposed via the rebuttable presumption that arises.[225] Failure to clarify the 'for profit' criterion and the consequent duty of care in this sense is likely to cause problems because the duty of care imposed via the rebuttable presumption may be infeasible and impractical, thus creating unrealistic expectations; and, moreover, it will conflict with fundamental rights, especially where it is impossible to monitor all online activity.[226]

Thirdly, the use of 'for profit' in relation to the 'knowledge' criterion must be validated. It is uncertain how a 'for profit' act leads to a presumption of 'knowledge' and, furthermore, whether this is a desirable mechanism for determining infringement. Coene argued that the 'for profit' criterion can be used as an indicator of whether a 'communication' was made knowingly. If the 'communication' is made 'for profit' it is more likely to be the result of a deliberate or knowing intervention by the organisation.[227] However, Coene's suggestion does not offer any more of a rationale than the CJEU's findings in *GS Media*. It is perhaps plausible to suggest that there is a link with 'knowledge' because doing an act 'for profit' suggests a sense of deliberateness and, moreover, that the operator is aware of the underlying details, including the works involved. However, copyright law has traditionally been strict liability, and as such, knowledge of the infringing act should have no bearing on infringement where the constituent elements of the act are present;[228] that is, an act of 'communication' to the 'public' without authorisation.

Notwithstanding the above, a more desirable outcome would be to remove 'for profit' as an express criterion of the communication to the public right. In the first place, copyright law has never required profitability as a precondition for liability.[229] While it is arguable that there is an underlying economic element involved in the justification of the exclusive rights,[230] copyright infringement

pursuit of profit is weaker; that is 'when linking is casual and not the main object of the site' – Savola (2017) 145–46 paras 40–44. See also, Clark and Dickenson (2017) 269–70, E Rosati, '*GS Media* and its Implications for the Construction of the Right of Communication to the Public within EU Copyright Architecture' (2017) 54(4) *Common Market Law Review* 1221, 1231, Midelieva (2017) 483–84; E Rosati, 'The CJEU Pirate Bay Judgment and its Impact on the Liability of Online Platforms' (2017) 39(12) *EIPR* 737, 740 and 743–44 and Leistner (2017) 330–32.

[225] Leistner argues that for the rebuttable presumption of knowledge to be proportional it is necessary to adopt an approach that involves reasonable and proportionate checks in the context of the defendant – Leistner (2017) 331.

[226] Peguera (2018) 16 and Leistner (2017) 330–31.

[227] Coene (2014) 5–6.

[228] Ginsburg argued that violation of a true property right does not require the right holder to establish knowledge – J Ginsburg, 'The Court of Justice of the European Union Creates an EU Law of Liability for Facilitation of Copyright Infringement: Observations on *Brein v Filmspeler* [C-527/15] (2017) and *Brein v Ziggo* [C-610/15] (2017)' Columbia Law and Economics Working Paper No. 572 (2017) 2 <https://papers.ssrn.com/sol3/papers.cfm?abstract_id=3024302> accessed 3 August 2018.

[229] Dusollier in Hugenholtz (2018) 183. Makeen also makes a similar argument in relation to the 'for profit' criterion applied to cases on the public performance right – Makeen (2016) 130–31.

[230] Depreeuw argues that the CJEU has developed an economic approach to its decision-making with regard to the communication to the public right and the issue of temporary copies – Depreeuw (2014) para 698. Mysoor also suggests that the focus should be on the economic significance of the 'communication' to the person or organisation making the 'communication' – Mysoor (2013) 181.

remains a strict liability cause of action. As such, if there is an unauthorised 'communication' made to a 'public' there should be an infringing act of 'communication to the public' unless it is subject to any exceptions and limitations. Secondly, the uncertainty surrounding the 'for profit' criterion disproportionately benefits right holders, given that the courts have appeared to utilise low thresholds in holding users accountable.

'For profit' should play no part in determining infringement. However, what 'for profit' can assist with is the normative development of the scope of the right. Acts that affect the earning capacity of right holders should come within the scope of the right.[231] Alternatively, acts such as simple and deep hyperlinking that do not affect the earning capacity of right holders should be excluded from the scope of the right of communication to the public. This will allow for a more proportional right, adequately balancing the competing interests of right holders and users. This approach can be justified if 'for profit' is viewed in a similar manner to the second step of the three-step test. 'For profit' may be understood in the context of whether the act of communication to the public is in conflict with a normal exploitation of the work.[232] A normal exploitation of the work means an action that would ordinarily require a licence from the right holder.

If it is the case that the act in question would normally be subject to a licence, then infringement should be established because the right holder is 'injured'. Following the normative approach suggested in the previous paragraph, courts should consider whether the act in question is done 'for profit' only in the context of deciding whether to include the act complained of within the scope of the right. This approach can be used as an objective means to determine the suitability of allowing infringement on the basis of some 'injury' suffered by the right holder. However, this is premised on the existence of a common understanding of what 'normal exploitation' includes, which makes it unsuitable for addressing new forms of exploitation that do not fit the mould of what is understood to be a normal exploitation, especially in the age of rapidly evolving technology. Likewise, this approach can be criticised as merely shifting analysis from the exceptions and limitation stage to the infringement stage, thus creating a de facto 'not for profit' or 'harmless communication' exemption within the scope of the right.[233]

Alternatively, it is also possible to construct an exception to the right of communication to the public using the concept of 'for profit'. This will be justifiable on the grounds that copyright infringement attracts strict liability and should not depend on the damage caused by the act. The only requirement is that one of the exclusive rights be breached in accordance with the criteria established by the Court, 'for profit' not being a necessary criterion. However, where infringement is committed

[231] Brison and Depreeuw argued that the economic approach to interpreting the communication to the public right should be broader than the sole question of whether an act is done 'for profit' – Brison and Depreeuw in Torremans (2017) 132.

[232] See Article 13 of the TRIPS Agreement and Article 5(5) of the ISD.

[233] See Makeen's discussion on the 'financial injury' criterion developed in the UK public performance case law – Makeen (2016) 131–32.

and there is no damage done to the right holder it may be justified to exempt the infringer from liability. AG Campos Sánchez-Bordona in *Renckhoff* suggested a similar approach in relation to subsequent uses of works made freely available on the Internet with authorisation; however, through the scope of the right itself. It was suggested that where the subsequent use of a work made freely available on the Internet is not 'for profit' and the user has no knowledge of the work being unauthorised, there should be no act of infringement where that use does not cause harm to the right holder. However, this approach was not followed by the CJEU.

In conclusion, 'for profit' should be removed as an express criterion of the communication to the public right, though it may be recycled for other useful purposes.

B. Usefulness of 'Knowledge'

Despite the CJEU ascribing a critical role to 'knowledge' in the communication to the public framework, it is not definitive that 'knowledge' is necessary. It is clear that the raison d'être for the introduction of the 'knowledge' requirement was to limit the consequences of the *Svensson* decision. However, it has been advocated that the 'new public' criterion should be abandoned. As such, the issue in *Svensson* will disappear if that suggestion is adopted and consequently, the need for the 'knowledge' requirement will also dissipate. However, if 'new public' is maintained, it remains questionable whether 'knowledge' is needed. Thus far, the use of 'knowledge' has been in clear-cut cases, notably in relation to The Pirate Bay – the most popular torrent website on the Internet – and in relation to hyperlinking examples that were obviously unauthorised given the notices received. In more subtle cases involving services not prone to infringing activity, media that are obscure or websites with significantly less content or less user traffic, it is unclear what standard of knowledge must be established and, furthermore, whether the 'knowledge' criterion will actually be useful given its lack of objectivity.[234] This is of importance because the CJEU has not expressly stated whether the standard of 'knowledge' is a duty-of-care-style 'ought to have known' requirement or an actual knowledge requirement.[235] This difficulty is expressly mentioned in *GS Media* with particular regard to works that are sub-licensed.[236] This is significant because it is often difficult to determine whether works have been uploaded to the Internet with authorisation.

In circumstances that are not clear-cut, or where no notice of the unauthorised nature of the works is given, acts of subsequent communication that are not

[234] JB Nordemann, 'Recent CJEU case law on communication to the public and its application in Germany: A new EU concept of liability' (2018) 13(9) *JIPLP* 744, 748 and Ohly (2018) 670.

[235] Clark and Dickenson (2017) 269.

[236] *GS Media* [2016] para 46.

'for profit' are unlikely to lead to a finding of communication to the public except where there is actual knowledge.[237] Therefore, in the absence of actual knowledge, the communication to the public right may become very limited in non-commercial contexts unless right holders engage in a 'notice and takedown' style approach.[238] This was alluded to in the AG's Opinion in *Renckhoff*.[239] The CJEU in *Renckhoff* also expressed a similar sentiment in a different context, by suggesting that hyperlinking to freely available works should not amount to infringement because the right holder could merely revoke consent of the initial upload and have the work removed.[240] However, where the right holder has not authorised the initial upload of their work, infringement should be found because the right holder will not have control over future uses.[241] The CJEU in *Renckhoff* adopted this perspective in justifying why infringement should be established for subsequent uploads of an authorised work already freely available on the Internet.[242]

From this, it can be said that the 'knowledge' requirement can prove to be an inhibitor to finding infringement and is thus unnecessary. When this is combined with the earlier discussion that the 'knowledge' requirement has been conflated with the 'communication' and 'new public' criteria and, furthermore, is superfluous, maintaining 'knowledge' as a stand-alone criterion is unjustified. As such, it should be omitted from the communication to the public framework.

C. 'Knowledge', the Duty of Care and the E-Commerce Directive

A further issue with the introduction of the 'knowledge' criterion is the creation of the resultant duty of care that is imposed on defendants who have actual knowledge or are tagged with a rebuttable presumption of knowledge via the 'for profit' criterion. This duty of care translates into a requirement that defendants monitor the content that they share via hyperlinks and torrent files, or else they face the risk of infringement.[243] This is because the establishment of 'knowledge' that the works in question are unauthorised or infringing will give rise to an act of communication to the public provided that the 'communication' and 'public'

[237] An example of this situation would be where an intermediary's service is used for both infringing and non-infringing uses. In this context the intermediary is aware of the risk of infringing uses, but is unaware of actual cases of infringement. See Ohly (2018) 673.

[238] J Smith and H Newton, 'Hyperlinking to material on the internet: the CJEU expands on the circumstances when it may amount to copyright infringement' (2016) 38(12) *EIPR* 768, 770 and Clark and Dickenson (2017) 270 and Quintais (2018) 23.

[239] *Renckhoff* [2018] Opinion of AG Campos Sánchez-Bordona, paras 73 and 82–85.

[240] *Renckhoff* [2018] para 30.

[241] ibid para 31.

[242] *Renckhoff* [2018] paras 28–29.

[243] Peguera (2018) 15–17, Midelieva (2017) 483 and Quintais (2018) 20.

elements are met.[244] However, the CJEU has not expressed what threshold of 'knowledge' is required or what standard of behaviour is expected.

This creates the first problem for the right of communication to the public. It is unclear what is required to establish infringement in non-obvious cases; that is, the cases where there is no evidence of specific unauthorised works or no actual knowledge of infringement. In contrast to the factual contexts in *GS Media* and *Ziggo*, where it was obvious that the files being shared were unauthorised, it is not clear how much 'knowledge' is required or how expansive the duty of care is. It was stated in the previous subsection that the threshold for 'knowledge' can range from the defendant 'ought to have known' to 'actual knowledge'. Thus, 'knowledge' in its present form is not useful in non-obvious cases of infringement because it is unknown how meticulous users must be in ensuring that no infringing files are being shared.[245] Given the absence of any threshold for the duty of care, Nordemann has suggested the adoption of a 'due diligence' standard, akin to the obligations of intermediaries under Article 8(3) of the ISD.[246] Nordemann's suggestion appears desirable because it is consistent with existing law under the ISD and therefore allows for legal certainty and consistency. Additionally, it affords a proportionate balance that does not place overly onerous demands on users and intermediaries. Nonetheless, it remains the case that the 'knowledge' requirement should be abandoned. The alternative to Nordemann's approach would be the use of the general duties of care found under secondary liability doctrines at the domestic level. However, this approach will be difficult to implement given the diversity of approaches across Member States, leading to legal uncertainty.

The second issue with the duty of care resulting from the use of the 'knowledge' criterion is conflict with the E-Commerce Directive.[247] The conflict arises because Article 15 of the E-Commerce Directive prevents the imposition of a general obligation to monitor transmitted information for intermediaries engaged in/as 'mere conduits', 'caching' and 'hosting'.[248] Therefore, the CJEU's post-*GS Media* use of 'knowledge' may be in direct contravention of Article 15 of the E-Commerce Directive because it effectively requires users to check whether the content they are sharing is authorised.[249] Despite this, the safe harbours under the E-Commerce Directive and the 'knowledge' criterion are functionally similar. They both determine liability, though from different starting points.[250] However, there are significant differences in the level of protection afforded since the safe

[244] *GS Media* [2016] paras 51 and 54, *Filmspeler* [2017] para 49 and *Ziggo* [2017] para 34 and 45.
[245] Ohly (2018) 673.
[246] Nordemann (2018) 749.
[247] Directive 2000/31/EC of the European Parliament and of the Council of 8 June 2000 on certain legal aspects of information society services, in particular electronic commerce, in the Internal Market [E-Commerce Directive] [2000] OJ L 178/1, 17.7.2000.
[248] See Articles 12–14 of the E-Commerce Directive.
[249] Peguera (2018) 13–14, Ohly (2018) 673 and *Ziggo* [2017] Opinion of AG Szpunar, para 52.
[250] Peguera describes the 'knowledge' criterion as a judicially created safe harbour for the right of communication to the public – Peguera (2018) 15.

harbours offer complete protection from liability; whereas, the absence of 'knowledge' only precludes the finding of primary liability under the harmonised EU right of communication to the public and leaves the possibility of secondary liability at the domestic level open.

The conflict of 'knowledge' with the E-Commerce Directive can also be described from a different perspective. Unlike Articles 12–14 of the E-Commerce Directive, which prevent the establishment of liability where there is no 'knowledge', the requirement of 'knowledge' for finding an act of 'communication to the public' means the burden of proof is different. Under the E-Commerce Directive, the onus is on the defendant to prove compliance with the conditions for exempting liability. By contrast, it is the claimant that has to prove the defendant had 'knowledge' in cases concerning the right of communication to the public.[251] This difference has significance for legal certainty as the burden of proof is reversed and, moreover, from a normative perspective there can be inconsistency. In instances where the safe harbours under Articles 12–14 of the E-Commerce Directive are unavailable, this should not necessarily mean that infringement of the communication to the public right should follow. Therefore, 'knowledge' should not be a definitive factor in finding infringement of the communication to the public right.

D. Overlap with Secondary Liability

Traditionally copyright law has not required knowledge or intention to establish primary infringement. This had led to the idea that infringement of the exclusive rights is strict liability in nature.[252] By contrast, knowledge has been restricted to the laws of secondary liability at the domestic level.[253] Therefore, adding a 'knowledge' criterion to the communication to the public framework has blurred the line between primary infringement and secondary liability, and created uncertainty as to whether EU copyright law still entails strict liability.[254] Apart from the attempt to fix the issue created in *Svensson*, it is arguable that the addition of the 'knowledge' requirement in *GS Media* was in part due to the absence of harmonised laws on secondary liability within the EU.[255] Consequently, to avoid a gap in the law, the

[251] Ginsburg (2017) 11.

[252] Goold describes this as the 'orthodox view', but goes on to criticise the orthodox view of copyright law by arguing for the fault-based nature of copyright infringement – P Goold, 'Is Copyright Infringement a Strict Liability Tort?' (2014) 30(1) *Berkeley Technology Law Journal* 306, 333, 338–53. See also: S Hetcher, 'The Immortality of Strict Liability in Copyright' (2013) 17(1) *Marquette Intellectual Property Law Review* 1 and A Dorfman and A Jacob, 'Copyright as Tort' (2011) 12(1) *Theoretical Inquiries in Law* 59.

[253] For example, see laws on accessory liability in the UK and störerhaftung in Germany under s 1004 of the German Civil Code.

[254] G Dimita, 'The WIPO right of making available' in P Torremans (ed), *Research Handbook on Copyright Law*, 2nd edn (Edward Elgar Publishing Ltd, 2017) 157.

[255] Note, Leistner argues that there is a minimal level of harmonisation with regard to secondary liability pertaining to intermediaries under Articles 12–15 of the E-Commerce Directive, Articles 9–13

CJEU expanded the scope of the communication to the public right to cover acts that should be addressed by secondary liability laws.[256]

Acts such as hyperlink and torrent file aggregation should be dealt with under secondary liability. This is because the aggregator does not actually provide any of the works and, as such, does not perform an act of 'communication' according to the refined transmission approach that has been supported in this book.[257] Rather, the aggregator makes it easier to access works. Where those works are unauthorised, and the aggregator has actual or presumed knowledge of such, the CJEU has unilaterally expanded the communication to the public right to address these situations. While this conflation of primary and secondary liability might be beneficial for right holders in allowing them to hold users and culpable business models accountable under a harmonised right, such an expansion amounts to the CJEU overstepping its powers by harmonising aspects of secondary liability under the scope of the communication to the public right without the input of the respective Member States or consideration of their domestic laws.[258]

Additionally, the approach adopted by the CJEU is not in accordance with the proposals made in this book. The expansion of the right of communication to the public to accommodate acts that should be dealt with under secondary liability has been to the detriment of users, given that the scope of the right is now disproportionately in favour of right holders and, moreover, the right itself is unclear and incoherent. This lack of certainty will have a spill-over effect at the domestic level as the scope of the EU communication to the public right will overlap with domestic rules on secondary liability, tort and copyright.[259] Therefore, it is unjustified and problematic to maintain the 'knowledge' requirement as a core element of the communication to the public right. Consequently, it is suggested that the EU should harmonise the law on secondary liability for copyright rather than expanding the scope of the communication to the public right.[260] By doing this it would reduce the burden placed on the communication to the public right and allow for a coherent reformulation of the right.

of Directive 2004/48/EC of the European Parliament and of the Council of 29 April 2004 on the enforcement of intellectual property rights, [2004] OJ L195/16 and Article 8 of the ISD – M Leistner, 'Structural aspects of secondary (provider) liability in Europe' (2014) 9(1) *JIPLP* 75.

[256] C Angelopoulos, *European Intermediary Liability in Copyright: A Tort-Based Analysis* (Kluwer Law International BV, 2017) 65–66. Also see Clark and Dickenson (2017) 277, Savola (2017) 143, para 23, Midelieva (2017) 487, Lim Saw (2018) 562, Ginsburg (2017) 3 and Nordemann (2018) 745. Note, AG Szpunar in his Opinion on *Ziggo* stated that failing to expand the scope of the communication to the public right to address torrent files would undermine the objective of harmonising EU copyright law, given the divergent approaches to secondary liability at the domestic level – *Ziggo* [2017] Opinion of AG Szpunar, para 3.

[257] Ohly argues that primary liability should be restricted to cases where the infringer uses the work himself – Ohly (2018) 675.

[258] Peguera (2018) 1213 and Nordemann (2018) 752.

[259] Ohly (2018) 671.

[260] See Angelopoulos (2017) Chapters 4 and 5, for discussion on introducing harmonised EU law on secondary liability.

E. Proposed Solution

The 'knowledge' and 'for profit' criteria should be removed from the communication to the public framework. These concepts may be helpful in developing the scope of the right but should not form part of the core requirements. In particular, the 'for profit' consideration has flexibility that can be utilised in shaping a more normative scope for the right or even possibly the creation of an exception.

VIII. Conclusion

This chapter detailed the development of the EU communication to the public right and identified the specific problems that exist with the scope of the right. The problems identified compromise the coherence and future development of the right. As such, several recommendations were made for the reform of the right. In summary, the recommendations are:

- The broad interpretation of the communication to the public right should be abandoned in lieu of a more clearly defined right;
- The term 'communication' should be defined as any act of transmission or provision of a work – 'provision' requiring direct contact with the work from the act of 'communication';
- The making available aspect should be clarified as a subset of the communication to the public right relating solely to on demand transmissions;
- The act of reception in public should be excluded from the scope of the communication to the public right. Instead, it should be governed under a harmonised public performance right;
- The 'new public' criterion should be replaced by the 'organisation other than the original one' criterion to govern all acts of subsequent communication;
- The 'for profit' criterion should be abandoned as an express aspect of the right of communication to the public; and
- The 'knowledge' requirement should be abandoned.

Chapter four will complement these recommendations by addressing: what the reformed right of communication to the public will look like; the relationship of the proposed right with the other harmonised exclusive rights, exceptions and limitations; and the mechanisms for completing the harmonisation of the right.

4

Structuring the Reformed Right of Communication to the Public Under EU Copyright Law

I. Introduction

Chapter three analysed the problems relating to the EU right of communication to the public and made several recommendations to resolve the issues. This chapter builds on the analysis by establishing the proposed reformed communication to the public right and, subsequently, sets out to reconcile the reformed right with the existing EU copyright law framework. This includes reconciling the proposed communication to the public right with the existing reproduction and distribution rights and the exceptions and limitations and, moreover, discussing the steps for completing the harmonisation of the communication to the public right. With this in mind it is argued that: the communication to the public right should be the sole applicable right in cases of non-material dissemination to a geographically dispersed 'public' and that the right should be codified under the ISD in the short term, with the ultimate goal being a codified right under a new copyright regulation.

II. The Reformed Right of Communication to the Public

Following the recommendations made in Chapter three, the determination of an act of communication to the public should be subject to the following requirements:

Step 1 – There must be an act of 'communication' – defined as 'any transmission or provision[1] of a protected work including the making available of that work in such a way that members of the public may access it from a place and at a time individually chosen by them'. The provision of access to a protected work is insufficient to constitute an act of 'communication'.

[1] 'Provision' meaning direct contact with the work from the act of 'communication'.

Step 2 – There must be a 'public' – defined as 'a fairly large and indeterminate number of persons who are geographically dispersed.'

Step 3 – If the act involves a subsequent 'communication' of a work, fresh authorisation must be sought if the act was conducted by an organisation other than the original one.

These three steps comprise the entire approach to determining infringement of the reformed communication to the public right, barring any applicable exceptions or limitations. The proposed criteria are compliant with the international copyright treaties and, moreover, offer a simpler and better balanced approach than what is currently applied by the CJEU.[2] The proposed right ensures that the interests of right holders are proportionately balanced with those of users and that the other competing interests discussed in Chapter one are adequately taken account of. The scope of the reformed right is also narrower than the currently applicable right, given the narrow interpretation of 'communication' guided by a refined transmission approach. This means that acts of hyperlinking and torrent files that caused the CJEU to overstretch the communication to the public right will fall outside the scope of the reformed right. As such, liability for hyperlink aggregators and torrent websites should be dealt with under secondary liability.

Thus, it is suggested that the provision containing the reformed right of communication to the public should reflect:

> Member States shall provide right holders with the exclusive right to authorise or prohibit any communication to the public of their works.
>
> (i) 'Communication' means the transmission or provision of the work. Mere access is insufficient for the purpose of the communication to the public right.
> (ii) Communication to the public includes the making available of works to the public in such a way that members of the public may access them from a place and at a time individually chosen by them.
> (iii) Acts of subsequent communication will require authorisation where the communication is made by an organisation other than the original one.
> (iv) Communication to the public does not include acts of reception in public or other acts of public performance.
> (v) 'Public' means a fairly large and indeterminate number of persons who are geographically dispersed.

It should be noted that the reformed right does not remove the need for the CJEU in matters concerning communication to the public. The CJEU still has a role to determine whether specific acts, especially relating to technologies not in existence at the time of this book, come within the scope of the reformed

[2] This approach is in keeping with the concept of a binary approach to establishing infringement, whereby an array of inconsistent and divergent complementary criteria such as 'new public', 'for profit' and 'knowledge' are avoided. See L Midelieva, 'Rethinking Hyperlinking: Addressing Hyperlinks to Unauthorized Content in Copyright Law and Policy' (2017) 39(8) *European Intellectual Property Review (EIPR)* 479, 486.

communication to the public right. Given the flexibility of the right, it is not expected that any new technologies will be able to 'break' the reformed right. Furthermore, the clear wording of the reformed right will avoid any problems of legal uncertainty or unwarranted expansion of the communication to the public right. However, it is acknowledged that the recommendations made for the reformed communication to the public right are ambitious and as such, its adoption will require significant political will. This is particularly because several of the recommendations conflict with the current trends existing in the *acquis communitaire* of EU copyright law.

III. Reconciling the Reformed Right with the Existing Copyright Framework

One of the primary interests underlying the development of EU copyright law has been the establishment of a high level of protection for right holders. The consequence of this has been the development of wide exclusive rights and broad interpretations combined with narrow approaches to exceptions and limitations.[3] As a result, there are instances where the exclusive rights of communication to the public, reproduction and distribution overlap or conflict. The implications of this include overregulation, uncertainty and incoherence. Therefore, it is necessary to clarify the relationship between the exclusive rights under EU copyright law. The clarification will be conducted from the perspective of making the reproduction and distribution rights compatible with the reformed communication to the public right that has been proposed. From the outset, it is suggested that the communication to the public right should be the sole applicable right governing the non-material dissemination of works to a geographically dispersed 'public'.

The relationship between the communication to the public right and the other exclusive rights has become a real concern because of the development of digital technology. In the analogue context, the delineation between the exclusive rights was clearer. The reproduction right covered the tangible copying of works and the distribution right dealt with the dissemination of tangible copies of works, while the communication to the public right addressed the non-material dissemination of works. However, with the advent of digital technology, notably the Internet, the boundaries between these rights have become increasingly blurred as digital copies become the norm. As a result, the reproduction right was expanded to include digital copies, including temporary copies.[4] The consequence of this is

[3] See Case C-435/12 *ACI Adam BV and others v Stichting de Thuiskopie and another* [2014] ECLI:EU:C:2014:254.

[4] See Article 2 of Directive 2001/29/EC of the European Parliament and of the Council of 22 May 2001 on the harmonisation of certain aspects of copyright and related rights in the information society [Information Society Directive], [2001] OJ L167/10, 22.6.2001.

the overlap between the reproduction right and the communication to the public right; in particular, the making available aspect that was designed to address digital, on demand technologies. Overlap has been described as the primary problem with the relationship between reproduction and communication to the public.[5] Therefore, it is necessary to clarify the relationship of these two rights in order to create a coherent copyright framework.

Additionally, the distribution and communication to the public rights conflict because the distribution right was extended to cover the online resale of software under the Computer Programs Directive[6] and moreover, was subjected to exhaustion.[7] This is of concern because the extension of the distribution right online can potentially overlap with the role of the communication to the public right. Furthermore, allowing the distribution right to be exhausted online may conflict with the communication to the public right. Therefore, this inconsistency must be clarified.

A. Reproduction and Communication to the Public

A significant overlap occurs between the reproduction right and the communication to the public right under the Information Society Directive (ISD).[8] Due to the inclusion of temporary copies under the Article 2 reproduction right, acts of 'communication' that should only be covered by the Article 3 communication to the public right can also implicate the reproduction right.[9] The reason for this is that every use of a digital work necessarily involves the making of temporary

[5] A Lucas Schloetter, 'The Acquis Communitaire in the Area of Copyright and Related Rights: Economic Rights' in T Synodinou (ed), *Codification of European Copyright Law: Challenges and Perspectives* (Kluwer Law International, 2012) 118.

[6] Council Directive 91/250/EEC of 14 May 1991 on the legal protection of computer programs, codified under: Directive 2009/24/EC of the European Parliament and of the Council of 23 April 2009 on the legal protection of computer programs [Computer Programs Directive] [2009] OJ L111/16, 5.5.2009.

[7] See Case C-128/11 *UsedSoft GmbH v Oracle International Corp* [2012] ECLI:EU:C:2012:407.

[8] European Commission, *Public Consultation on the review of the EU copyright rules* (2014) 11–12.

[9] M Makeen, *Copyright in a Global Information Society: The Scope of Copyright Protection Under International, US, UK and French Law* (Kluwer Law International, 2000) 308–14, J Ginsburg, 'Can Copyright Become User-Friendly? Review: Jessica Litman, Digital Copyright (2001)' (2002) 25 *Columbia Journal of Law & Arts* 71, 83, T Aplin, *Copyright Law in the Digital Society* (Hart Publishing, 2005) 113, Institute for Information Law, *The Recasting of Copyright & Related Rights for the Knowledge Economy* (University of Amsterdam, 2006) 48, Institute for Information Law, *Study on the Implementation and Effect in Member States' Laws of Directive 2001/29/EC on the Harmonisation of Certain Aspects of Copyright and Related Rights in the Information Society* (University of Amsterdam, 2007) 25, M van Eechoud *et al*, *Harmonizing European Copyright Law: The Challenges of Better Lawmaking* (Kluwer Law International, 2009) 75 and 88, A Ohly, 'Economic rights' in E Derclaye (ed), *Research Handbook on the Future of EU Copyright* (Edward Elgar Publishing Ltd, 2009) 217 and T Aplin, '"Reproduction" and "Communication to the Public" Rights in EU Copyright Law: *FAPL v QC Leisure*' (2011) 22(1) *King's Law Journal* 209, 212.

copies in order to facilitate the transmission and reception of the work.[10] This includes the making of temporary copies in the RAM of a computer, memory of a cable decoder box, on the screen of a television and even in the course of retransmitting broadcasted signals.[11] The consequence of this is that the reception of a work communicated to the public can potentially result in infringement of the reproduction right by the end user.

The danger with this possibility is that copyright law has traditionally never interfered with the use or consumption of copyright works by private end users.[12] It has never been the case that reading a book or watching or listening to radio or television programmes involved reproductions and/or copyright infringement.[13] However, the inclusion of temporary copies under the scope of the reproduction right means that the reading of e-books, tuning in to digital programming or streaming works on the Internet can potentially attract copyright liability.[14] Litman has termed the development of this 'use right' as an 'exclusive right to read' and further argues that the reproduction right has evolved into something more encompassing than envisioned under any previous copyright law.[15]

This resulting overlap has several implications for EU copyright law, including: overregulation, the creation of an imbalanced copyright framework, 'double dipping' and legal uncertainty. The EU legislature tried to mitigate the fears of overlap by providing the temporary copy exception under Article 5(1).[16]

[10] M Lehmann, 'Digitisation and Copyright Agreements' in I Stamatoudi and P Torremans (eds), *Copyright in the New Digital Environment: Volume 8: The Need to Redesign Copyright* (Sweet & Maxwell, 2000) 195.

[11] M Walter and S von Lewinski, *European Copyright Law: A Commentary* (Oxford University Press, 2010) 968, para 11.2.18, Institute for Information Law (2007) 23, Institute for Information Law (2006) 47–48, S Depreeuw, *The variable scope of the exclusive economic rights in copyright* (Kluwer Law International, 2014) 207, para 300, M Hart, 'The Copyright in the Information Society Directive: an overview' (2002) 24 *EIPR* 58, 58, Aplin (2011) 213, J Litman, 'The Exclusive Right to Read' (1995) 13 *Cardozo Arts & Entertainment Law Journal* 29, 31, van Eechoud *et al* (2009) 75, J Litman, *Digital Copyright* (Prometheus Books 2001) 174, 178, G Mazziotti, *EU Digital Copyright Law and the End-User* (Springer, 2008) 59 and Legal Advisory Board (LAB), *Reply to the 1995 Green Paper on Copyright and Related Rights in the Information Society* (1995) <http://www.echo.lu/legal/en/ipr/reply/reply.html> accessed 6 May 2013.

[12] Institute for Information Law (2007) 23, Institute for Information Law (2006) 69, PB Hugenholtz, 'Caching and copyright: the right of temporary copying' (2000) 10 *EIPR* 482, 486, Depreeuw (2014) 207, para 300, S Dusollier, 'Technology as an imperative for regulating copyright: from the public exploitation to the private use of the work' [2005] *EIPR* 201, 201, G Westkamp, 'Transient Copying and Public Communications: The Creeping Evolution of Use and Access Rights in European Copyright Law' (2004) 36 *George Washington International Law Review* 1057, 1102, PB Hugenholtz, 'Adapting copyright to the information superhighway' in PB Hugenholtz (ed), *The Future of Copyright in a Digital Environment* (Kluwer Law International, 1996) 93, Litman (1995) 31, Litman (2001) 177 and Institute for Information Law, *Copyright and Electronic Document Delivery Services – Background document* (1993) para 2.3.

[13] Makeen (2000) 284 and 309 and *Public Relations Consultants Association Ltd v Newspaper Licensing Agency Ltd* [2013] UKSC 18, para 36 (Lord Sumption).

[14] Institute for Information Law (2007) 23, Institute for Information Law (2006) 54, Ohly in Derclaye (2009) 217 and Hugenholtz in Hugenholtz (1996) 92.

[15] Litman (1995) 40 and M Kretschmer, 'Digital copyright: the end of an era' (2003) 25 *EIPR* 333, 337.

[16] Institute for Information Law (2006) 48.

Furthermore, the CJEU allayed some of the overlap fears in *PRCA v NLA*.[17] Nonetheless, there is an increasing consensus that the traditional copyright framework should not sustain both broad rights.[18] As a result, it is necessary to discuss the implications of the overlap problem in more detail and suggest recommendations to remedy the problem.

The overlap of these two rights leads to overregulation and creates an imbalanced copyright framework because it disproportionately benefits right holders contrary to Recital 31 of the ISD. Right holders have the ability to control the dissemination and use of their works so that users may potentially be forced to obtain permission to receive works even though the initial communication to the public of that work was authorised. This compromises some of the key interests for users discussed in Chapter one, notably their ability to engage with works of cultural or educational value and the development of the information society. The fundamental right to access information may also be prejudiced. There is also the concern that digital technologies are prejudiced because they are subject to possible restrictions that are not applicable to fundamentally similar analogue technologies. As such, new forms of exploitation and business models may be discouraged, to the detriment of the public interest.

The concern for new forms of exploitation being prejudiced is legitimate because the overlap problem has created an artificial distinction between the protection afforded to digital works and that to analogue works. Whereas, in the analogue context a single use of a work is subject to a single exclusive right, the use of a digital work can fall under the scope of both the reproduction and the communication to the public rights. The consequence of this is that digital right holders have more power and stand to earn more copyright revenue than their analogue counterparts. This is problematic for legal certainty and fairness because there is no express benefit for digital works under the law and, moreover, copyright law ought to be technology-neutral. However, digital works are clearly favoured, given that they stand to benefit from a greater level of protection under EU copyright law.[19] This creates inequality between owners of digital works and owners of analogue works, which has implications for the general principles of legal certainty and proportionality as well as for the rights of equality and non-discrimination under the Charter of Fundamental Rights of the EU.[20] As a result, it is necessary to restrict the scope of the reproduction right so that it does not overlap with the communication to the public right and overregulate the conduct of users. Failure to remedy this situation will perpetuate the imbalanced copyright framework and continue the copyright incoherence.

[17] Case C-360/13 *Public Relations Consultants Association Ltd v Newspaper Licensing Agency Ltd* [2014] ECLI:EU:C:2014:1195.

[18] Institute for Information Law (2006) 55 and van Eechoud *et al* (2009) 89.

[19] Westkamp (2004) 1103–04.

[20] Articles 20 and 21 of the Charter of Fundamental Rights of the EU.

Right holders disproportionately benefitting from the overlap can also be manifested in the form of unjustified double dipping.[21] This means that right holders are potentially able to claim multiple licensing fees for a single use of a work.[22] For example, an online film streaming service may have to obtain licences to communicate the movie to the public as well as a reproduction licence because temporary copies are made in the course of uploading and communicating the work online. From the end user perspective, after purchasing access to the film service, the user may then have to pay for a reproduction licence to actually watch the film because temporary copies are made in the RAM of the computer and on the screen. Therefore, the right holder may be able to claim up to three licence fees for the dissemination and consumption of their film, solely because any use of a digital work necessarily involves the making of temporary copies that are actionable under Article 2 (but for being exempted under Article 5(1)) of the ISD.[23]

If right holders are allowed to double dip by demanding two or more licence fees for a single use of a work, this makes the copyright licensing process more expensive, cumbersome and inefficient.[24] The reason for this is that all the exclusive rights of a particular work may not vest in the same entity.[25] For example in the UK, a user will have to secure the communication to the public licence and the reproduction licence from two different collecting societies. This increases administrative costs because the process of rights clearing becomes more bureaucratic and costly for users.[26] The CJEU in *PRCA v NLA* somewhat eased these fears by holding that copies made in the cache and on display screens are exempted from copyright liability.[27] The Court reached this conclusion by establishing that the cached and on screen copies were exempted via the Article 5(1) temporary copy exception because there was no justification for requiring Internet users to obtain further permission to watch the already authorised communication.[28] Following the decision in *PRCA v NLA*, it should be the case that any temporary copy made in the course of availing oneself of an act of authorised communication to the public should not be actionable under the reproduction right.[29]

[21] Institute for Information Law (2007) 25.

[22] Institute for Information Law (2006) 54, G Glisson, 'A Practitioner's Defense of the White Paper' (1996) 75 *Oregon Law Review* 277, 282 and Ginsburg (2002) 83.

[23] Note, this is unlikely to occur for authorised sources.

[24] Institute for Information Law (2007) 24–25, M Lemley, 'Dealing with Overlapping Copyrights on the Internet' (1997) 22 *University of Daytona Law Review* 548, 568–72 and Ohly in Derclaye (2009) 217.

[25] Ginsburg (2002) 83.

[26] S Dusollier, 'Realigning Economic Rights with Exploitation of Works: The Control of Authors over the Circulation of Works in the Public Sphere' in PB Hugenholtz (ed), *Copyright Reconstructed: Rethinking Copyright's Economic Rights in a Time of Highly Dynamic Technological and Economic Change* (Kluwer Law International BV, 2018) 171.

[27] *PRCA v NLA* [2014] paras 25–63 – The CJEU held that it was unnecessary for Internet users to obtain a licence to receive what was already authorised to be communicated.

[28] ibid paras 59–61.

[29] The decision in *PRCA v NLA* was seen as a victory for common sense – S James, 'And breathe … you can continue browsing the Internet, as the CJEU hands down its decision in PRCA v NLA (Meltwater)' (2014) 20(6) *Computer and Telecommunications Law Review* 169, 171. According to Lord

However, temporary copies made in the course of utilising an unauthorised communication to the public will be subject to the overlap problem and possibly the resultant double dipping.[30]

The overlap problem also causes legal uncertainty because it is unclear whether the reproduction right, communication to the public right or both rights should apply in cases concerning the dissemination of digital works.[31] What contributes to the lack of certainty is that the traditional copyright framework was not designed to address a single use with multiple infringements.[32] In the analogue context the individual exclusive rights were designed to address distinct acts. In particular, the reproduction right was limited to tangible or physical reproduction, as opposed to the communication to the public and public performance rights that addressed non-material acts. However, the expansion of the reproduction right to accommodate digital technology blurred the distinctiveness between these rights, as both rights can cover non-material uses of works.[33] Therefore, the scope and application of the reproduction right is in need of amendment in order to become more certain about the contexts in which it should apply.

B. Reconciling Reproduction and the Reformed Communication to the Public Right

It has been made clear that the overlap between the reproduction and communication to the public rights has implications for the coherency of EU copyright law. As such, it is imperative that the relationship of these two rights be clarified to balance the interests of right holders and users and to instil greater legal certainty. In order to achieve this, the overlap problem must be removed. EU copyright law has already attempted to mitigate and remove the overlap problem by virtue of the Article 5(1) temporary copy exception under the ISD and the CJEU's interpretation of that provision in *PRCA v NLA*. However, it is argued that these approaches are insufficient to resolve the overlap problem.

Article 5(1) of the ISD is the sole means of restricting the reproduction right from becoming a 'use right'.[34] Therefore, it is entrusted with the responsibility of keeping the reproduction right within reasonable bounds[35] and

Sumption, any other result would turn millions of ordinary users into infringers – *PRCA v NLA* [2013] paras 35–36 (per Lord Sumption).

[30] Case C-527/15 *Stichting Brein v Jack Frederik Wullems (also trading under the name Filmspeler)* [2017] ECLI:EU:C:2017:300, paras 64–72.

[31] van Eechoud *et al* (2009) 84 and Makeen (2000) 301.

[32] Lemley (1997) 568.

[33] Ginsburg (2002) 83.

[34] Depreeuw (2014) 208, para 302.

[35] The initial aim of the temporary copy exception was to neutralise the unwanted side-effects of the broad reproduction right – Institute for Information Law (2007) 31.

preventing overregulation.[36] Despite its importance, it is generally accepted that Article 5(1) is complex[37] and it has even been described as convoluted.[38] Nonetheless, the CJEU established five cumulative criteria that must be satisfied in order to benefit from the exception. The copy must be:

- Temporary;
- Transient or incidental;
- An integral and essential part of a technological process;
- Produced for the sole purpose of enabling a transmission in a network between third parties by an intermediary or a lawful use of a work or protected subject matter; and
- Have no independent economic significance.[39]

Failing to adhere to all five criteria would mean that the copy in question is subject to liability under the broad Article 2 reproduction right. In addition to the five cumulative criteria, the CJEU also held that Article 5(1) must be interpreted strictly.[40] The strict interpretation is for two main reasons. Firstly, the temporary copy exception must adhere to the three-step test as required by Article 5(5), which limits the exception to certain special cases.[41] Secondly, the CJEU in *Infopaq* stated that it is settled case law that any derogation from an established principle must be interpreted strictly.[42] This was followed in *ACI Adam* where the CJEU held that the exceptions and limitations provided in Article 5(2) of the ISD must be interpreted strictly.[43] In addition to the strict interpretation, the CJEU also requires that the temporary copy made is compliant with the individual aspects of the three-step test.[44] Before *PRCA v NLA*, it was assumed that if a copy complied

[36] Aplin (2005) 102.

[37] Article 5(1) is complex because it was a compromise designed to strike a fair balance between right holders and users rather than 'a demarcation logically deducted from the nature of the traditional reproduction right' – Institute for Information Law (2007) 31, citing European Commission, *Communication from the Commission to the European Parliament Concerning the common position of the Council on the adoption of a Directive of the European Parliament and the Council on the harmonisation of certain aspects of copyright and related rights in the Information Society* (SEC(2000) 1734 final, 2000) 3.

[38] H Cohen Jehoram, 'European copyright law ever more horizontal' (2001) 32 *International Review of Intellectual Property and Competition Law (IIC)* 532, 540.

[39] Case C-5/08 *Infopaq International A/S v Danske Dagblades Forening* [2009] ECLI:EU:C:2009:465, paras 54–55.

[40] ibid paras 56–58. Reaffirmed by the CJEU in: Cases C-403/08 and C-429/08 *Football Association Premier League (FAPL) and others v QC Leisure and others* and *Karen Murphy v Media Protection Services Ltd* [2011] ECLI:EU:C:2011:631, paras 162–64, Case C-302/10 *Infopaq International A/S v Danske Dagblades Forening* [2012] ECLI:EU:C:2012:16, para 27 [*Infopaq 2*] and *PRCA v NLA* [2014] paras 23–24. For more discussion on 'strict interpretation' see: Case C-98/06 *Freeport plc v Olle Arnoldsson* [2007] ECLI:EU:C:2007:595, para 35, Case C-145/10 *Eva-Maria Painer v Standard Verlags GMBH and others* [2011] ECLI:EU:C:2011:798, paras 74, 133 and *PRCA v NLA* [2014] para 24.

[41] *Infopaq* [2009] para 58.

[42] ibid para 56.

[43] *ACI Adam* [2014] para 23.

[44] See *PRCA v NLA* [2014] paras 54–62.

with Article 5(1), it automatically satisfied Article 5(5).[45] However, the CJEU in *PRCA v NLA* placed greater reliance on the three-step test by assessing whether web browsing or caching was in accordance with Article 5(5).[46]

Notwithstanding the general approach outlined, it is important to note that the CJEU in *PRCA v NLA* departed from the rigidity of strictly interpreting exceptions.[47] This is because the CJEU considered the practical implications of the decision rather than solely taking a literal approach to the exception. This was a positive development because it allowed the Court to apply a more normative and flexible approach to the temporary copy exception and in doing so, arrive at the correct decision.[48] Furthermore, the CJEU was correct to ensure that the purpose and effectiveness of the exception was upheld. Despite this victory for common sense, *PRCA v NLA* did not remove the root of the overlap problem. The wide reproduction right and the technical framing of the temporary copy exception, coupled with its strict interpretation, remain the law. This approach is antithetical to common sense decision-making and is weighted too much in favour of right holders, given that users must fit within a very limited exception in order to avoid liability for a technical act that is an essential part of using digital works.[49]

But for the CJEU's judicial activism in departing from the strict interpretation of Article 5(1) in *PRCA v NLA*, the outcome could have been detrimental to users of digital works and more generally EU e-commerce. Therefore, it must be said that the current framework for addressing temporary copies is still undesirable despite the decision in *PRCA v NLA*, because it is uncertain whether the CJEU will also depart from the required strict interpretation approach in other cases. If reference is made to *Filmspeler*, the Court in that case held that the Article 5(1) temporary copy exception does not apply to the streaming of unauthorised works on media players preloaded with add-ons to access infringing content.[50] As such, in cases where the consumed work is unauthorised, it is possible that overlapping rights can be invoked. *Filmspeler* therefore demonstrated the undesirable consequences of the existing law, whereby the temporary copy exception was held inapplicable to the use of film players involving unauthorised works.[51]

Furthermore, if *PRCA v NLA* was about a technology not discussed under Recital 33 it is unclear whether the CJEU would depart and, moreover, be justified in departing from the strict interpretation approach. It is important to note that

[45] *Infopaq 2* [2012] para 56.

[46] *PRCA v NLA* [2014] paras 54–62.

[47] Derclaye argues that the inconsistency of the CJEU's decision-making is the inevitable result of the court trying to achieve a reasonable and balanced result in a specific case – E Derclaye, 'The Court of Justice copyright case law: *quo vadis*?' (2014) 36 *EIPR* 716, 722.

[48] James (2014) 171 – James argues that public policy played a role in the decision of the CJEU in convincing them to depart from the strict interpretation approach, as a means of achieving the desired end result.

[49] T Cook and L Brazell, *Copyright Directive: UK Implementation* (Jordan Publishing Ltd, 2004) 20, para 2.44.

[50] *Filmspeler* [2017] para 72.

[51] ibid paras 63–71.

the decision in *PRCA v NLA* was achieved through a purposive and policy-driven use of the three-step test. From a legal certainty stand point it is not desirable to depend on such judicial activism or the subjectivity of the Court in order to reach the correct decision.[52] It would have been more desirable and legally sound to address the overlap problem expressly in the main text of the judgment rather than in the conclusion of the case where the overall decision was being justified by virtue of the three-step test.

Another concern that must be raised is that an overly strict interpretation of Article 5(1) can in effect operate as an access right that would negatively prejudice users as very few transient copies would be exempted.[53] This could raise the costs of using digital works and/or curtail their use; the consequence being that Article 5(1) may fall foul of the aim to achieve a fair balance between right holders and users as designated under Recital 31. and thus conflict with fundamental rights such as access to information and cultural works. Hence, the interpretation of Article 5(1) is stuck between two difficult alternatives. On the one hand, too strict an interpretation of Article 5(1) would render the provision useless to many users and in doing so undermine the use of some forms of technology. On the other hand, achieving desirable results may require a wide interpretation of Article 5(1) that is not in accordance with the traditional strict interpretation approach that is applied to exceptions and other derogations under EU law. Taking the problems with Article 5(1) and its interpretation together, what is required is a rethink of the scope of the reproduction right to avoid the overlap problem completely, rather than mitigating the issue with an exception or through judicial activism.

Aside from the current EU approach to resolving the overlap problem, scholars have made alternative suggestions. Litman has suggested that a positive right for users to read or use works be implemented so that the temporary copies made in the course of using digital works are exempt from copyright liability.[54] This suggestion would not be a desirable solution because it merely sidesteps the problem by patching the existing law rather than solving the root of the problem; that is, the scope of the reproduction right. Westkamp adopted a different perspective and questioned whether copyright law should develop into a comprehensive access or 'use right'.[55] Several authors have developed this idea of an access right.[56]

[52] The inconsistencies of CJEU decision-making make it difficult to predict the future direction of EU copyright law – Derclaye (2014) 722.

[53] Aplin (2011) 213, Westkamp (2004) 1103 and E Derclaye, 'Infopaq International A/S v Danske Dagblades Forening (C-5/08): wonderful or worrisome? The impact of the ECJ ruling in Infopaq on UK copyright law' (2010) 32(5) *EIPR* 247, 251.

[54] Litman (2001) 183 and Ginsburg (2002) 85.

[55] Westkamp (2004) 1058.

[56] See Z Efroni, *Access Right: The Future of Digital Copyright Law* (Oxford University Press, 2011), Westkamp (2004), J Ginsburg, 'Essay: From Having Copies to Experiencing Works: The Development of an Access Right in US Copyright Law' (2003) 50 *Journal of the Copyright Society of the USA (J Copyright Soc'y USA)* 113, M Landeau, 'Has the Digital Millennium Copyright Act Really Created a New Exclusive Right of Access?: Attempting to Reach a Balance Between Users' and Content Providers'

However, it would mean a reorganisation or abandonment of the traditional copyright framework and as such, would be too ambitious an approach for the EU to pursue given the already existing discrepancies between the common law copyright countries and the civil law *droit d'auteur* countries. Alternatively, Lemley discussed the adoption of a right of net transmission where communications made over the Internet are solely addressed by that right, as opposed to the traditional reproduction or public performance rights. However, this proposal in its entirety is not helpful because the communication to the public right already covers Internet transmissions. Only the latter aspect of the suggestion is useful: the reproduction right should be restricted from applying to copies made in the course of Internet transmissions.[57]

Makeen also makes a similar suggestion to Lemley. He argued that the scope of the reproduction right should not be expanded to address digital works on the Internet or, more generally, copying in non-material form. Makeen suggested that to apply the reproduction right instead of or alongside the communication to the public right to cover the use of online works would be incorrect because the intention of right holders placing their works online is to communicate them rather than reproduce them.[58] As a result, the logical approach is to rely solely on the communication to the public right or else risk a reappraisal of the categorisation of exclusive rights in copyright law.[59] He went on to state that the support for the use of the reproduction right on the Internet by collecting societies is fuelled by the self-interest of earning more revenue, potentially through double dipping.[60] However, Lemley and Makeen's suggestions only address part of the overlap problem. In order to completely solve this problem a more holistic redefinition of the scope of the reproduction right is needed,[61] such as that proposed by the Wittem Group: 'The right of reproduction is the right to reproduce the work in any manner or form, including temporary reproduction insofar as it has independent economic significance.'[62]

The Wittem Group's proposed provision maintains the core of the existing reproduction right and adds a 'carve out' for exempting certain temporary copies from the scope of the right, in lieu of the temporary copy exception under Article 5(1).[63] It does this by expressly using the language of the fifth criterion of Article 5(1), as well as implicitly adopting the 'lawful use' aspect of the fourth

Rights' (2002) 49 *J Copyright Soc'y USA* 277, Litman (1995), S Olswang, 'Accessright: an evolutionary path for copyright into the digital era?' (1995) 17 *EIPR* 215 and T Heide, 'Copyright in the EU and US: What "Access-Right"?' (2001) 48 *J Copyright Soc'y USA* 363.

[57] Lemley (1997) 582–83. Makeen also holds this opinion – Makeen (2000) 308.

[58] Makeen (2000) 311–12 – copyright consistency argument.

[59] ibid 312–313.

[60] ibid 312.

[61] Depreeuw also shares this viewpoint – Depreeuw (2014) 233 para 332.

[62] See Wittem Group, 'European Copyright Code' (2011) 33(2) *EIPR* 76. A similar approach to exempting temporary copies is also adopted in the Dutch Copyright Act 1912 (as amended) under Article 13a of the Auteurswet.

[63] Wittem Group (2011) fn 46.

criterion in its interpretation of the term 'independent'.[64] In one way this can be seen as adopting the approach that temporary copies made for the purpose of ordinary uses of works do not have 'independent economic significance'. For example, the temporary copies made in the course of watching or listening to a work should not constitute an act of reproduction because those temporary copies are not made/used for any additional or alternative use. Applying this approach to the *Filmspeler* situation should produce a finding of no reproduction infringement even though the works were unauthorised, because the temporary copies were not of any independent economic significance; that is, the users of the film players were not deriving any economic benefit from the temporary copies. Economic benefit could, however, be derived from making additional copies or making the unauthorised work available to the public.

The Wittem Group notes that the rule of Article 5(1) is absorbed into the 'carve out' of the proposed reproduction right.[65] This suggests that the five criteria of Article 5(1) are still relevant in determining whether a temporary copy is an actionable reproduction. But, the application of the Article 5(1) criteria will be contributory indications of 'independent economic significance' rather than being a cumulative test as is the case under Article 5(1). Despite this, it would seem that the Wittem Group's reproduction right abandons the technical approach and criteria of Article 5(1) (the first three criteria) and instead, focuses on the purpose ('lawful use') for which the temporary copy was made and its economic significance to the responsible individual. Nonetheless, the Wittem Group's suggestion is still incapable of preventing overlap with the communication to the public right if emphasis is placed on the unauthorised nature of works, leading to a finding of unlawful use as in *Filmspeler*.[66]

In order for the Wittem proposal to be effective, the concept of unlawful use has to be interpreted more broadly to address the purpose of the use rather than the nature of the work; that is, authorised or unauthorised. Furthermore, it is necessary to adopt the Wittem Group proposal in tandem with Lemley and Makeen's suggestion to solely apply the communication to the public right in cases involving digital dissemination of works. However, to develop a more comprehensive right, it is suggested that the reformed communication to the public right should be the sole applicable right in cases involving the non-material dissemination of works to a geographically dispersed 'public'. This approach will ensure that there is no overlap between the reproduction and communication to the public rights

[64] ibid fn 45.

[65] ibid fn 43.

[66] Quintais and Rendas describe this as a requirement of lawfulness of source, which only privileges copies made from lawful sources – JP Quintais and T Rendas, 'EU copyright law and the Cloud: *VCAST* and the intersection of private copying and communication to the public' (2018) 13(9) *Journal of Intellectual Property Law & Practice (JIPLP)* 711, 717. Also see: *ACI Adam* [2014] paras 20–58, Case C-463/12 *Copydan Båndkopi v Nokia Danmark A/S* [2015] ECLI:EU:C:2015:144, paras 74–79 and Case C-572/13 *Hewlett-Packard Belgium SPRL v Reprobel SCRL* [2015] ECLI:EU:C:2015:750, paras 57–64.

and, furthermore, no conflation of acts of communication to the public and public performance. As a result, it is important to emphasise that the communication to the public right only applies in cases where the 'public' is geographically dispersed from the act of 'communication'.

Despite these recommendations, approaching such a reform is difficult. Although a holistic reform of the reproduction right is desirable, this may be deemed too ambitious an approach.[67] However, it is essential to pursue this reform to ensure that content distributors and end users are not subjected to overregulation. Furthermore, adopting the proposed approach will establish a better balanced framework, accounting for all the various competing interests and pressures. In order to achieve this result, the best method of implementation in the short term will be to add a recital to the ISD clearly stating that acts of non-material dissemination made to a geographically dispersed 'public' that invoke the communication to the public right should be excluded from the scope of the reproduction right. This approach will allow the reproduction right to remain applicable to digital acts of copying that are not made to a 'public'; that is, a fairly large and indeterminate number of people. Consequently, right holders will have adequate protection of their works online.

C. Distribution and Communication to the Public

The conflict between the distribution and communication to the public rights originated with the use of the distribution right under the Computer Programs Directive to address the online resale of used software in *Usedsoft v Oracle*.[68] This is an issue because there is no communication to the public right under the Computer Programs Directive and consequently, there is uncertainty as to how the online dissemination of computer programs should be addressed. If it is the case that the distribution right was extended online to compensate for the lack of a communication to the public right under the Computer Programs Directive, the resultant conflict is primarily to do with the online exhaustion of the distribution right. This is because the communication to the public right is not subject to online exhaustion.[69] Thus, it is necessary to clarify the scope of the distribution right under the Computer Programs Directive and under the ISD and in doing so, to clarify the role of the communication to the public right in relation to software and more generally to the resale of digital works online. With this in mind, the recommendation that the communication to the public right should be the sole applicable right governing the dissemination of digital works to a 'public' will be followed.

[67] A fuller discussion on the reform of the reproduction right exceeds the scope of this book, which focuses on the development of the communication to the public right.

[68] *Usedsoft v Oracle* [2012] paras 59 and 61.

[69] Public Consultation on the review of the EU copyright rules (2014) 13.

The CJEU expanded the distribution right under the Computer Programs Directive to address the instance of the online resale of a computer program because the act of selling and reselling computer programs online was considered analogous to the tangible sale of a computer program on a CD or DVD.[70] However, it should be noted that the 'resale' was actually about the transfer of the licence to use the computer program from the initial buyer to a new buyer. Thus, the copyright work was not directly involved. Instead, the licence being transferred was simply the means to render the computer program usable.[71] From this perspective the transfer of the licence for money was akin to a typical act of resale.[72] Given the analogy adopted by the Court, it is questionable whether it was necessary to engage in the discussion concerning the online exhaustion of the distribution right and, furthermore, it must be asked why the communication to the public right under the ISD was exhausted in relation to the resale of software online.[73]

In reaching its decision, the CJEU in *Usedsoft* concluded that the downloading of the computer program from the claimant's website and the sale of the user licence formed an indivisible whole[74] and moreover, amounted to a transfer in ownership of the software copy in question.[75] The Court also reasoned that the situation was a *lex specialis* so that the Article 4(2) distribution right under the Computer Programs Directive should apply even though the Article 3(1) communication to the public right under the ISD could apply.[76] Furthermore, the finding that ownership of the software copy transferred from Oracle to the user meant that the communication to the public right would no longer be applicable. However, this interpretation of the factual scenario is wrong because the Court incorrectly exhausted the right holder's ability to enforce the communication to the public right.[77] The Court's decision is underlined by the assumption that each copy of the software is its own separate work and as such when it is purchased by a consumer, the transfer of ownership means that Oracle's exclusive rights are

[70] *Usedsoft v Oracle* [2012] para 47. Benabou argues that it is dangerous to apply analogical reasoning between analogue and digital exhaustion because the nature of the goods is different, rival versus non-rival, respectively. As such, the application of exhaustion would not have the same impact – V Benabou, 'Digital Exhaustion of Copyright in the EU or Shall We Cease Being so Schizophrenic' in I Stamatoudi (ed), *New Developments in EU and International Copyright Law* (Kluwer Law International BV, 2016) 356.

[71] *Usedsoft v Oracle* [2012] para 26.

[72] Bechtold argued that the CJEU's decision in *Usedsoft* was demonstrative of a functional approach which allowed the Court to expand the existing law to arrive at the 'right' conclusion – S Bechtold, 'Deconstructing Copyright' in PB Hugenholtz (ed), *Copyright Reconstructed: Rethinking Copyright's Economic Rights in a Time of Highly Dynamic and Technological and Economic Change* (Kluwer Law International BV, 2018) 70.

[73] For discussion on *Usedsoft* and online exhaustion, see P Mysoor, 'Exhaustion, non-exhaustion and implied licence' (2018) 49(6) *IIC* 656, 677–80.

[74] *Usedsoft v Oracle* [2012] para 44.

[75] ibid para 52.

[76] ibid para 51.

[77] ibid para 52.

transferred/exhausted in relation to that *copy*. However, this fails to take into account the fact that what is sold is merely a copy of the original work that is retained by Oracle.[78]

The CJEU's finding that Oracle could not stop the resale of the used computer program licences was correct.[79] However, the exclusion/exhaustion of the communication to the public right was incorrect regardless of what justification was provided, because Article 3(3) of the ISD precludes the exhaustion of the right. Moreover, the absence of a communication to the public right under the Computer Programs Directive meant that the Article 3(1) communication to the public right under the ISD would remain applicable despite the ISD being designated without prejudice to the Computer Programs Directive. Consequently, the distribution right under the Computer Programs Directive should merely take precedence over the ISD rather than precluding the applicability of the communication to the public right.[80]

The root of the problem with the decision in *Usedsoft* and its consequential uncertainty was the Court's failure to differentiate the two different acts of making the computer program available and selling the licence to use the computer program (on Oracle's website). This is an important distinction to make for the act of reselling the computer program because the resale by Usedsoft only involved the licence; the computer program itself was not directly involved in the resale. Hence, it was unnecessary to discuss the communication to the public right or raise any discussion concerning online exhaustion of the distribution right. The traditional principles concerning the distribution right, including exhaustion, could have been directly applicable. Had copies of Oracle's software been provided together with the licences by Usedsoft, the situation would have been different and would only then have raised questions of actual online exhaustion of the *work* and/or the applicability of the communication to the public right.[81]

Notwithstanding the above arguments, the issues raised in *Usedsoft* are of more general importance. The extension of the distribution right online for computer programs or any other subject-matter and the inclusion of online exhaustion will conflict with the proposed reformed right of communication to the public. The traditional exclusive rights were designed to address specific forms of exploitation. The distribution right was designed to address the material dissemination of tangible copies of works, whereas the communication to the public right was designed to cover the non-material dissemination of works. Therefore, allowing the distribution right to address all dissemination of intangible copies will create

[78] The CJEU's findings in *Usedsoft* has caused a reaction in the software industry whereby there has been a shift toward service-based subscriptions in lieu of permanent licences – Benabou in Stamatoudi (2016) 358.

[79] *Usedsoft v Oracle* [2012] para 72.

[80] See Article 1(2)(a) of the ISD.

[81] Benabou argued that exhaustion in the digital sphere requires simplicity and predictability and as such, it only makes sense where the user has acquired 'ownership' of the work in the analogue sense – Benabou in Stamatoudi (2016) 377.

legal uncertainty by blurring the distinction between the two rights, creating overlap. In addition, such an approach will be in contravention of the recommendation that the communication to the public right should be the only exclusive right applicable to the dissemination of digital works to a 'public'.

Consequently, it is important to clarify that the *Usedsoft* decision should not affect the application of the communication to the public right. Furthermore, in the interests of ensuring that the scope of the exclusive rights is proportionately balanced and that there is legal certainty and consistency, especially where there are namesake rights across Directives, it is necessary to limit the extension of the distribution right so that it is not applied to the online dissemination of copies where a 'public' is involved. However, this is not to say that the use of the distribution right online will be negligible. In the context of reselling digital works online, there will often be no act of 'communication to the public' because the 'communication' or 'public' aspect is not met. For example, in the *Usedsoft* situation, the communication to the public right will not be infringed because Usedsoft did not actually 'communicate' the work; they only provided the user licence to make the software operable. Conversely, had Usedsoft made available the software in conjunction with the licence, this could have potentially constituted an act of 'communication to the public'.

Alternatively, if the factual scenario concerned the resale of a computer program from one private individual to another, this will not constitute an act of communication to the public because there is no 'public'. As such, the distribution right retains value in private one-on-one scenarios and is distinguished from the making available aspect of the right of communication to the public.[82] In conclusion, right holders should not be able to stop the online resale of legitimately purchased digital works. However, this does not equate to an exhaustion of their other exclusive rights because this will destroy the market for right holders.[83]

D. Exceptions and Limitations and Communication to the Public

The exhaustive list of exceptions and limitations applicable to the right of communication to the public are found under Article 5(3) of the ISD. In light of the changes proposed via the reformed right of communication to the public, it is possible that the list of exceptions and limitations will also have to be amended.[84]

[82] ibid 371–72.

[83] ibid 354 and 378. However, Benabou notes that the reproduction right should not apply in instances of online exhaustion because the distribution right would have already covered the transaction. This is true, but should be framed within the parameters of the single transaction and not subsequent copies – ibid 375.

[84] A fuller discussion of exceptions and limitations exceeds the scope of this book. The emphasis here is placed on clarifying the exclusive right. Accordingly, only suggestions are made as to the further development of exceptions and limitations.

Article 5(3) provides general exceptions and limitations that are applicable to both the communication to the public and reproduction rights. It should be recalled that the reformed right omitted the 'new public' and 'for profit' criteria, as well as limiting the interpretation of 'communication' to acts of transmission or provision of the work. The scope of the reformed right is narrower and simpler than the existing right of communication to the public. However, the introduction of the 'organisation other than the original one' criterion for acts of subsequent communication does make it easier to establish an act of communication to the public. This is because any act of 'subsequent communication' by a third party without authorisation will amount to an act of communication to the public.

Therefore, if the EU legislature desires to further limit the applicability of the communication to the public right, it was mentioned in Chapter three, section VII.A that the concept of 'for profit' may still have a role to play, at least normatively, in defining the scope of the communication to the public right or determining whether a party should be held liable for infringement. It is possible that a refined version of the 'for profit' concept can be a latent consideration by the CJEU or alternatively, it can form the basis for an express exception. Similarly, in Chapter three, section VI.A it was mentioned that the concept of 'new public' could also be developed into an exception. Should the EU legislature wish to further develop the exceptions and limitations for the communication to the public right, these two concepts may be a good starting point. Alternatively, the CJEU can use the three-step test as a general exception to achieve the end goal of limiting a party's liability under the communication to the public right where necessary.

The three-step test is already legislated for under Article 5(5) of the ISD. However, Article 5(5) is limited to an interpretation tool to ensure that the exhaustive list of exceptions and limitations under Articles 5(2) and (3) are interpreted in a restricted manner that does not unfairly prejudice right holders.[85] Despite this, the three-step test has been used at the domestic level by several Member States as a flexible test where there is no specific applicable provision.[86] This will offer a flexible means to restrict the imposition of liability in cases where would-be infringers should not face liability. This is because the constitution of the three-step test involves carefully determined criteria aimed at balancing the interests of right holders and users. As such, it takes account of what amounts to normal uses of the work and the impact of that use on the right holder, and moreover, restricts the context to special cases.[87]

[85] See *FAPL v QC Leisure* [2011] para 181, *Filmspeler* [2017] para 63 and Case C-256/16 *VCAST Ltd v RTI SpA* [2017] ECLI:EU:C:2017:913, para 31. Also see Recital 44 of the ISD.

[86] Such EU countries include: Croatia, France, Spain, Portugal and Greece. Mexico and Australia have also adopted the test. See D Gervais, *(Re)structuring Copyright: A Comprehensive Path to International Copyright Reform* (Edward Elgar Publishing Ltd, 2017) 73–74.

[87] Further development of exceptions and limitations for the right of communication to the public exceeds the scope of this book.

IV. Completing the Harmonisation of the Communication to the Public Right

The right of communication to the public was developed in a piecemeal fashion across four Directives and the extensive case law of the CJEU, as demonstrated in Chapter two. In furtherance of the EU's harmonisation agenda for copyright law and the achievement of a communication to the public right that is proportionately balanced and certain, it is necessary to complete the harmonisation of the right. The ideal recommendation would be that the reformed communication to the public right is codified in a copyright regulation in a neutral manner so that it is applicable to all forms of copyright and related subject-matter regardless of the technology involved.[88] However, the difficulty of achieving this may prove prohibitive and consequently, a more viable approach in the short term will be discussed first.

It is advocated that the right of communication to the public should be codified in one provision under the ISD and should be equally applicable to all types of subject-matter, including related rights, and be technology-neutral.[89] Such an approach will ensure a non-discriminatory and adequate level of protection for all types of right holders. Additionally, it will ensure certainty because the communication to the public right will be subject to consistent interpretations in all contexts. Adopting this approach is justifiable and compatible with the necessary copyright considerations; notably, the international copyright obligations of the EU via the Berne Convention and WIPO Copyright Treaty because those Treaties provide for minimum rights. Therefore, it is possible and indeed desirable to provide for a greater level of protection, especially in the context of the removal of compulsory licensing.

The issue of upward harmonisation was dealt with by the CJEU in *C More Entertainment*, where it was held that Member States are free to provide a greater level of protection than that provided under the Directives.[90] Thus, Member States are free to provide exclusive rights instead of compulsory licensing. However, this must be interpreted in accordance with the CJEU's earlier finding in *Svensson* that 'communication to the public' should not be interpreted to include a wider range of acts than those provided under Article 3 of the ISD.[91] Notwithstanding the

[88] Adopting a codified form of the reformed communication to the public right under a regulation is the preferred method of harmonisation because regulations are the strongest instruments available under EU law other than the Treaties themselves – F Gotzen, 'The European Legislator's Strategy in the Field of Copyright Harmonization' in T Synodinou (ed), *Codification of European Copyright Law: Challenges and Perspectives* (Kluwer Law International, 2012) 46.

[89] Gotzen describes the amendment of the ISD as the most straightforward approach to further harmonisation or codification of EU copyright law – ibid 51.

[90] Case C-279/13 *C More Entertainment AB v Linus Sandberg* [2015] ECLI:EU:C:2015:99, paras 35–37.

[91] Case C-466/12 *Nils Svensson and others v Retriever Sverige AB* [2014] ECLI:EU:C:2014:76, para 33.

maximal harmonisation of the scope of the communication to the public right, this does not affect the upward harmonisation of the right, which is justified given its pursuit of furthering the internal market, an EU Treaty objective. Consequently, the proposal to adopt a single harmonised communication to the public right under one Directive is attainable.

In proposing a single harmonised right of communication to the public for all subject-matter, it is necessary to justify the individual aspects in more detail. In the first place it is essential to highlight that the reformed communication to the public right is available for both copyright works and related subject-matter. This is not an overly controversial issue under EU copyright law because Article 3 of the ISD already contains provisions on both copyright and related subject-matter. But, there may be some concern in adopting this approach because copyright and related rights at the international level have traditionally been separate, as per the Berne Convention and the Rome Convention and the WCT and WPPT. However, this should not prove to be an insurmountable issue because the protection of copyright and of related rights have been conflated before, for example, in the UK Copyright, Designs and Patents Act (CDPA) 1988.

Secondly, the subject-matter-specific approach of EU copyright law should be abandoned in relation to the communication to the public right. It is necessary to make it expressly clear that all subject-matter is covered by a single communication to the public right. Aside from the Satellite and Cable Retransmission Directive, Database Directive, Rental and Lending Right Directive and the ISD, there is also the Computer Programs Directive to consider. As such, the reformed communication to the public right should expressly address all copyright and related subject-matter, including databases and computer programs, in a single provision. This aggregated communication to the public right has special significance for computer programs because there is no right of communication to the public under the Computer Programs Directive. It can be argued that the ISD *does* supplement the protection afforded by the Computer Programs Directive because it is without prejudice to the existing provisions of the Computer Programs Directive.[92] Therefore, the protection granted under the ISD can only step in where the Computer Programs Directive does not provide protection, as in the case of the communication to the public right. A similar approach should be adopted for the other Directives, as the complete harmonisation of the communication to the public right must be accompanied by the express removal of any provisions concerning communication to the public. In other words, the reformed communication to the public right should be codified under the ISD.[93] This should be clarified in an express manner for the avoidance of doubt.

[92] See Article (2)(a) of the ISD.

[93] See P Jougleux, 'The Plurality of Legal Systems in Copyright Law: An Obstacle to a European Codification?' in T Synodinou (ed), *Codification of European Copyright Law: Challenges and Perspectives* (Kluwer Law International, 2012) 58–60.

Thirdly, it is important that the communication to the public right is an unfettered, exclusive right. This is in the interest of securing a high level of protection for right holders. As a result, there will be no requirement of payment of an entrance fee to make the right actionable as in Article 8(3) of the Rental and Lending Right Directive. Furthermore, Article 8(2) of the Rental and Lending Right Directive must be abolished so that there is no possibility of a compulsory licensing mechanism. There are no anticipated problems with these suggested changes from a practical perspective because the means through which the communication to the public and public performance of works are licensed already exist. Collecting societies already play a significant role in the licensing of copyright works; therefore, the abolition of the compulsory licensing mechanism is not expected to cause any alterations to the way works – in particular, phonograms/music – are licensed. It may be the case that broadcasters oppose this suggestion; however, the works that they use can also be subject to collective licensing in the interest of avoiding individual negotiations with right holders.

The reformed communication to the public right should comprise one provision governing all the types of copyright and related rights works, including computer programs and databases, with no compulsory licensing mechanism.[94] Adopting this approach eliminates the possibility of inconsistent interpretation of the communication to the public right across Directives and ensures a high level of protection for right holders. It also ensures greater legal certainty because there is only one provision on communication to the public which is applicable to all types of copyright and related subject-matter. Additionally, the removal of the compulsory licensing mechanism will not be detrimental to users because the mechanism of collective licensing is already available.[95] Although harmonising the right into a single provision is an ambitious project, it is possible through Article 118 of the TFEU[96] and will be given impetus by the EU's pursuit of a digital single market.[97]

[94] This approach is similar to that provided under the Wittem Group's European Copyright Code – see Articles 1.1 and 4.5.

[95] It should be noted that the EU legislature is moving in the direction of mandating the use of collective management organisations in certain contexts – see Article 3 of European Commission, *Proposal for a Regulation of the European Parliament and of the Council laying down rules on the exercise of copyright and related rights applicable to certain online transmissions of broadcasting organisations and retransmissions of television and radio programmes* (COM(2016) 594 final, 2016).

[96] Consolidated Version of the Treaty on the Functioning of the European Union (2012).

[97] PB Hugenholtz, 'The Wittem Group's European Copyright Code' in T Synodinou (ed), *Codification of European Copyright Law: Challenges and Perspectives* (Kluwer Law International, 2012) 353 and R Hilty, 'Reflections on a European Copyright Codification' in T Synodinou (ed), *Codification of European Copyright Law: Challenges and Perspectives* (Kluwer Law International, 2012) 356–57. Also see European Commission, *Communication from the Commission to the European Parliament, the Council, the European Economic and Social Committee and the Committee of the Regions: A Digital Single Market Strategy for Europe* (COM(2015) 192 final, 2015).

A. A More Ambitious Approach to Harmonisation

It was suggested above that the most achievable mode of completely harmonising the reformed communication to the public right would be through the codification of a single provision under the existing ISD. This approach is easily workable because it respects the traditions of the Member States by allowing them to implement the right provided under the ISD on their own terms. However, the consequence of this is that there is the possibility of transposition or implementation errors, which in turn compromise the achievement of uniform protection and thus the furthering of the internal market.[98] As such, it is suggested that a greater level of harmonisation is required for true, complete harmonisation of the communication to the public right; otherwise less than ideal results would ensue.[99]

The alternative harmonisation option is the codification of the communication to the public right under a copyright regulation.[100] The unification of EU copyright law is not discussed because it is too ambitious an approach in the current context.[101] This is because the unification route for copyright law will require significant political desire and will entail extensive negotiations over the substance and form of the unified framework, which is unlikely to be limited to aspects of copyright law. EU copyright unification will have to include other areas, such as moral rights, enforcement, contracting and collective rights management.[102] It is also the case that there will be a need for transitional measures to facilitate the movement from national copyright and *droit d'auteur* laws to the unified framework.[103] If these reasons are added to the lessons learnt from copyright law-making at the international level, it is clear that the process of unification is a formidable task; notably, because of the plurality of constitutional and copyright interests that must be taken account of at the EU level. In particular,

[98] Hugenholtz argues that the mode of harmonisation via Directives employed by the EU is subject to more far-reaching problems including: inefficient reaction times, ratcheting of domestic legislation to meet EU requirements, and legal uncertainty. See PB Hugenholtz, 'Is Harmonization a Good Thing? The case of the Copyright *Acquis*' in A Ohly and J Pila (eds), *The Europeanization of Intellectual Property Law* (Oxford University Press, 2013) 64–67.

[99] Hilty in Synodinou (2012) 357.

[100] The unification of EU copyright law is not discussed in this book because it is too ambitious an approach. However, see the European Copyright Society's letter to Günther Oettinger, the Commissioner for Digital Economy and Society – European Copyright Society, 'Unification of copyright law' <http://www.ivir.nl/syscontent/pdfs/78.pdf> accessed 10 August 2016, Gotzen in Synodinou (2012) 52, Hilty in Synodinou (2012) 356–63 and E Derclaye and T Cook, 'An EU Copyright Code: what and how, if ever? [2011] 3 *IPQ* 259.

[101] Derclaye and Cook suggest that EU copyright unification would make the previous harmonization measures seem 'extremely easy by comparison' – Derclaye and Cook (2011) 269. Alternatively, Strowel describes it as a more ambitious project – A Strowel, 'Towards a European Copyright Law: Four Issues to Consider' in I Stamatoudi and P Torremans (eds), *EU Copyright Law: A Commentary* (Edward Elgar Publishing Ltd, 2014) para 21.28.

[102] Hilty in Synodinou (2012) 359–72.

[103] Derclaye and Cook (2011) 262–64.

balancing the interests of the copyright and *droit d'auteur* countries will be difficult, as experienced at the international level.[104] This is compounded by the fact that unification necessarily involves a substantial loss of autonomy in terms of copyright law-making.[105]

Therefore, it is suggested that a non-unifying codification process under a regulation would be a more achievable goal and should be pursued in the long run.[106] The regulation option is desirable because it removes the potential concerns about transposition and implementation errors that affect the directive approach and, moreover, is not limited to unification measures.[107] Regulations unlike directives, are directly binding on Member States so that there is no need to implement the provisions of the regulation through legislation.[108] This is in the interest of furthering the internal market and the harmonisation agenda for EU copyright law because it limits the possibility of divergent interpretations or applications of the law facilitated by liberal or incorrect implementation of EU law.[109] A regulation requires all Member States to apply the right using the same wording and structure provided in the proposed regulation. Furthermore, adopting the reformed communication to the public right under a regulation is unlikely to unreasonably prejudice the copyright and *droit d'auteur* traditions of the Member States, because these interests will be taken into account in the conceptualisation and legislation of the proposed regulation. Moreover, those interests are already embedded in the reformed right of communication to the public.

Lastly, it is also important to note that the possibility of codifying the communication to the public right in a regulation is plausible given that its adoption would only require a qualified majority (55 per cent majority) in favour.[110] This is facilitated by Article 118 of the Treaty on the Functioning of the European Union (TFEU). Therefore, it is recommended that in the long run the reformed

[104] Should the UK leave the EU, it is arguable that unification may become more attainable. However, there will still be other common law copyright countries such as Ireland and additionally, not all the *droit d'auteur* countries are the same. For example, France and Germany have different *droit d'auteur* frameworks.

[105] Hilty in Synodinou (2012) 359.

[106] See Strowel in Stamatoudi and Torremans (2014) paras 21.25–21.27.

[107] Adopting the codified communication to the public right under a regulation would not mean unification because the territoriality of copyright remains unaffected. A similar non-unifying regulation approach was adopted in Regulation (EC) No 469/2009 of the European Parliament and of the Council of 6 May 2009 concerning the supplementary protection certificate for medicinal products (codified version).

[108] P Craig and G de Búrca, *EU Law: Text Cases, and Materials*, 6th edn (Oxford University Press, 2015) 107, D Chalmers, G Davies and G Monti, *European Union Law*, 3rd edn (Cambridge University Press, 2014) 112, 'Regulations, Directives and other acts' <https://europa.eu/european-union/law/legal-acts_en> accessed 10 August 2016 and 'Applying EU law' <http://ec.europa.eu/info/law-making-process/applying-eu-law_en> accessed 10 August 2016.

[109] Gotzen in Synodinou (2012) 51–52.

[110] 'Qualified majority voting and the ordinary legislative procedure' <http://eur-lex.europa.eu/legal-content/EN/TXT/?uri=URISERV:ai0015> accessed 10 August 2016 and E Rosati, 'Towards an EU-wide copyright? (Judicial) pride and (legislative) prejudice' [2013] *IPQ* 47, 66.

communication to the public right should be codified in a new copyright regulation, given the benefits it holds for ensuring legal certainty.[111]

B. Other Issues in Need of Harmonisation

In addition to the codification of the reformed right of communication to the public, it is also necessary to harmonise the public performance right and secondary liability under EU copyright law. Given the proposed adjustments to the scope of the communication to the public right it is necessary to harmonise these two other areas to limit the gaps in the law. In fact, it is such gaps which actually influenced the unjustifiable expansion of the communication to the public right in the first place. Therefore, developing a coherent right of communication to the public requires significant adjustments to the scope of the existing EU copyright framework as demonstrated in this chapter.[112]

V. Conclusion

This chapter addressed the general issues concerning the EU copyright framework in which the reformed communication to the public right will be based. This included reconciling the reformed communication to the public right with the existing reproduction and distribution rights and exceptions and limitations. It was advocated that the reformed right of communication to the public should be the sole exclusive right applicable to acts of non-material disseminations made to a geographically dispersed 'public'. It was also discussed that to complete the harmonisation of the reformed communication to the public right, it is necessary to codify the right. In the short term the codification should be done under the ISD, but the more preferable long-run approach would be the adoption of a copyright regulation including the codified reformed right.

[111] A regulation is achievable given that it exists for EU trade mark law.

[112] Given that focus is placed on the communication to the public right, in-depth discussion on the other aspects of EU copyright law exceeds the scope of this book.

5

Locating and Establishing Responsibility for the Act of Communication to the Public

I. Introduction

Following the critique of the existing right of communication to the public in Chapters two and three and the subsequent proposal of a reformed right of communication to the public in Chapter four, it is necessary to clarify where the act of 'communication to the public' occurs and who is responsible for that act because this has not been expressly addressed in the existing law.[1] This issue is important because it has implications for the application and enforcement of the right, especially in relation to establishing jurisdiction and applicable law, which will be discussed in Chapter six. Therefore, it is necessary to localise where the act of communication to the public occurs and provide a clear means of establishing who is the responsible party.

Under the current EU legislation pertaining to the communication to the public right, only the Satellite and Cable Retransmission Directive expressly states where the act of communication to the public occurs. Article 1(2)(b) of the Satellite and Cable Retransmission Directive indicates that the act occurs in the country where the broadcast is emitted. However, no equivalent provision exists for the general communication to the public right under the ISD or the communication to the public right for related subject-matter under the Rental and Lending Right Directive. Hence, it is an open question where the act occurs, particularly because the Article 3 communication to the public right under the ISD is wider in scope given that it includes the making available aspect. In order to determine where the act of 'communication to the public' occurs, including its making available aspect, it is recommended that the place of localisation incorporates both aspects of the communication to the public right: transmission and reception. Consequently, the act should be localised in the country(ies) of reception. This is necessary because the reformed communication to the public right requires an act of transmission or provision of the work plus potential reception.

[1] European Commission, *Public Consultation on the review of the EU copyright rules* (2014) 10–11.

In terms of who is responsible for the act of communication to the public, it is assumed that the communicator of the work is responsible. However, it is unclear what action is required to make a person the communicator. In the existing case law, the communicator is taken to mean the person or organisation who intervenes to give access to the protected work.[2] Determining who is responsible is fairly uncomplicated in cases involving broadcasting organisations and hotels where traditional and analogue forms of communication to the public are involved, such as terrestrial broadcasting, satellite broadcasting and cable retransmission. However, in digital contexts such as on the Internet, the situation is not as clear. For example, if a person uploads a photograph subject to copyright on his private website and that website is subsequently hacked allowing the hacker to embed the photograph on another website, who is responsible for the act of communication to the public? In such a scenario, it is recommended that the person responsible should be the hacker who breached the private website's security because it is the hacker who actively initiates the 'communication'. In this way, passive parties, including intermediaries and end users who do not actively participate in *providing* the work to the public, are absolved from liability. This is an important development in the interest of preventing unwarranted overregulation of business models and technologies that passively interact with the dissemination of copyright works.

Therefore, it is advocated that the person responsible for an act of communication to the public should be the person who actively initiates the 'communication' of the work. As for where the act occurs, it should be localised in the country(ies) of reception so as to account for the complete act of the transmission or provision of the work plus potential reception.

II. Where Does the Act of Communication to the Public Occur?

It has never been expressly stated where the act of 'communication to the public' occurs due to the fact that the right remains undefined in the existing legislation. At the time the communication to the public right was first introduced under the Rome Revision of the Berne Convention in 1928, there was no real issue of cross-border infringement. Despite developments in technology, the framework of the right was never updated to specify where the act occurs despite the possibility of cross-border infringement. Instead, where the act occurs has been interpreted by way of the theories used to establish the applicable law. This practice still exists. However, it is proposed that the question of where the act of communication to the public occurs should be separate to the determination of applicable law.

[2] Case C-306/05 *Sociedad General de Autores y Editores de España (SGAE) v Rafael Hoteles SL* [2006] ECLI:EU:C:2006:764, para 42.

Nonetheless, it is important to look at the traditional theories that establish the applicable law because they provide guidance about where the act of communication to the public should occur.[3]

The first discussion, both at the international and EU levels, concerning the issue of locating the act of communication to the public was in relation to traditional broadcasting and satellite broadcasting. Despite the absence of any express law on this issue at the international level, the EU chose to adopt a modified version of the Emission theory in determining where the act of satellite broadcasting occurs under the Satellite and Cable Retransmission Directive 1993.[4] Article 1(2)(b) of the Satellite and Cable Retransmission Directive, prima facie, suggests that the act of communication to the public by satellite broadcast occurs in the country of emission, thus following the Emission theory.[5] However, Makeen argues that the Satellite and Cable Retransmission Directive did not strictly adopt the Emission theory because aspects of the Communication theory were also incorporated.[6] Notwithstanding this, the issue of where the general right of communication to the public takes place has been left unaddressed at both the EU and international levels due to the fact that the right has been left undefined.[7] It has been proposed in this book that the reformed communication to the public right should be defined as an act of transmission or provision of the work plus potential reception.

From the above definition, it is possible that the place where the act occurs can be interpreted from the perspective of the place where the transmission originated or the places where the reception is potentially receivable or actually received. However, a distinction must be made in instances involving interventions by third parties for the purpose of making subsequent communications, as was the case in *Rafael Hoteles*. Subsequent acts of 'communication', such as cable retransmission, amount to a separate act of communication to the public different from the initial 'communication'; that is, the broadcast. As such, where the initial 'communication' occurs and where the subsequent 'communication' occurs is different. This distinction was ignored in *FAPL v QC Leisure*, given that the CJEU considered that the act of 'communication' originated at the football stadium where the broadcast was emitted, despite the fact that the act in question was the subsequent act of reception

[3] Although the Emission, Bogsch and Communication theories ultimately focus on the determination of the applicable law, in the course of establishing what the applicable law should be, they provide guidance about where the act of communication to the public occurs.

[4] M Makeen, *Copyright in a Global Information Society: The Scope of Copyright Protection Under International, US, UK and French Law* (Kluwer Law International, 2000) 219.

[5] W Rumphorst, 'The EC Directive on satellite broadcasting and cable retransmission' in H Cohen Jehoram, P Keuchenius and J Seignette (eds), *Audiovisual media and copyright in Europe* (Kluwer, 1994) 17–18.

[6] Makeen (2000) 219–20 – Makeen argues that the provision of an exclusive right for satellite broadcasting in place of the possibility of compulsory licensing resulted in the adoption of aspects of the Communication theory because the location of the act in the country of emission is premised on the existence of the exclusive right.

[7] See Articles 11, 11bis and 14 of the Berne Convention and Article 8 of the WIPO Copyright Treaty. Also see T Aplin, *Copyright Law in the Digital Society* (Hart Publishing, 2005) 131.

in public that occurred in the pub.[8] Where the intervention amounts to a direct representation of the work to a gathered public there is no act of 'communication', since acts of reception are excluded from the scope of the reformed communication to the public right.

The possibility of different locations where the act of communication to the public can be said to occur and the possibility of multiple acts stemming from one initial act are real concerns because a number of different countries become relevant[9] – transmission/emission country, server country and reception country(ies). This makes it difficult to determine where the act(s) of infringement actually occurs in the absence of clear and express guidance.[10] Thus, it is important to separate the different acts of communication to the public and identify one particular point where the act occurs, in the interest of attaining consistent and certain results. This is especially important because acts of communication to the public can be ubiquitous, thus making the potential for inconsistent results palpable.

Therefore, it is necessary to establish a clear approach for determining where the act of communication to the public occurs under the scope of the reformed right, in order to ensure that right holders are able to enforce their exclusive rights under EU copyright law, especially where the alleged infringement is ubiquitous. To ensure an adequate level of protection for right holders, it is necessary that they are able to enforce the reformed right of communication to the public regardless of where the act originated, provided the work is receivable within the EU. Moreover, a clear approach will also allow users to plan their communication activities accordingly. Failure to provide a harmonised approach to where the act occurs will undermine the reformed communication to the public right's aim to develop a coherent framework that is certain and proportionate.

With this background in mind, the Bogsch theory, the Communication theory and the Emission theory will be examined to help ascertain where the act of 'communication to the public' occurs. Although these theories ultimately lead to the establishment of what the applicable law should be, they do provide information about where the act of communication to the public occurs. However, it is advocated that determining where the act of communication to the public occurs should be separate to establishing what the applicable law is. As such, the choice of applicable law will turn on where the act of communication to the public is located. Therefore, establishing where the act of communication to the public occurs must be completed before determining what the applicable law is.

[8] Cases C-403/08 and C-429/08 *Football Association Premier League (FAPL) and others v QC Leisure and others* and *Karen Murphy v Media Protection Services Ltd* [2011] ECLI:EU:C:2011:631, para 203.

[9] P Goldstein and PB Hugenholtz, *International Copyright: Principles, Law and Practice*, 3rd edn (Oxford University Press, 2014) 124.

[10] P de Miguel Asensio, 'The Private International Law of Intellectual Property and of Unfair Commercial Practices: Convergence of Divergence?' in S Leible and A Ohly (eds), *Intellectual Property and Private International Law* (Mohr Siebeck, 2009) 142.

A. The Bogsch Theory

The Bogsch theory comprises six principles. Bogsch stated that firstly, satellite broadcasting is equal to broadcasting in the sense of Article 11bis of the Berne Convention. Secondly, broadcasting is a means of communication to the public by wireless diffusion. Given that the terms 'communication to the public' and 'diffusion' were used, this meant that the narrower concept of 'emission' was not applicable. Consequently, broadcasting must be understood as occurring where communication to the public occurs, which in the case of satellite broadcasting is in all the footprint countries where the signal is potentially receivable. Thirdly, the national law of each footprint country is applicable in order to ensure that the law of the territory in which the act of communication to the public occurs, applies.[11] If the law of the specific footprint country is inapplicable, the consequence could be the application of another country's law to acts occurring within the footprint's territory. Fourthly, where a satellite broadcast has de minimis overspill into a country, the copyright law of that country should not be taken into account. Fifthly, it is the sole responsibility of the person or organisation that gives the order for the broadcast to comply with the relevant copyright laws. Lastly, the Bogsch theory is based on the latest revision of the Berne Convention.[12]

In simple terms, under the Bogsch theory, the act of communication to the public, in relation to broadcasting and satellite broadcasting, occurs in the footprint countries that can receive the broadcasts. This finding can be inferred from the second and third principles of the Bogsch theory, where it is expressly stated that the act of communication to the public occurs in the footprint countries and consequently the applicable law is equally that of the footprint countries. This aspect of the Bogsch theory can be criticised on the grounds that it ignores the entire transmission or emission aspect of a broadcast.[13] However, this criticism can be addressed if the act of communication to the public is understood to be completed in the footprint countries. Slightly altering the perspective in this way takes accounts of the fact that the transmission occurred, but focus is placed on the potential reception of the work because that is what completes the act and as such, that is where the infringement occurs. In other words, the Bogsch theory localises

[11] The actual wording of this criterion by Bogsch was framed as: 'otherwise, a communication to the public in one country would be governed by the national law of another country, a result contrary to the principle of national treatment'. According to Makeen, this statement confused 'national treatment' with 'applicable law'. See Makeen (2000) 194.

[12] WIPO, 'Report of the Group of Experts on the Copyright Aspects of Direct Broadcasting by Satellite' (1985) 5 *Copyright* 180, 181, para 12, Makeen (2000) 194 and M Ficsor, 'Direct Broadcasting by Satellite and the Bogsch Theory' (1990) 18 *International Business Law (Int'l Bus Law)* 258, 259.

[13] The communication to the public right even in the traditional sense was considered to be the act of emission plus potential reception – WIPO, 'Preparatory Document for and Report of the WIPO/UNESCO Committee of Governmental Experts on Audiovisual Works and Phonograms' (1986) 7 *Copyright* 218, 233, paras 90–91. Also see Makeen (2000) 195.

the act of communication to the public in the footprint countries because the act is contingent on the prospect of its potential reception.

It can be argued that the Bogsch theory's approach to where the act occurs should not be applied to the reformed right of communication to the public because it fails to take into account a situation where the right holder in the footprint country is not the actual owner of the copyright work, but rather a licensee, for example. The problem with this is that the actual owner (licensor) of the work should also be taken into account in the clearance of rights.[14] This argument can be rebutted because the actual owner of the copyright work should consider this when licensing or assigning the work to other third-party right holders. As a result, this is not really a problem for the use of the approach derived from the Bogsch theory.

B. The Communication Theory

The Bogsch theory was 'modified' in 1986 during the meeting of the World Experts on Audiovisual Works and Phonograms. Instead of the act of satellite broadcasting solely occurring in the footprint countries, as suggested by Bogsch in 1985, it was suggested that the act of broadcasting takes place in both the country of emission *and* the country of reception.[15] The inclusion of the country of emission as one of the places where the act of communication to the public by satellite broadcasting occurs was justified on two grounds. Firstly, it was argued that traditional analogue broadcasting was judged on the basis of the location of the broadcaster's headquarters or where the emission took place. Given that satellite broadcasting is considered equivalent to traditional broadcasting under Article 11bis of the Berne Convention, similar logic should therefore be applied to satellite broadcasting.[16]

However, the application of this rationale to satellite broadcasting should be contested because the two technologies are not really comparable; the reason being that an act of traditional broadcasting originates and ends in the same country for the most part. In other words, the country of reception for a traditional broadcast would be the same as the country of emission. Thus, the place where the act occurs is identical regardless of whether emphasis is placed on the act of emission or the act of (potential) reception. This is not the case for satellite broadcasting because the country of emission is singular; however, the reach of the satellite broadcast is multi-national/global.[17] Therefore, placing focus on the emission country alone in

[14] Ficsor (1990) 259.

[15] Preparatory Document for and Report of the WIPO/UNESCO Committee of Governmental Experts on Audiovisual Works and Phonograms (1986) 231, para 86 and Ficsor (1990) 259.

[16] Preparatory Document for and Report of the WIPO/UNESCO Committee of Governmental Experts on Audiovisual Works and Phonograms (1986) 231, para 87.

[17] Makeen (2000) 199, Ficsor (1990) 261.

the satellite broadcasting context will provide very different results compared with when focus is placed on the footprint countries alone. The same logic applies in relation to Internet transmissions, given that it is a ubiquitous technology.

The second justification given for the adoption of the country of emission, *in addition to* the countries of reception, as the locality of the communication was that the act of broadcasting should not be polarised in the sense solely of an act of emission or alternatively, an act of reception. The act of broadcasting by its inherent nature necessitates both aspects.[18] As such, the law must account for both in the determination of where the act takes place. This rationale is more persuasive. However, it complicates the issue because there are two sets of laws that need to be taken account of – the country of emission and the country(ies) of (potential) reception. To resolve this conflict it was stated that the applicable law should be the one that is more favourable to the right holder.[19] If the extent of protection offered by the law of the country of emission and the laws of the countries of reception is the same then there is no problem and either law is applicable, with the one to be chosen being the one most favourable to the right holder.[20] Bogsch then suggested that the applicable law issue should be simplified by solely applying the emission country's law where it offers an exclusive right.[21] This mode of reasoning gave rise to the Communication theory.[22]

However, Makeen has suggested that the Communication theory is not simply a modified version of the Bogsch theory, but rather a completely separate theory. He argues that while the Bogsch theory was consistent in its designation of the footprint countries as the place where the act of broadcasting occurred, the Communication theory, by contrast, is simply a convenient choice-of-law rule.[23] This argument would appear to be valid if one considers that the act of broadcasting can be held to have occurred in both the country of emission and the countries of reception, but the location of the act is dependent on the level of protection granted in the respective countries. In other words, where the act takes place is subject to the existence of strong or effective applicable law, which is problematic for two reasons.

It should not be the case that an act of communication to the public can occur in two different places. This problem is exacerbated under the Communication theory because the location of the act is chosen as a matter of practical convenience. While the application of the Communication theory might ultimately be

[18] Preparatory Document for and Report of the WIPO/UNESCO Committee of Governmental Experts on Audiovisual Works and Phonograms (1986) 232, paras 90–91, Ficsor (1990) 261.

[19] Preparatory Document for and Report of the WIPO/UNESCO Committee of Governmental Experts on Audiovisual Works and Phonograms (1986) 231, Principle AW14 and 232, para 92, Makeen (2000) 195.

[20] Preparatory Document for and Report of the WIPO/UNESCO Committee of Governmental Experts on Audiovisual Works and Phonograms (1986) 232, para 92.

[21] ibid 233 and Makeen (2000) 195–96.

[22] This is why Makeen argues that the EU did not adopt a pure version of the Emission theory under the Satellite and Cable Retransmission Directive.

[23] Makeen (2000) 196.

satisfactory in practice, it does not properly solve the question of where the act of communication to the public occurs, other than mentioning that both the country of emission and countries of reception must be taken into account and moreover, that the act of communication to the public can occur in either place. In this way, the Communication theory fails to reflect the understanding that the act of communication to the public involves an act of potential transmission plus potential reception.[24] Therefore, it should be the case that each act of communication to the public occurs in one place that is clearly defined for the purpose of consistency and certainty. In instances where there are multiple successive acts of communication to the public via subsequent communications, each of these subsequent acts must be addressed separately. In this way, that individual act will also be isolated to one place.

Additionally, determining where the act of communication to the public occurs under the Communication theory is illogical because of the circularity in reasoning. The circularity is a consequence of how the Communication theory operates in practice. It is worth reiterating that the Communication theory establishes that the act of communication to the public can occur in both the country of emission and the countries of reception. Then, as a matter of applicable law, the law of the country of emission should solely apply, provided that it offers protection in the form of an exclusive right. Should this not be the case, the law of the footprint country with the strongest level of protection should apply. If this guidance is followed, it can be inferred that the place where the act occurs is in the country of emission, provided there is an exclusive right of communication to the public. Alternatively, the act of communication to the public will be taken to occur in the footprint country which has the strongest level of protection.

From this, the Communication theory establishes that the place where the act of communication to the public occurs is subject to the potential choice of applicable law. This method of determining where the act took place is illogical because the concept of 'communication to the public' then has no real bearing on the designation of the place where the act occurs. Instead, the place of the act is dependent on which implicated country has the strongest or most effective laws. From this it can be said that the Communication theory is really just a convenient choice-of-law rule. The desirable position to adopt would be that the applicable law is informed by the place where the act occurs. However, the only way to achieve this is to adopt an express definition for communication to the public. Failing to do this will perpetuate the circularity in reasoning because what constitutes an act of communication to the public will have to be determined by a specific law which in turn cannot be selected unless it is implicated by virtue of the localisation of the act to a particular country.

Notwithstanding these criticisms, it has been argued that the Communication theory should be applied to the existing right of communication to the public,

[24] Preparatory Document for and Report of the WIPO/UNESCO Committee of Governmental Experts on Audiovisual Works and Phonograms (1986) 232 para 91.

including its making available aspect, for the purpose of determining applicable law and consequently where the act takes place. Ficsor and Aplin both suggest that the Communication theory is best suited to governing the dissemination of works over the Internet.[25] However, the Communication theory is not suited to the reformed communication to the public right because the operation of the Communication theory conflicts with the definition of the right. The fact that the act under the Communication theory may occur in the country of emission or countries of reception as a matter of convenience is problematic because the location of the act should be determined in a single consistent manner. Thus, the Communication theory is ill suited for the reformed right because it does not produce certainty and, furthermore, can end up disregarding important aspects of the right; namely the transmission or the reception aspect.

C. The Emission Theory

The Emission theory was proposed as the alternative to the Bogsch and Communication theories. The primary argument advanced by Rumphorst was that there should only be the possibility of a single applicable law. As its name suggests, it argues that the act of communication to the public by satellite broadcast occurs in the country of emission and, consequently, the applicable law should be the law of the emission country. This is supported by the argument that the country of emission always regulated traditional acts of broadcasting. Therefore, the same reasoning should be applied to satellite broadcasting. However, this analogy is invalid because satellite broadcasting is not comparable to traditional broadcasting, given that the footprint countries extend far beyond the country of emission.[26] Regardless, Rumphorst argued that the Emission theory was the best means for determining where the act occurs and consequently the applicable law because of the problems associated with the Communication Theory.[27]

(i) Criticism of the Emission Theory

In analysing the Emission theory, it must be said that the application of the Emission theory in its original context is incompatible with the notion of the reformed communication to the public right. The right of communication to the public has traditionally been understood as an act of transmission plus

[25] M Ficsor, *The Law of Copyright and the Internet: The 1996 WIPO Treaties, their Interpretation and Implementation* (Oxford University Press, 2002) 508–09, Aplin (2005) 133.

[26] Makeen (2000) 199.

[27] W Rumphorst, 'Broadcasting of Films Via Satellite' (1990) 4 *EBU Review* 34, 34–38. Also, see Makeen (2000) 199–203 – Makeen provides a good summary of the problems with the Communication theory advocated by the proponents of the Emission theory. However, Makeen goes on to dismiss these criticisms raised by the advocates for the Emission theory.

potential reception.[28] Therefore, the Emission theory's failure to take into account the reception aspect of communication to the public results in the wrongful location of the act in the country of emission alone. Any theory relating to the reformed communication to the public right must take account of both the act of transmission and the act of reception. The second problem with the Emission theory is that locating the act within the country of emission could encourage parties responsible for the communication of copyright works to set up in countries that offer less stringent copyright protection;[29] the potential result being a race to find the country with the lowest level of protection. While it may be argued that organisations may set up in a particular country for reasons other than the strength of its copyright law, such as: tax, labour, telecommunications regulations and competition law concerns,[30] the reality is that copyright law shopping remains an important concern.[31]

Notwithstanding these two criticisms of the Emission theory, the EU adopted a modified version of the Emission theory in relation to satellite broadcasting under Article 1(2)(b) of the Satellite and Cable Retransmission Directive.[32] Article 1(2)(b) states that:

> The act of communication to the public by satellite occurs solely in the Member State where, under the control and responsibility of the broadcasting organization, the programme-carrying signals are introduced into an uninterrupted chain of communication leading to the satellite and down towards the earth.[33]

Reference to Recital 14 of the Satellite and Cable Retransmission Directive suggests that the Emission theory was selected to avoid the application of the laws of all the footprint countries concurrently. Moreover, Makeen argued that the Emission theory is a better fit for the context of an internal market than the Bogsch or Communication theories.[34] The reason for this is that EU copyright law is harmonised to a large extent and as such, locating the act of communication to the public in the country of emission is unproblematic because there

[28] Preparatory Document for and Report of the WIPO/UNESCO Committee of Governmental Experts on Audiovisual Works and Phonograms (1986) 232, para 91.

[29] Makeen (2000) 203 and S Plenter, 'Choice of law rules for copyright infringements in the global information infrastructure: a never-ending story?' (2001) 23(7) *European Intellectual Property Review* 313, 315.

[30] Rumphorst (1994) 22.

[31] Makeen (2000) 2003, Aplin (2005) 133, A Lucas, 'Applicable Law in Copyright Infringement Cases in the Digital Environment' (2005) *e-Copyright Bulletin* 1, 11, P Geller, 'Conflicts of Laws in Cyberspace: Rethinking International Copyright' (1997) 44 *Journal of the Copyright Society of the USA* 103, 112 and M Burnstein, 'Conflicts on the Net: Choice of Law in Transnational Cyberspace' (1996) 29 *Vanderbilt Journal of Transnational Law* 75, 89.

[32] Makeen (2000) 219–20.

[33] Article 1(2)(d)(i) and (ii) of the Satellite and Cable Retransmission Directive deal with the situations where the satellite uplink occurs in a country outside the EU that does not provide the same level of protection as within the EU.

[34] Makeen (2000) 217. This claim is contested in criticising the potential application of the Emission theory to the reformed communication to the public right.

is no opportunity for forum shopping. This is because all Member States are required to adopt the same minimum level of protection in relation to acts of satellite broadcasting. Therefore, there ought to be equal protection available across the EU regardless of what Member State the broadcast originates from. As a result, it is unnecessary to consider the footprint countries. As such, it was not the case that the Emission theory was better than the Bogsch or Communication theories;[35] rather, locating the act in the country of emission was workable in the EU context and hence, the Emission theory was seen as compatible.

However, it has been argued that Article 1(2)(b) of the Satellite and Cable Retransmission Directive did not implement a pure version of the Emission theory. Makeen argued that aspects of the Communication theory are incorporated into the Satellite and Cable Retransmission Directive.[36] This claim is persuasive because the Directive provides an exclusive right for satellite broadcasting and excludes the possibility of compulsory licensing. In this way, the Directive latently follows the advice given by Bogsch in simplifying the Communication theory so that the emission country's laws apply where it offers protection in the form of an exclusive right.[37]

The question remains whether the Emission theory should be extended to cover the reformed right of communication to the public? As it stands, the Emission theory is only applicable to satellite broadcasting. Therefore, all acts under the existing Article 3 communication to the public right of the ISD are largely open to interpretation, subject to any existing rulings by the CJEU.[38] Therefore, it must be considered whether the Emission theory should be extended to include all types of communication to the public under EU copyright law for the purpose of the proposed reformed communication to the public right that is codified?

(ii) Further Criticism of the Emission Theory

In addition to the two problems discussed above, there are other issues with the Emission theory that prevent it from being an ideal choice for the determination of where the reformed communication to the public right occurs. It must be remembered that the Emission theory was conceived in a different technological and legal context. As such, the foundational arguments in support of the Emission theory are not as persuasive as they once were. Moreover, it will be argued that the Emission theory does not sit comfortably with the reformed communication to the public right.

[35] Makeen (2000) 217.

[36] ibid 219–20.

[37] Preparatory Document for and Report of the WIPO/UNESCO Committee of Governmental Experts on Audiovisual Works and Phonograms (1986) 233.

[38] Case C-170/12 *Peter Pinckney v KDG Mediatech* [2013] ECLI:EU:C:2013:635, Case C-387/12 *Hi Hotel HCF SARL v Uwe Spoering* [2014] ECLI:EU:C:2014:215 and Case C-441/13 *Pez Hejduk v EnergieAgentur.NRW GmbH* [2015] ECLI:EU:C:2015:28.

The first argument against the application of the Emission theory is that the origin of an act of communication to the public is not always clear, especially where the Internet is involved.[39] For example, files distributed on the Internet may not necessarily be sent as one whole file from one location. It may be the case that the file is broken up into many parts that are transmitted from many different places. This occurs with P2P applications. To put it differently, traditional satellite broadcasting operated on a point-to-multipoint basis,[40] whereas, modern digital technology can operate on a multipoint-to-multipoint basis. Therefore, merely stating that the act of communication to the public under the reformed right occurs in the country of emission may not be helpful where the nature of modern technology may produce several 'emission' countries. In fact, it can be argued that the number of emission countries can be as numerous as the number of footprint countries. From this, the raison d'être of the Emission theory that only one country's law should be applicable is undermined by the nature of modern technology.

This argument that the Emission theory was developed in a context where it was relatively easy to identify the place of the emission is given further impetus if it is considered that the parties responsible for acts of communication to the public were mostly large broadcasters. The consequence of this is that fixed, large entity broadcasters were the focal point for locating the act of communication to the public. The place where the act occurs was inextricably tied to the place where the broadcaster actually emitted the signal or the place where the broadcaster had its headquarters. By contrast, modern acts of communication to the public are not limited to large corporate entities like broadcasting organisations, but now include individual users who are capable of disseminating copyright works on a scale equal to or greater than that of a traditional broadcaster. Furthermore, identifying where the act of transmission occurred is not as simple as in the satellite broadcasting context. The upload or uplink of an act of 'communication' can be mobile, resulting in increased and/or more complicated cross-border activity.[41] As a result, the person responsible for an emission can be a moving target in contrast to the fixed broadcaster in the traditional sense. This has been facilitated by the development of technology, notably the Internet, which has allowed electronic dissemination of copyright works on a global scale.[42]

In addition to this, new technologies have eroded the distinction between content distributors and receivers. Moreover, persons can easily switch roles knowingly or unknowingly.[43] For example, in P2P networks, users can be both

[39] Aplin (2005) 133, A Reindl, 'Choosing Law in Cyberspace: Copyright Conflicts on Global Networks' (1998) 19 *Michigan Journal of International Law* 799, 835.

[40] The phrase 'point-to-multipoint' is derived from Makeen (2000) 283.

[41] Consider the example of a work being uploaded on the go, in a car that is driving across the borders of various Member States.

[42] P Torremans, 'Copyright jurisdiction under EU private international law' in P Torremans (ed), *Research Handbook on Copyright Law*, 2nd edn (Edward Elgar Publishing Ltd, 2017) 557.

[43] Reindl (1998) 800.

receivers and distributors interchangeably or simultaneously. Furthermore, ordinary Internet users are receivers when they are accessing copyright works online, for example by watching YouTube videos. However, they are also able to upload videos to YouTube and as such, can be content disseminators as well. The implication of this for the Emission theory is that the simplicity and effectiveness traditionally associated with locating the act of communication to the public in the emission country is no longer justified. The reality is that it is difficult to monitor individual users and moreover, it is inefficient to do so. Consequently, there is no benefit in focusing on the country of emission alone as opposed to the countries of reception, especially since the perpetrators of acts of communication to the public are not limited to large broadcasting organisations which possess valuable assets.

A third criticism of the Emission theory relates to its failure to take account of the potential reception aspect of the communication to the public right. As a result, the whole act of communication to the public is not taken into account. The consequence of solely focusing on the act of emission is that the 'public' aspect of communication to the public is ignored. This has important implications not only for the choice of jurisdiction and applicable law, but also for evidential purposes. In order to complete an act of communication to the public, there must be potential reception of the 'communication' by a large and indeterminate number of people.[44] It must be ascertained whether the potential audience exists in order to establish an actionable communication to the public and, moreover, make a coherent decision in choosing jurisdiction and applicable law.[45] Simply focusing on the country of emission could lead to the reformed communication to the public right being reduced to a right of communication or an access right. Thus, the Emission approach is incomplete for the determination of where the act of communication to the public takes place.

The Emission theory is also ill suited for the determination of where the reformed communication to the public right occurs for the purpose of infringement proceedings because it disregards the 'public' requirement. The issue with this is that an act of communication to the public may be located in a country that is far removed from where the harm of the infringement is ultimately concluded.[46] This then creates problems for obtaining evidence in relation to how many people

[44] This is the definition of 'public' as set out in the case law and accepted in this book – Case C-89/04 *Mediakabel BV v Commissariaat voor de Media* [2005] ECLI:EU:C:2005:348, para 30, Case C-192/04 *Lagardère Active Broadcast v Société pour la perception de la rémunération équitable (SPRE), Gesellschaft zur Verwertung von Leistungsschutzrechten mbH (GVL)* [2005] ECLI:EU:C:2005:475, para 31 and Case C-135/10 *Societa Consortile Fonografici (SCF) v Marco del Corso* [2012] ECLI:EU:C:2012:140, para 84.

[45] Supporters of the Emission theory will argue that the potential audience will be taken into account in the licensing process. However, this has nothing to do with infringement proceedings, especially where the 'communication' is made without the consent of the right holder.

[46] For example, by locating the act in the country of emission, it may be the case that there are actually no recipients (actual or potential) in that country. Therefore, the act of communication to the public technically did not occur in that country.

were actually capable of receiving the communication because the court in the emission country will have to rely on evidence from another jurisdiction. In the absence of this information, liability under the communication to the public right cannot be established. Therefore, in order to establish a coherent framework to determine where the reformed act of communication to the public occurs, it must be reiterated that both the 'communication' and 'public' aspects must be considered equally. This is necessary to prevent the misleading idea that the act of transmitting a work alone is sufficient to establish where the act of communication to the public occurs.

Lastly, it is argued that even in the instance of the reformed communication to the public right coupled with complete harmonisation through the codification of the right, the Emission theory is still not an ideal choice. According to Makeen, in the context of the Berne Convention the only way that the application of the Emission theory would work in designating the country of emission as the place where the act of communication to the public occurred without the complication of forum shopping would be in a situation where compulsory licensing is abolished and copyright law is harmonised in relation to duration, moral rights, authorship/ownership, protection of performers, producers and broadcasters.[47] Similarly, in the context of the EU, Makeen suggests that for the Emission theory to work 'a minimum level of copyright protection had to be recognised'.[48]

However, both of Makeen's suggestions are insufficient. The reason for this is that even in the instance of a codified approach as proposed for the reformed right of communication to the public, Member States still have the freedom to implement EU copyright obligations of their own accord. This is of particular concern where the reformed right is manually incorporated into domestic law. While the reformed communication to the public right addresses the issue of compulsory licensing and proposes a codified approach, the other issues raised by Makeen are not fully harmonised. Furthermore, in the absence of a copyright Regulation at the EU level there will remain room for divergence at the domestic level of the various Member States.

It may be the case that the domestic application of the right is subject to imperfect implementation, such as different wordings, as well as different forms of interpretation due to the different legal traditions present in the EU. Although the intervention of the CJEU's case law may limit these concerns, it remains an issue because the EU cannot advise on every situation and, moreover, the courts of some Member States tend to disregard or misapply the decisions of the CJEU.[49] Similarly, existing domestic laws often tend to conflict with EU copyright law and

[47] Makeen (2000) 208–09.

[48] ibid 217.

[49] For example, the UK courts were initially resistant to the 'author's own intellectual creation' concept. In *The Newspaper Licensing Agency Ltd and others v Meltwater Holding BV and others* [2011] EWCA Civ 890, para 20 per Jackson LJ, it was held that *Infopaq* did not qualify the long-standing UK test on originality.

the decisions of the CJEU.[50] Therefore, the Emission theory remains a less than ideal choice in the absence of an EU copyright Regulation or a unitary approach to EU copyright law.

Even though the reformed right resolves the definitional problems experienced by the existing right, as long as Member States are allowed to interpret their existing legislation in line with the reformed right or alternatively have the freedom to implement the reformed right in their own way, there will be inconsistencies. For example, in France, the communication to the public right falls under the general performance right.[51] This is in contrast to the UK that provides a specific communication to the public right.[52] Similarly, specific technologies or acts, such as P2P, hyperlinking and streaming, are treated differently in various Member States.[53] In order for the Emission theory to be appropriate, an EU copyright Regulation is required at minimum.[54] Anything short of this level of uniformity will allow for differences in protection that will result in the same problems previously discussed and, as a result, it will limit the effectiveness of the Emission theory. However, this is unlikely to be achieved at present, given the absence of plans to codify EU copyright law generally or produce a copyright Regulation.[55]

The application of the Emission theory is not ideal even though this book has proposed a reformed communication to the public right that is codified. The issue lies with the disconnect between the reformed right, its implementation at the national level and its subsequent interpretation, given the absence of an EU copyright Regulation or a unitary approach to EU copyright law.

[50] This was the case in *Football Association Premier League Ltd v QC Leisure (No 3)* [2012] EWHC 108 (Ch) and *Football Association Premier League Ltd and others v QC Leisure and others* [2012] EWCA Civ 1708, where the interpretation of the Article 3 communication to the public right under the ISD conflicted with the UK's provisions on communication to the public, performance in public and the relevant defences available under the Copyright, Designs and Patents Act 1988 (CDPA).

[51] Article L122-2 Intellectual Property Code 1992.

[52] s 20 CDPA 1988.

[53] With particular regard to hyperlinks, a number of different approaches have been tried successfully and unsuccessfully. Successful approaches include: primary infringement under the communication to the public right, the reproduction right and the distribution right, secondary liability for authorising in the UK – *Paramount Home Entertainment International Ltd and others v British Sky Broadcasting Ltd and others* [2013] EWHC 3479 (Ch), breach of duty of care in the Netherlands – *Greenstijl v Sanoma* (2013) Gerechtshof Amsterdam, 19 November 2013, ECLI:NL:GHAMS:2013:4019, contributory infringement in Italy – *Sky Italia Srl v DaBo e Telecom Italia Spa* (2010) Trib Milano, 20 March 2010, n 3639 and unfair competition in Austria – *R v Vorarlberg Online* (2001) unreported.

[54] Although the interpretation of the communication to the public right is meant to be uniform and consistent with the findings of the CJEU, the fact that Member States have flexibility in the way that they implement the copyright Directives inevitably leaves room for inconsistency through the use of different language or domestic legal norms and traditions. As such, it is necessary to codify copyright law in a Regulation, so that the law does not require implementation or transposition. The reformed communication to the public right that is maximally harmonised remains insufficient for the purposes of applying the Emission theory.

[55] The EU legislature's focus is on producing a Regulation for the cross-border portability of online content – Commission, *Making EU copyright rules fit for the digital age – Questions and Answers* (MEMO 15/6262, 2015) and Commission, *Proposal for a Regulation of the European Parliament and of the Council on ensuring the cross-border portability of online content services in the internal market* (COM(2015) 627 final, 2015).

D. A Suitable Theory for the Reformed Right – The Completion Theory

Determining where the act of the reformed communication to the public right occurs must account for three considerations. Firstly, it must take account of the complete notion of communication to the public. Therefore, it must consider the transmission or provision of the work plus the potential reception of that work. Failing to do this would mean that the method of locating the act is incompatible with the understanding of the reformed communication to the public right. Secondly, it must designate that the act of communication to the public occurs in a single, clearly defined place.[56] Thirdly, the method must be technology-neutral.[57] In considering these three criteria, it must be remembered that the purpose of isolating and locating the act is to clearly inform jurisdictional competence and the substantive applicable law. Thus, the method in which the act of communication to the public is located should not facilitate or encourage the 'cherry picking' of the most lenient copyright jurisdictions and laws.

Of the three traditional theories previously discussed, none are capable of satisfying all the above-listed criteria. However, the Bogsch theory is closest to what is required to designate where the act of the reformed communication to the public right occurs. This is because the Bogsch theory locates the act in the footprint countries, which takes into account the whole communication to the public process – transmission and reception. As a result, the proposed Completion theory draws inspiration from the Bogsch theory. The Completion theory is so named because it locates the act of communication to the public in the country or countries where the act is completed; that is, in the countries of potential reception, given that a completed act of communication to the public entails the transmission or provision of a work plus its potential reception. The act is only completed where it is potentially receivable or actually received.[58] Ginsburg also suggests this point of view by highlighting that the inclusion of the making available aspect under the communication to the public right would point toward the country of receipt being the place where the act occurs.[59]

[56] It is not required that only one country's laws can be applicable.

[57] None of the three traditional theories are capable of meeting this criterion because they are all constructed with satellite broadcasting in mind. For this reason, none of the traditional theories are suitable to be applied because satellite broadcasting is not comparable to online transmissions – P Schonning, 'Applicable Law in Transfrontier On-Line Transmissions' (1996) 170 *Revue Internationale du Droit d'Auteur.(RIDA)* 21, 37–39.

[58] In order to prove actual or potential reception, the onus will fall on the claimant to adduce evidence to support his claim. This evidentiary burden is also important in establishing that there was a 'public' for the purposes of finding infringement. Therefore, in the absence of this evidence, there is no chance of proving infringement at the later stage in the court seised.

[59] J Ginsburg, 'The (New?) Right of Making Available to the Public' in D Vaver and L Bently (eds), *Intellectual Property in the New Millennium, Essays in Honour of William R Cornish* (Cambridge University Press, 2004) 236–37 – Ginsburg suggests that argument can be made that the act of communication to the public occurs in the country of receipt, given the inclusion of the making available aspect, which ties the act to the place and time chosen by the user.

The Completion theory follows the crux of the Bogsch theory, in that the requisite act occurs in the footprint countries.[60] Consequently, both theories are subject to the criticism that locating the act in the countries of reception creates the problem that claims can be brought anywhere, in the context of the Internet age. This is because Internet technologies are ubiquitous and works made available online can be used or accessed in potentially any country. Thus, the issue is that defendants may be forced to fight litigation on multiple fronts or face judgments in default.[61] However, this criticism assumes that claimants will more often than not choose to sue in every country possible and that this is a viable option for claimants. But, this is not efficient; instead it is more likely the case that claimants will bring claims where they are most likely to succeed and where they will get a desirable remedy.[62]

It must not be forgotten that establishing jurisdiction is only one part of the overall process in enforcing the reformed right; the claimant must still prove actual infringement. Establishing jurisdiction does not necessarily mean that there exists the requisite 'public' aspect in the country of the court seised. Furthermore, claimants must also bear in mind the potential consequences of bringing unjustified litigation or more generally a weak claim. For example, in the UK, the claimant will have to consider liability for abuse of process,[63] summary judgment for the defendant[64] and declarations of non-infringement.[65]

However, the location of the act of communication is the only substantial similarity between the two approaches and the Completion theory differs from the Bogsch theory in several ways. In the first place, the Completion theory is primarily focused on establishing the place where the act of the reformed communication to the public right occurs. This is in contrast to the Bogsch theory that states where the act occurs and designates the applicable law based on the place of the act. Under the Completion theory, establishing where the act occurs does not necessarily lead to the determination of the applicable law. This is because the determination of applicable law is addressed separately (Chapter seven) to the location of the act under the framework proposed in this chapter.

[60] The act of transmission is implicit because in its absence, there can be no potential reception.

[61] A Metzger, 'Jurisdiction in Cases Concerning Intellectual Property Infringements on the Internet' in S Leible and A Ohly (eds), *Intellectual Property and Private International Law* (Mohr Siebeck, 2009) 255–56.

[62] R Matulionyte, 'The Law Applicable to Online Copyright Infringements in the ALI and CLIP Proposals: A Rebalance of Interests Needed?' (2011) 2 *Journal of Intellectual Property, Information Technology and E-Commerce (JIPITEC)* 26, 27.

[63] See *Sullivan v Bristol Film Studios* [2012] EWCA Civ 570, applying *Jameel (Yousef) v Dow Jones & Co Inc* [2005] EWCA Civ 75.

[64] See *Robin George Le Strange Meakin v British Broadcasting Corporation and others* [2010] EWHC 2065 (Ch).

[65] See *Point Solutions Ltd v Focus Business Solutions Ltd and Focus Solutions Group PLC* [2005] EWHC 3096 (Ch). Declarations of non-infringement are recognised for Community trade mark and design rights where applicable under national laws. See Article 81 Council Regulation (EC) No 6/2002 of 12 December 2001 on Community designs and Article 96 Council Regulation (EC) No 207/2009 of 26 February 2009 on the Community trade mark (codified version).

The second difference is that the Completion theory is technology-neutral, meaning that it has been developed in a manner that allows it to address any instance involving the communication to the public right regardless of the technology involved. This is different to the Bogsch theory that was developed specifically with broadcasting, and subsequently satellite broadcasting, in mind. The advantage of the Completion theory being technology-neutral is that it has flexibility in addressing new technologies. By contrast, using the Bogsch theory for modern and future technologies requires drawing an analogy between traditional broadcasting and the technology in question. This is evidenced by the logic of the Bogsch theory's application to satellite broadcasting, where it was argued that satellite broadcasting should be treated as analogous to traditional broadcasting.

This is problematic for modern technologies that are on demand or 'pull' technologies because they are conceptually different to the traditional 'push' or broadcasting technologies. This claim is supported by the fact that it was uncertain whether the traditional communication to the public right extended to on demand technologies. As such, the making available aspect became a necessity.[66] Consequently, the logic of the Bogsch theory should not be stretched to induce a finding that traditional broadcasting and on demand technologies are analogous. Instead, the technology-neutral approach of the Completion theory is a more coherent and desirable approach to adopt even though the location of the act under the Bogsch theory may produce the same results in some circumstances.

Thirdly, the Completion theory has no de minimis principle. Unlike the Bogsch theory, the Completion theory does not require a threshold principle because it is unconcerned with applicable law or actual infringement. Instead, the focus is solely based on determining where the act of communication to the public occurs and who is responsible for that act. As such, once there is a transmission or provision of the work plus potential reception, the act is located where the potential reception exists. The questions pertaining to whether there is an actionable 'communication', a 'public' and ultimately actual infringement, are not subject to the Completion theory. Instead, this is for the court seised to decide. Fourthly, the Completion theory does not designate any specific rule on who is responsible for the clearing of rights. It must be reiterated that the Completion theory is primarily concerned with where the act of communication to the public occurs.[67]

[66] S Ricketson and J Ginsburg, *International Copyright and Neighbouring Rights: The Berne Convention and Beyond*, 2nd edn (Oxford University Press, 2006) para 12.49, S Depreeuw, *The variable scope of the exclusive economic rights in copyright* (Kluwer Law International, 2014) para 501, T Dreier, 'Copyright Digitized: Philosophical Impacts and Practical Implications for Information Exchange in Digital Networks' in *WIPO Worldwide Symposium on the Impact of Digital Technology on Copyright and Neighboring Rights* (1993) 193 and Commission, *Copyright and Related Rights in the Information Society* (Green Paper COM(95) 382 final, 1995) 56 [Green Paper for the ISD].

[67] Having said that, the onus of clearing licences will most likely fall on the person responsible for initiating the transmission, or in other words, the person liable for the act of communication to the public.

E. Responsibility for Acts of Communication to the Public

In addition to locating where the act of communication to the public occurs, the Completion theory also establishes who is responsible for that act. Under the Bogsch theory knowledge of the responsible party is assumed. Whereas, under the Completion theory it is proposed that the person responsible for an act of communication to the public is the person who actively initiated the act of 'communication to the public'. This requirement of 'active initiation' is conceptually derived from the 'intervention' concept used by the CJEU to determine whether there was a 'communication' in *FAPL v QC Leisure*.[68] 'Active initiation' means that the person involved ordered or orchestrated the copyright work to be placed into a process resulting in its transmission or provision.[69] Therefore, 'active initiation' is more specific than 'intervention' as used by the CJEU because it requires the responsible party to be actively and directly involved in the act of 'communication'.

The requirement of 'active initiation' is important because it ensures that Internet service providers (ISP) and other mere technical facilitators, such as persons who provide communication facilities, are not responsible for the act of communication to the public where their role is limited to facilitating the transmission over their physical facilities or network systems.[70] This is because they are not actively involved with the content that is subject to the act of communication to the public. Instead, their role is passive because they merely follow the active initiator's commands, with no control over what is included in the transmission. In the absence of the active initiator's actions, ISPs and other third parties will not be involved because there are no instructions or initial act to follow.

However, if the service providers were to become involved in the selection of content or alternatively, gave instructions for the 'communication' of the work, this would place them within the definition of 'active initiation'. Therefore, under the Completion theory the person or organisation who selects what is broadcast,

[68] *FAPL v QC Leisure* [2011] paras 195–96. The CJEU also confusingly uses the term 'intervention' to establish a 'new public' in *SGAE v Rafael Hoteles* [2006] para 42 and Case C-466/12 *Nils Svensson and others v Retriever Sverige AB* [2014] ECLI:EU:C:2014:76, paras 27 and 31. This is highlighted by AG Wathelet in Case C-160/15 *GS Media BV v Sanoma Media Netherlands BV and others* [2016], Opinion of AG Wathelet ECLI:EU:C:2016:221, paras 55–60.

[69] 'Active initiation' is concerned with the determination of who is responsible for an act of communication to the public; whereas, the CJEU's use of 'intervention' in *SGAE v Rafael Hoteles* and *Svensson* exists on the assumption that the responsible party has already been identified. This is because the 'intervention' approach is concerned with establishing that a 'new public' exists. This is evidenced if one considers that the CJEU combines the 'intervention' approach with 'but for' logic in determining whether there is a 'new public'. In *SGAE v Rafael Hoteles* [2006] para 42, it is stated that: 'In the absence of that intervention, its customers, although physically within that area, would not, in principle, be able to enjoy the broadcast work'. Therefore, the responsible party is already established. This is in contrast to *FAPL v QC Leisure* [2011] paras 195–96, where the CJEU uses the same term 'intervention' to establish an act of 'communication'. This also implicitly suggests who is responsible for the act of 'communication'.

[70] This is consistent with Recital 27 of the ISD.

decides whether retransmission occurs, or makes available a work, will be the person responsible for the act of 'communication to the public'. Establishing the responsible party under the Completion theory in this way is both necessary and justified because its overarching purpose is to assist in the enforcement of the communication to the public right. In this way, it informs the jurisdiction and applicable law to be used. Therefore, the Completion theory has a vital role in the enforcement of the reformed communication to the public right.

F. Justifying the Completion Theory

There are several reasons why it is valuable to adopt the Completion theory. One of the strongest reasons is that locating the act of communication to the public in the footprint countries ensures that right holders can enforce the reformed communication to the public right within the EU. This will ensure that right holders have adequate protection over their works by being able to bring claims within the EU regardless of where the communication originated. Furthermore, the possibility of users 'cherry picking' where they transmit from will be limited, since the act occurs where the work can be received. Thus, EU copyright law will always be relevant once works are potentially receivable in the EU.

It is also the case that the Completion theory is technology-neutral and less complicated than the Bogsch theory because it is not premised on analogising the act/technology concerned to traditional forms of broadcasts. The Completion theory offers a simple means for determining where the act of the reformed communication to the public right takes place without the rigid rules of the Bogsch theory. In this way, it is responsive to changes in technology, but maintains certainty in relation to the place where the act occurs. Therefore, the principle of legal certainty is upheld, and a proportionate level of protection is ensured for right holders.

The Completion theory accounts for the whole process of communication to the public (transmission or provision of the work plus potential reception), clearly designates where the act of communication to the public occurs (footprint countries) and is technology-neutral. It also contributes to the reformed communication to the public's framework by identifying the party responsible for an act of communication to the public.

III. Conclusion

This chapter established the mechanism by which to determine where the act of 'communication to the public' occurs and, moreover, who is responsible for that act. Using the Completion theory for this purpose has helped establish a simple and certain way to enforce the reformed communication to the public right, with particular attention being paid to the development of technology. It was demonstrated that relying on the old theories to discern where the act occurs was insufficient and as such it was necessary to develop a new approach: the Completion theory. The Completion theory is justifiable because it is technology-neutral, clearly identifies a single location where the act occurs and accounts for the complete act of communication to the public. As such, it will be used to help inform the determination of jurisdiction and applicable law that will be discussed in Chapters six and seven.

6

Enforcing the Reformed Right of Communication to the Public: Choice of Jurisdiction

I. Introduction

Thus far, this book has critically analysed the existing right of communication to the public and proposed a reformed right. Included in the proposal are the means to legislate, interpret and apply the right in a more proportionate and certain manner; how to reconcile the reformed right with the existing EU copyright law framework; and the mechanism by which to determine where the act of 'communication to the public' occurs and who is responsible. In order to create a coherent framework for the reformed communication to the public right it is also necessary to clarify the rules concerning choice of jurisdiction and applicable law because these issues affect the enforcement of the right. Therefore, this chapter focuses on the development of clear and consistent rules to determine what court should have jurisdiction in cases concerning the reformed right of communication to the public.[1]

The international copyright treaties provide no assistance in relation to the establishment of jurisdiction and applicable law. As such, reliance is placed solely on the EU rules. This chapter criticises the approach adopted by the EU in relation to the establishment of jurisdiction in copyright cases and in doing so proposes its own method for the determination of jurisdiction. Adopting effective and coherent rules in this regard has attained increased significance due to the ubiquity of digital technology, in particular the Internet.[2] The EU rules for the establishment of jurisdiction require improvement, given that they are not copyright-specific and, moreover, suffer from inherent problems. In order to establish an ideal

[1] The existing EU communication to the public right will be referenced where necessary. In all other circumstances the communication to the public right discussed is the proposed reformed right.

[2] R Matulionyte, 'Enforcing Copyright Infringements Online: In Search of Balanced Private International Law Rules' (2015) 6 *Journal of Intellectual Property, Information Technology & E-Commerce Law (JIPITEC)* 132 and P Torremans, 'Private International Law Issues on the Internet' in I Stamatoudi (ed), *New Developments in EU and International Copyright Law* (Kluwer Law International BV, 2016) 380.

framework for copyright law, the rules concerning jurisdiction should not be grouped under the heading of IP or general tort law. This is because copyright law is not necessarily synonymous with either of these general groupings. Instead, copyright-specific rules should be enacted, preferably under a copyright Directive or Regulation. Furthermore, the rules proposed should be certain, proportionate and technology neutral. The existing EU rules on jurisdiction and applicable law fail to meet these criteria, especially with regard to the application and enforcement of the communication to the public right. Therefore, it is necessary to propose a different set of rules.

In proposing a framework for the determination of jurisdiction and applicable law in relation to alleged infringements of the reformed communication to the public right, it is suggested that it must first be determined where the act complained of takes place.[3] It is essential to establish where the act occurs because it is a decisive element in the determination, firstly, of which country has jurisdiction, and secondly, of what the applicable law should be.[4] With regard to this, the Completion theory discussed in Chapter five is applied. Under the Completion theory, the act occurs in the country(ies) of receipt, since the act of 'communication to the public' is only completed where there is actual or potential reception. Furthermore, the Completion theory also provides the answer to who is responsible for the act. It is held that the responsible party should be the one who actively initiates the act of communication to the public.

Subsequent to determining where the act occurs and who is responsible, only then can the issues of jurisdiction and applicable law be competently established. As such, it is advocated that in addition to the general rule on jurisdiction pertaining to the domicile of the defendant, a copyright specific rule should be adopted based on where the alleged act occurred or where it is likely to occur. The next chapter will address the issue of applicable law.

[3] Establishing where the act of communication to the public takes place has added importance in determining the jurisdiction of the court seised because the infringement provides information about the defendant. It may be the case that the infringement occurs within the territory of a particular state, but the court seised may not have jurisdiction to hear a claim against that defendant. For example, this can be seen in the application of Article 7(2) of the Regulation (EU) No 1215/2012 of the European Parliament and of the Council of 12 December 2012 on jurisdiction and the recognition of judgments in civil and commercial matters (recast) [Brussels Regulation Recast (BRR)] where the defendant must be domiciled in a Member State regardless of the fact that the infringement may not have occurred in that Member State. If the defendant is not domiciled in a Member State, then a claim for jurisdiction under Article 7(2) cannot be made. In this situation that defendant will be subject to the domestic law of the court seised, subject to Article 6 of the BRR.

[4] P de Miguel Asensio, 'The Private International Law of Intellectual Property and of Unfair Commercial Practices: Convergence of Divergence?' in S Leible and A Ohly (eds), *Intellectual Property and Private International Law* (Mohr Siebeck, 2009) 181 and S Neumann, 'Ubiquitous and Multistate Cases in P Torremans (ed), *Research Handbook on Cross-Border Enforcement of Intellectual Property* (Edward Elgar Publishing, 2014) 521.

II. Establishing Jurisdiction in EU Copyright Cases – The Current Approach

With knowledge of where the act of communication to the public occurred and who is responsible for it, the next step in enforcing the right in a case for alleged infringement is to establish the jurisdiction of the court seised. The current method of doing this under EU law is through the provisions of the Brussels Regulation Recast (BRR). However, it will be argued that the BRR is not the best means to determine jurisdiction in relation to cases of alleged infringement of the reformed communication to the public right because it is problematic in relation to the more complex aspects of EU copyright law.[5] This is because the BRR has inherent problems and, additionally, there are alternative frameworks that provide better approaches to the issue of jurisdiction. Thus, it is argued that a copyright-specific rule should be adopted to take account of the nuances of EU copyright law.

The need for copyright-specific rules pertaining to jurisdiction has become increasingly important with the advent of digital technology, in particular, the Internet, which has allowed for ubiquitous infringement. As such, it is important that the courts of EU Member States are in a position to effectively manage copyright infringement cases. This begins with courts being able to claim jurisdiction. Therefore, this section will explore how jurisdiction is established in EU copyright cases. This will include analysis of the current application of the BRR to copyright cases, focusing in particular on the application of Article 7(2) of the BRR. The problems concerning the application of the BRR will also be discussed.

Subsequent to this, the ALI Principles on jurisdiction[6] and the Max Planck CLIP Principles[7] will be compared with the existing BRR, with the aim of suggesting a more appropriate means for establishing jurisdiction in cases involving copyright infringement, namely, in relation to the reformed communication to the public right.[8] The result will be a proposed framework that should ensure certainty

[5] P Torremans, 'Copyright jurisdiction under EU private international law' in P Torremans (ed), *Research Handbook on Copyright Law*, 2nd edn (Edward Elgar Publishing Ltd, 2017) 573.

[6] American Law Institute, *Intellectual Property: Principles Governing Jurisdiction, Choice of Law, and Judgments in Transnational Disputes* (2008) [ALI Principles]. See F Beckstein, 'The American Law Institute Project on Intellectual Property: Principles Governing Jurisdiction, Choice of Law, and Judgments in Transnational Disputes' in S Leible and A Ohly (eds), *Intellectual Property and Private International Law* (Mohr Siebeck, 2009) for a brief overview of the ALI Principles.

[7] European Max Planck Group, *Principles on Conflict of Laws in Intellectual Property* (2011) [CLIP Principles].

[8] Only the ALI Principles and the CLIP Principles will be addressed, given that the ALI Principles have their origins in the failed Hague Draft Convention on Jurisdiction and, subsequently, the WIPO Draft Convention on Jurisdiction – R Dreyfuss and J Ginsburg, 'Draft Convention on Jurisdiction and Recognition of Judgments in Intellectual Property Matters' (2002) 77 *Chicago-Kent Law Review* 1065, R Dreyfuss, 'The ALI Principles on Transnational Intellectual Property Disputes: Why Invite Conflicts?' (2005) 30(3) *Brooklyn Journal of International Law (Brook J Int'l L)* 819 and F Dessemontet, 'A European Point of View on the ALI Principles – Intellectual Property: Principles Governing Jurisdiction, Choice of Law, and Judgments in Transnational Disputes' (2005) 30(3) *Brook J Int'l L* 849, 854.

and predictability, a proportionate balancing of the relevant competing interests and technological neutrality.[9]

A. The Brussels Regulation Recast

The sole purpose of the BRR is to determine the jurisdiction of courts to hear disputes in the area of civil and commercial liability.[10] The BRR is unconcerned about the issue of applicable law. With this in mind, there is a general rule for establishing jurisdiction and separate rules governing specific circumstances. The general rule under Article 4(1) of the BRR states that the defendant can be sued in the Member State in which he is domiciled,[11] regardless of his nationality. This default rule means that the court of a Member State can claim jurisdiction over a case of copyright infringement where the alleged infringer is domiciled in that country, regardless of where the actual infringement took place, inclusive of EU-wide infringement.[12]

In specific circumstances, there are special provisions that can apply in lieu of the default rule.[13] These circumstances include cases where there are multiple defendants (Article 8(1)), tortious infringements (Article 7(2)) or defendants who are not domiciled in the EU (Article 6(1)). Where there are multiple defendants who have their domicile in Member States, Article 8 of the BRR allows the claimant to sue those defendants in the court of any Member State where at least one other defendant is domiciled. This allows the claimant to potentially sue all the defendants in one Member State provided that: 'the claims are so closely connected that it is expedient to hear and determine them together to avoid the risk of irreconcilable judgments resulting from separate proceedings.'[14] The interpretation

For the Hague Draft Convention see: Hague Conference on Private International Law, *Preliminary Draft Convention on Jurisdiction and Foreign Judgments in Civil and Commercial Matters* (1999) adopted by the Special Commission on 30 October 1999. See Beckstein in Leible and Ohly (2009) 15–16 for a brief discussion on the failure of the Hague Draft Convention. For the WIPO Draft Convention see: WIPO, *Draft Convention on Jurisdiction and Recognition of Judgments in Intellectual Property Matters* (2001).

[9] Subsumed within these criteria are other factors such as efficiency and simplicity. See P Jurčys, 'International Jurisdiction in Intellectual Property Disputes' (2012) 3(3) *JIPITEC* 174, 184.

[10] Case C-68/93 *Fiona Shevill and others v Presse Alliance SA* [1995] ECLI:EU:C:1995:61, para 37.

[11] The term 'domiciled' is not defined in the Regulation. However, in terms of its ordinary dictionary meaning, it can be interpreted as: 'the place where one has his home or permanent residence, to which, if absent, he has the intention of returning'. See Oxford English Dictionary, 'Domicile': <http://www.oed.com/view/Entry/56682?rskey=gK6cV3&result=1#eid> accessed 20 November 2015.

[12] Torremans in Stamatoudi (2016) 382.

[13] Where the special rules apply, for example, Article 7(2) of the BRR, the claimant can derogate from the general rules in accordance with Article 5.

[14] This requirement was developed in Case C-189/87 *Athanasios Kalfelis v Bankhaus Schroder, Munchmeyer, Hengst und Co and others* [1988] ECLI:EU:C:1988:459, paras 8–12, borrowing the language from Article 22 of the Brussels Convention on jurisdiction and the enforcement of judgments in civil and commercial matters of 27 September 1968 [Brussels Convention]. The close connection requirement was then incorporated into Article 6(1) of Council Regulation (EC) No 44/2001 of 22 December 2000 on jurisdiction and the recognition and enforcement of judgments in civil and commercial matters [Brussels Regulation] [2001] OJ L12/1, 16.1.2001, and later Article 8(1) of the BRR.

of this requirement covers situations where: 'separate trial and judgment would involve the risk of conflicting decisions, without necessarily involving the risk of giving rise to mutually exclusive legal consequences.'[15] In other words, cases involving multiple defendants domiciled in the EU should be litigated together to prevent the possibility of conflicting decisions even where the ultimate legal consequences would not be so different. The use of Article 8(1) is to be limited to situations where the defendants commit the same infringement and are subject to the same laws, so that it is expedient to hear the cases together to avoid the risk of irreconcilable judgements.[16]

By virtue of copyright infringement being *considered* a tort, Article 7(2) of the BRR allows the claimant in a copyright suit to sue a defendant (if domiciled in a Member State) where the 'harmful event occurred or may occur'. The concept of 'harmful event' was interpreted to mean the place where the damage occurred or the place of the event giving rise to the harm.[17] This interpretation was designed to justify the attribution of jurisdiction to a particular court based on the existence of a close linking factor between the Member State of the court seised and the dispute at hand.[18] In practice what this means is that the claimant can bring his claim in the Member State where liability for the act can be established[19] or alternatively, the place where the act causing the damage originated. It is possible that the place where liability can be established and the place of the event giving rise to the harm could be the same and as such, be a single Member State.

In the digital context, the question of where jurisdiction can be established may be difficult to determine. This is a result of the pervasive nature of disseminating material on the Internet, whereby a single act can have effects in multiple countries. The CJEU has offered different solutions to this issue based on the type of rights involved. For personality rights, the CJEU allowed litigants to bring a claim where their centre of interest exists with the additional possibility that a single claim can cover all damage within the EU.[20] Alternatively, for registered trade

[15] Case C-406/92 *The owners of the cargo lately laden on board the ship 'Tatry' v The owners of the ship 'Maciej Rataj'* [1994] ECLI:EU:C:1994:400, para 58.

[16] Case C-539/03 *Roche Nederland BV and others v Frederick Primus and Milton Goldenberg* [2006] ECLI:EU:C:2006:458, paras 27–36. Note, this example was in the case of EU patent law. Torremans argues that this should be unproblematic in the context of EU copyright law, given the extent of harmonisation. As such, there should not be a risk of irreconcilable decisions, which has led to Article 8(1) of the BRR being easier to apply via the 'softening' of its criteria – Torremans in Stamatoudi (2016) 386–92.

[17] Case C-21/76 *Handelskwekerij v Mines de Potasse d'Alsace* [1976] ECLI:EU:C:1976:166, paras 17–25 in relation to Article 5(3) of the Brussels Convention. This interpretation was accepted under the Brussels Regulation in Cases C-509/09 and C-161/10 *eDate Advertising GmbH v X and Oliver Martinez and another v MGN Ltd* [2011] ECLI:EU:C:2011:685, para 41 and later in the copyright case of Case C-170/12 *Peter Pinckney v KDG Mediatech* [2013] ECLI:EU:C:2013:635, para 26.

[18] *Shevill v Presse Alliance* [1995] para 19 in relation to Article 5(3) of the Brussels Convention, Case C-189/08 *Zuid-Chemie BV v Philippo's Mineralenfabriek NV/SA* [2009] ECLI:EU:C:2009:475, para 24 in relation to the Brussels Regulation and *Pinckney* [2013] para 27 in the copyright context.

[19] *Zuid-Chemie* [2009] para 26.

[20] *eDate Advertising* [2011] paras 48–49.

mark law, claims can be brought where the trade mark in question is registered[21] even when the alleged act of infringement originates outside of the Member State of registration.[22] Furthermore, if the court seised is located in the country of the trade mark's registration it has the ability to take into account all damage relating to the infringement of the trade mark in question.

In contrast to personality rights and trade mark law, copyright law has no 'centre of interest' or registration requirement and, as such, it has been treated differently by the CJEU with regard to the scope of damage that the court can consider. The CJEU in *Pinckney* limited the scope of damage that the court could consider to the damage that occurred within the Member State of the court seised.[23] *Hejduk* affirmed the finding from *Pinckney* in stating that a Member State's court is limited to considering damage caused by the infringement in its own territory because the copyright protection bestowed on the work is limited to its own territory.[24] Therefore, other Member States' courts retain jurisdiction to address damage in their own territories because they are better placed to ascertain the validity of rights, infringement and the nature of damage within their own territories.[25] However, it will be argued that courts in copyright cases should be able to adopt an EU-wide consideration of damage.

Lastly, where the domicile of the defendant is not a Member State, Article 6 of the BRR states that the domestic laws of the relevant Member State will determine whether the court seised has jurisdiction. Despite the historical rhetoric of the BRR by virtue of its derivation from the Brussels Convention, there are several problems with the framework for establishing jurisdiction. Many of these issues are exposed and exacerbated in the digital context, particularly with reference to the reformed communication to the public right.

B. Problems with the Brussels Regulation Recast for EU Copyright Law

(i) Domicile Requirement

If one focuses on the wording of Articles 4, 5, 7 and 8 of the BRR, it is apparent that there is the consistent requirement that the defendant has his 'domicile' in

[21] Case C-523/10 *Wintersteiger AG v Products 4U Sondermaschinenbau GmbH* [2012] ECLI:EU:C:2012:220, paras 28–29.

[22] From *Wintersteiger*, it can be seen that damage to trade marks occurs at the place of its registration. This justifies the establishment of jurisdiction in the country of registration even though the act of infringement originated elsewhere. This reasoning is consistent with the fact that Article 24(4) of the BRR grants exclusive jurisdiction to a court of the Member State where an IP right is registered in cases involving the registration or validity of such IP rights – Case C-4/03 *Gesellschaft für Antriebstechnik mbH & Co KG v Lamellen und Kupplungsbau Beteiligungs KG* [2006] ECLI:EU:C:2006:457.

[23] *Pinckney* [2013] para 45.

[24] Case C-441/13 *Pez Hejduk v EnergieAgentur.NRW GmbH* [2015] ECLI:EU:C:2015:28, para 36.

[25] ibid para 37.

a Member State. Thus, the concept of 'domicile' is essential under the BRR. Yet, the term 'domicile' remains undefined in the BRR. Although Article 63 defines 'domicile' in the context of a company, Article 62 reserves the interpretation of 'domicile' concerning individuals as a matter for the court seised to determine based on its domestic law. Consequently, this provides the opportunity for inconsistent decisions even though the general law is harmonised. Despite the absence of an express definition, it has been suggested that 'domicile' refers to a stable establishment or substantial residence.[26] As a matter of certainty, an express definition for the term 'domicile' should be adopted.

Recital 15 of the BRR states that the rules of jurisdiction should be generally based on the defendant's domicile, so much so that jurisdiction should always be available on this ground (save in a few well-defined instances).[27] The rationale provided for the reliance on 'domicile' is primarily based on ensuring fairness for defendants. It is argued that establishing jurisdiction on the basis of the defendant's domicile ensures predictability about where a suit may be brought and, additionally, allows the defendant the best opportunity to defend himself.[28] Using the 'domicile' requirement in this way ensures there is certainty as to where a claim can be brought. In order to balance the interests of the claimants and defendants, the court seised is allowed to assert 'unlimited jurisdiction' where jurisdiction is established on the basis of the defendant's domicile under Article 4(1). By this it is meant that parallel infringements and damages occurring in other territories can be taken account of by the court seised.[29]

However, use of 'domicile' assumes there is certainty about where the act of alleged infringement occurs and where its implications are felt and, secondly, that the defendant has resources in the country of his domicile.[30] It may be the case that these considerations are over-simplified and taken for granted to the extent that establishing jurisdiction in the country of the defendant's domicile offers no practical advantage. As such, Recital 16 goes on to state that there should be alternative grounds for jurisdiction based on a close connection between the court and the action. This approach was suggested under Article 4(2) of the Proposal for a Regulation on jurisdiction and the recognition and enforcement of judgments in civil and commercial matters.[31] The proposed Article 4(2) would have allowed defendants not domiciled in a Member State to be sued in a Member

[26] P Stone, *EU Private International Law*, 3rd edn (Edward Elgar Publishing Ltd, 2014) 68.

[27] Stone describes the 'domicile' requirement as the principal connecting factor used in the BRR – ibid 52.

[28] This was the rationale adopted by the CJEU in Case C-26/91 *Jakob Handte & Co GmbH v Traitements Mécano-chimiques des Surfaces SA* [1992] ECLI:EU:C:1992:268, para 14.

[29] A Metzger, 'Jurisdiction in Cases Concerning Intellectual Property Infringements on the Internet' in S Leible and A Ohly (eds), *Intellectual Property and Private International Law* (Mohr Siebeck, 2009) 253.

[30] Stone (2014) 53.

[31] European Commission, *Proposal for a Regulation of the European Parliament and of the Council on jurisdiction and the recognition and enforcement of judgments in civil and commercial matters* (COM(2010) 748 final, 2010) 23.

State where special jurisdiction could be established. For example, this would have meant that the current Article 7(2) could apply to defendants not domiciled in a Member State. However, this proposal was rejected and the 'domicile' requirement remained intact.

It is not being suggested that the 'domicile' requirement should be removed as the default rule. Rather, it is argued that the establishment of special jurisdiction should not require the defendant be 'domiciled' in a Member State. This suggestion may be seen as controversial because the 'domicile' requirement is ordinarily a central aspect of private international law. However, changes in technology require alterations in the way jurisdiction is established. While 'domicile' has been central to the BRR, it is not the only justifiable means for establishing jurisdiction; nor is it the most suitable in the current context. The 'domicile' requirement makes the provisions on special jurisdiction too EU-centric, since only persons domiciled in a Member State may be sued under Article 7(2). This approach is inconsistent with the aim of securing a high level of protection for right holders because the 'domicile' requirement restricts who they can sue.

With developments in technology increasing the prevalence of ubiquitous infringements by persons outside the EU, the effectiveness of the 'domicile' requirement must be scrutinised. The problem is that the 'domicile' requirement complicates the enforcement of EU copyright law, given that claimants will have to rely on domestic laws to establish jurisdiction pursuant to Article 6 where the defendant is not domiciled in the EU. Diverse modes of establishing jurisdiction in this regard conflict with the EU's pursuit of an internal market and its harmonisation agenda.[32] Thus, adopting a harmonised approach for the treatment of persons not domiciled in the EU will provide for greater certainty and efficiency. Any reform in this area will have to place more emphasis on the act than on the actor, which will be to the benefit of right holders. This is because the reach of the courts will be wider in terms of their ability to adjudicate on unauthorised uses of works. An additional benefit of adopting this approach is the avoidance of the problems caused by the absence of an express definition for 'domicile'. Therefore, in the interests of achieving a high level of protection for right holders and achieving further harmonisation of EU law for the purpose of the internal market,

[32] For example, in the UK, establishing jurisdiction over persons not domiciled in the EU is subject to the common law. The rules provide that an English court can establish jurisdiction where the defendant is properly served process within the UK – see *HRH Maharanee Seethadevi Gaekwar of Baroda v Wildenstein* [1972] 2 WLR 1077. Alternatively, jurisdiction can be established over a defendant not domiciled in the EU even where they are outside the UK subject to the permission of the court pursuant to Practice Direction 6B, paragraph 3.1 of the Civil Procedure Rules. By contrast, Germany governs the establishment of jurisdiction for defendants not domiciled in the EU via the German Code of Civil Procedure (Zivilprozessordnung) – see ss 12–34. Similarly, France addresses jurisdiction subject to the Code of Civil Procedure – see Articles 42–48. See K Bonacorsi, 'Not at Home with "At-Home" Jurisdiction' (2014) 37(6) *Fordham International Law Journal* 1821 and E Treppoz, 'Does size matter? A comparative study of jurisdictional rules applicable to domestic and Community IP rights' in P Stone and Y Farah (eds), *Research Handbook on EU Private International Law* (Edward Elgar Publishing Ltd, 2015) 157–62.

the 'domicile' requirement in the area of special jurisdiction should be abandoned. This will provide a more effective enforcement framework for EU copyright law.

Establishing jurisdiction on the basis of the infringement (Article 7(2)) or establishing jurisdiction for multiple defendants in one Member State (Article 8(1)) should not hinge on whether the defendant in question is domiciled in a Member State.[33] Instead, it should be sufficient that there is a close connection between the court seised and the claim brought. From this, focus should be on the act in question and not the actors. This would satisfy the criteria set out in Recital 16 of the BRR. Moreover, it would enable right holders to attain a greater level of protection because they will not be limited in bringing claims under EU copyright law on the basis of the domicile of the defendant.

The suggestion to remove the 'domicile' requirement for cases of special jurisdiction involving copyright law can be supported by other frameworks concerning IP law. The EU Regulations concerning Community designs[34] and Community trade marks[35] have specific provisions on the establishment of jurisdiction. Both Regulations are structured in such a way that if the defendant is not domiciled in a Member State, this is not detrimental to the claimant's action. The 'international jurisdiction' provision is configured in such a way that jurisdiction can be established on the basis of the defendant's domicile or establishment, the claimant's domicile or establishment or at the court of the European Union Intellectual Property Office (EUIPO, formerly OHIM).[36] This approach reduces the central importance of the defendant's domicile by relegating it to one of three potential considerations.

Alternatively, Article 2:202 of the CLIP Principles and section 204(1) of the ALI Principles provide a more radical approach, whereby the 'domicile' requirement is completely removed. Instead of focusing on the actors involved, both these provisions are solely concerned with the act in question. Adopting either the approach used for the EU community rights or alternatively, the approach of the proposed international principles will both be in accordance with the objectives set out in this section, namely to ensure a high level of protection for right holders. This is because the reach of claimants will not be limited by the requirement that the defendant be domiciled in a Member State. In this way, the ubiquitous nature of copyright infringement will be taken into account. Having said that, it would be preferable to adopt a similar approach to that applied under Article 2:202 of the CLIP Principles because it offers a simple and effective way of establishing jurisdiction.

[33] Torremans argues that relying on domicile in establishing jurisdiction for cases of multi-party infringement is unsuitable – Torremans in Stamatoudi (2016) 382.

[34] Council Regulation (EC) No 6/2002 of 12 December 2001 on Community designs.

[35] Council Regulation (EC) No 207/2009 of 26 February 2009 on the Community trade mark (codified version).

[36] Article 82 Community Designs Regulation and Article 97 Community Trade Mark Regulation.

(ii) Ubiquitous Infringement and Consideration of Damage

Digital uses of copyright works have facilitated the occurrence of ubiquitous infringement. This is because the reach of the Internet is global and as such, a work uploaded in one country has the potential to be accessed anywhere that has an Internet connection. Moreover, these acts are not limited to persons domiciled in the EU. The consequences of this are conflict with the EU's territorially-oriented rules concerning jurisdiction[37] and, furthermore, an unnecessarily complicated and problematic legal framework.[38] In response to the ubiquity issue courts have relied on a targeting criterion to establish jurisdiction.[39]

In the trade mark context, the CJEU in *L'Oreal v eBay* required that the act of infringement must be directed/targeted at a specific Member State in order to establish jurisdiction in that country.[40] This was also initially followed in the copyright context in *Football Dataco v Sportradar*.[41] Similarly, at the domestic level the targeting approach has also been applied, whereby UK courts only have jurisdiction to hear a claim for infringement of the communication to the public right where the act is targeted at the UK.[42] If the targeting approach is followed, it means that the act in question is not viewed as ubiquitous. Instead, that act is related to a particular country and, as such, will be addressed by the laws of that country.

However, the CJEU in *Pinckney* departed from the targeting approach for copyright law and relied on a less rigid, access approach, whereby jurisdiction can be established once the infringing act is accessible in that Member State.[43] Notwithstanding this, it is suggested that it is necessary to expressly address ubiquitous infringement in the proposed rules for establishing jurisdiction in relation to EU copyright law. In the first place, Stamatoudi and Torremans argue that the EU rules on private international law are inadequate in addressing the context of the digital era, especially in the context of ubiquitous infringement.[44] In particular, this is

[37] Fawcett and Torremans describe this conflict as '[a] real clash' – J Fawcett and P Torremans, *Intellectual Property and Private International Law*, 2nd edn (Oxford University Press, 2011) 535 para 10.05. Also see, A Reindl, 'Choosing Law in Cyberspace: Copyright Conflicts on Global Networks' (1998) 19 *Michigan Journal of International Law* 799, 807 and J Ginsburg, 'Copyright Without Borders? Choice of Forum and Choice of Law for Copyright Infringement in Cyberspace' (1997) 15 *Cardozo Arts & Entertainment Law Journal* 153.

[38] P Schonning, 'Applicable Law in Transfrontier On-Line Transmissions' (1996) 170 *Revue Internationale du Droit d'Auteur (RIDA)* 21, 21 and M Burnstein, 'Conflicts on the Net: Choice of Law in Transnational Cyberspace' (1996) 29 *Vanderbilt Journal of Transnational Law* 75, 87.

[39] Torremans argues that a territorial approach in the Internet context is undesirable because it would mean litigating on a country-by-country basis, which could make exclusive rights unenforceable – Torremans in Torremans (2017) 565.

[40] Case C-324/09 *L'Oreal SA and others v eBay International AG and others* [2011] ECLI:EU:C:2011:474, para 64.

[41] Case C-173/11 *Football Dataco Ltd and others v Sportradar GmbH and another* [2012] ECLI:EU:C:2012:642, paras 36–43.

[42] *EMI Records Ltd v British Sky Broadcasting Ltd* [2013] EWHC 379 (Ch), paras 48–51.

[43] *Pinckney* [2013] para 42.

[44] I Stamatoudi and P Torremans, *EU Copyright Law: A Commentary* (Edward Elgar Publishing, 2014) 1060.

caused by the 'domicile' requirement and the absence of a ubiquitous infringement provision. The 'domicile' requirement of the BRR limits whom right holders can hold accountable. If a claim is brought against a person not domiciled in the EU, the establishment of jurisdiction is subject to the domestic jurisdiction rules of the court seised (Article 6). This restricts the development of a more harmonised approach to EU copyright law because a large number of alleged infringement cases will be subject to diverse domestic laws concerning the treatment of defendants not domiciled in the EU. Therefore, in the interest of combatting ubiquitous infringement, especially by non-EU persons, and to achieve a more harmonised copyright framework, the laws concerning jurisdiction need to be amended to expressly address instances of ubiquitous infringement in a non-EU-centric manner.

The above argument concerning the removal of the 'domicile' requirement can be supported on the basis that the establishment of jurisdiction on the premise of the 'domicile' of the defendant is questionable, because the more pertinent issue is whether there is a close connection between the court seised and the act complained of. It is arguable that the reason for the 'domicile' requirement under the BRR is to ensure certainty for defendants and to increase the chance that the defendant has assets in the Member State of the court seised. However, this reasoning is not persuasive in justifying the necessity of the 'domicile' requirement. If the rule is clear that defendants can be sued in any Member State where there is a close connection to the act complained of, this does not compromise the certainty element that defendants supposedly benefit from under the current rules of the BRR. Similarly, the need for 'domicile' is increasingly undermined if the aim of suing a defendant is broadened to focus not solely on obtaining damages, but rather to include or focus on stopping the infringement. If the primary aim does not concern financial remedies, then the need for 'domicile' is greatly weakened because the defendant having assets is not necessary.[45]

Furthermore, there is the issue concerning the consideration of damage in relation to EU copyright cases. If jurisdiction is established under Article 7(2) of the BRR, the court seised can only address damage within its territory due to the territorial nature of copyright law.[46] However, this is a naïve approach to adopt because it prejudices right holders' ability to achieve a high level of protection for their works and moreover, is an inefficient way of addressing infringement. The current rules do not provide an effective or efficient means for addressing acts of ubiquitous infringement. A more desirable approach would be that the court seised should be able to take into account all damage caused by the alleged infringement throughout the EU and, additionally, be able to grant EU-wide injunctions.[47]

[45] For example, consider the availability of novel remedies such as 'live injunctions' in the UK. See *Football Association Premier League Ltd v British Communication Plc* [2017] EWHC 480 (Ch).

[46] *Pinckney* [2013] para 45.

[47] EU-wide injunctions are possible in relation to Community-wide rights – Community trade marks, design rights and patents. See Case C-235/09 *DHL Express France SAS v Chronopost SA*

The availability of EU-wide injunctions also has the added importance of being able to address instances of threatened ubiquitous infringement. This suggested approach will provide an efficient means for litigating copyright claims, so that right holders can obtain an effective remedy without the administrative burden of multiple claims in different Member States. If this approach is adopted, a high level of protection for right holders will be established because they will be able to hold infringers accountable under one claim. Additionally, the ubiquitous nature of copyright infringement will be acknowledged under an express provision.[48]

Courts seised in an EU copyright case should have the ability to take account of all damage occurring within the EU. The CLIP Principles and the ALI Principles adopt approaches similar to what is advocated in this subsection. Article 2:203(2) of the CLIP Principles provides the option that in cases of infringement by ubiquitous media, the court seised may have jurisdiction over infringements in other states, provided that the infringements have no substantial effect in the state where the defendant is habitually resident. It must also be the case that substantial activities have been carried out in furtherance of the infringement in the territory of the court seised and there is substantial harm in the territory of the court seised in relation to the ubiquitous infringements taken as a whole. If these criteria are met, then the court seised can address the damage for the infringement as a whole.

Section 204(1) of the ALI Principles also offers the option for the court seised to take account of all damage where the defendant substantially acted or made substantial preparatory acts to initiate or further an alleged infringement in that country. These alternative frameworks offer different means of addressing the issues concerning ubiquitous infringement, the 'domicile' requirement and the consideration of damage. Thus, it will be recommended that the law on jurisdiction should reflect something similar to the alternative provisions discussed in this subsection. This is because ubiquitous acts are often committed by persons not domiciled in the EU. Furthermore, it is worth considering the implementation of EU-wide injunctions for copyright law.

(iii) Article 7(2) of the Brussels Regulation Recast and Copyright Cases

In order to gain a better understanding of the copyright-specific criticisms directed at the BRR, it is necessary to analyse Article 7(2). Pursuant to Article 7(2),

[2011] ECLI:EU:C:2011:238, *Mattel Inc v Woolbro (Distributors) Ltd* [2003] EWHC 2412 (Ch), *Apple vs. Samsung Re: Galaxy Tab 8.9*: Landgericht Düsseldorf, Urteil vom 15.09.2011 Az.: 14c O 219/11, Oberlandesgericht Düsseldorf, Urteil vom 31. Jan. 2012, Az. I 20 U 126/11 and *Apple vs. Samsung Re: Galaxy Tab 10.1*: Landgericht Düsseldorf, Urteil vom 09.09.2011, Az. 14c O 194/11, Oberlandesgericht Düsseldorf, Urteil vom 31. Jan. 2012, Az. I 20 U 175/11.

[48] In the long term, the ideal situation will be the codification of copyright law into a Community-wide right. This will provide for EU-wide protection, as is the case with the other Community rights.

the establishment of jurisdiction in copyright cases is dependent on the 'place where the harmful act occurred'.[49] The application and interpretation of this concept will be analysed by looking at four key EU copyright cases – *Football Dataco v Sportradar*, *Pinckney*, *Hi Hotel*[50] and *Hejduk*. With this in mind, 'the place where the harmful event occurred' has been interpreted to mean 'the place where the damage occurred and the place of the event giving rise to the harm'.[51] It is important to note that this phrase refers to two distinct situations; that is, 'where the damage occurred' *or* 'the place of the event giving rise to the harm'.

Notwithstanding this, it should be said that the CJEU in *Pinckney* stated that jurisdiction in cases of alleged copyright infringement:

> is already established in favour of the court seised if the Member State in which that court is situated protects the copyrights relied on by the plaintiff and that the alleged damage may occur within the jurisdiction of the court seised.[52]

The underlying reasoning for this was that courts which recognise the subsistence of copyright and offer protection against the alleged act of infringement are in the best position to adjudicate on the case.[53] This reasoning is similar to that used in the cases involving registered IP rights. For example, the CJEU in the patent case *Zuid-Chemie* held that the place where damage occurs is the place where the event in question may give rise to liability.[54] Similarly, in the trade mark case *Wintersteiger*, the CJEU stated that the place where the damage occurred is the country where the mark is registered.[55] The CJEU has been consistent in its reasoning that jurisdiction can be established where the rights are recognised; and where those rights can be infringed in the manner alleged in the claim. Thus, this has created certainty for both claimants and defendants.

Nonetheless, in the copyright context it is still necessary for claimants to validate the jurisdiction of the court on the basis that the infringing event originated in the Member State of the court seised or that the damage occurred in that Member State. The issue of where the infringing event originated has been largely unproblematic and has been interpreted to mean the causal event for the harmful act that occurred or will occur.[56] Despite this, it should be noted that it is unclear whether jurisdiction established in this manner allows the court seised to take account of all damage throughout the EU. By contrast, establishing jurisdiction on the basis of where the damage occurred has produced conflicting views. This is evidenced in comparing *Football Dataco v Sportradar* against *Pinckney* and *Hejduk*. In *Football Dataco v Sportradar*, the CJEU established that in order to locate an act of

[49] For an overview of Article 7(2) see Stone (2014) Chapter 4.
[50] Case C-387/12 *Hi Hotel HCF SARL v Spoering* [2014] ECLI:EU:C:2014:215.
[51] *Pinckney* [2013] para 26.
[52] *Pinckney* [2013] para 43.
[53] *Zuid-Chemie* [2009] para 24, *Wintersteiger* [2012] para 28 and *Pinckney* [2013] para 46.
[54] *Zuid-Chemie* [2009] para 26.
[55] *Wintersteiger* [2012] para 27.
[56] *Hi Hotel* [2014] para 27 and *Hejduk* [2015] para 24.

infringement, that act must target or be directed to the particular Member State.[57] In other words, infringement can only occur in the specified country if the act was targeted at that country. In the absence of such localisation, the court seised cannot establish jurisdiction.

The targeting approach used by the CJEU in *Football Dataco v Sportradar* was based on the *Pammer*[58] decision, where the Court, in interpreting Article 15(1)(c) of the Brussels Regulation (now Article 17(1)(c) of the BRR), held that the mere accessibility of a website was insufficient to establish jurisdiction.[59] This approach was also followed in the trade mark case of *L'Oreal v eBay*, where the use of trade marks online would not invoke EU law unless the use of the marks was targeted at Member States.[60] Similarly, UK courts have followed the targeting approach in establishing jurisdiction to hear cases concerning the infringement of the communication to the public right.[61] The targeting approach has been justified on the basis that it limits forum shopping and ensures that courts seised have a close connection to the alleged infringement.[62] Furthermore, the reduction in enforcement possibilities provides a better balance between the interests of right holders and users, because the targeting requirement aids legal certainty and foreseeability for users by reducing the possibility of litigation in countries where there is little or no harm.[63] This mitigates the possibility of right holders bullying weaker defendants into disadvantageous positions.[64]

Thus, it was anticipated that *Pinckney* would follow *Football Dataco v Sportradar*, given the prospects of certainty and predictability for online users in particular. However, the CJEU in *Pinckney* adopted a contrasting view and held that to establish jurisdiction on the basis of the place where the damage occurred, there is no requirement of targeting. Instead, it is sufficient that the copyright work is accessible in the country of the court seised.[65] However, if jurisdiction is established on this ground, the consideration of damage by the court seised is limited to damage present in the territory of that court.[66] This approach was followed in *Hejduk*.[67]

[57] *Football Dataco v Sportradar* [2012] paras 36–39.

[58] Cases C-585/08 and C-144/09 *Peter Pammer v Reederei Karl Schluter GmbH & Co KG* [2010] ECLI:EU:C:2010:740.

[59] ibid paras 69 and 74–76 and *Football Dataco v Sportradar* [2012] paras 36–40.

[60] *L'Oreal v eBay* [2011] para 64.

[61] *EMI v Sky* [2013] paras 48–51, followed in *1967 Ltd v British Sky Broadcasting Ltd* [2014] EWHC 3444 (Ch) para 21.

[62] Torremans argues that it is unlikely that a claimant would have suffered damage in a country where he did not act or target – Torremans in Torremans (2017) 565.

[63] Matulionyte (2015) 136.

[64] Torremans argues that right holders should not be allowed to bring claims in every Member State where there is harm, as this will disadvantage weaker defendants – Torremans in Stamatoudi (2016) 384.

[65] *Pinckney* [2013] para 42.

[66] ibid para 45.

[67] *Hejduk* [2015] paras 33–34 and 36.

The CJEU's failure to follow the targeting approach from *Football Dataco v Sportradar* may be attributed to the criticisms that can be levied against the notion of 'targeting'. Matulionyte discussed the difficulties with defining and quantifying what 'targeting' means. The evidence required to prove 'targeting' is more suitable to a substantive discussion concerning infringement and as such, the evidentiary threshold is burdensome to the parties at a preliminary stage of the court dispute.[68] Additionally to this, the targeting approach is inconsistent with the norms of ubiquitous copyright infringement, where there is often no identifiable target audience. While it can be argued that targeting can be determined on the basis of the language of the communication, the type of advertisements involved and even the content being infringed, these factors do not preclude the possibility of infringement in other countries. Moreover, these factors are not definitive evidence of 'targeting', given the widespread use of languages such as English or the versatility of advertisements and furthermore, the increasing pursuit of cross-border sales on the Internet.[69]

Despite the criticism levied against the targeting approach, the access approach has also been subjected to criticism. It has been argued that the access approach adopted in *Pinckney* is problematic because it facilitates forum shopping and abuse by claimants, who may sue in cases where success is unlikely. The width of 'access' in relation to the Internet means that a lawsuit could be established in potentially every single Member State. Therefore, users will be unable to predict where they can be sued.[70] A further implication of this includes the absence of a close connection between the court seised and the act complained of.[71] These criticisms should be dismissed because the problem of using the access approach for forum shopping is overstated. The reality is that the establishment of jurisdiction is only the first step to obtaining a remedy for an alleged breach of copyright. It remains the case that infringement still has to be proved within the territory for which protection is claimed. For example, this would require actual evidence of an act of communication to the public. It is also the case that the consideration of damage under the access approach is limited to the harm that occurred within the chosen Member State. As such, this will influence right holders into bringing claims where it is efficient to do so.[72]

In a practical sense the targeting and access approaches are not so different, because they have developed internal restricting factors to prevent forum shopping abuse. The targeting approach prohibits the establishment of jurisdiction in non-targeted countries, implementing a de minimis approach. However, the wide interpretation of 'targeting' means that many Internet transmissions will be held to be pan-European in the absence of clear evidence specifying a particular

[68] Matulionyte (2015) 136.
[69] ibid 136–37.
[70] Torremans in Torremans (2017) 564
[71] Matulionyte (2015) 133–34.
[72] ibid 135.

Member State(s). By contrast, the access approach serves to limit forum shopping by restricting the consideration of damage to the harm that occurred in the Member State. Rational right holders are likely to bring their claims in countries where they are likely to succeed and obtain a desirable remedy. Furthermore, baseless claims will be addressed at the domestic level using mechanisms such as summary judgments, abuse of process and declarations of non-infringement. As such the fear of mass forum shopping is likely unfounded.

In resolving the conflict between the targeting and access approaches, it is suggested that the access approach be adopted as the determinant for establishing jurisdiction on the basis of where the damage occurred. However, a de minimis threshold should be added to further limit baseless claims. The justification for this is that the access approach is better suited to the realities of the Internet. If the targeting approach is adopted, there may be significant consequences for the operation of the reformed communication to the public right because it will limit enforcement to countries targeted by the 'communication' despite the ubiquity of online transmissions. This could amount to de facto exhaustion of the communication to the public right in non-targeted countries in contravention of Article 3(3) of the ISD. Therefore, adopting the access approach with a de minimis threshold will ensure that right holders can enforce their rights where infringements occur. This is counterbalanced by users having protection from simultaneous de minimis claims in multiple countries and increased foreseeability and predictability as to where they may be sued.[73]

For the establishment of certainty these suggestions must be made express in the law.

(iv) The Need for Copyright-Specific Rules

Copyright law and more generally IP law are categorised under the heading of 'tort' for the purpose of establishing jurisdiction under Article 7(2) of the BRR. Although copyright law does ordinarily fall within the scope of tort law, it is debatable whether it should be separately addressed for the purpose of establishing jurisdiction. This book will not contest the notion that copyright law is part of tort law.[74] However, it will be argued that there should be copyright-specific rules pertaining to the establishment of jurisdiction. Copyright-specific rules will allow for more coherence because the specifics of copyright law can be taken into account, in particular, the unregistered nature of copyright, the prevalence of

[73] Torremans argues that the introduction of filters for determining jurisdiction would improve foreseeability and predictability – Torremans in Torremans (2017) 565.

[74] This issue exceeds the scope of the book. However, see P Goold, 'Is Copyright Infringement a Strict Liability Tort?' (2015) 30(1) *Berkeley Technology Law Journal* 305, W Gordon, 'Of Harms and Benefits: Tort, Restitution and Intellectual Property' (2003) 34 *McGeorge Law Review* 541, S Hetcher, 'The Immortality of Strict Liability in Copyright' (2013) 17(1) *Marquette Intellectual Property Law Review* 1 and A Dorfman and A Jacob, 'Copyright as Tort' (2011) 12 *Theoretical Inquiries in Law* 59.

ubiquitous infringement and the intricacies of the different exclusive rights, such as the reformed communication to the public right. Adopting such an approach is justifiable and achievable in light of the Regulations on Community trade marks and Community design rights respectively.[75]

Currently, the generic tortious rule under Article 7(2) of the BRR takes insufficient account of the features of EU copyright law, notably, the possibility of ubiquitous infringement. Furthermore, in order to achieve a more effective EU copyright framework it would be beneficial to adopt jurisdictional rules specific to EU copyright law. It may be the case that the copyright-specific rules largely resemble the traditional rules, as is the case with the WIPO Draft Convention on Jurisdiction, which closely mirrored the Hague Draft Convention on Jurisdiction. The subject-specific approach is desirable because it creates additional certainty for copyright law, as well as providing the possibility of creating subject-specific rules where necessary. Consequently, it is recommended that copyright-specific rules on jurisdiction be adopted so that the nuances of copyright infringement can be accommodated. This would include managing the specific exclusive rights, in particular, the reformed communication to the public right that is proposed in this book. Additionally, this approach will allow for the range of justificatory considerations that exist within EU copyright law to be better taken into account.

III. Establishing Jurisdiction for the Reformed Communication to the Public Right

In order to establish a coherent EU copyright law framework, all the relevant rules must be compatible. It has been stated that the proposed reformed communication to the public right should be the sole right applicable to the non-material dissemination of works where there is a geographically dispersed 'public'. As a result, the proposed rules on establishing jurisdiction must take account of nuances such as the scope of the reformed right, the ubiquity of digital copyright infringement and the notion of the Completion theory. Currently, relevant parts of the BRR are in conflict with the reformed communication to the public right. The conflict begins with the reliance on the EU domicile of the defendant. This is problematic because acts of communication can originate anywhere in the world and still have a global impact. It is particularly important to note that illegitimate communications tend to originate from outside the EU.[76] Therefore, in the absence of a harmonised

[75] See Article 82 of the Community Designs Regulation and Article 97 of the Community Trade Mark Regulation.

[76] For example, a BBC article reported that 25% of illegal football live streams originate from servers located in Belize. Additionally, more than 60% of the live streams analysed came from five countries: Belize, Switzerland, The Netherlands, Sweden and Canada – BBC, 'Illegal football streams are "dangerous", study says' (1 February 2016) <http://www.bbc.co.uk/news/technology-35434765> accessed 2 February 2016.

rule to regulate acts committed by persons not domiciled in the EU, there is a likelihood that the establishment of jurisdiction will be inconsistent, given the dependence on the varying domestic laws of the Member States. Consequently, it is argued that the 'domicile' requirement should be abandoned in special jurisdiction cases in order to ensure right holders have adequate protection and that there is consistency in the determination of jurisdiction for cases involving the reformed communication to the public right.

Secondly, the CJEU's interpretation of Article 7(2) of the BRR conflicts with the concept of where the act of communication to the public right occurs under the reformed right. The current interpretation of Article 7(2) allows for the establishment of jurisdiction in any Member State where the damage occurred or the place of the event giving rise to the harm.[77] In most ordinary tortious circumstances, establishing the place of the harm or the place of the event giving rise to the harm is unproblematic. In the context of the reformed communication to the public right this is more complicated because the Completion theory dictates that the act of 'communication to the public' occurs in the country(ies) of receipt and as such, the establishment of jurisdiction should be guided accordingly. However, the duality of Article 7(2) allows for the reintroduction of the Emission theory if the place of the event giving rise to the harm is applied. This can be evidenced by the CJEU's findings in *Hejduk*, where the place of the event giving rise to the harm, in terms of an act of communication to the public, was held to be where the activation of the process for the technical display of the photographs on the website occurred; that is, where the upload of the works occurred.[78]

The unsuitability of the Emission theory for the reformed communication to the public right was discussed in Chapter five, section IV. The main point to note is that the infringement of the communication to the public right involves two elements: an act of 'communication' and its potential reception, unlike the other exclusive rights that require a single act to establish infringement. As such, to create consistency a minor adjustment to the interpretation of Article 7(2) will suffice. It is suggested that Article 7(2) be interpreted to mean the place where the act occurs or the place where the harm occurs. This subtle change in language, from the place of the event giving rise to the harm to where the act occurred, will prevent the reintroduction of the Emission theory in interpreting the reformed communication to the public right while it will not affect the other exclusive rights. In other words, the place of the event giving rise to the harm and where the act occurred will be the same for an act of reproduction or distribution because a single action is required for infringement; that is, an act of copying or issuing copies to the public. Furthermore, there is no conflict between where the harm occurs and where the act occurs because the harm will not always be felt where the act occurs.

[77] *Pinckney* [2013] para 26.
[78] *Hejduk* [2015] para 24.

Thirdly, there is no provision covering ubiquitous infringement, and consequently, right holders have to bring multiple claims to achieve EU-wide remedies. Ideally, right holders should be able to bring a single claim against an act of ubiquitous infringement in one Member State, which is capable of covering all damage within the EU. This option should be available on the condition that there has been a substantial act by the defendant in the territory of the court seised and, furthermore, the result of the act is significant damage or a significant risk of damage. If this is the case, the court seised should be able to determine infringement and award remedies on the basis of the impact of the act on the EU as a whole. This is in the interest of furthering the internal market and ensuring right holders are able to benefit from a high level of protection. If this remedy is available, it will also make it clear to users that they face liability for the totality of their infringing acts within the EU. Therefore, it will ensure certainty as to where and how jurisdiction can be established. Furthermore, it will offer a more proportionate and effective mechanism for litigation instead of having to file multiple lawsuits across EU Member States. This approach has been employed in relation to personality rights.[79]

From the above discussion it is necessary to reform the existing approach to establishing jurisdiction under the BRR in order to produce a coherent and copyright compatible approach.

A. New Rules for Establishing Jurisdiction in EU Copyright Cases

It is desirable to introduce a copyright-specific means of establishing jurisdiction for cases of alleged copyright infringement due to the problems with the existing provisions of the BRR and the need for compatibility with the nuances of EU copyright law, in particular, the reformed right of communication to the public. The availability of alternative frameworks that deal with the issue of jurisdiction in an IP-specific context also furthers the call for the introduction of new rules. Consequently, the proposed structure will reflect aspects of the alternative frameworks on jurisdiction that were previously discussed, as well as embody the criteria highlighted in the introduction to this chapter – certainty, proportionality and technological neutrality. However, the proposed framework will not necessarily change everything about the current BRR framework. The general rule concerning the domicile of the defendant is maintained. Instead, emphasis is placed on the rule pertaining to special jurisdiction in the copyright context. It is recommended that the proposed changes be adopted in a copyright-specific Directive like the ISD or alternatively and more preferably a separate Regulation on the establishment of jurisdiction and applicable law for EU copyright law.

[79] *eDate Advertising* [2011] para 52.

With that in mind, the following changes are proposed:

General Rule

Persons domiciled in a Member State may, whatever their nationality, be sued in the courts of that Member State.

(a) Domicile means a close and stable connection between the person and the place in question.

The general rule under the proposed framework largely remains the same as that under Article 4(1) of the BRR. It is worth maintaining this core rule because relying on the defendant's domicile as a method to establish jurisdiction provides both defendants and claimants with certainty and predictability as to where they may sue or be sued. The domicile rule also achieves a balanced approach to the interests of both parties because it offers one place where the claim can be brought with surety. Therefore, the knowledge of both parties is equal. Furthermore, the domicile rule is unaffected by the nature of the infringement and as such is technology-neutral.

With this in mind, the proposed domicile rule meets the criteria set out for attaining an effective choice of jurisdiction rule. However, there are only two differences between the proposed rule and the original rule under the BRR. The first difference is that the term 'domicile' is defined. The definition is taken from Recital 23 of the Regulation on jurisdiction, applicable law, recognition and enforcement of decisions and acceptance and enforcement of authentic instruments in matters of succession and on the creation of a European Certificate of Succession.[80] Recital 23 states that: 'The habitual residence thus determined should reveal a close and stable connection with the State concerned taking into account the specific aims of this Regulation.' Although this sentence addresses 'habitual residence', it can be argued that 'domicile' and 'habitual residence' have been used as substitute terms.[81]

While there may be subtle differences in the meanings of 'domiciled' and 'habitually resident', they ultimately aim to achieve the same outcome; that is, to establish a close and stable connection to a particular place. According to the Borrás Report on the Brussels Regulation II, 'habitual residence' should be interpreted as: 'the place where the person had established, on a fixed basis, his permanent or habitual centre of interests, with all the relevant facts being taken

[80] Recital 23 of Regulation (EU) No 650/2012 of the European Parliament and of the Council of 4 July 2012 on jurisdiction, applicable law, recognition and enforcement of decisions and acceptance and enforcement of authentic instruments in matters of succession and on the creation of a European Certificate of Succession [Regulation on jurisdiction, applicable law, recognition and enforcement] [2012] OJ L201/107, 27.7.2012.

[81] Compare the BRR, which uses 'domicile', to the alternative frameworks discussed that use 'habitual residence' to similar effect – Hague Draft Convention on Jurisdiction, ALI Principles and the CLIP Principles.

into account for the purpose of determining such residence'.[82] In comparing 'domicile' to 'habitual residence' it can be stated that 'domicile' has an intention requirement in establishing the connection between the person and the place. In other words, the person involved must have the intention that the place in question is his permanent residence. As such, there is a continuing relationship with that place; whereas, 'habitual residence' is more about 'a close and stable connection' between the person and the place in question.[83] In contrast to 'domiciled', 'habitual residence' does not necessarily require any future intention to hold permanent residence at the place in question. It must simply be established that the person has had sufficient connection with that place. From this comparison it can be said that 'habitually resident' sets a lower standard than 'domiciled' and perhaps is part of the reason that 'habitual residence' is used in the international conventions.

However, as stated, the ultimate goal of either term is to ensure that the defendant has a close and stable connection with the territory in which he is to be sued. The term 'domicile' is used as a matter of consistency with existing EU law. However, the definition provided is akin to the interpretation of 'habitual residence' given by Borrás. The second difference is the replacement of the word 'shall' with 'may'. The use of the term 'shall' implies that the defendant must be sued in the Member State that he is domiciled in.[84] From the perspective of the claimant, this suggests that he can only sue the defendant in the state that the defendant is domiciled. Although, it is the general rule that the defendant can be sued in the Member State of his domicile, it is not the only Member State he can be sued in.[85] As such, it is misleading to use the word 'shall'.

Lastly, it should be noted that if jurisdiction is established on the ground of the defendant's domicile, it remains the case that the court seised has the ability to take an EU wide account of damage. However, an EU-wide consideration of damage in this context is not necessarily justified, given that the infringement is not necessarily connected to the place of the court seised. This can negatively affect the balance of interests between claimants and defendants by unfairly favouring the claimant at the expense of the territoriality of copyright law. For an EU-wide consideration of damage to be justified, it must be the case that the court with jurisdiction has a strong and direct link with the infringement. However, this is not provided by the domicile link. It should be noted that emphasis should be placed on the act of infringement and not the actor involved.

[82] A Borrás, *Explanatory report on the Convention, drawn up on the basis of Article K.3 of the Treaty on European Union, on Jurisdiction and the Recognition and Enforcement of Judgments in Matrimonial Matters* (98/C 221/04) (1998) para 32.

[83] Recital 23 of Regulation on jurisdiction, applicable law, recognition and enforcement.

[84] K Adams, *A Manual of Style for Contract Drafting*, 3rd edn (American Bar Association, 2013) 43–50. See discussion on how the term 'shall' should be used.

[85] In fact, a defendant in a case of ubiquitous infringement may be sued in multiple Member States simultaneously.

Infringement Rule

A claimant may sue a defendant in any Member State where the defendant is alleged to have committed an act of copyright infringement or is likely to commit an act of copyright infringement.

(a) Where a claimant brings an infringement action against a person, the claimant may also proceed in that same court against other defendants where:
   (i) that defendant has caused or is likely to cause infringement in any Member state; and
   (ii) the claims are so closely connected that it is expedient to hear and determine them together to avoid the risk of irreconcilable judgments resulting from separate proceedings.

(b) The court with jurisdiction will have the ability to take account of all damages occurring or likely to occur in the EU as a result of the alleged copyright infringement, if the defendant substantially acted within the Member State of the court seised.

(c) In all other circumstances the court with jurisdiction will only have control over damage suffered within their own Member State.

This proposed provision largely departs from the rule contained in Article 7(2) of the BRR. Firstly, the rule is copyright-specific, as opposed to being considered a subset of tortious acts. Secondly, the requirement that the defendant be domiciled in a Member State is abandoned. As such, anyone who commits or is likely to commit an act of copyright infringement can be sued in the Member State where the act occurs regardless of his nationality, residence or where he initiated the act. Thus, this makes it easier for right holders to hold defendants accountable subject to EU copyright law because any defendant who commits an infringement within the EU can be sued in the court of a Member State that is sufficiently connected.[86]

This means that the proposed rule departs from the language of Article 7(2) that allows jurisdiction to be established where the 'harmful event' occurred. As was discussed, 'harmful event' was interpreted to mean the place where the damage occurred or the place of the event giving rise to the harm.[87] By contrast, the proposed provision focuses on the act of infringement; that is, where the infringement occurred or where the harm of the infringement is felt. As previously discussed, such an approach will be consistent with the reformed right of communication to the public and its accompanying Completion theory. Furthermore, it will not prejudice the operation of the other existing exclusive rights.

[86] Neuman argues that a rule on special jurisdiction 'presupposes a close, but not necessarily the closest, connection'. See S Neumann, 'Intellectual Property Rights Infringements in European Private International Law: Meeting the Requirements of Territoriality and Private International Law' (2011) 7(3) *Journal of Private International Law* 583, 591.

[87] *Handelskwekerij v Mines de Potasse d'Alsace* [1976] paras 17–25 in relation to Article 5(3) of the Brussels Convention. This interpretation was accepted under the Brussels Regulation in *eDate Advertising* [2011] para 41 and later in the copyright case of *Pinckney* [2013] para 26.

Thirdly, the multiple defendants rule is reworked and relocated under the general infringement provision. This reworked provision maintains the central idea that defendants should be tried together where it is efficient and justified to do so. However, the provision differs from Article 8(1) of the BRR on three main grounds. The domicile requirement is completely abandoned in order to be consistent with the general infringement provision proposed. Similarly, there is no requirement that the subsequent defendants be domiciled in any Member State. Therefore, this provision is available for anyone who fits the criteria of paragraphs (a)(i) and (ii) irrespective of where he originates, acts or is domiciled.

This allows defendants who are not domiciled in the EU to be held accountable within the EU where their acts cause infringement or are likely to cause infringement and those acts are closely connected or the same as that of the initial defendant. In this way, multi-party ubiquitous infringements are taken into account such as, P2P file sharing. This is compatible with the reformed communication to the public right because it allows right holders and courts seised to claim jurisdiction over defendants regardless of where they originate, reside or communicate works from. Consequently, a high level of protection is achieved because defendants are unable to hide behind the shield of insufficient jurisdiction and moreover, the effectiveness of forum shopping for anti-copyright safe havens is limited. The third difference concerns the structure, whereby the proposed provision allows for easier reading, which ensures clarity and ease of application for the rule.[88]

Furthermore, the interpretation of Article 7(2) resulting in the court's control over damage being limited to damage that occurred within the territory of the court seised is removed. The precedent set in *Pinckney* that was followed in *Hi Hotel* and *Hejduk*,[89] is replaced by subsection (b) that allows courts to claim jurisdiction over all damage resulting from the act of infringement complained of, where the defendant has substantially acted within the territory of the court seised. The 'substantially acted' requirement is necessary because it provides the justification for why the court seised should have jurisdiction to take account of damage throughout the EU. Where the defendant carries out a substantial act in a Member State, it provides the court seised in that Member State with a sufficiently close connection to the infringement as a whole, including damage caused in other Member States.

In order to determine what constitutes a 'substantial act', reliance should be placed on considerations such as where the act was targeted and the origin of the act.[90] The targeting approach that was used in *Football Dataco v Sportradar* could

[88] The layout adopted reflects the approach used in the ALI Principles and the Draft WIPO Convention on Jurisdiction.

[89] In these cases, the Court reasoned that the court seised only had jurisdiction to consider damage within its territory because of the territorial nature of EU copyright law. In other words, the protection afforded to the copyright work was limited to that particular Member State. See *Pinckney* [2013] paras 45–47, *Hi Hotel* [2014] para 38 and *Hejduk* [2015] para 36.

[90] Matulionyte (2015) 134–37.

be applied in the context that if the act of communication was targeted at a particular Member State, that Member State should have the ability to take account of all damage occurring in the EU because the defendant would have calculated his efforts to ensure the communication reached the desired audience and as such, this constitutes a substantial act for the purpose of the provision. Alternatively, 'substantially acted' can be interpreted to mean any actual or potential transmission or provision of a work originating from within a Member State. For example, if a work is uploaded to the Internet in the UK without authorisation and subsequently shared across the EU, this will constitute a substantial act in the UK for the purposes of the jurisdiction infringement rule.

Focusing on where the act of transmission originated may appear to run counter to the Completion theory; however, this is not the case because the situation at hand has nothing to do with locating the act. Instead, the act of transmission provides justification for why the court seised should have jurisdiction over all damage in the EU. The act of transmission is the connecting factor between the Member State of the court seised and the damage in the other Member States. By contrast, if the work that was communicated to the public was merely *received* in the Member State of the court seised there should be no possibility for the court seised to take account of damage throughout the EU. This is because there was no 'substantial act' by the defendant in the Member State of receipt. Rather, there was merely infringement in that Member State by virtue of applying the Completion theory.

IV. Conclusion

The proposed provisions on establishing jurisdiction in cases of copyright infringement were designed to solve the problems identified in relation to the BRR. In particular, the provisions are meant to establish a better balance between the rights of claimants and defendants by ensuring that right holders have a high level of protection for their copyright works and have an efficient way of enforcing their copyright. This must be counterbalanced with users having certainty about where they may be sued and the extent of damages they can be liable for. Moreover, the provisions are technology-neutral. As such, the criteria for setting out an effective jurisdiction rule are met.

7

Enforcing the Reformed Right of Communication to the Public: Choice of Applicable Law

I. Introduction

The previous chapter discussed the establishment of jurisdiction and proposed new rules for determining jurisdiction in EU copyright law cases. This chapter is complementary as it aims to establish clear and consistent rules concerning the applicable law in EU copyright law cases. Similarly to jurisdiction, there is no express assistance provided in relation to the establishment of the applicable law for copyright law. Under the Berne Convention 1971,[1] Article 5(2), the so-called applicable law provision, is ambiguous at best in setting out the applicable law. Similarly, the drafters of the WIPO Copyright Treaty 1996[2] stated without reason that: 'it would be inappropriate to include provisions in the protocol on such aspects of private international law as the question of applicable law'.[3] Makeen described this excuse as 'lame' because the language of Article 5(2) of the Berne Convention supplied a general choice of law rule. Thus, there was no inhibiting reason preventing the creation of a choice of law rule.[4]

Consequently, the issue of applicable law was left within the competence of contracting states' domestic laws,[5] thus allowing the EU to adopt its own approach.

[1] Berne Convention for the Protection of Literary and Artistic Works 1971.

[2] WIPO Copyright Treaty 1996 (adopted in Geneva on 20 December 1996).

[3] WIPO, 'Committee of Experts on a Possible Protocol to the Berne Convention: Fourth Session (Geneva, December 5 to 9, 1994)' (1994) 11 *Copyright* 214, 227, para 90.

[4] It is perhaps arguable that the legislature's view on the WIPO Copyright Treaty was primarily focused on copyright-specific rules as opposed to more general rules on private international law. From this perspective it was not important or the right time to discuss rules on applicable law. Furthermore, the EU countries were uninterested in adopting an international rule on applicable law for broadcasts because they had recently implemented the Satellite and Cable Retransmission Directive whereby a modified version of the Emission theory was adopted. See M Makeen, *Copyright in a Global Information Society: The Scope of Copyright Protection Under International, US, UK and French Law* (Kluwer Law International, 2000) 207.

[5] It must be noted that before the issue was excluded from the draft WIPO Copyright Treaty, a majority of the Committee seemed to be in favour of applying the Emission theory to acts of satellite broadcasting in order to determine the applicable law. However, it was noted that where the owner

In the interest of ensuring certainty and a proportionate balance of interests between right holders and users, there is a need for reform of the rules concerning applicable law in the EU copyright context. It is suggested that the *lex protectionis* should be applied as the standard applicable law. Furthermore, in instances of multi-country infringement, all the individual infringements should be subjected to one applicable law in one claim. The applicable law in this instance will be determined subject to the existence of a substantial connection with the overall infringement.

II. Establishing Applicable Law in EU Copyright Cases – The Current Approach

Due to the prevalence of digital and ubiquitous infringements, the method by which applicable law is chosen has increased importance.[6] This is because acts of copyright infringement committed on the Internet are unlikely to be territorially limited and this consequently poses the central problem of how to reconcile different competing domestic laws.[7] In other words, which law should apply in cases where an infringement spans multiple territories? Unlike analogue technology where the act of infringement and the consequent harm were often confined to the same territory, the modern norm is that an act of copyright infringement involving Internet technologies is ubiquitous and extends beyond territorial boundaries. As such, it is necessary that the rules on applicable law are capable of addressing such forms of ubiquitous infringement in an effective manner.[8]

However, the current approach to applicable law for IP rights under the Rome II Regulation[9] fails to achieve effective outcomes with regard to ubiquitous infringement. Thus, a different framework will be proposed to provide adequate

of broadcast rights in a reception country was different to the owner in the country of emission, the owners in reception countries should be taken into account – Committee of Experts on a Possible Protocol to the Berne Convention (1994) 227, para 89.

[6] R Matulionyte, 'Enforcing Copyright Infringements Online: In Search of Balanced Private International Law Rules' (2015) 6 *Journal of Intellectual Property, Information Technology & E-Commerce Law* 132, 132.

[7] The central reason for rules on conflict of laws is to resolve the conflicts between different domestic territorial copyright laws that may apply to a cross-border action – F Dessemontet, 'Conflict of Law for Intellectual Property in Cyberspace' (2001) 18(5) *Journal of International Arbitration* 487, J Ginsburg, 'Copyright Without Borders? Choice of Forum and Choice of Law for Copyright Infringement in Cyberspace' (1997) 15 *Cardozo Arts & Entertainment Law Journal* 153, 153 and M Burnstein, 'Conflicts on the Net: Choice of Law in Transnational Cyberspace' (1996) 29 *Vanderbilt Journal of Transnational Law* 75, 87.

[8] American Law Institute, *Intellectual Property: Principles Governing Jurisdiction, Choice of Law, and Judgments in Transnational Disputes* (2008) Part III [ALI Principles] – Applicable Law.

[9] Regulation (EC) No 864/2007 of the European Parliament and of the Council of 11 July 2007 on the law applicable to non-contractual obligations (Rome II) [Rome II Regulation] [2007] OJ L199/40, 31.7.2007.

protection. This section advocates that in order for the determination of applicable law to be coherent and effective it is necessary to take into account the ubiquitous nature of copyright infringement and the territorial approach of copyright law. In pursuing a more coherent and effective choice of law rule, academics set different benchmarks for achieving optimal results. For example, van Eechoud suggests that choice of law rules should accommodate 'utility, legal certainty and substantive justice'.[10] Ginsburg highlights that choice of law rules must mandate a nexus between the claim and the actors or the activities.[11] Reindl argues that a plurality of interests must be taken account of, including: enforcement, users, right holders, practicality and the economic impact. Furthermore, the choice of law approach must be flexible, but predictable.[12] Burnstein states that any choice of law rule should achieve certainty and fairness. Similarly, Neumann suggests that it is necessary for a choice of law rule to be consistent, certain, avoid *dépeçage*[13] and have a close connection to the act or actors. From all these different criteria, a general list can be constructed. The choice of law rule should be: efficient, sufficiently connected, certain, and proportionately balanced between claimants and defendants.

Incorporating the above considerations, it will be argued that the *lex protectionis* approach should be adopted as the means for determining the applicable law and should govern the procedural law, infringement and remedies.[14] This is in accordance with the existing Rome II Regulation. To support the continued use of the *lex protectionis*, it is necessary to explain why the other approaches – *lex fori*, *lex loci delicti* and the country of origin principle – are not suitable.[15] Subsequent to this, a new framework for the determination of applicable law under EU copyright law will be proposed. The proposed framework serves to address the shortcomings of the Rome II Regulation in relation to EU copyright law.

[10] M van Eechoud, *Choice of Law in Copyright and Related Rights* (Kluwer Law International, 2003) 16.

[11] J Ginsburg, 'Global Use/Territorial Rights: Private International Law Questions of the Global Information Infrastructure' (1995) 42 *Journal of the Copyright Society of the USA* 318, 337.

[12] See A Reindl, 'Choosing Law in Cyberspace: Copyright Conflicts on Global Networks' (1998) 19 *Michigan Journal of International Law* 799, 799–802.

[13] *Dépeçage* normally refers to a situation where the laws of different countries are applied to different aspects in an individual case. For example, in a copyright infringement case, UK law may apply to issues of subsistence, but French law may apply to the issue of infringement and lastly, German law may apply to the issue of remedies. See W Reese, 'Dépeçage: A Common Phenomenon in Choice of Law' (1973) 73(1) *Columbia Law Review* 58, for a discussion on the meaning of the term *dépeçage*.

[14] Although the *lex protectionis* is capable of addressing both subsistence and infringement issues, this chapter will only address the *lex protectionis* in the context of infringement cases because the focus of the book is on the communication to the public right. As such, it exceeds the scope of this book to address the subsistence aspect of the *lex protectionis* approach in any detail.

[15] The *lex loci delicti* approach is discussed together with the *lex protectionis*, given that there is overlap between the two in relation to the choice of law in infringement cases.

A. The Traditional Approaches

The traditional approaches to the conflict of laws dilemma in relation to copyright law include the *lex fori*, *lex loci delicti* and *lex protectionis* approaches.[16] The *lex fori* states that the applicable law is that of the country where protection is claimed;[17] that is, the law of the forum country, or in other words, the country where the claim is brought. For example, if a claim for copyright infringement is brought in the UK, the *lex fori* will dictate that UK copyright law applies to the substantive issues of infringement in that case.

Alternatively, the *lex loci delicti* establishes the applicable law on the basis of where the harm or infringing act occurred.[18] However, as will be discussed later, there is a circularity in reasoning in using the *lex loci delicti*, given that it requires the location of the act before being able to establish what the applicable law is. The circularity in reasoning exists because location cannot occur without interpreting what the law is, which is determinant on establishing the applicable law. This is of particular importance with regard to the communication to the public right. An example of using the *lex loci delicti* would be where a claim is brought in the UK and the act of infringement occurred in France; the applicable law would be French law because the harm occurred in France. As a result, the UK court would have to apply French law to determine the substantive issues in the case.

As for *lex protectionis*, the applicable law is established as the law of the country for which protection is claimed.[19] To put it differently, this means the law of the country where the claimant would like to obtain protection. This is different to the *lex fori* because focus is placed on the country where protection is desired. For example, an infringement of communication to the public may occur in Germany. The claimant brings the claim in the UK because the defendant is domiciled there. The claimant argues for protection in Germany; consequently the UK court will have to use German law to find whether infringement has occurred. On the face of it, this approach resembles the *lex loci delicti*. However, as will be discussed later, the two approaches should not be used interchangeably.

B. Country of Origin Principle

In addition to the traditional approaches, there is also the country of origin approach that has been discussed by Matulionyte, Plenter, Reindl and Dessemontet. Unlike the traditional approaches, there is no common understanding of

[16] It is worthy to note that the issue of applicable law in cross-border cases often never materialised due to jurisdictional bars that prevented courts from hearing such claims.

[17] Makeen describes the *lex fori* as 'the laws of the place of litigation' – Makeen (2000) 189, fn 60.

[18] ibid 189, fn 61.

[19] J Fawcett and P Torremans, *Intellectual Property and Private International Law*, 2nd edn (Oxford University Press, 2011) 676, para 12.22 and van Eechoud (2003) 105.

what the country of origin principle means. Thus, each advocate for a 'country of origin' principle suggests something different. Matulionyte suggests that the rule of *lex originis* or country of origin be considered, so that the only applicable law is that of where the copyright work originated, regardless of where it is exploited; that is, the law of the country where the copyright work was made or from which its author originates. However, this approach is contrary to national treatment because authors are thereby treated differently on the basis of their nationality or where they created their works, as opposed to being treated the same as authors in the forum country. This interpretation of the country of origin principle is also impractical because using multiple works in the exact same way can attract different applicable laws.[20]

Similarly, Plenter's approach argues that the country of origin principle requires the applicable law to be that of the place where the work was first published or uploaded. It is argued that this makes the applicable law foreseeable from the beginning. However, it relies too heavily on analogue concepts of tangible publication. In the context of Internet technologies, the place where the work is uploaded may be uncertain and difficult to trace and, moreover, allows the uploading party to cherry-pick where the work is made available online.[21] The consequence of this is that the country of upload may be selected for its low levels of copyright protection. As a result, Plenter's version of the country of origin principle is not desirable.

Alternatively, the approach to the country of origin principle proposed by Reindl is based on where the act of infringement originates.[22] This finding is premised on the assumption that there is a workable definition of the right that is allegedly infringed.[23] Reindl, like Plenter, argues that such a rule has the advantage of predictability. However, in similar fashion to Plenter's approach, Reindl's country of origin principle also suffers from the difficulty of pinpointing where an act originated on the Internet. This is particularly problematic for Internet technologies which involve a multitude of users interacting with parts of a work, as is the case with P2P-based technologies. To avoid this problem Reindl suggests that the country of transmission can be determined by the location of the user responsible for the act, thus shifting the emphasis onto the behaviour and domicile of the would-be defendant.[24] But this creates the identical problem faced by Plenter's approach, namely, that cherry-picking of laws may result, given that users will look to set up and/or transmit from countries with low levels of copyright protection.[25] Therefore, Reindl's country of origin approach is also unsuitable to act as the choice of law approach.

[20] Matulionyte (2015) 138–39.

[21] S Plenter, 'Choice of law rules for copyright infringements in the global information infrastructure: a never-ending story?' (2001) *European Intellectual Property Review (EIPR)* 313, 315.

[22] That is, the country in which the transmission was emitted – Reindl (1998) 833.

[23] Reindl (1998) 832.

[24] ibid 833 and 835–36.

[25] Matulionyte (2015) 139.

Lastly, Dessemontet suggests that the country of origin principle concerns the residence or domicile of the author. In other words, the location of the author should dictate the applicable law. Dessemontet's application of the country of origin principle as the means to determine the applicable law is made on two grounds: firstly, that the 'country of origin' is a concept fundamental to the Berne Convention and as such cannot be twisted into different meanings; secondly, it is argued that the residence or domicile of the author offers a significant point of contact. As such, it is 'natural' to extend the country of origin of the work to determine applicable law because it offers the main point of contact with the copyright work in question.[26] However, this approach would appear to be focused on issues of subsistence rather than infringement.

Consequently, it is not justifiable to extend the reasoning in the infringement context because the 'main point of contact' argument is not persuasive outside the subsistence context. This is because the emphasis shifts to the defendant and the act committed, rather than the copyright work itself and any subsequent infringement. Additionally, Ginsburg argued that the use of 'country of origin' in this manner is an unlikely candidate for a choice of law rule and goes against the traditions of the Berne Convention. The main problem with Dessemontet's country of origin approach is that the applicable law would be variable regardless of the similarity in infringement at hand.[27] Cases involving the exact same act would be subject to different laws depending on where the author of the work in question is from. Thus, the results would be inconsistent.

Despite the four contrasting approaches to the country of origin principle as a choice of law rule, they all excel in the certainty department. However, they fail to meet the other three criteria set out for an ideal choice of law rule. All four suggestions seem to be better suited for issues of subsistence than infringement. The consequence of this is that their potential use as a choice of law rule is undermined by the lack of sufficient connection in instances of infringement proceedings. Placing focus on the location of the author or origination of the work, or the act leading to the infringement, does not take account of the nature of the infringement, especially in the context of the reformed communication to the public right. Therefore, the sufficient connection criterion is not met in the infringement context.

Secondly, the various rules suggested by Plenter and Reindl allow for cherry-picking of copyright protection to some extent because the rules are based on where the work or act originated. The consequence of this is that defendants may choose places with low copyright protection to make works available. This gives the defendant an unfair advantage over the claimant as he can control the level of redress available to the claimant. Lastly, the country of origin principle in its various forms does not offer an effective choice of law rule because it fails to take into account the various nuances of modern-day infringement, notably the

[26] Dessemontet (2001) 502.
[27] Ginsburg (1995) 336.

prevalence of online infringement that is ubiquitous. This is the case because emphasis is placed on the actors and their location rather than the act/infringement as a whole. In order to achieve a consistent and efficient choice of law approach, emphasis must be placed on the alleged infringement and its accompanying nuances. As a result, the country of origin approach in its various forms does not provide a suitable method of determining the applicable law.[28]

C. Dismissing the *Lex Fori*

The *lex fori* states that the applicable law should be the law of the country where protection is claimed. In other words, the domestic law of the court seised should apply to the case in question. This approach worked well in the analogue context because it was ordinarily the case that the place where an infringement originated, the place where the resultant damage occurred and the territory of the court seised were all the same place. As such, there was no need to consider the application of any other laws.[29] However, with developments in technology and the increasing prevalence of ubiquitous infringement, the *lex fori* approach is ill-suited for modern application. Even before the advent of the Internet, the development of satellite technology created doubt about the *lex fori* approach because of the fact that a single satellite broadcast could cover multiple footprint countries, thus implicating multiple countries' laws. Nevertheless, it can be argued that the application of the *lex fori* approach has some benefit.

The primary advantage with using the *lex fori* approach is that judges are most comfortable while applying their own domestic law.[30] As a result, the use of the *lex fori* approach should avoid major errors in law and other misunderstandings given the court's pre-existing level of familiarity with its own law. However, this advantage of using the *lex fori* should not be overstated in the context of EU copyright law. The advantage of using the *lex fori* approach discussed above relates to the international context where copyright laws are widely diverse. By contrast, in the EU copyright context the courts of Member States should already be familiar with EU copyright laws because they have to apply them by virtue of the EU having competence to legislate in the area of copyright law under Article 118 of

[28] Note, the country of origin approach has been proposed by the EU legislature in relation to ancillary online retransmissions of broadcasters – see Article 2 of European Commission, *Proposal for a Regulation of the European Parliament and of the Council laying down rules on the exercise of copyright and related rights applicable to certain online transmissions of broadcasting organisations and retransmissions of television and radio programmes* (COM(2016) 594 final, 2016).

[29] E Ulmer, *Intellectual Property Rights and the Conflict of Laws* (Kluwer Law, 1978) 10 and S Ricketson and J Ginsburg, *International Copyright and Neighbouring Rights: The Berne Convention and Beyond*, 2nd edn (Oxford University Press, 2006) 1299, para 20.10.

[30] B Svantesson, *Private International Law and the Internet*, 2nd edn (Kluwer Law International, 2007) 384, O Kahn-Freund, *General problems of private international law* (Sijthoff, 1976) 321 and Makeen (2000) 189–90.

the TFEU.[31] Furthermore, the statutory law is supplemented by the decisions of the CJEU and the domestic case law that applies the CJEU's decisions. What this means is that the courts of Member States are already in the habit of using EU copyright law provisions and decisions.

This view of EU copyright law may be criticised as idealistic because several issues remain concerning how EU copyright law is dealt with at the Member State level. Given the cultural and legal diversity of the EU, there exist problems with regard to the interpretation and application of laws at the domestic level. For example, there are common law countries such as the UK and Ireland who may address EU law differently to the other civil law countries of mainland Europe. Similarly, the diversity in languages means that there is the possibility of translation and transposition errors. However, the CJEU has attempted to mitigate these problems by requiring that EU copyright law be interpreted in a 'uniform and autonomous manner'.[32]

Nonetheless, divergences may still occur. Such divergences can take the form of existing laws wrongly being interpreted as consistent with the EU law. For example, the initial approach of UK courts in relation to the concept of 'author's own intellectual creation', developed in the seminal case of *Infopaq*,[33] had an uncertain beginning in the UK. Despite the importance of the *Infopaq* decision, the UK's early approach to 'author's own intellectual creation' was one of reluctance because the long-standing UK law test of 'labour, skill and judgement' was held to be compatible.[34] However, this reluctance is gradually ebbing away as UK courts are becoming more open to applying 'author's own intellectual creation'.[35] Another example of divergence between EU copyright law and domestic law is the UK's approach to the communication to the public right. The scope of the UK communication to the public right does not match that of the EU communication to the public right, given that UK copyright also has an exclusive right of public performance. As such, where acts of reception in public belong has been a debated issue under UK law.[36]

[31] Consolidated Version of the Treaty on the Functioning of the European Union (2012).

[32] See Case C-5/08 *Infopaq International A/S v Danske Dagblades Forening* [2009] ECLI:EU:C:2009:465, para 27 for copyright law generally. In the context of the communication to the public right see Case C-306/05 *Sociedad General de Autores y Editores de Espana (SGAE) v Rafael Hoteles SL* [2006] ECLI:EU:C:2006:764, para 31.

[33] *Infopaq* [2009] para 37.

[34] See *The Newspaper Licensing Agency Ltd and others v Meltwater Holding BV and others* [2011] EWCA Civ 890, para 20 per Jackson LJ, where Jackson LJ held that *Infopaq* did not qualify the long-standing UK test on originality. For contrasting arguments see E Rosati, *Originality in EU Copyright: Full Harmonization through Case Law* (Edward Elgar Publishing Ltd, 2013) Chapter 3 and A Rahmatian, 'Originality in UK copyright law: the old "skill and labour" doctrine under pressure' (2013) 44(1) *International Review of Intellectual Property and Competition Law (IIC)* 4.

[35] See *SAS Institute Inc v World Programming Ltd* [2010] EWHC 1829 (Ch), *Temple Island Collections Ltd v New English Teas Ltd* [2012] ECDR 11 and *T & A Textiles and Hosiery Ltd v Hala Textile UK Ltd and others* [2015] EWHC 2888.

[36] See *Football Association Premier League Ltd v QC Leisure (No 3)* [2012] EWHC 108 (Ch) and *Football Association Premier League Ltd and others v QC Leisure and others* [2012] EWCA Civ 1708.

With this in mind, caution should be applied in stating that domestic courts are comfortable in applying EU copyright law. It should be remembered that in the absence of a codified Regulation on copyright or a unitary copyright law, accompanied by flawless translation and transposition, there is still room for errors to be made. However, the absence of a codified Regulation or a unitary EU copyright law does not undermine the argument that the courts of Member States are capable of effectively and efficiently using EU copyright law. The maximal harmonisation of the reformed communication to the public right, its suggested codification and the interpretive guidelines set by the CJEU ought to minimise any discrepancies in the law among Member States.

The second argument in favour of applying the *lex fori* approach for copyright law is that a literal interpretation of Article 5(2) of the Berne Convention requires it. This interpretation is derived from the wording: 'the extent of protection, as well as the means of redress afforded to the author to protect his rights, shall be governed exclusively by the laws of the country where protection is claimed'.[37] Interpreting Article 5(2) in the literal sense is also supported by the fact that the language of 'the country where protection is claimed' is used seven times throughout the Berne Convention. Koumantos argued that it would be contradictory to interpret the phrase in different ways throughout the Berne Convention. Therefore, a literal interpretation of Article 5(2) leads to the conclusion that the *lex fori* approach should be followed.[38]

However, this argument is contestable. In the first place, it has been questioned whether Article 5(2) actually concerns the applicable law. Some academics have argued that the Berne Convention did not try to address the general question concerning the conflict of laws and as such, leaves it open for contracting states to enact their own rules concerning private international law.[39] Makeen adopted a nuanced viewpoint of this in arguing that Article 5(2) does provide a conflict of laws rule, albeit limited to cases of infringement and thus excludes contractual claims.[40] Consequently, the argument that the *lex fori* approach is supported by a literal interpretation of Article 5(2) is open to criticism.

The second difficulty with the literal interpretation of Article 5(2) relates to whether Article 5(2) was intended to establish a general *lex fori* rule. Instead of expressly using the term '*lex fori*', the drafters of the provision in the Berlin Revision of the Berne Convention (1908) preferred to use the phrase: 'the country

[37] J Ginsburg and E Treppoz, *International Copyright Law: US and EU Perspectives* (Edward Elgar Publishing Ltd, 2015) 653, van Eechoud (2003) 103, Plenter (2001) 317, G Koumantos, 'Private International Law and the Berne Convention' (1988) 24 *Copyright* 415, 426, Ricketson and Ginsburg (2006) 1299, para 20.10 and European Commission, *Final Report to the Study on Intellectual Property and the Conflict of Laws* (2000) ETD/99/B5-3000/E/16, Second Part, 19.

[38] Koumantos (1988) 426.

[39] Ricketson and Ginsburg (2006) 1294, para 20.03 and 1298, para 20.09, van Eechoud (2003) 95 and 108, Ginsburg (1995) 331, Dessemontet (2001) 489, 502 and de Miguel Asensio in Leible and Ohly (2009) 17.

[40] Makeen (2000) 187–90.

where protection is claimed', thus employing the *lex loci protectionis* or *lex loci delicti*.[41] Makeen suggested that the initial drafting of Article 5(2) was made on the assumption that the *lex fori*, *lex protectionis* and *lex loci delicti* would more often than not coincide.[42] This would suggest that Article 5(2) requires a modern reinterpretation, in order to take account of the fact that its underlying rationale is no longer valid in the digital and ubiquitous infringement context.

In addition to the legislative history outlined, it has been more generally argued that Article 5(2) should be interpreted in a purposive manner. Under this interpretation, it is argued that Article 5(2) should be read as 'the country for which protection is claimed', given that the rule was designed to provide a conflict of law rule to address infringement cases (thus excluding claims in contract). However, in using the purposive interpretation there has still been uncertainty as to whether the provision meant the *lex protectionis*[43] or the *lex loci delicti*[44] approach. If our understanding of Article 5(2) is limited to instances of infringement then the narrower *lex loci delicti* approach would be correct, given that it solely concerns where the harm occurs. Alternatively, if Article 5(2) has a wider scope than just infringement proceedings, the *lex protectionis* approach is applicable because it is equally capable of addressing subsistence matters.[45] The wording of Article 5(2), 'the extent of protection, as well as the means of redress afforded to the author to protect his rights' would suggest that the provision is not limited to cases of infringement because it concerns the scope of protection more generally.

More than the purposive approach, it must also be said that the rationale that the *lex fori*, *lex protectionis* and *lex loci delicti* would more often than not coincide with the same country/applicable law must be rejected in the modern context where ubiquitous infringement is the norm. In the analogue context, for example a terrestrial broadcast, the place where the broadcast originated and was received was likely to be the same country. In this sense the defendant was located in that country, the infringement occurred there, and the claimant wanted redress all in the same territory. However, the modern reality is that the place of the infringement, the place where the claim is brought and where protection is wanted may equate to different places. This is the case in relation to ubiquitous media because a single act can lead to potential infringements in a large number of countries.

[41] Makeen (2000) 191, citing A Lucas, *Traité de la Propriété Littéraire et Artistique* (Litec, 1994) 889–90.

[42] Makeen (2000) 190–91. Also see van Eechoud (2003) 104.

[43] Fawcett and Torremans (2011) 676, para 12.22, Ulmer (1978) 10–11, van Eechoud (2003) 95, A Lucas, 'Applicable Law in Copyright Infringement Cases in the Digital Environment' (2005) *e-Copyright Bulletin* 1, 3, Plenter (2001) 518, P de Miguel Asensio, 'The Private International Law of Intellectual Property and of Unfair Commercial Practices: Convergence of Divergence?' in S Leible and A Ohly (eds), *Intellectual Property and Private International Law* (Mohr Siebeck, 2009) 17 and G Dinwoodie, 'Developing a Private International Intellectual Property Law: The Demise of Territoriality?' (2010) 51 *William & Mary Law Review* 711, 718.

[44] Ginsburg and Treppoz (2015) 653 and Reindl (1998) 805.

[45] If Article 5(2) only covered matters of copyright infringement, there would be no debate, given that the *lex loci delicti* would be the apparent choice of law rule under the provision.

For example, the claimant may bring a case in the UK because the defendant is domiciled there; however, the claimant may want to invoke French law because a better remedy can be obtained. The laws of these two countries must also be balanced against the fact that the law of any other country where infringement occurred may also be applicable. This example serves to demonstrate that the reach of modern forms of infringement can be multi-territorial. As such, a number of laws can become applicable. Hence, a more nuanced approach is required that acknowledges the fact that the use of digital technology will more than likely result in ubiquitous infringement. Consequently, the establishment of a general *lex fori* approach must be refuted and, moreover, it should be stated that the modern digital context necessitates a purposive interpretation of Article 5(2).

Furthermore, there is also a consistency argument for using the *lex fori* approach, in order to be consistent with the determination of remedies or redress. It is ordinarily the case that the procedural law of the court seised determines the redress available to a claimant, that is, the *lex fori* is applied. Thus, argument is made that the substantive applicable law should be consistent with the law used to determine the remedy for that infringement.[46] Therefore, applying any law other than the domestic law of the court seised would create inconsistency between the establishment of infringement and the remedy for that infringement. This reasoning can be supported from the wording of Article 5(2) wherein it is stated that: 'the extent of protection, as well as the means of redress afforded to the author to protect his rights, shall be governed exclusively by the laws of the country where protection is claimed'. Hence, both the scope of protection and of redress should be governed by the same applicable law on a literal interpretation.

However, in arguing for the application of the *lex fori* as a means of achieving consistency, the result will be in conflict with established private international law. This is because the application of the *lex fori* contravenes the basic private international law principle of a 'close connection'.[47] The potential implication is that the law applied may be illogical because it is unconnected to the act complained of.[48] This is a problem for defendants because they will be unable to predict what law may apply to their actions. Thus, use of the *lex fori* is likely to create a fairness problem whereby the predictability of the rules concerning applicable law is compromised, creating uncertainty and inconsistent results.[49]

Therefore, it is argued that adopting the *lex fori* approach shifts the balance of power too much in favour of the claimant, who may bring a claim in a certain forum for strategic advantage rather than on the basis of coherent legal requirement. But, this problem is perhaps overstated with regard to EU copyright law. The reason for this is twofold. Firstly, a claimant will only be able to bring a claim

[46] Final Report to the Study on Intellectual Property and the Conflict of Laws (2000) Second Part, 20.
[47] ibid.
[48] Plenter (2001) 317, Ricketson and Ginsburg (2006) 1293, para 20.02 and Ginsburg and Treppoz (2015) 558.
[49] Svantesson (2007) 384.

in a particular forum if they have satisfied the criterion that the defendant is domiciled in that country or the defendant infringed or is likely to infringe in that country. Therefore, fear of the *lex fori* approach resulting in unrestricted forum shopping for the purpose of cherry-picking applicable law[50] is minimised because the rules concerning the establishment of jurisdiction proposed in the previous chapter mitigate this possibility. Moreover, claimants are more likely to bring claims where they have a reasonable chance of success. Given that claimants still have to establish jurisdiction and prove actual infringement, fears of excessive forum shopping can be dismissed because claimants are likely to restrict their litigation to countries where they have a strong claim and the possibility of effective redress.[51]

Similarly, the likelihood of forum shopping can be reduced because EU copyright law is to a large extent harmonised. Furthermore, the proposed reformed communication to the public right in this book is maximally harmonised and accompanied by the suggestion of codification. The consequence of this is that the application of the *lex fori* as opposed to the application of the *lex protectionis* or the *lex loci delicti* in relation to the reformed right of communication to the public should make no difference because the scope and interpretation of the exclusive rights ought to be the same across Member States. However, if the exclusive rights are not subject to maximal harmonisation and/or codification, then the application of the *lex fori* approach can be problematic because the existence of diverse domestic laws would allow for varying interpretations and applications of the right, leading to different results. As such, claimants will choose courts that offer an interpretation most conducive to their claim.

That aside, van Eechoud argues that forum shopping will always exist because it is inevitable that claimants will prefer one forum over another where there is the option of choice.[52] Forum shopping in this regard may relate to the efficiency of court procedure, availability of remedies, location of the defendant and other factors unrelated to the issue of substantive applicable law. This becomes particularly relevant in the context of ubiquitous infringement where the infringement occurs in multiple countries, allowing claimants to bring their claim in the place most beneficial to themselves, provided the criteria for establishing jurisdiction are met. Equally, it can be argued that forum shopping affects the other two traditional approaches to applicable law (*lex protectionis* and *lex loci delicti*) because ubiquitous infringement offers a choice of where to bring a claim. Therefore, the only real solution to the problem of forum shopping is to minimise the differences between applicable fora.[53]

[50] Makeen (2000) 191–92, Ginsburg (1995) 337, Reindl (1998) 806 and Burnstein (1996) 89.

[51] Matulionyte (2015) 135 – Given that EU copyright law is territorial, claimants are likely to restrict their claims to the countries where they are able to obtain an effective remedy. Otherwise, the claim will be of limited value to the claimant.

[52] van Eechoud (2003) 17.

[53] The issue of minimising the differences between various fora is outside the scope of this book. The book is only concerned with the question of applicable law, particularly in relation to the reformed communication to the public right.

Another issue with the *lex fori* approach is that its use can result in a situation where compulsory licensing mechanisms are expanded beyond their proper scope. For example, Article 11bis(2) of the Berne Convention requires states to impose a compulsory licensing system 'only in the countries where they have been prescribed', in lieu of the exclusive right concerning the restricted uses of broadcasts outlined in Article 11bis(1). Thus, applying the *lex fori* approach can lead to a situation where the compulsory licensing mechanism of Country A is applied to an act that occurred in Country B. This is a problem because the compulsory licensing mechanism should be restricted to acts that occur within Country A. Failure to restrict the application of the compulsory licensing mechanism would contravene Article 11bis(2) and, furthermore, allow for the creation of unjustifiable extraterritorial effects.[54]

This issue is avoided under the reformed communication to the public right for EU copyright law because there is no compulsory licensing mechanism. But, the principle behind the problem remains a concern if the reformed right is not subject to maximal harmonisation or codification. As discussed previously, if Member States have different means of applying the reformed communication to the public right, there may be the problem that these interpretations are unjustifiably extended to acts that did not occur within the jurisdiction of the court seised. Again, this fear may be limited by the criteria for establishing jurisdiction, in particular, where jurisdiction is established on the grounds that the infringement occurred or is likely to occur in the territory of the court seised. In this case, the court seised is justified in applying its own laws in accordance with the *lex fori* approach. However, this is not necessarily the case where jurisdiction is established on the grounds of the defendant's domicile.[55]

Lastly, there is concern that the use of the *lex fori* approach in conjunction with the rules on establishing jurisdiction proposed in the previous chapter can produce inconsistent results. Where jurisdiction is established on the grounds that the infringement occurred or is likely to occur in that country, in accordance with the infringement rule provided under Chapter six, section III.A, there may be overlap between the *lex fori*, *lex loci delicti* and *lex protectionis*. The reason for this is that there is a close connection between the act and the applicable law of the forum country and, as such, the choice of applicable law could be the same under any of the three approaches. In this scenario, the criteria for an ideal choice of law rule are met and consequently the use of the *lex fori* is unproblematic.

However, where jurisdiction is established on the basis of the domicile of the defendant the argument above is not as persuasive because the law of the country where the defendant is domiciled may have nothing to do with the act of infringement. Therefore, where the infringement does not occur in the country of the defendant's domicile there is no close connection and as such, no justification for applying the *lex fori* because the criterion relating to a sufficiently close connection

[54] Makeen (2000) 191–92.
[55] Matulionyte (2015) 138.

is not met. As a result, the use of the *lex fori* approach will allow for inconsistent results based on the manner in which jurisdiction is established, thereby creating an unfair situation for defendants where the determination of the applicable law is inconsistent.

From this discussion it can be said that the *lex fori* approach is workable where the court seised has established jurisdiction on the grounds that the act of infringement occurred or is likely to occur within its territory. This is because the four criteria for an effective choice of law rule are met – efficiency, sufficient connection, certainty and proportionate balance between the interests of claimant and defendant. In this scenario it may be the case that the *lex fori*, *lex protectionis* and *lex loci delicti* overlap. However, where jurisdiction is established on the grounds of domicile, the arguments for using the *lex fori* approach are weakened because the connection between the act complained of and the law being applied under the *lex fori* approach may be too remote or non-existent. Therefore, in this context the criteria of sufficient connection and proportionate balance are not met because the choice of law will be inconsistent even though the premise of the *lex fori* is predictable since the choice of law is tied to one specific place: the place where the claim is brought.

As a result, the *lex fori* approach is not the best means to determine the applicable law. This is because the use of the *lex fori* in conjunction with the proposed rules for establishing jurisdiction will produce incoherent results that are not in accordance with the ideal criteria that are highlighted. A coherent choice of law rule must meet the four criteria set out above on a comprehensive and consistent basis, as well as be compatible with the other proposed rules in this book.

D. Why Adopt the *Lex Protectionis*?

(i) Distinguishing lex protectionis *from* lex loci delicti

Having dismissed the application of the *lex fori* approach in the previous subsection, it is proposed that the *lex protectionis* approach be adopted to determine the applicable law in cases involving EU copyright law. The applicable law under the *lex protectionis* approach is that of the country for which protection is claimed. Unlike the *lex loci delicti*, the *lex protectionis* approach is not limited to cases of infringement,[56] but concerns all aspects of copyright law.[57] Consequently, it is important to avoid using the terms *lex protectionis* and *lex loci delicti* interchangeably for two main reasons. Firstly, the *lex protectionis* approach is wider than the

[56] *Lex loci delicti commissi* (abbreviated to *lex loci delicti*) literally means the law of the place where the offence was committed; that is, the law of the place where the copyright infringement occurred.

[57] M van Eechoud, 'Alternatives to the *lex protectionis* as the Choice-of-Law Rule for Initial Ownership of Copyright' in J Drexl and A Kur (eds), *Intellectual Property and Private International Law – Heading for the Future* (Hart Publishing, 2005) 289.

lex loci delicti approach and should be respected as such.[58] This is because the *lex protectionis* is able to address issues concerning both infringement and subsistence, whereas the *lex loci delicti* is limited to acts of infringement.[59] It may be argued that the interchangeable use of these two terms derives from the fact that the question of applicable law mostly arises in infringement cases.

The concern about the interchangeable use of the *lex protectionis* and *lex loci delicti* approaches is evidenced by the general uncertainty concerning Article 5(2) of the Berne Convention. It has been subject to much academic debate what Article 5(2) actually conveys. As previously discussed, some have argued that Article 5(2) does not address the general conflict of laws issue and therefore leaves it open to contracting states to apply their own private international law.[60] Alternatively, it has been argued by others that Article 5(2) should be read literally and thus purveys the *lex fori* approach.[61] There is also a third perspective where it can be argued that Article 5(2) indicates the *lex protectionis*[62] or *lex loci delicti* approach on a purposive interpretation.[63]

The argument that Article 5(2) establishes the *lex protectionis* or *lex loci delicti* approach is based on the purposive interpretation that the phrase 'where protection is claimed' should be read as: *for which protection is claimed.*[64] This interpretation is made on the basis that the applicable law should reflect where the infringement occurred or the place where protection is wanted. The argument is that in the analogue era the place where the claim was brought more often than not coincided with where the harm or infringement occurred and, consequently, also where protection was wanted.[65] Hence, the wording of 'where protection is claimed' implied the place where the infringement or harm occurred as opposed to the *lex fori.*[66] However, with the development of digital technology and the possibility of ubiquitous infringement it is not necessarily the case that these various approaches will overlap. This is because the country for which protection is

[58] van Eechoud (2003) 104.

[59] Fawcett and Torremans (2011) 677, para 12.26.

[60] Ricketson and Ginsburg (2006) 1294, para 20.03 and 1298, para 20.09, van Eechoud (2003) 95 and 108, Ginsburg (1995) 331, Dessemontet (2001) 489 and de Miguel Asensio in Leible and Ohly (2009) 17.

[61] Ginsburg and Treppoz (2015) 653, van Eechoud (2003) 103, Plenter (2001) 317, Koumantos (1988) 426, Ricketson and Ginsburg (2006) 1299, para 20.10 and Final Report to the Study on Intellectual Property and the Conflict of Laws (2000) Second Part, 19.

[62] Fawcett and Torremans (2011) 676, para 12.22, van Eechoud (2003) 95, de Miguel Asensio in Leible and Ohly (2009) 17 and Dinwoodie (2010) 718.

[63] Ginsburg and Treppoz (2015) 653, Reindl (1998) 805 and P Schonning, 'Applicable Law in Transfrontier On-Line Transmissions' (1996) 170 *Revue Internationale du Droit d'Auteur (RIDA)* 21, 29.

[64] Ulmer (1978) 11, Fawcett and Torremans (2011) 676, para 12.22, van Eechoud (2003) 95, Lucas (2005) 3 and Final Report to the Study on Intellectual Property and the Conflict of Laws (2000) Second Part, 19–20, Plenter (2001) 518 and Dessemontet (2001) 490.

[65] S Neumann, 'Intellectual Property Rights Infringements in European Private International Law: Meeting the Requirements of Territoriality and Private International Law' (2011) 7(3) *Journal of Private International Law* 583, 589, R Arnold, 'Cross-border enforcement: the latest chapter' [1999] *Intellectual Property Quarterly* 389, 396 and Ginsburg and Treppoz (2015) 558.

[66] Ricketson and Ginsburg (2006) 1293, para 20.02 and van Eechoud (2003) 104.

claimed could be one of a number of countries where infringement occurs and moreover, this may also differ from where the claim is brought. The point to note is that the *lex protectionis* and the *lex loci delicti* are not the same.

Secondly, the terms *lex protectionis* and *lex loci delicti* should not be used interchangeably due to the circularity in reasoning that prejudices the application of the *lex loci delicti*. In order to determine the applicable law under the *lex loci delicti* approach, it is first necessary to establish the act of infringement and where it occurs. The reason for this is that the applicable law under the *lex loci delicti* is solely dependent on where the act of infringement occurs. However, establishing where the act occurs is equally dependent on the choice of applicable law because the location of the infringing act depends on the interpretation of a chosen law. Gaudrat phrases this conundrum by stating that the applicable law is determined by the infringement of the copyright and that same law defines whether or not there is an infringement.[67]

It is arguable that the *lex loci delicti* is unproblematic in terms of the reproduction right because it is universally accepted that the act of reproduction involves an act of copying. Similarly, acts of distribution concern the issuing of copies to the public. Both the reproduction and distribution rights are comparable because they involve one clear point of contact for proving infringement, the act of copying or the issuing of copies, respectively. As such, it is easy to ascertain in general where the act of infringement originated without any reference to express law. By contrast, the existing communication to the public right is problematic. There is no clear understanding of what the right entails or where it occurs because it is undefined. Furthermore, acts of communication to the public involve two distinct points of contact: the transmission or provision of the work and the reception. When this uncertainty is combined with the circularity of the *lex loci delicti* approach, the result is impracticality in using the *lex loci delicti* as the choice of law rule.[68] Even in the context of the reformed right of communication to the public that is codified and its location made clear through the Completion theory, the *lex loci delicti* remains unfavourable because of the ubiquitous nature of infringement and differences in other copyright elements. Given that infringement can occur in multiple countries simultaneously, it remains the case that the applicable law can be arbitrarily chosen based on factors other than the exclusive rights, which can have serious consequences for the ultimate decision on infringement.[69]

[67] P Gaudrat, 'Protection of the Author in Relation to a Retransmission by Satellite of his Work' (1980) 104 *RIDA* 2, 10.

[68] Svantesson (2007) 385.

[69] Austin argues that if domestic courts are forced to concern themselves with exactly where acts of infringement occur, the legal process is likely to become unmanageable. This applies equally to the finding of infringement and the determination of applicable law. See G Austin, 'Global networks and domestic laws: some private international law issues arising from Australian and US liability theories' in A Strowel (ed), *Peer-to-Peer File Sharing and Secondary Liability in Copyright Law* (Edward Elgar Publishing Ltd, 2009) 143.

Although the circularity in reasoning diminishes the attractiveness of the *lex loci delicti* approach, in particular at the international level,[70] it must be noted that its potential negative impact in the overall EU copyright framework is mitigated. Given that there is a minimum level of harmonisation with regard to EU copyright law, the practical choice of choosing one EU Member States' law over another is not so significant. This is because all the Member States must offer the minimum harmonised level of protection to right holders. However, this assumes that there is consistent interpretation and application of EU copyright law at the domestic level of the various Member States. However, for the issues with the *lex loci delicti* to become superfluous, it will be necessary for EU copyright law to be maximally harmonised and codified beyond the exclusive rights;[71] that is, the law on subsistence, exclusive rights, exceptions and limitations and moral rights should be completely harmonised. In the absence of such an approach the application of the *lex loci delicti* will remain problematic due to differences in interpretation and application and scope of protection of the law. Therefore, even in the aftermath of the proposed reformed right of communication to the public, the *lex loci delicti* remains an unacceptable choice of law rule.

(ii) Understanding lex protectionis

Applying the *lex protectionis* completely avoids the circularity dilemma associated with the *lex loci delicti* because emphasis is not placed on establishing where the infringing act occurred. Instead, the claimant can choose where he is claiming protection.[72] In this regard, the burden falls on the claimant to adduce the necessary evidence to prove infringement and damage relevant to the country for which protection is claimed. From this, it is arguable that the *lex protectionis* creates another problem in that it does not verify whether copyright protection subsists and furthermore, whether there has been an infringement.[73] However, to do this would create the same circularity in reasoning problem experienced under the *lex loci delicti*. Thus, Neumann argued that the *lex protectionis* approach

> offers a clear and easy way to determine the law applicable to the infringement of IP rights as no further determination and localisation of the allegedly infringing acts, involving different notions of infringement in national substantive IP law, is required at the conflict-of-laws level.[74]

[70] Specifically at the international level because there is not a great deal of harmonisation, particularly with regards to the communication to the public right.

[71] Makeen (2000) 303, Final Report to the Study on Intellectual Property and the Conflict of Laws (2000) Second Part, 24 and Reindl (1998) 811.

[72] This is how the *lex protectionis* approach under Article 8 of the Rome Regulation II is applied. See P Savola, 'The ultimate copyright shopping opportunity – jurisdiction and choice of law in website blocking injunctions' (2014) 45(3) *IIC* 287, 299–300 and A Peukert, 'The coexistence of trade mark laws and rights on the Internet, and the impact of geolocation technologies' (2016) 47(1) *IIC* 60, 74.

[73] Neumann (2011) 584.

[74] ibid 589.

Having distinguished the *lex protectionis* from the *lex loci delicti*, it is necessary to note that the *lex protectionis* has been the preferred approach for determining applicable law in the area of IP law. In fact, Recital 26 of the Rome II Regulation states that, 'the universally recognised principle of the *lex loci protectionis* should be preserved'.[75] Although this claim is disputable,[76] it remains the case that the *lex protectionis* is an internationally accepted conflict of laws rule for IP law.[77] Article 8(1) of the Rome II Regulation implemented the *lex protectionis* approach for matters concerning non-contractual obligations arising from infringements of IP law within the EU.[78] Similarly, section 301 of the ALI Principles and Article 3:601 of the CLIP Principles both provide the *lex protectionis* as the means to determine applicable law in their proposals.[79] This legislative history reinforces the popularity of the *lex protectionis* approach for the determination of the applicable law in IP cases. The popularity of the *lex protectionis* approach is justified when one considers the advantages that it possesses in itself and as opposed to the competing choice of law rules namely, the *lex loci delicti* and *lex fori*, which have been previously discussed.

Given that the *lex protectionis* approach is suggested as the best solution for the choice of law issue in relation to infringement cases, it is necessary to demonstrate that the *lex protectionis* satisfies the ideal criteria highlighted – efficiency, sufficient connection, certainty and proportionate balance between the interests of claimants and defendants. The *lex protectionis* approach satisfies the efficiency criterion because of its wide scope and minimal formalistic requirements.[80] Under the *lex protectionis* approach, the claimant must simply establish the country or countries where he is claiming protection.[81] This process avoids any cumbersome legal decision-making in comparison to the *lex loci delicti*, where there exists circularity in reasoning in determining the applicable law. By comparison, establishing the applicable law is quick and simple under the *lex protectionis* and, moreover, flexible due to the absence of any formalistic requirements.[82] Nonetheless, the *lex protectionis* is criticised because its simplicity and lack of clear scope in establishing the applicable law allows for uncertain results in the context of ubiquitous

[75] de Miguel Asensio argues that the territorial nature of copyright law requires that the *lex protectionis* be the basic conflict of laws rule – de Miguel Asensio in Leible and Ohly (2009) 17.

[76] Neumann argues that the reasoning used by the EU Commission and legislature, as highlighted in Recital 26 of the Rome II Regulation, is unsatisfactory and insufficient – Neumann (2011) 587.

[77] ibid 590.

[78] The implementation of the *lex protectionis* for IP is questionable because Article 8 is limited to infringement proceedings. However, the wording is sufficiently wide to distinguish it from the *lex loci delicti*.

[79] European Max Planck Group, *Principles on Conflict of Laws in Intellectual Property* (2011) [CLIP Principles].

[80] C Otero Garcia-Castrillion, 'Choice of law in IP: Rounding off territoriality' in P Torremans (ed), *Research Handbook on Cross-border Enforcement of Intellectual Property* (Edward Elgar Publishing Ltd, 2014) 445.

[81] Peukert (2016) 74 and Savola (2014) 299–300.

[82] Neumann (2011) 589.

infringements, since the claimant can choose to invoke the law of any country in which the infringement occurred.[83]

However, claimants will only invoke the law of a country where they have a reasonable chance of establishing a connection between the act complained of and that country's copyright law. The required connection involves the claimant being able to satisfy the provisions governing subsistence and infringement under the law of the country for which protection is claimed. What this means is that claimants will only invoke a country's laws where they are likely to succeed. In fact, the *lex protectionis* will often offer the closest connection between the infringement and choice of law.[84] Thus, the absence of any filtering mechanism in the *lex protectionis* to stop inadmissible claims is otiose. To put it differently, the criticism that the *lex protectionis* allows claimants to invoke potentially any country's law in cases of ubiquitous infringement is overstated because claimants will only designate an applicable law that is beneficial to them.

Additionally, the interests of defendants are fairly balanced with those of claimants in relation to the establishment of applicable law in EU copyright cases because it is certain and predictable what the scope of the law will be regardless of what Member State's law is applied.[85] This is due to the minimum level of harmonisation in EU copyright law. However, where an element of unfairness may exist is in relation to the extraterritorial effects of certain remedies.[86] For example, an injunction granted against a defendant in one court to take down a website may result in the website becoming inaccessible in all other countries.[87] This is unfair to defendants because the remedy granted using the law of the country for which protection is claimed may have a disproportionate impact by affecting other countries in which protection is not claimed.

This problem is not exclusive to the *lex protectionis* approach because the territorial nature of copyright law and the prevalence of ubiquitous infringement mean that a single act can affect multiple countries. It remains the case that even if the *lex fori* or *lex loci delicti* were to be applied, extraterritorial consequences could occur because a single act of infringement can affect multiple countries and

[83] R Fentiman, 'Choice of Law and Intellectual Property' in J Drexl and A Kur (eds), *Intellectual Property and Private International Law – Heading for the Future* (Hart Publishing, 2005) 144–45, van Eechoud in Drexl and Kur (2005) 297, van Eechoud (2003) 104 and R Matulionyte, 'The Law Applicable to Online Copyright Infringements in the ALI and CLIP Proposals: A Rebalance of Interests Needed?' (2011) 2 *JIPITEC* 26, 27.

[84] Neumann (2011) 589–90.

[85] Neumann (2011) 589. Matulionyte argues the opposite by claiming that the ability of claimants to bring a claim anywhere causes uncertainty – Matulionyte (2011) 27. However, in applying the Completion theory, it becomes clear where an act of communication to the public occurs and moreover, defendants should bear the responsibility of engaging in acts of ubiquitous infringement. It is fair that an act that affects multiple countries should be able to be litigated in multiple countries.

[86] Matulionyte argues that using the *lex protectionis* approach tends to have extraterritorial effects – Matulionyte (2011) 27 and Matulionyte2 (2011) 187.

[87] This would depend on whether the injunction is directed at the website operator or at an Internet Service Provider (ISP), for example. If directed at an ISP, the injunction will remain territorially limited.

consequently, any remedy granted to cure such a ubiquitous act will also likely have extraterritorial effect.[88] By contrast, claimants may also consider themselves disadvantaged under the *lex protectionis* approach where they are granted judgment, but are unable to enforce that judgment in another territory.[89] From these two issues, both right holders and users need to take into account the territorial issues that arise in EU copyright law.

Following the above discussion, the *lex protectionis* meets the criteria set out for an effective choice of law rule. In addition to this, it is also important to mention that the *lex protectionis* approach is consistent with the territorial nature of copyright law. It was previously mentioned that one of the primary problems with copyright law is how to reconcile the territorial nature of copyright law with the ubiquitous nature of copyright infringement, the issue being that the laws of copyright are confined to the territory from which they originate.[90] However, an act of copyright infringement may extend beyond the boundaries of a particular territory.[91] Consequently, the choice of law employed must be able to take account of such occurrences.[92] Thus, in applying the *lex protectionis* approach, the court must be able to apply law that has a connection with the act complained of. Failure to facilitate this would be contrary to copyright law because it would mean that other laws are given extraterritorial effect. In other words, an act of infringement may be governed by a law that is unconnected with it.

This is a possibility under the *lex fori* approach because the place where the claim is brought may be completely unconnected to where the act complained of occurred. Thus, the potential consequence is that the law of the court seised is applied to an infringement outside of its territory, thereby disrespecting the territorial nature of copyright law. This is of particular importance where domestic copyright laws provide for compulsory licensing or exceptions and limitations beyond the scope of Article 5 of the Information Society Directive. The *lex protectionis* is, however, competent at ensuring that the territoriality of copyright law is respected because the applicable law subject to Article 15(c) of the Rome II Regulation covers both the determination of infringement and remedy.[93] This approach is also found under section 301(1) of the ALI Principles and Article 3:601(2)(b) of the CLIP Principles. Determining the remedy under the same law used to determine the infringement is desirable because it reduces the chance of *dépeçage*.

[88] R Matulionyte, *Law Applicable to Copyright: A Comparison of the ALI and CLIP Proposals* (Edward Elgar Publishing Ltd, 2011) 187 [Matulionyte2].

[89] M Ficsor, 'Direct Broadcasting by Satellite and the Bogsch Theory' (1990) 18 *International Business Law* 258, 261

[90] Ginsburg (1995) 330.

[91] Austin in Strowel (2009) 124, M van Eechoud et al, *Harmonizing European Copyright Law: The Challenges of Better Lawmaking* (Kluwer Law International, 2009) 308–09, A Ohly, 'Choice of Law in the Digital Environment – Problems and Possible Solutions' in J Drexl and A Kur (eds), *Intellectual Property and Private International Law – Heading for the Future* (Hart Publishing, 2005) 241, Fawcett and Torremans (2011) 925–26, para 18.07.

[92] Neumann (2011) 588.

[93] This is also the approach adopted under Article 5(2) of the Berne Convention.

Thus, where the *lex protectionis* is employed, the procedural law of the *lex fori* is prevented from seeping back in with regards to the determination of remedies. Thus, the territoriality of copyright law is respected and preserved because the applicable law is designated by the claimant or court on the basis that protection is being claimed in a particular country and as such, that country's law should be applicable.[94] Furthermore, the *lex protectionis* approach also respects the principle of national treatment as set down in Article 5(1) of the Berne Convention. This is because claimants who invoke another country's laws are treated the same as domestic persons of that country, regardless of their nationality or where the claim is brought.

Despite the virtues of the *lex protectionis*, however, it is not necessarily the case that it is effective in practice. Applying the law of one country in another country's court can be problematic. It is often difficult to enforce judgments handed down in one country in another country.[95] As a result, using the *lex protectionis* to apply laws foreign to those of the court seised may not be the most effective means of enforcing one's copyright at the international level. However, at the EU level this is not as troublesome because EU copyright law has been minimally harmonised through the copyright *acquis communitaire*. As such, the domestic courts of Member States have experience in dealing with EU copyright law that ought to be reflected at the domestic level of all the Member States. Moreover, the development of EU copyright law has been held to be autonomous and independent. Thus, the scope of the exclusive rights and exceptions and limitations is subject to the approaches of the CJEU and not the individual courts of Member States.

Nonetheless, in order to solve the issues raised in this subsection, it is necessary to expressly address acts of ubiquitous infringement under the choice of law rules. This will resolve the uncertainty surrounding the use of the *lex protectionis* with regard to the issues of extraterritorial effects and concerns about enforcing judgments in other jurisdictions. However, it must be noted that the onus remains on claimants to carefully consider where to bring their claims and what applicable law to invoke. Following the above discussion about the *lex protectionis* approach, it is advocated that the approach should continue to be followed for EU copyright law. However, an amended copyright-specific rule, containing an express provision addressing ubiquitous infringement, should be adopted in lieu of Article 8 of the Rome II Regulation.

III. Establishing Applicable Law for the Reformed Communication to the Public Right

The rules concerning the determination of applicable law are of particular importance to the enforcement of the reformed communication to the public right

[94] de Miguel Asensio in Leible and Ohly (2009) 17.
[95] Ficsor (1990) 261.

because of the ubiquitous nature of digital technology, notably, the Internet. As such, single acts of communication often implicate multiple countries and, moreover, acts of Internet communication can affect all countries with free Internet access. Consequently, it is necessary for the EU rules concerning applicable law to accommodate ubiquitous acts of infringement that arise under the reformed communication to the public right, in order to ensure the development of a coherent copyright system.

A. New Rules for Establishing Applicable Law in EU Copyright Cases

It has been argued that the determination of applicable law for EU copyright law should continue to follow the *lex protectionis* approach. However, in the interest of developing an effective, copyright-specific approach, the existing Article 8 of the Rome II Regulation is insufficient. Article 8 only addresses cases of infringement and in a very limited capacity; whereas, the copyright-specific provision should be capable of addressing both infringement and subsistence issues in the interest of achieving complete copyright harmonisation to ensure copyright consistency within the internal market.[96] Furthermore, acts of ubiquitous infringement should be expressly addressed. Consequently, it is necessary to propose a new provision to address the question of applicable law for EU copyright law. Similarly to the provisions proposed for jurisdiction in Chapter six, it is recommended that this provision be adopted in a new piece of copyright legislation or under a copyright-specific Regulation.

The new provisions on applicable law should read as follows:

<u>General Rule</u>

The law applicable to all matters concerning copyright law shall be the law of the country for which protection is claimed.

(a) 'All matters' for the purpose of this provision include the determination of subsistence, infringement and remedies.
(b) Without prejudice to the multi-country infringement rule, the court may derogate from the general rule and apply the law of the forum for all matters, if that law has a sufficient connection to the alleged infringement.

The proposed general rule reflects the approach taken under section 301 of the ALI Principles and Article 3:601 of the CLIP Principles in comprehensively applying the *lex protectionis*. Unlike Article 8 of the Rome II Regulation, the proposed

[96] It is necessary to reiterate that the scope of this thesis prevents detailed discussion about subsistence issues because focus is solely on the exclusive right of communication to the public. As such, the proposed rules on establishing applicable law will primarily focus on the infringement aspect.

provision can address both infringement and subsistence issues. Additionally, the assessment of damage and the determination of remedies are also expressly included under a single uniform provision. This is in contrast to the split provision approach adopted under the Rome II Regulation, where Article 8 establishes the applicable law and then Article 15(c) details that the established applicable law also governs the determination of damage and remedies. Having a single law that addresses all these issues is necessary for the avoidance of *dépeçage*.

However, paragraph (b) of the proposed rule is a novel concept introduced to the general rule for the purpose of promoting efficient litigation of copyright infringement cases. Paragraph (b) allows courts to apply their own law where the *lex protectionis* is capable of coinciding with the *lex fori*. In other words, if the *lex fori* in the case at hand was an option under the *lex protectionis*, the *lex fori* should be applied. As far as possible, courts should try to apply their own law given that they are most efficient when doing so. The application of domestic law in this regard ought to further reduce the possibility of forum shopping and cherry-picking of laws, as well as increase the efficiency with which copyright cases are decided.

This is achievable because the burden of establishing that another country's laws apply can be avoided if the situation allows. Moreover, courts should be more efficient and accurate in applying their own law. It should be noted that in the ideal scenario this is merely an additional safeguard and an efficiency issue. In the context of the reformed communication to the public right, this should not have any impact on the determination of infringement because the law ought to be applied and interpreted in a uniform manner, given that its proposed form is codified.

Multi-country Infringement Rule

In cases involving multi-country infringement carried out through ubiquitous media such as the Internet, the court may apply the law of the country where substantial activities in furtherance of the infringement as a whole have been carried out, to cover all the resultant acts of infringement.

- *(a) 'Multi-country infringement' covers acts that are capable of occurring in multiple countries simultaneously or successively.*
- *(b) Notwithstanding the applicable law chosen pursuant to this section, either party may prove that the law of one or more of the countries implicated in the action differs from the chosen applicable law. The court shall take into account such difference(s) in determining the scope of liability and remedies.*

This rule on multi-country infringement has become necessary in order to account for ubiquitous media that facilitate infringements in multiple countries. The consequence of the prevalence of ubiquitous infringement is litigation in multiple countries for the same act of infringement (affecting multiple countries).[97]

[97] Otero García-Castrillón in Torremans (2014) 458.

Therefore, in the interest of efficiency, claimants should be able to bring one claim under one applicable law to enforce their exclusive rights. As such, the multi-country infringement rule is the means to provide a more fair, efficient and certain way to litigate cases of ubiquitous infringement.

In practice the multi-country infringement rule will allow the court to apply a single law to cover all the infringements that arise from a single ubiquitous act. In the context of the reformed communication to the public right, this will provide an efficient means of protection for right holders because they will not have to file multiple claims in different Member States.[98] Using the rules on jurisdiction from Chapter six and the multi-country infringement rule outlined here, acts of ubiquitous infringement can be addressed in one claim. The interests of right holders and defendants are also fairly balanced because litigation can be centralised in a predictable manner subject to the close connection requirement and, furthermore, the risk of overcompensation is reduced as the court can address all damage in a single claim.

The rule concerning multi-country infringements is proposed as an alternative to the ubiquitous infringement concept that is advocated by the ALI Principles and CLIP Principles. Although different in name, the multi-country infringement rule is designed to address similar issues to the ubiquitous infringement provisions proposed by the ALI Principles and CLIP Principles. Matulionyte suggests that the ALI Principles and CLIP Principles' ubiquitous infringement provisions require both ubiquitous activity and multi-state infringement.[99] In other words the activity involved must have a worldwide reach and the infringements must occur in multiple countries.[100] However, using the term 'ubiquitous infringement', though reflective of modern technologies including the Internet and Internet-based technologies, does lead to difficult questions. Matulionyte asked several questions including: Is ubiquitous infringement designed to address the Internet specifically? What happens in instances where a work made available on the Internet is not available worldwide or is targeted to specific countries? What types of acts constitute 'ubiquitous'?[101]

By adopting the 'multi-country infringement' approach, these issues and their problematic implications are avoided. Focus is placed on the 'multi-country' aspect of the infringement rather than the specific nature of the activity. This implicitly requires ubiquitous media to be involved; however, emphasis is not placed on this. Rather, the important point is that a single act, regardless of the technology

[98] G Austin, 'Private International Law and Intellectual Property Rights: A Common Law Overview' at *WIPO Forum on Private International Law and Intellectual Property* (Geneva, 30 and 31 January 2001) 13, para 34.

[99] Neumann adopts a similar interpretation of 'ubiquitous' by suggesting it has to be worldwide in reach or 'virtually in every state'. If this is not the case, then it should be considered 'multistate infringement' – S Neumann, 'Ubiquitous and Multistate Cases in P Torremans (ed), *Research Handbook on Cross-Border Enforcement of Intellectual Property* (Edward Elgar Publishing, 2014) 497.

[100] Matulionyte2 (2011) 178–81.

[101] ibid 178–79.

involved, is capable of occurring in multiple countries without the need for further intervention. Therefore, there is no need for the act to be worldwide or 'virtually in every state'.[102] Furthermore, the word 'capable' is important because it is not necessary that the multiple infringements occur at the exact same time. Instead, it is necessary that there is the possibility that infringement can occur in multiple countries jointly (on the basis of the single act).

In addition to this, using 'multi-country' as the title of the provision rather than 'ubiquitous' also resolves the issue relating to quantifying 'ubiquitous'. The question is: how many countries need to be implicated to consider an act ubiquitous? According to the ALI Principles, which sets a low threshold, ubiquitous means multiple countries are involved.[103] However, the CLIP Principles adopted a higher threshold, requiring that the infringement 'arguably takes place in every State'.[104] In this regard, the proposed provision is more closely related to the ALI Principles and this is evidenced by its name, which in turn more closely reflects the objective of the provision; that is, to provide an efficient means of adjudicating infringement cases that have a multi-territorial impact.

Following the change in name, the term 'multi-country infringement' is also defined, unlike the term 'ubiquitous infringement' that is left undefined in both the ALI Principles and the CLIP Principles. As already noted, 'multi-country infringement' means any act that is capable of occurring simultaneously or successively. This allows the provision to cover any technology, provided that it allows for infringement in multiple countries without the need for any additional act. This would in principle include acts of making available online such as on demand activities, live streaming or Internet retransmissions and, alternatively, satellite broadcasts. However, application of this provision would depend on the factual situation allowing for multi-country infringement. For example, if a work is geo-blocked, this would not indicate multi-country infringement if that work cannot be accessed in multiple countries. As a whole, the definition provided ensures the provision is technology-neutral and indicates its central purpose.

In addition to the above differences, the proposed multi-country infringement provision also departs from the ALI Principles and CLIP Principles' approach in another significant way. Both approaches require that the applicable law under the ubiquitous infringement provision should have a close connection (ALI Principles) or the closest connection (CLIP Principles) with the infringement in question. Determining this connection is subject to a number of relevant factors. Under the ALI Principles, the relevant factors, though non-exhaustive, include: where the parties reside; where the parties' interests are centred; the extent of the activities and investment of the parties; and the principal market toward which the parties targeted their activities. Alternatively, the CLIP Principles set as the

[102] The distinction adopted by Neumann between 'ubiquitous infringement' and 'multistate infringement' is followed – Neumann in Torremans (2014) 497.

[103] See section 321 of the ALI Principles.

[104] See Article 3:603 of the CLIP Principles.

relevant factors, again in a non-exhaustive list: the infringer's habitual residence or place of business; the place where the substantial activities in furtherance of the infringement occurred; and the place where the harm caused by the infringement is substantial in relation to the infringement as a whole.

However, the proposed multi-country provision in this chapter departs from this relevant factor approach and sets a single requirement for the courts to assess; that is, where substantial activities in furtherance of the infringement as a whole have been carried out. This method was chosen because it is compatible with the approach adopted for the establishment of jurisdiction in allowing all damages to be taken into account by one court. Secondly, it ensures a predictable and consistent way of determining whether the multi-country infringement provision can apply. This difference in approach is characterised by the fact that the provisions concerning applicable law focus on the act of infringement and not the actor responsible for it. As such, this ensures that the applicable law has a sufficient nexus to the act that it will apply to, in order to comply with the sufficient connection requirement, set out as a criterion for an ideal choice of law rule.

As for paragraph (b), it establishes a 'retreat to territoriality' rule akin to section 321(2) of the ALI Principles and Article 3:603(3) of the CLIP Principles. The structure of this paragraph largely reflects that of the above mentioned provisions and achieves the same effect. That is, to allow the parties involved to invoke the laws of other Member States where the result may differ to that determined under the applicable law chosen under the multi-country infringement provision.[105] Given the absence of a unitary copyright law, the provision maintains the underlying territoriality of the existing copyright laws.[106] However, in the instance of the reformed communication to the public right, this provision can be seen as a check and balance because the proposed right is codified. Consequently, there is limited opportunity for major divergences in the law of the various Member States.

Maintaining the territoriality of EU copyright law raises a number of concerns. It is not disputed that the multi-country infringement rule or the ubiquitous infringement rules can produce a more efficient means of litigation. Instead, there is some concern whether the ultimate outcome will be any different to the current situation. In the first place, the multi-country infringement provision is not mandatory; it can be invoked at the discretion of the claimant or the court. This is evidenced by using the word 'may' instead of 'shall'. As such, a claimant may choose to pursue the ordinary *lex protectionis* approach.

This concern is compounded by the fact that remedies under the existing *lex protectionis* approach in the EU can have extraterritorial effects albeit unjustifiably in some cases. Therefore, it must be asked whether the employment of the multi-country infringement provision and/or the ubiquitous infringement provisions ultimately differs from the ordinary *lex protectionis* approach.[107] Regardless

[105] Matulionyte2 (2011) 187–88.
[106] ibid 188–89.
[107] ibid 189.

of whether there is a difference in the ultimate result, the multi-country infringement rule will provide a more justifiable method of achieving the end goal that is compliant with the criteria set out for an ideal choice of law rule. Therefore, there is definitely a need for the newly proposed rules.

IV. Conclusion

This chapter explored the existing rules concerning the determination of applicable law in the EU copyright context. Although it was suggested that the *lex protectionis* should continue to be the general means for determining applicable law, it was advocated that the rules needed to expressly accommodate acts of ubiquitous infringement. As such, a multi-country infringement rule was proposed in order to allow claimants to bring one claim under one law to govern ubiquitous infringements. With that in mind, the proposed rules on applicable law form part of a coherent framework with the rules on jurisdiction discussed in Chapter six.

The proposals for the redesign of the existing rules on jurisdiction and applicable law were made in response to the increasing digital nature of copyright law and the accompanying acts of ubiquitous infringement. Of particular concern in this regard is the operation of the communication to the public right that was reformed in this book. Thus, the proposal of a new, reformed communication to the public right equally required new rules on jurisdiction and applicable law to construct a coherent framework for its interpretation, application and enforcement. Consequently, to effectively enforce the act of communication to the public, the act must firstly be located, jurisdiction must then be established, and finally the applicable law determined.

8

Applying the Reformed Right of Communication to the Public: Case Studies

I. Introduction

This book has made several proposals for the development of a reformed right of communication to the public under EU copyright law. In order for the reformed right to be coherent and effective in its interpretation, application and enforcement, it was suggested that: there is a need for comprehensive reform of the scope of the communication to the public right (Chapters two, three and five); the reformed right must be reconciled with the framework of EU copyright law (Chapter four); and the existing rules on jurisdiction and applicable law should accommodate the nuances of EU copyright law, in particular, the possibility of ubiquitous infringement (Chapters six and seven). The recommendations proposed in this book were guided by the competing interests present in EU copyright law and the principles of certainty and proportionality discussed in Chapter one. Consequently, the result is the proposal of a comprehensive framework for the governance of acts of communication to the public:

- Is there an act of 'communication'?
  - Does the act involve a transmission or provision of the work? Provision is taken to mean direct contact with the work.
  - If the 'communication' is a subsequent communication, was it made by an organisation other than the original one?
- If there is an actionable 'communication', is there a 'public'?
  - Is there a fairly large and indeterminate number of people that are geographically dispersed from the place of 'communication'?
- If there is an actionable 'communication' to a 'public', where does the act occur and who is the responsible party?
  - Location – Where the act is completed; that is in the country(ies) of receipt, in accordance with the Completion theory.
  - Responsibility – The person who actively initiated the act.

- Where can jurisdiction be established?
  - Is the defendant domiciled in the EU?
  - Where did the infringement occur or where is it likely to occur?
  - Did the defendant substantially act within the Member State of the court seised (for the purpose of taking an EU-wide account of damage)?
- What is the applicable law?
  - *Lex protectionis* – the law of the country for which protection is claimed.
  - Can the multi-country infringement rule be applied?

Where the act complained of falls outside the scope of the reformed right of communication to the public, there may still exist the possibility of secondary liability. This is important because the act in question may harbour culpable behaviour. Therefore, in the interest of securing a high level of protection for right holders, secondary liability can provide residual protection in the absence of primary infringement. However, secondary liability is not harmonised at the EU level;[1] and as such it is subject to the domestic laws of the relevant Member State.[2]

With the above framework in mind, this chapter sets out to illustrate how the reformed right of communication to the public should be applied. The use of the reformed right will be illustrated using a number of scenarios from existing case law and situations that are expected to arise.

[1] Secondary liability differs by Member State. For example, the UK has authorisation and joint tortfeasance under tort law, Germany has *störerhaftung, täterhaftung, mittäter and teilnehmer* under the German Civil Code and France has special liability regimes for hosts and editors and *le droit commun* (general rules of tort law). See C Angelopoulos, *European Intermediary Liability in Copyright: A Tort-Based Analysis* (Kluwer Law International BV, 2017).

[2] Despite the relevance of secondary liability, it is not discussed in the book, since the focus is on the development of the communication to the public right and primary infringement. For discussion on secondary liability see: A Strowel (ed), *Peer-to-Peer File Sharing and Secondary Liability in Copyright Law* (Edward Elgar Publishing Ltd, 2009), P Davies, *Accessory Liability* (Hart Publishing, 2015), G Williams *Joint torts and contributory negligence: A study of concurrent fault in Great Britain, Ireland and the common law dominions* (Stevens & Sons, 1951), M Leistner, 'Common Principle of Secondary Liability' in A Ohly (ed), *Common Principles of European Intellectual Property Law* (Mohr Siebeck, 2012), M Leistner, 'Structural aspects of secondary (provider) liability in Europe' (2014) 9(1) *Journal of Intellectual Property Law & Practice (JIPLP)* 75, L Oswald, 'Secondary Liability for Intellectual Property Law Infringement in the International Arena: Framing the Dialogue' in R Bird and S Jain (eds), *The Global Challenge of Intellectual Property Rights* (Edward Elgar Publishing Ltd, 2008), S Barazza, 'Secondary liability for IP infringement: converging patterns and approaches in comparative case law' (2012) 7(12) *JIPLP* 879, P Davies, 'Accessory liability: protecting intellectual property rights' [2011] *Intellectual Property Quarterly (IPQ)* 390, G Dinwoodie, R Dreyfuss and A Kur, 'The Law Applicable to Secondary Liability in Intellectual Property Cases' (2010) 42 *New York University Journal of International Law & Politics* 201, JB Nordemann, 'Internet Copyright Infringement: Remedies Against Intermediaries – The European Perspective on Host and Access Providers' (2012) 59 *Journal of the Copyright Society of the USA* 773, P Davies, 'Accessory liability for assisting torts' (2011) 70(2) *Cambridge Law Journal* 353, A Kur, 'Secondary Liability for Trademark Infringement on the Internet: The Situation in Germany and Throughout the EU' (2014) 37 *Columbia Journal of Law & the Arts* 525, C Angelopoulos, 'Beyond the safe harbours: harmonizing substantive intermediary liability for copyright infringement in Europe' [2013] *IPQ* 253 and JB Nordemann, 'Liability for Copyright Infringements on the Internet: Host Providers (Content Providers) – The German Approach' (2011) *Journal of Intellectiual Property, Information Technology & E-Commerce Law* 37.

II. *Rafael Hoteles* – Acts of Cable Retransmission

What happened – A hotel set up a central antenna where it received television broadcasts and subsequently retransmitted the received signals by cable to individual television sets in its hotel rooms.[3]

Original finding – The CJEU held that the act of cable retransmission to the hotel rooms was an act of communication to the public because the customers of the hotel amounted to a 'new public'. This finding was made on the basis that the hotel guests would not have been able to access the broadcast but for the hotel's intervention, even though they were in a physical space where the broadcast was receivable.[4]

Revised finding – In applying the revised right of communication to the public to the factual scenario from *Rafael Hoteles*, the end result will be the same as that derived by the CJEU, but via a different means. There is an act of communication to the public because the cable retransmission amounts to a subsequent act of 'communication' made by an 'organisation other than the original one'; that is, the hotel was a third party different from the initial broadcaster. As such, authorisation is required from the right holder.

III. *FAPL v QC Leisure* – Acts of Reception in Public

What happened – A pub showed a live broadcast football match to its patrons via a television screen and speakers installed in the pub.[5]

Original finding – The CJEU held that the act of playing the broadcast in the pub was an act of communication to the public because the broadcast was shown to a 'new public'. This is because the 'public' contemplated by the right holder when granting permission for the initial broadcast consisted of persons in their private homes or family circles.[6]

Revised finding – Applying the revised right of communication to the public to the factual situation in *FAPL v QC Leisure* leads to a different outcome from that of the CJEU's decision. The act of reception in public should fall outside the scope of the communication to the public right because the 'public' is physically gathered at the place where the 'communication' originates. Unlike the CJEU's finding that the 'communication' originated where the football match was played (at the stadium where the broadcast originated),[7] under the framework of the reformed

[3] Case C-306/05 *Sociedad General Autores y Editores (SGAE) v Rafael Hoteles SA* [2006], Opinion of AG Sharpston, ECLI:EU:C:2006:479, paras 17–19.

[4] Case C-306/05 *Sociedad General de Autores y Editores de España (SGAE) v Rafael Hoteles SA* [2006] ECLI:EU:C:2006:764, para 41.

[5] Cases C-403/08 and C-429/08 *Football Association Premier League (FAPL) and others v QC Leisure and others and Karen Murphy v Media Protection Services Ltd* [2011] ECLI:EU:C:2011:631, para 183.

[6] *FAPL v QC Leisure* [2011] para 198.

[7] ibid paras 200–203.

right, the place of 'communication' is where the actor complained of transmits or provides the work. In this case, the act in question is the playing of the football broadcast in the pub, and as such the act of 'communication' is the playing of the work on the television. Consequently, the 'communication' occurs in the pub where the 'public' is physically gathered. In the absence of the requisite 'public' element, there is no act of communication to the public requiring authorisation.

Alternative solution – This type of act should be covered by the exclusive right of public performance at the domestic level, given that there is no harmonised right of public performance at the EU level.

IV. *ITV v TVCatchup* – Acts of Internet Retransmission ('Simulcasting')

What happened – TVCatchup streamed ITV's free-to-air broadcasts on its Internet application that streams live television broadcasts near simultaneously.[8]

Original finding – The CJEU held that the 'simulcasting' of a free-to-air broadcast on the Internet was an act of communication to the public requiring authorisation because it was done using a specific technical means different from the initial communication.[9]

Revised finding – If the reformed right of communication to the public was applied in this factual context, the ultimate result would be the same as the CJEU's decision. The defendant should be found liable for an act of communication to the public. However, the finding of liability would be based on the fact that the act of streaming a live broadcast on the Internet is an act of subsequent 'communication', invoking the 'organisation other than the original one' criterion. Given that TVCatchup is a different entity to ITV, this would mean that there is an act of communication to the public requiring authorisation from the right holders of the works contained within the broadcasts. Internet rebroadcasts should be treated in the same manner as ordinary rebroadcasts or satellite rebroadcasts.

V. *Svensson* – Hyperlinks

What happened – The defendant ran a website which provided clickable hyperlinks to newspaper articles on external websites. The articles being linked to were

[8] Case C-607/11 *ITV Broadcasting Ltd and others v TVCatchup Ltd* [2013] ECLI:EU:C:2013:147, para 9.

[9] ibid paras 24–26.

made freely available on their host websites with the permission of the right holder.[10]

Original finding – The CJEU held that the provision of clickable hyperlinks[11] to works freely available on the Internet did not amount to an act of communication to the public because the works were not made available to a 'new public'. This is because works made freely available on the Internet are accessible by all users of the Internet and this would have been taken into account by the right holder when authorising the initial upload of the work.[12]

Revised finding – The application of the reformed right of communication to the public would give rise to the same finding as the CJEU's in *Svensson*. That is, there should be no act of communication to the public. However, this finding is based on the premise that there is no act of 'communication' where simple or deep hyperlinks are involved. This is because simple hyperlinks do not involve a transmission or provision of the work. The simple hyperlink merely takes the user to the location where the work can already be found as opposed to offering direct contact. Consequently, there is no act of communication to the public.

VI. *GS Media* – Hyperlinks

What happened – The defendant wrote articles which included hyperlinks to photographs made freely available online without the permission of the right holder.[13]

Original finding – The CJEU held that hyperlinking to works made freely available online without authorisation amounted to an act of communication to the public where the hyperlinker had 'knowledge' of the infringing nature of the work being linked to. The CJEU interpreted 'knowledge' to mean actual knowledge, or imputed knowledge where the act of hyperlinking is done 'for profit'. Therefore, in the absence of 'knowledge' there can be no act of communication to the public. However, in this case, the defendant had actual knowledge that the photographs were uploaded without permission and moreover, the act of hyperlinking was done 'for profit'.[14] Consequently, the act of hyperlinking to unauthorised photos made freely available was an act of communication to the public.

[10] Case C-466/12 *Svensson and others v Retriever Sverige AB* [2014] ECLI:EU:C:2014:76, para 8.

[11] See A Strowel and N Ide, 'Liability with Regard to Hyperlinks' (2001) 24 *Columbia VLA Journal of Law & the Arts* 403, 407–09, for a brief discussion on the different types of hyperlinks.

[12] ibid paras 27–28.

[13] Case C-160/15 *GS Media BV v Sanoma Media Netherlands BV and others* [2016] Opinion of AG Wathelet ECLI:EU:C:2016:221, paras 7–15.

[14] ibid paras 47–51 and 54.

Revised finding – Similarly to the revised finding in *Svensson*, the application of the reformed communication to the public right in the *GS Media* fact scenario will also give rise to a finding of no infringement. The hyperlinks in question merely took the users to the place where the unauthorised photographs could be located. This deep hyperlink did not transmit or provide the works and as such does not amount to a 'communication'. Therefore, there can be no finding of communication to the public.

Alternative solution – Posting of simple or deep hyperlinks to unauthorised content should be addressed using the laws on secondary liability at the domestic level, given the absence of any harmonised EU approach.

VII. *Filmspeler* – Media Players

What happened – The defendant sold media players pre-loaded with add-ons containing hyperlinks that allowed users to access streams of broadcast channels and audio-visual works on demand. The content accessible through the media player included both authorised and unauthorised sources.[15]

Original finding – The CJEU held that the sale of media players with 'knowledge' that the installed add-ons (containing hyperlinks to freely accessible websites) allowed access to unauthorised content meant that there was an infringement of the communication to the public right.[16]

Revised finding – If the revised right of communication to the public were applied to the facts of *Filmspeler*, the decision would have been different to that of the CJEU. A finding of no communication to the public should ensue because the installation of the add-ons which contained the hyperlinks does not amount to an act of 'communication'. The add-ons do not transmit or provide the work. The situation is analogous to the provision of simple or deep hyperlinks which redirect the user to the original source of the unauthorised content, from which the work is then streamed. Although the operation of the media player makes it easy to play unauthorised works, the add-ons merely offer indirect contact with the works.

It should also be noted that the media player itself is not subject to primary infringement as it amounts to providing physical facilities and as such falls outside the scope of the communication to the public right.

Alternative solution – The provisions of add-ons with 'knowledge' of the unauthorised nature of the works being linked to should be addressed by domestic laws on secondary liability.

[15] Case C-527/15 *Stichting Brein v Jack Frederik Wullems (acting under the name of Filmspeler)* [2017] ECLI:EU:C:2016:938, paras 15–18.

[16] ibid para 42 and *Ziggo* [2017] paras 50–52.

VIII. *Ziggo* – Torrent Files

What happened – The Pirate Bay operated a website that indexed torrent files.[17] Ninety to ninety-five per cent of the torrent files shared were concerned with unauthorised works.[18]

Original finding – The CJEU held that the management of an online sharing platform that indexes torrent files is an act of communication to the public, given that The Pirate Bay could not be unaware that the platform provided access to unauthorised works.[19]

Revised finding – Applying the revised communication to the public right to the facts of *Ziggo* would lead to a different outcome than that arrived at by the CJEU. The CJEU focused its decision on the organisation of The Pirate Bay website and its indexing of the torrent files, which made it less complex to share infringing works.[20] However, emphasis should have been specifically placed on the nature of the torrent files. Like simple and deep hyperlinks, torrent files merely provide information concerning where to find content and the instructions to obtain it.[21] From this there is no transmission or provision of works. Consequently, there is no act of 'communication' and as such, no communication to the public.

Alternative solution – Given that the operators of The Pirate Bay knew that 90 to 95 per cent of torrent files shared on their website involved unauthorised works, they are culpable. However, their culpability should be dealt with under the secondary liability laws available at the Member State level.

IX. *VCAST* – Time Shifting

What happened – VCAST was a television service provider that had an online function allowing users to record television programmes that were stored in external cloud storage for later watching (time shifting).[22] The user was then able to watch the recorded programmes on demand.

Original finding – The issue of communication to the public was not the central aspect of *VCAST*. However, the CJEU held that the recording of television

[17] Case C-610/15 *Stichting Brein v Ziggo BV and XS4All Internet BV* [2017] ECLI:EU:C:2017:456, paras 9–12.

[18] Case C-610/15 *Stichting Brein v Ziggo BV and XS4ALL Internet BV* [2017] Opinion of AG Szpunar ECLI:EU:C:2017:99, para 23.

[19] *Ziggo* [2017] para 45.

[20] ibid para 36.

[21] See the expert report by Michael Walsh of Kerna Communication Ltd that was quoted by Arnold J in *Dramatico Entertainment Ltd v British Sky Broadcasting Ltd* [2012] EWHC 268 (Ch), para 19, for a description of the torrent process. Also see the description of the torrent process in *Roadshow Films Pty Ltd v iiNet Ltd* [2011] FCAFC 23, paras 46–63.

[22] Case C-256/16 *VCAST Ltd v RTI SpA* [2017] ECLI:EU:C:2017:913, paras 14–15.

programmes and the subsequent making available of those programmes on demand was an act of communication to the public because it involved a different technical means of communication and as such required authorisation.[23]

Revised finding – The application of the revised right of communication to the public to the *VCAST* fact-pattern leads to divergence from the reasoning adopted by the CJEU, although the ultimate conclusion remains the same. The act of making available a recorded television programme (time shifting) amounts to a new and separate act of 'communication' that requires fresh authorisation. The provision of television content and the ability to record that content gives rise to an act of communication to the public because the overall concept is analogous to the provision of on demand content.[24] As such, it amounts to an act of making available separate to the original act of broadcasting.

However, establishing liability for the act of communication to the public for time shifting the broadcasted content is dependent on VCAST being responsible for the act of making available. This is of particular importance given that the cloud storage was provided by a third party.[25] Nonetheless, the available facts suggest that VCAST was the only party involved in making the works available and moreover, was the party who initiated the 'communication'.[26]

Alternative scenario – If VCAST did not provide both the content and the means to time shift the broadcasted content, there would be no act of communication to the public because the works would not be made available in a way that is accessible at a time and place of the user's choice. In the instance where the means to time shift the works were provided without the provision of any content, this would amount to the mere provision of facilities. Therefore, this would fall outside the scope of the communication to the public right, following Recital 27 of the Information Society Directive.[27] In the scenario that VCAST provided only the mechanism to time shift without any content, liability would depend on the domestic laws concerning secondary liability if there was 'knowledge' of illegitimate works being communicated. This finding is justified because the provider only plays a passive role in the communication process and as such does not

[23] ibid paras 46–49.

[24] R Giblin and J Ginsburg, 'We (Still) Need to Talk About *Aereo*: New Controversies and Unresolved Questions After the Supreme Court's Decision' (2015) 38 *Colum JL & Arts* 109, 131–32.

[25] For more on cloud computing see A Cheung and R Weber (eds), *Privacy and Legal Issues in Cloud Computing* (Edward Elgar Publishing Ltd, 2015).

[26] The issue of time shifting has troubled courts in various countries including: the US – *WNET and others v Aereo* (2013) 712 F 3d 676, *ABC v Aereo* (2014) 134 S Ct 2498, *Cartoon Network LP v CSC Holdings Inc* (2008) 536 F 3d 121 and *Fox Broadcasting Company Inc v Dish Network LLC* (2014) 747 F 3d 1060; Singapore – *RecordTV Pte Ltd v Mediacorp TV Singapore Pte Ltd* [2010] SGCA 43; and Australia – *Singtel Optus Pty Ltd v National Rugby League Investments Pty Ltd (No 2)* [2012] FCA 34 and *National Rugby League Investments Pty Ltd v Singtel Optus Pty Ltd* [2012] FCAFC 59. Courts have come up with a range of diverse approaches to 'resolve' the problem.

[27] This finding is similar to that in the analogue recording device cases concerning the right of reproduction. See *Sony Corporation of America v Universal City Studios Inc* (1984) 464 US 417 and *CBS Songs Ltd v Amstrad Consumer Electronics Plc* [1988] 2 WLR 1191.

actively initiate the making available of works. To hold otherwise would stem the growth of new communicative technologies.

X. Embedded Hyperlinks

Fact pattern – A website embeds a photograph from a third-party website onto its home page. The photograph was made freely available on the third-party website with the consent of the right holder.

Suggested finding – Applying the reformed right of communication to the public to this scenario, it should amount to communication to the public because the embedding of the work directly provides that work to the user. The user does not have to positively act to experience the work. Unlike simple and deep hyperlinks that redirect the user to the location where the work can be found, embedded hyperlinks bring the work to the user.[28] As such, there is a provision of the work. The act of embedding a work can be interpreted as a substitute for the original upload. Alternatively, from a practical standpoint, it can be interpreted as an act equivalent to cable retransmission or rebroadcasting because it is a subsequent use of the work that is dependent on the existence of the initial act of communication.

Given that acts of subsequent communication require authorisation where they are made by an 'organisation other than the original one', the act of embedding should be treated in a similar fashion. Thus, if the act of embedding was done by a third party, it should require authorisation. Furthermore, liability in this instance is justified because it ensures that the reformed right of communication to the public is not exhausted. Even though the work is freely available with consent, that consent only extends to the initial upload and does not cover subsequent reuses of the work. If this is not followed, the right holder will lose control over where his work is placed.[29]

XI. Direct to Download Hyperlinks

Fact pattern – A freely accessible website places a hyperlink on its home page; when it is clicked a music file is automatically downloaded. The music file is an unauthorised copy of a popular song.

Suggested finding – The application of the reformed right of communication to the public to this fact pattern should lead to a finding of infringement. This is because clicking the hyperlink leads to the file being downloaded which amounts

[28] Stanford Copyright and Fair Use, 'Connecting to Other Websites' <http://fairuse.stanford.edu/overview/website-permissions/linking/> accessed 4 March 2015.

[29] With this finding it will become important to discuss issues such as implied consent.

to a transmission of the work, given that the user directly obtains the work from the hyperlink. As such there is an actionable 'communication', given that the work is made available to the public.

XII. Circumventing Access Restrictions

Fact pattern – A user uploads some photographs to his personal cloud storage, which has no public access. A hacker gains access to the cloud storage and shares a hyperlink allowing third parties to gain access to the user's photographs.

Suggested finding – The act in question from this fact scenario amounts to a circumvention of technological protection measures. The act will likely lead to infringement of the rules implemented at the domestic level in accordance with Article 6(1) of the Information Society Directive. However, in terms of liability under the reformed right of communication to the public, the result should be that there is no infringement. This is because the hyperlink, although allowing access to what were originally protected works, does not transmit or provide the works and as such, does not amount to an act of 'communication'. The hyperlink in this sense is equivalent to a deep hyperlink, which also does not come within the concept of 'communication'. In this scenario liability should be established for circumventing the technological protection measure.

Alternative solution – The person who circumvents the access restrictions of the cloud storage to provide access to the protected works via hyperlink can be liable under the domestic laws on secondary liability. This is because the responsible party is facilitating or encouraging copyright infringement.

XIII. Conclusion

This chapter demonstrated how the reformed right of communication to the public should be applied. It illustrated how a normative approach to the right would produce different outcomes to that of the CJEU's decisions. The reformed right was also applied in three instances which have yet to be addressed at the EU level – embedded hyperlinks; direct to download hyperlinks; and acts circumventing access restrictions. Taken together, all the examples used in this chapter and the subsequent responses to them portray what the results of a more coherent, certain and proportionate right ought to be.

Conclusion

I. The Recommendations

This book proposed recommendations for the creation of a more coherent, certain and proportionate right of communication to the public under EU copyright law. Previous studies of this subject have not considered the impact of modern digital and communications technologies; nor have they dealt with the competing legal influences stemming from EU law and external copyright law frameworks. The review of CJEU rulings related to the communication to the public right clearly demonstrates that the right requires comprehensive reform. The proposals for reform include significant structural changes to the scope, application and enforcement of the EU communication to the public right.

The research conducted demonstrates that the reformed right must be compatible with the EU copyright law framework, inclusive of the considerations general to EU law. Consequently, any EU copyright provision must take into account, balance and reconcile the various competing pressures and interests present in the conceptualisation, enactment and application of the law. These considerations include: the internal market; fundamental rights; the general principles of EU law; obligations under the international copyright treaties; the domestic *droit d'auteur* and copyright traditions of the Member States; and the specific goals and requirements for EU copyright law designated in the *acquis communitaire*. Although these pressures and interests often conflict, they must be reconciled in order to produce an effective law that is certain and proportionate. In particular, the interests of right holders and users should be balanced alongside the EU's goal of furthering the internal market.

With those interests in mind, this book recommended the following changes to the existing EU communication to the public right:

- The broad interpretation of the communication to the public right should be abandoned in lieu of a more clearly defined right;
- The term 'communication' should be defined as any act of transmission or provision of a work. Provision requires direct contact with the work;
- The making available aspect should be clarified as a subset of the communication to the public right, relating solely to on demand transmissions;
- The act of reception in public should be excluded from the scope of the communication to the public right. Instead, it should be governed under a harmonised public performance right;

- The 'new public' criterion should be replaced by the 'organisation other than the original one' criterion to govern acts of subsequent communication;
- The 'for profit' criterion should be abandoned; and
- The 'knowledge' requirement should be disregarded.

In addition to remedying the specific problems relating to the scope of the communication to the public right, it is also necessary to reform the structure of the communication to the public right. Given that the communication to the public right is one of a number of harmonised exclusive rights, it is important to ensure that the reformed communication to the public right does not overlap or conflict with the other exclusive rights; namely, the reproduction and distribution rights. Given the increased prominence of the communication to the public right due to advancements in digital technology, the reproduction and distribution rights should be restricted, so that the reformed communication to the public right is the sole applicable right in cases of digital dissemination to a 'public'.

Furthermore, the reformed communication to the public right should be further harmonised through codification under the Information Society Directive in the short term. In the long term, EU copyright law should be codified under a copyright Regulation. This approach would bind all Member States to the wording of a single provision applicable to all forms of subject-matter without the need for transposition and implementation. As a result, the negative effects of divergent domestic laws and their interpretations would be mitigated. Such a provision must also clarify where an act subject to the reformed communication to the public right occurs and who is responsible for that act. The Completion theory states that the act of communication to the public occurs in the country(ies) of reception, because an act of communication to the public involves an act of transmission or provision of the work plus potential reception. The act is only completed in the country(ies) of actual or potential reception; therefore, that is the location where the act should be held to have occurred. Furthermore, the party who actively initiated the transmission or provision of the work should be responsible for the act of communication to the public, in order to protect passive intermediaries from liability.

Specific rules on jurisdiction and applicable law are also necessary in order to establish an effective means for the application and enforcement of the reformed right. In particular, the proposed provisions seek to address the existing EU jurisdiction rules' unnecessary reliance on the EU domicile of the defendant and the failure of the rules on jurisdiction and applicable law to take into account ubiquitous infringement and its impact across multiple Member States. Therefore, the EU-centric focus of the rules on jurisdiction is removed. While the general rule that the defendant may be sued in the Member State of his domicile is maintained, the special jurisdiction rule concerning where the infringement occurred does not have any requirement that the defendant be domiciled in the EU. Alternatively, the rules on both jurisdiction and applicable law are reformulated to account for ubiquitous infringement. Thus, the court with jurisdiction is capable of taking an EU-wide account of damage, provided the defendant substantially acted in that Member State. Similarly, the court seised has the ability to apply the single applicable law of the Member State where the defendant substantially acted if the infringement affects multiple Member States.

Thus, this book provides an original, holistic approach to reforming the communication to the public right under EU copyright law from its conception to its application and enforcement.

II. Implications

If accepted in part or whole, these proposals for a reformed communication to the public right would have significant implications for the existing case law of the CJEU and the *acquis communitaire* of EU copyright law. While the ultimate findings of liability established by the CJEU in employing the existing communication to the public right in prior cases may not all be overturned, the process by which those decisions were made will be radically changed. This is because key aspects of the communication to the public right have been modified; notably, defining the term 'communication' in terms of the transmission or provision of the work, the abandonment of the 'new public' criterion in lieu of the 'organisation other than the original one' criterion, and the removal of the 'knowledge' and 'for profit' criteria. Should the reformed right be adopted, the CJEU will be forced to establish a new line of case law for the application and enforcement of the communication to the public right.

In addition to the changes to the scope of the communication to the public right, the proposed rules on jurisdiction and applicable law will also have a significant impact on the way the communication to the public right is litigated. The ability of courts to take an EU-wide account of damage and the possibility of a single applicable law applying to multi-country infringements across the EU will affect where right holders bring infringement claims and consequently, how and where users can be sued. The proposed rules provide a more efficient approach to litigation, whereby ubiquitous acts can be addressed in one case rather than multiple cases across Member States. Furthermore, the proposed rules make it easier to establish jurisdiction in the EU and ensure that EU copyright law is applicable.

In looking at the reformed communication to the public right and the proposed rules on jurisdiction and applicable law cumulatively, the most significant changes to be expected will be in relation to the notorious hyperlinking and torrent file cases and acts of reception in public. In these cases, if the reformed communication to the public right is applied, the reasoning to be applied by the CJEU will be very different, as illustrated in Chapter eight. Furthermore, defendants will be subject to the proposed rules on jurisdiction and applicable law, which address ubiquitous acts that lead to multi-country infringements and which allow for an EU-wide account of damage.

Overall, it has been argued that the proposals made in this book will provide right holders with adequate protection to enforce their rights under EU copyright law. These rules also provide greater clarity and guidance to technology developers, businesses and users concerning what actions will be subject to liability, thus allowing them greater certainty in their exploits. Hence, the proposed rules will provide for a certain and proportionately balanced system.

III. Final Comments

The changes proposed in the book are ambitious, but not impossible. While these proposals may go against the current trends of the EU legislature and the CJEU, they are supported by serious academic inquiry. Therefore, any chance for the proposals made in this book to be adopted would require significant political will. Yet, the advantages of providing a coherent and effective right, striking a delicate balance between all the competing pressures and interests, would be far-reaching and worth the political efforts. It is, of course, understood that the reforms suggested in this book are not the end of the road for EU copyright law; more must be done. This book focused solely on primary liability under the reformed communication to the public right. As such, there are other areas of EU copyright law that require consideration. The most prominent areas requiring attention include:

- The implications of adopting the proposed Regulation on rules for certain online transmissions[1] and the proposed Directive on copyright in the Digital Single Market;[2]
- A more detailed appraisal and rebalancing of the existing exclusive rights;
- The introduction of an exclusive right of public performance;
- Introduction of harmonised rules on secondary liability;
- The pursuit of a codified copyright Regulation;
- The concept of implied licensing and the right of communication to the public; and

[1] European Commission, *Proposal for a Regulation of the European Parliament and of the Council laying down rules on the exercise of copyright and related rights applicable to certain online transmissions of broadcasting organisations and retransmissions of television and radio programmes* (COM(2016) 594 final, 2016).

[2] European Commission, *Proposal for a Directive of the European Parliament and of the Council on copyright in the Digital Single Market* (COM(2016) 593 final, 2016).

- An impact assessment on the relationship of the exclusive rights and contracting and licensing mechanisms.[3]

In moving forward with future reforms, one of the central arguments of this book should have a far-reaching impact – the future development of EU copyright law should take as its starting point the framework consisting of the constitutional pressures and copyright interests that influence EU copyright law. As demonstrated in this book using the example of the communication to the public right, the efficacy of EU copyright law is dependent on the law striking the right balance between the competing interests of right holders, users and the aims of the EU.

[3] See A Strowel, 'Towards a European Copyright Law: Four Issues to Consider' in I Stamatoudi and P Torremans (eds), *EU Copyright Law: A Commentary* (Edward Elgar Publishing Ltd, 2014) paras 21.30–21.48.

BIBLIOGRAPHY

Books

K Adams, *A Manual of Style for Contract Drafting*, 3rd edn (American Bar Association, 2013)

G Alexander and E Peñalver, *An Introduction to Property Theory* (Cambridge University Press, 2012)

C Angelopoulos, *European Intermediary Liability in Copyright: A Tort-Based Analysis* (Kluwer Law International BV, 2017)

T Aplin, *Copyright Law in the Digital Society* (Hart Publishing, 2005)

G Beck, *The Legal Reasoning of the Court of Justice of the EU* (Hart Publishing Ltd, 2012)

J Bengoetxea, *The legal reasoning of the European Court of Justice: towards a European jurisprudence* (Clarendon Press, 1993)

J Bentham, *An Introduction to the Principles of Morals and Legislation* (White Dog Publishing, 2010)

R Bird and S Jain (eds), *The Global Challenge of Intellectual Property Rights* (Edward Elgar Publishing Ltd, 2008)

S Bottomley and D Kinley (eds) *Commercial Law and Human Rights* (Ashgate Publishing Ltd, 2001)

B Bouckaert and G De Geest (eds), *Encyclopedia of Law and Economics Volume II* (Edward Elgar Publishing Ltd, 2000)

J Boyle, *Shamans, Software and Spleens* (Harvard University Press, 1996)

D Chalmers, G Davies and G Monti, *European Union Law*, 3rd edn (Cambridge University Press, 2014)

ASY Cheung and RH Weber (eds), *Privacy and Legal Issues in Cloud Computing* (Edward Elgar Publishing Ltd, 2015)

H Cohen Jehoram, P Keuchenius and J Seignette (eds), *Audiovisual media and copyright in Europe* (Kluwer, 1994)

T Cook and L Brazell, *Copyright Directive: UK Implementation* (Jordan Publishing Ltd, 2004)

P Craig and G de Búrca, *EU Law: Text Cases, and Materials*, 6th edn (Oxford University Press, 2015)

K Davies, *Understanding European Union Law*, 3rd edn (Routledge-Cavendish, 2007)

P Davies, *Accessory Liability* (Hart Publishing, 2015)

S Depreeuw, *The variable scope of the exclusive economic rights in copyright* (Kluwer Law International, 2014)

E Derclaye (ed), *Research Handbook on the Future of EU Copyright* (Edward Elgar Publishing Ltd, 2009)

G Dinwoodie, *Secondary Liability of Internet Service Providers* (Springer, 2017)

P Drahos, *A Philosophy of Intellectual Property* (Dartmouth Publishing Company, 1996)

T Dreier and PB Hugenholtz, *Concise European Copyright Law* (Kluwer Law International, 2006)

J Drexl and A Kur (eds), *Intellectual Property and Private International Law – Heading for the Future* (Hart Publishing, 2005)

Z Efroni, *Access Right: The Future of Digital Copyright Law* (Oxford University Press, 2011)

N Emiliou, *The principle of proportionality in European Law – a comparative study* (Kluwer Law International, 1996)

J Fawcett and P Torremans, *Intellectual Property and Private International Law*, 2nd edn (Oxford University Press, 2011)

M Ficsor, *Copyright in the Asia-Pacific Region: Reprography and digital Copying* (Australian Copyright Agency Limited, 1995) p 151, 'Digital Technology and Copyright'.

—— *The Law of Copyright and the Internet: The 1996 WIPO Treaties, their Interpretation and Implementation* (Oxford University Press, 2002)

R Frey (ed), *Utility and Rights* (Basil Blackwell Ltd, 1985)

C Geiger (ed), *Research Handbook on Human Rights and Intellectual Property* (Edward Elgar Publishing Ltd, 2015)

D Gervais, *(Re)structuring Copyright: A Comprehensive Path to International Copyright Reform* (Edward Elgar Publishing Ltd, 2017)

J Ginsburg and E Treppoz, *International Copyright Law: US and EU Perspectives* (Edward Elgar Publishing Ltd, 2015)

P Goldstein and PB Hugenholtz, *International Copyright: Principles, Law, and Practice*, 3rd edn (Oxford University Press, 2013)

A Gosseries, A Marcano and A Strowel (eds), *Intellectual Property and Theories of Justice* (Palgrave Macmillan, 2008)

X Groussot, *General Principles of Community Law* (Europa Law Publishing, 2006)

S Halpern and P Johnson, *Harmonising Copyright Law and Dealing with Dissonance* (Edward Elgar Publishing Ltd, 2014)

GWF Hegel, *Elements of the Philosophy of Right*, A Wood (ed) (Cambridge University Press, 2012)

H Howe and J Griffiths (eds), *Concepts of Property in Intellectual Property Law* (Cambridge University Press, 2013)

PB Hugenholtz (ed), *Copyright Reconstructed: Rethinking Copyright's Economic Rights in a Time of Highly Dynamic and Technological and Economic Change* (Kluwer Law International BV, 2018)

—— *The Future of Copyright in a Digital Environment* (Kluwer Law International, 1996)

O Kahn-Freund, *General problems of private international law* (Sijthoff, 1976)

S Leible and A Ohly (eds), *Intellectual Property and Private International Law* (Mohr Siebeck, 2009)

J Litman, *Digital Copyright* (Prometheus Books, 2001)

J Locke, *Two Treatises of Government*, Peter Laslett (ed) (Cambridge University Press, 2010)

A Lucas, *Traité de la Propriété Littéraire et Artistique* (Litec, 1994)

M Makeen, *Copyright in a Global Information Society: The Scope of Copyright Protection Under International, US, UK and French Law* (Kluwer Law International, 2000)

R Matulionyte, *Law Applicable to Copyright: A Comparison of the ALI and CLIP Proposals* (Edward Elgar Publishing Ltd, 2011)

G Mazziotti, *EU Digital Copyright Law and the End-User* (Springer, 2008)

J Mill, *Utilitarianism*, 7th edn (Longmans, Green and Co, 1879)

—— *Utilitarianism, On Liberty, Considerations On Representative Government*, G Williams (ed) (Everyman's Library, 1996)

S Munzer (ed), *New Essays in the Legal and Political Theory of Property* (Cambridge University Press, 2001)

R Nozick, *Anarchy, State and Utopia* (Basic Books Inc, 1974)

A Ohly and J Pila (eds), *The Europeanization of Intellectual Property Law* (Oxford University Press, 2013)

R Posner, *Economic Analysis of Law*, 9th edn (Wolters Kluwer Law & Business, 2014)

A Ramalho, *The Competence of the European Union in Copyright Lawmaking: A Normative Perspective of EU Powers for Copyright Harmonisation* (Springer International Publishing Switzerland, 2016)

A Rand (ed) *Capitalism: The Unknown Ideal* (Signet, 1967)

J Reinbothe and S von Lewinski, *The WIPO Treaties 1996: the WIPO Copyright Treaty and the WIPO Performances and Phonograms Treaty: commentary and legal analysis* (Butterworths LexisNexis, 2002)

J Riordan, *The Liability of Internet Intermediaries* (Oxford University Press, 2016)

E Rosati, *Originality in EU Copyright: Full Harmonization through Case Law* (Edward Elgar Publishing Ltd, 2013)

S Ricketson and J Ginsburg, *International Copyright and Neighbouring Rights: The Berne Convention and Beyond* (Oxford University Press, 2006)

S Shmanske, *Public Goods, Mixed Goods and Monopolistic Competition* (Texas A&M University Press, 1991)

JJC Smart and B Williams, *Utilitarianism: for and against* (Cambridge University Press, 1973)

I Stamatoudi (ed), *New Developments in EU and International Copyright Law* (Kluwer Law International, 2016)
I Stamatoudi and P Torremans (eds), *Copyright in the New Digital Environment: Volume 8: The Need to Redesign Copyright* (Sweet & Maxwell, 2000)
—— *EU Copyright Law: A Commentary* (Edward Elgar Publishing Ltd, 2014)
P Stone, *EU Private International Law*, 3rd edn (Edward Elgar Publishing Ltd, 2014)
P Stone and Y Farah (eds), *Research Handbook on EU Private International Law* (Edward Elgar Publishing Ltd, 2015)
A Strowel (ed), *Peer-to-Peer File Sharing and Secondary Liability in Copyright Law* (Edward Elgar Publishing Ltd, 2009)
B Svantesson, *Private International Law and the Internet*, 2nd edn (Kluwer Law International, 2007)
T Synodinou (ed), *Codification of European Copyright Law: Challenges and Perspectives* (Kluwer Law International, 2012)
P Torremans (ed), *Intellectual Property and Human Rights: Enhanced Edition of Copyright and Human Rights* (Kluwer Law International, 2008)
—— *Research Handbook on Copyright Law*, 2nd edn (Edward Elgar Publishing Ltd, 2017)
—— *Research Handbook on Cross-Border Enforcement of Intellectual Property* (Edward Elgar Publishing, 2014)
T Tridimas, *The General Principles of EU Law*, 2nd edn (Oxford University Press, 2006)
E Ulmer, *Intellectual Property Rights and the Conflict of Laws* (Kluwer Law, 1978)
M van Eechoud, *Choice of Law in Copyright and Related Rights* (Kluwer Law International, 2003)
M van Eechoud et al, *Harmonizing European Copyright Law: The Challenges of Better Law Making* (Kluwer Law International, 2009)
D Vaver and L Bently (eds), *Intellectual Property in the New Millennium, Essays in Honour of William R Cornish* (Cambridge University Press, 2004)
M Walter and S von Lewinski, *European Copyright Law: A Commentary* (Oxford University Press, 2010)
G Williams, *Joint torts and contributory negligence: A study of concurrent fault in Great Britain, Ireland and the common law dominions* (Stevens & Sons, 1951)

Contributions to Edited Books

D Attas, 'Lockean Justifications of Intellectual Property' in A Gosseries, A Marcano and A Strowel (eds), *Intellectual Property and Theories of Justice* (Palgrave Macmillan, 2008)
G Austin, 'Global networks and domestic laws: some private international law issues arising from Australian and US liability theories' in A Strowel (ed), *Peer-to-Peer File Sharing and Secondary Liability in Copyright Law* (Edward Elgar Publishing Ltd, 2009)
S Bechtold, 'Deconstructing Copyright' in PB Hugenholtz (ed), *Copyright Reconstructed: Rethinking Copyright's Economic Rights in a Time of Highly Dynamic and Technological and Economic Change* (Kluwer Law International BV, 2018)
F Beckstein, 'The American Law Institute Project on Intellectual Property: Principles Governing Jurisdiction, Choice of Law, and Judgments in Transnational Disputes' in S Leible and A Ohly (eds), *Intellectual Property and Private International Law* (Mohr Siebeck, 2009)
V Benabou, 'Digital Exhaustion of Copyright in the EU or Shall We Cease Being so Schizophrenic' in I Stamatoudi (ed), *New Developments in EU and International Copyright Law* (Kluwer Law International BV, 2016)
F Brison and S Depreeuw, 'The right of "communication to the public" in the European Union' in P Torremans (ed), *Research Handbook on Copyright Law*, 2nd edn (Edward Elgar Publishing Ltd, 2017)
DL Burk, 'The Market for Digital Piracy' in B Kahin and C Nesson (eds), *Cyberspace: Information Policy and the Global Information Infrastructure* (MIT Press, 1997)

R Burrell and E Hudson, 'Property Concepts in European Law: The Case for Abandonment' in H Howe and J Griffiths (eds), *Concepts of Property in Intellectual Property Law* (Cambridge University Press, 2013)

J Christoffersen, 'Human rights and balancing: The principle of proportionality' in C Geiger (ed), *Research Handbook on Human Rights and Intellectual Property* (Edward Elgar Publishing Ltd, 2015)

P de Miguel Asensio, 'The Private International Law of Intellectual Property and of Unfair Commercial Practices: Convergence of Divergence?' in S Leible and A Ohly (eds), *Intellectual Property and Private International Law* (Mohr Siebeck, 2009)

E Derclaye, 'Intellectual Property Rights and Human Rights: Coinciding and Cooperating' in P Torremans (ed), *Intellectual Property and Human Rights: Enhanced Edition of Copyright and Human Rights* (Kluwer Law International, 2008)

G Dimita, 'The WIPO right of making available' in P Torremans (ed), *Research Handbook on Copyright Law*, 2nd edn (Edward Elgar Publishing Ltd, 2017)

P Ducoulombier, 'Interaction between human rights: Are all human rights equal?' in C Geiger (ed), *Research Handbook on Human Rights and Intellectual Property* (Edward Elgar Publishing Ltd, 2015)

S Dusollier, 'Realigning Economic Rights with Exploitation of Works: The Control of Authors over the Circulation of Works in the Public Sphere' in PB Hugenholtz (ed), *Copyright Reconstructed: Rethinking Copyright's Economic Rights in a Time of Highly Dynamic Technological and Economic Change* (Kluwer Law International BV, 2018)

R Fentiman, 'Choice of Law and Intellectual Property' in J Drexl and A Kur (eds), *Intellectual Property and Private International Law – Heading for the Future* (Hart Publishing, 2005)

W Fisher, 'Theories of Intellectual Property' in S Munzer (ed), *New Essays in the Legal and Political Theory of Property* (Cambridge University Press, 2001)

C Geiger, 'Copyright's fundamental rights dimension at EU level' in E Derclaye (ed), *Research Handbook on the Future of EU Copyright* (Edward Elgar Publishing Ltd, 2009)

—— 'The Role of the court of Justice of the European Union: Harmonizing, Creating and sometimes Disrupting Copyright Law in the European Union' in I Stamatoudi (ed), *New Developments in EU and International Copyright Law* (Kluwer Law International, 2016)

P Geller, 'Conflicts of Law in the Cyberspace' in PB Hugenholtz (ed), *The Future of Copyright in a Digital Environment* (Kluwer Law International, 1996)

T Georgopoulos, 'The Legal Foundations of European Copyright Law' in T Synodinou (ed), *Codification of European Copyright Law: Challenges and Perspectives* (Kluwer Law International, 2012)

D Gervais, 'Intellectual Property and Human Rights: Learning to Live Together' in P Torremans (ed), *Intellectual Property and Human Rights: Enhanced Edition of Copyright and Human Rights*, 2nd edn (Kluwer Law International, 2008)

J Ginsburg, 'The (New?) Right of Making Available to the Public' in D Vaver and L Bently (eds), *Intellectual Property in the New Millennium, Essays in Honour of William R Cornish* (Cambridge University Press, 2004)

F Gotzen, 'The European Legislator's Strategy in the Field of Copyright Harmonization' in T Synodinou (ed), *Codification of European Copyright Law: Challenges and Perspectives* (Kluwer Law International, 2012)

R Hilty, 'Reflections on a European Copyright Codification' in T Synodinou (ed), *Codification of European Copyright Law: Challenges and Perspectives* (Kluwer Law International, 2012)

PB Hugenholtz, 'Adapting copyright to the information superhighway' in PB Hugenholtz (ed), *The Future of Copyright in a Digital Environment* (Kluwer Law International, 1996)

—— 'Is Harmonization a Good Thing? The case of the Copyright *Acquis*' in A Ohly and J Pila (eds), *The Europeanization of Intellectual Property Law* (Oxford University Press, 2013)

—— 'The Wittem Group's European Copyright Code' in T Synodinou (ed), *Codification of European Copyright Law: Challenges and Perspectives* (Kluwer Law International, 2012)

PB Hugenholtz and M Kretschmer, 'Reconstructing Rights: Project Synthesis and Recommendations' in PB Hugenholtz (ed), *Copyright Reconstructed: Rethinking Copyright's Economic Rights in a Time of Highly Dynamic and Technological and Economic Change* (Kluwer Law International BV, 2018)

P Jougleux, 'The Plurality of Legal Systems in Copyright Law: An Obstacle to a European Codification?' in T Synodinou (ed), *Codification of European Copyright Law: Challenges and Perspectives* (Kluwer Law International, 2012)

D Kallinikou, 'CJEU Policy and Practice in the Field of European Copyright Law' in T Synodinou (ed), *Codification of European Copyright Law: Challenges and Perspectives* (Kluwer Law International, 2012)

M Lehmann, 'Digitisation and Copyright Agreements' in I Stamatoudi and P Torremans (eds), *Copyright in the New Digital Environment: Volume 8: The Need to Redesign Copyright* (Sweet & Maxwell, 2000)

M Leistner, 'Common Principles of Secondary Liability' in A Ohly (ed), *Common Principles of European Intellectual Property Law* (Mohr Siebeck, 2012)

A Lucas-Schloetter, 'Is there a concept of European copyright law? History, evolution, policies and politics and the *acquis* communautaire' in I Stamatoudi and P Torremans (eds), *EU Copyright Law: A Commentary* (Edward Elgar Publishing Ltd, 2014)

—— 'The Acquis Communitaire in the Area of Copyright and Related Rights: Economic Rights' in T Synodinou (ed), *Codification of European Copyright Law: Challenges and Perspectives* (Kluwer Law International, 2012)

M Martin-Prat, 'An Introduction – The EU Copyright Agenda' in I Stamatoudi (ed), *New Developments in EU and International Copyright Law* (Kluwer Law International, 2016)

P Menell, 'Intellectual Property: General Theories' in B Bouckaert and G De Geest (eds), *Encyclopedia of Law and Economics Volume II* (Edward Elgar Publishing Ltd, 2000)

A Metzger, 'Jurisdiction in Cases Concerning Intellectual Property Infringements on the Internet' in S Leible and A Ohly (eds), *Intellectual Property and Private International Law* (Mohr Siebeck, 2009)

S Neumann, 'Ubiquitous and Multistate Cases in P Torremans (ed), *Research Handbook on Cross-Border Enforcement of Intellectual Property* (Edward Elgar Publishing, 2014)

A Ohly, 'A Fairness-Based Approach to Economic Rights' in PB Hugenholtz (ed), *Copyright Reconstructed: Rethinking Copyright's Economic Rights in a Time of Highly Dynamic and Technological and Economic Change* (Kluwer Law International BV, 2018)

—— 'Choice of Law in the Digital Environment – Problems and Possible Solutions' in J Drexl and A Kur (eds), *Intellectual Property and Private International Law – Heading for the Future* (Hart Publishing, 2005)

—— 'Economic rights' in E Derclaye (ed), *Research Handbook on the Future of EU Copyright* (Edward Elgar Publishing Ltd, 2009)

L Oswald, 'Secondary Liability for Intellectual Property Law Infringement in the International Arena: Framing the Dialogue' in R Bird and S Jain (eds), *The Global Challenge of Intellectual Property Rights* (Edward Elgar Publishing Ltd, 2008)

C Otero Garcia-Castrillion, 'Choice of law in IP: Rounding off territoriality' in P Torremans (ed), *Research Handbook on Cross-border Enforcement of Intellectual Property* (Edward Elgar Publishing Ltd, 2014)

J Poort, 'Borderlines of Copyright Protection: An Economic Analysis' in PB Hugenholtz (ed), *Copyright Reconstructed: Rethinking Copyright's Economic Rights in a Time of Highly Dynamic and Technological and Economic Change* (Kluwer Law International BV, 2018)

A Rand, 'Patents and Copyrights' in A Rand (ed) *Capitalism: The Unknown Ideal* (Signet, 1967)

S Ricketson, 'Intellectual Property and Human Rights' in S Bottomley and D Kinley (eds), *Commercial Law and Human Rights* (Ashgate Publishing Ltd, 2001)

J Rosén, 'How Much Communication to the Public is "Communication to the Public"?' in I Stamatoudi (ed), *New Developments in EU and International Copyright Law* (Kluwer Law International BV, 2016)

W Rumphorst, 'The EC Directive on satellite broadcasting and cable retransmission' in H Cohen Jehoram, P Keuchenius and J Seignette (eds), *Audiovisual media and copyright in Europe* (Kluwer, 1994)

S Shiffrin, 'Lockean Arguments for Private Property' in S Munzer (ed), *New Essays in the Legal and Political Theory of Property* (Cambridge University Press, 2001)

E Stavang, 'Some Thoughts on Economic Reasoning in Appellate Courts and Legal Scholarship' in K Mathis (ed), *Law and economics in Europe: foundations and applications* (Springer, 2013)

A Strowel, 'Reconstructing the Reproduction and Communication to the Public Rights: How to Align Copyright with Its Fundamentals' in PB Hugenholtz (ed), *Copyright Reconstructed: Rethinking Copyright's Economic Rights in a Time of Highly Dynamic and Technological and Economic Change* (Kluwer Law International BV, 2018)

—— 'Towards a European Copyright Law: Four Issues to Consider' in I Stamatoudi and P Torremans (eds), *EU Copyright Law: A Commentary* (Edward Elgar Publishing Ltd, 2014)

P Torremans, 'Copyright jurisdiction under EU private international law' in P Torremans (ed), *Research Handbook on Copyright Law*, 2nd edn (Edward Elgar Publishing Ltd, 2017)

—— 'Private International Law Issues on the Internet' in I Stamatoudi (ed), *New Developments in EU and International Copyright Law* (Kluwer Law International BV, 2016)

—— 'When the Court of Justice of the European Union sets about defining exclusive rights: copyright *quo vadis*?' in P Torremans (ed), *Research Handbook on Copyright Law*, 2nd edn (Edward Elgar Publishing Ltd, 2017)

E Treppoz, 'Does size matter? A comparative study of jurisdictional rules applicable to domestic and Community IP rights' in P Stone and Y Farah (eds), *Research Handbook on EU Private International Law* (Edward Elgar Publishing Ltd, 2015)

M van Eechoud, 'Alternatives to the *lex protectionis* as the Choice-of-Law Rule for Initial Ownership of Copyright' in J Drexl and A Kur (eds), *Intellectual Property and Private International Law – Heading for the Future* (Hart Publishing, 2005)

Articles

O Afori, 'Proportionality: a new mega standard in European copyright law' (2014) 45(8) *IIC* 889

C Angelopoulos, 'Beyond the safe harbours: harmonizing substantive intermediary liability for copyright infringement in Europe' [2013] *IPQ* 253

T Aplin, '"Reproduction" and "Communication to the Public" Rights in EU Copyright Law: *FAPL v QC Leisure*' (2011) 22(2) *KLJ* 209

E Arezzo, 'Hyperlinks and making available right in the European Union: What future for the Internet after *Svensson*?' (2014) 45(5) *IIC* 524

R Arnold, 'Cross-border enforcement: the latest chapter' [1999] *IPQ* 389

A Baker, 'EU Copyright Directive: can a hyperlink be a "communication to the public"?' (2014) *Computer and Telecommunications Law Review* 100

S Barazza, 'Secondary liability for IP infringement: converging patterns and approaches in comparative case law' (2012) 7(12) *JIPLP* 879

K Bonacorsi, 'Not at Home with "At-Home" Jurisdiction' (2014) 37(6) *Fordham International Law Journal* 1821

D Brennan, 'Fair price and public goods: a theory of value applied to retransmission' (2002) 22 *International Review of Law and Economics* 347

M Burnstein, 'Conflicts on the Net: Choice of Law in Transnational Cyberspace' (1996) 29 *Vand J Transnat'l L* 75

B Clark and J Dickenson, 'Theseus and the labyrinth? An overview of "communication to the public" under EU copyright law: after Reha Training and GS Media: Where are we now and where do we go from here?' (2017) 39(5) *EIPR* 265

B Coene, 'What about the mirrored glass disco ball? Delimiting the right of communication to the public in copyright and related rights' (2014) 18/2014 ICRI Working Paper Series

H Cohen Jehoram, 'European copyright law ever more horizontal' (2001) 32(5) *IIC* 532

JP Conley and CS Yoo, 'Nonrivalry and Price Discrimination in Copyright Economics' (2009) 157 *U Pa L Rev* 1801

J Cornides, 'Human Rights and Intellectual Property: Conflict or Convergence?' (2004) 7(2) *Journal of World Intellectual Property* 135

P Davies, 'Accessory liability for assisting torts' (2011) 70(2) *CLJ* 353

—— 'Accessory liability: protecting intellectual property rights' [2011] *IPQ* 390

N de Boer, L Dijkman and S van Kampen, 'The Changing Role of Principles in the European Multilayered Legal Order: Conference Report of the Symposium "Principles and the Law", Utrecht University, 25 May 2011' (2012) 20(2) *European Review of Private Law* 425

S de Vries, 'Balancing Fundamental Rights with Economic Freedoms According to the European Court of Justice' (2013) 9(1) *Utrecht Law Review* 169

E Derclaye, 'Infopaq International A/S v Danske Dagblades Forening (C-5/08): wonderful or worrisome? The impact of the ECJ ruling in Infopaq on UK copyright law' (2010) *EIPR* 247

—— 'The Court of Justice copyright case law: quo vadis?' (2014) 36(11) *EIPR* 716

E Derclaye and T Cook, 'An EU Copyright Code: what and how, if ever? [2011] 3 *IPQ* 259

H Desbois and A Francon, 'Copyright and the Dissemination by Wire of Radio and Television Programmes' (1975) 86 *RIDA* 3

F Dessemontet, 'A European Point of View on the ALI Principles – Intellectual Property: Principles Governing Jurisdiction, Choice of Law, and Judgments in Transnational Disputes' (2005) 30(3) *Brook J Int'l L* 849

—— 'Conflict of Law for Intellectual Property in Cyberspace' (2001) 18(5) *Journal of International Arbitration* 487

W Dibble, 'Justifying intellectual property' (1994) *UCL Juris Rev* 74

G Dimita, 'Six characters in search of infringement: potential liability for creating, downloading, and disseminating .torrent files' (2012) 7(6) *JIPLP* 466

G Dinwoodie, 'Developing a Private International Intellectual Property Law: The Demise of Territoriality?' (2010) 51 *Wm & Mary L Rev* 711

G Dinwoodie, R Dreyfuss and A Kur, 'The Law Applicable to Secondary Liability in Intellectual Property Cases' (2010) 42 *NYU J Int'l & Pol* 201

R Dittrich, 'On the interpretation of Article 11bis(1) and (2) of the Berne Convention' (1982) 18 *Copyright* 294

A Dorfman and A Jacob, 'Copyright as Tort' (2011) 12 *Theoretical Inq L* 59

R Dreyfuss, 'The ALI Principles on Transnational Intellectual Property Disputes: Why Invite Conflicts?' (2005) 30(3) *Brook J Int'l L* 819

R Dreyfuss and J Ginsburg, 'Draft Convention on Jurisdiction and Recognition of Judgments in Intellectual Property Matters' (2002) 77 *Chi-Kent L Rev* 1065

M du Bois, 'Justificatory Theories for Intellectual Property Viewed through the Constitutional Prism' (2018) 21 *PELJ/PER* 1

S Dusollier, 'Technology as an imperative for regulating copyright: from the public exploitation to the private use of the work' (2005) 27 *EIPR* 201

M Favale, M Kretschmer and P Torremans, 'Is there an EU Copyright Jurisprudence? An Empirical Analysis of the Workings of the European Court of Justice' (2016) 79(1) *MLR* 31

M Ficsor, 'Direct Broadcasting by Satellite and the Bogsch Theory' (1990) 18 *Int'l Bus Law* 258

—— '*Svensson* and the CJEU's "new public" theory: what the EU may learn from the US to avoid judicisal lapse' (23rd Annual Fordham Intellectual Property Law & Policy Conference, 2015)

—— '*Svensson*: honest attempt at establishing due balance concerning the use of hyperlinks – spoiled by the erroneous "new public" theory' (2018) available at <http://www.copyrightseesaw.net/en/papers?page=3> accessed 8 August 2018

B Friedman, 'From Deontology To Dialogue: The Cultural Consequences Of Copyright' (1995) 13 *Cardozo Arts & Ent LJ* 157

U Furgal, 'Ancillary right for press publishers: an alternative answer to the linking conundrum?' (2018) 13(9) *JIPLP* 700

D Gaudel, 'Teledistribution' (1974) 81 *RIDA* 119

P Gaudrat, 'Protection of the Author in Relation to a Retransmission by Satellite of his Work' (1980) 104 *RIDA* 2

C Geiger, '"Constitutionalising" intellectual property law? The influence of fundamental rights on intellectual property in the European Union' (2006) 37(4) *IIC* 371

—— 'Fundamental rights, a safeguard for the coherence of intellectual property law?' (2004) 35(3) *IIC* 268

—— 'Intellectual property shall be protected!? Article 17(2) of the Charter of Fundamental Rights of the European Union: a mysterious provision with an unclear scope' (2009) 31(3) *EIPR* 113

P Geller, 'Conflicts of Laws in Cyberspace: Rethinking International Copyright' (1997) 44 *J Copyright Soc'y USA* 103

R Giblin and J Ginsburg, 'We (Still) Need to Talk About *Aereo*: New Controversies and Unresolved Questions After the Supreme Court's Decision' (2015) 38 *Colum JL & Arts* 109

J Ginsburg, 'Can Copyright Become User-Friendly? Review: Jessica Litman, Digital Copyright (2001)' (2002) 25 *Colum JL & Arts* 71

—— 'Copyright Without Borders? Choice of Forum and Choice of Law for Copyright Infringement in Cyberspace' (1997) 15 *Cardozo Arts & Ent LJ* 153

—— 'Essay: From Having Copies to Experiencing Works: The Development of an Access Right in US Copyright Law' (2003) 50 *J Copyright Soc'y USA* 113

—— 'Global Use/Territorial Rights: Private International Law Questions of the Global Information Infrastructure' (1995) 42 *J Copyright Soc'y USA* 318

—— 'Hyperlinking and "making available"' (2014) 36(3) *EIPR* 147

—— 'The Court of Justice of the European Union Creates an EU Law of Liability for Facilitation of Copyright Infringement: Observations on *Brein v Filmspeler* [C-527/15] (2017) and *Brein v Ziggo* [C-610/15] (2017)' (2017) 2 <https://papers.ssrn.com/sol3/papers.cfm?abstract_id=3024302> accessed 3 August 2018

G Glisson, 'A Practitioner's Defense of the White Paper' (1996) 75 *Or L Rev* 277

P Goold, 'Is Copyright Infringement a Strict Liability Tort?' (2014) 30(1) *Berkeley Technology Law Journal* 306

W Gordon, 'Of Harms and Benefits: Tort, Restitution and Intellectual Property' (2003) 34 *McGeorge L Rev* 541

F Gotzen, 'Cable television and copyright in Belgium: A study of the Belgian law in relation to the Berne Convention and the Treaty of Rome' (1982) 18 *Copyright* 307

J Griffin, 'Copyright evolution – creation, regulation and the decline of substantively rational copyright law' [2013] *IPQ* 234

J Griffiths, 'Constitutionalising or harmonizing? The Court of Justice, the right to property and European copyright law' (2013) *EL Rev* 65

—— 'Copyright law after *Ashdown* – time to deal fairly with the public' [2002] 3 *IPQ* 240

M Hart, 'The Copyright in the Information Society Directive: an overview' (2002) 24 *EIPR* 58

V Hazan, 'The body other than the original broadcaster in cable transmissions' (1984) 20 *Copyright* 228

JG Head, 'Public Goods and Public Policy' (1962) 17 *Public Finance* 197

T Heide, 'Copyright in the EU and US: What "Access-Right"?' (2001) 48 *J Copyright Soc'y USA* 363

L Helfer, 'Human Rights and Intellectual Property: Conflict or Coexistence' (2003) 5 *Minn Intell Prop Rev* 47

—— 'The New Innovation Frontier? Intellectual Property and the European Court of Human Rights' (2008) 49 *Harvard Int'l LJ* 1

—— 'Toward a Human Rights Framework for Intellectual Property' (2007) 40 *UC Davis L Rev* 971

S Hetcher, 'The Immortality of Strict Liability in Copyright' (2013) 17(1) *Marquette Intellectual Property Law Review* 1

E Hettinger, 'Justifying Intellectual Property' (1989) 18 *Philosophy & Public Affairs* 31

R Hilty, 'Copyright in the internal market' (2004) *IIC* 760

PB Hugenholtz, 'Harmonisation or Unification of European Union Copyright Law' (2012) 38(1) *Monash University Law Review* 4

PB Hugenholtz and S Van Velze, 'Communication to a new public? Three reasons why EU copyright law can do without a "new public"' (2016) 47(7) *IIC* 797

J Hughes, 'The Philosophy of Intellectual Property' (1989) 77 *Geo LJ* 287

R Hurt and R Schuchman, 'The Economic Rationale of Copyright' (1966) 56 *The American Economic Review* 421
S James, 'And breathe… you can continue browsing the Internet, as the CJEU hands down its decision in PRCA v NLA (Meltwater)' (2014) CTLR 169
J Jans, 'Proportionality Revisited' (2000) 27(3) Legal Issues of Economic Integration 239
P Jurčys, 'International Jurisdiction in Intellectual Property Disputes' (2012) 3(3) *JIPITEC* 174
B Jütte, 'The beginning of a (happy?) relationship: copyright and freedom of expression in Europe' (2016) 38(1) *EIPR* 11
G Karnell, 'The Berne Convention between authors' rights and copyright economics – an international dilemma' (1995) 26(2) *IIC* 193
K Koelman, 'Copyright law and economics in the EU Copyright Directive: is the droit d'auteur passe?' (2004) 35(6) *IIC* 603
T Koji, 'Emerging Hierarchy in International Human Rights and Beyond: From the Perspective of Non-derogable Rights' (2001) 12(5) *EJIL* 917
G Koumantos, 'Private International Law and the Berne Convention' (1988) 24 *Copyright* 415
M Kretschmer, 'Digital copyright: the end of an era' (2003) 25 *EIPR* 333
A Kur, 'Secondary Liability for Trademark Infringement on the Internet: The Situation in Germany and Throughout the EU' (2014) 37 *Colum JL & Arts* 525
L Lacey, 'Of Bread and Roses and Copyrights' (1989) *Duke LJ* 1532
M Landeau, 'Has the Digital Millennium Copyright Act Really Created a New Exclusive Right of Access?: Attempting to Reach a Balance Between Users' and Content Providers' Rights' (2002) 49 *J Copyright Soc'y USA* 277
M Landes and R Posner, 'An Economic Analysis of Copyright Law' (1989) 18 *J Legal Stud* 325
M Leistner, 'Closing the Book on the Hyperlinks: Brief Outline of the CJEU's Case Law and Proposal for European Legislative Reform' (2017) 39(6) *EIPR* 327
—— 'Copyright law on the internet in need of reform: hyperlinks, online platforms and aggregators' (2017) 12(2) *JIPLP* 136
—— 'Structural aspects of secondary (provider) liability in Europe' (2014) 9(1) *JIPLP* 75
M Lemley, 'Dealing with Overlapping Copyrights on the Internet' (1997) 22 *U Daytona L Rev* 548
P Letai, 'Don't think twice, it's all right: toward a new copyright protection system' (2014) 5(7) *Journal of Business Economics* 1012
C Lim Saw, 'Linking on the internet and copyright liability: a clarion call for doctrinal clarity and legal certainty' (2018) 49(5) *IIC* 536
F Lima and P Akester, 'The economic dimension of the digital challenge: a copyright perspective' [2005] 1 *IPQ* 69
J Litman, 'The Exclusive Right to Read' (1995) 13 *Cardozo Arts & Ent LJ* 29
A Lucas, 'Applicable Law in Copyright Infringement Cases in the Digital Environment' (2005) *e-Copyright Bulletin* 1
G Lunney Jr, 'Reexamining Copyright's Incentives-Access Paradigm' (1996) 49 *Vand L Rev* 483
E Mackaay, 'Economic Incentives in Markets for Information and Innovation' (1990) 13 *Harv JL & Pub Pol'y* 867
M Makeen, 'The Controversy of Simultaneous Cable Retransmission to Hotel Rooms Under International and European Copyright Laws' (2010) 57 *J Copyright Soc'y USA* 59
—— 'Rationalising performance "in public" under UK copyright law' [2016] *IPQ* 117
—— 'The Controversy of Simultaneous Cable Retransmission to Hotel Rooms Under International and European Copyright Laws' (2010) 57 *J Copyright Soc'y USA* 59
R Matulionyte, 'Enforcing Copyright Infringements Online: In Search of Balanced Private International Law Rules' (2015) 6 *JIPITEC* 132
—— 'The Law Applicable to Online Copyright Infringements in the ALI and CLIP Proposals: A Rebalance of Interests Needed?' (2011) 2 *JIPITEC* 26
P McBride, 'The "new public" criterion after Svensson: the (ir)relevance of website terms and conditions' [2017] 3 *IPQ* 262

P Mezei, 'Enter the matrix: the effects of CJEU case law on linking and streaming technologies' (2016) 11(10) *JIPLP* 778

L Midelieva, 'Rethinking hyperlinking: addressing hyperlinks to unauthorized content in copyright law and policy' (2017) 39(8) *EIPR* 479

P Morvan, 'What's a Principle?' (2012) 20(2) *European Review of Private Law* 313

P Mysoor, 'Exhaustion, non-exhaustion and implied licence' (2018) 49(6) *IIC* 656

—— 'Unpacking the right of communication to the public: a closer look at the international and EU copyright law' [2013] *IPQ* 166

S Neumann, 'Intellectual Property Rights Infringements in European Private International Law: Meeting the Requirements of Territoriality and Private International Law' (2011) 7(3) *Journal of Private International Law* 583

JB Nordemann, 'Internet Copyright Infringement: Remedies Against Intermediaries – The European Perspective on Host and Access Providers' (2012) 59 *J Copyright Soc'y USA* 773

—— 'Liability for Copyright Infringements on the Internet: Host Providers (Content Providers) – The German Approach' (2011) 2 *JIPITEC* 37

—— 'Recent CJEU case law on communication to the public and its application in Germany: A new EU concept of liability' (2018) 13(9) *JIPLP* 744

A Ohly, 'The broad concept of "communication to the public" in recent CJEU judgements and the liability of intermediaries: primary, secondary or unitary liability' (2018) 13(8) *JIPLP* 664

S Olswang, 'Accessright: an evolutionary path for copyright into the digital era?' (1995) 17 *EIPR* 215

T Palmer, 'Are Patents and Copyrights Morally Justified? The Philosophy of Property Rights and Ideal Objects' (1990) 13 *Harv JL & Pub Pol'y* 817

M Peguera, 'Hyperlinking under the lens of the revamped right of communication to the public' (2018) 34(5) *Computer Law & Security Review* 1099

K Perset, 'The Economic and Social Role of Internet Intermediaries' (OECD Study, DSTI/ICCP (2009)9/Final)

A Peukert, 'Intellectual property as an end in itself' (2011) 33 *EIPR* 67

—— 'The coexistence of trade mark laws and rights on the Internet, and the impact of geolocation technologies' (2016) 47(1) *IIC* 60

S Plenter, 'Choice of law rules for copyright infringements in the global information infrastructure: a never-ending story?' (2001) 23(7) *EIPR* 313

O Pollicino, 'Legal Reasoning of the Court of Justice in the Context of the Principle of Equality Between Judicial Activism and Self-restraint' (2004) 5(3) *German Law Journal* 283

J Quintais, 'Untangling the hyperlinking web: In search of the online right of communication to the public' (2018) *J World Intellect Prop* 1 [advanced access]

JP Quintais and T Rendas, 'EU copyright law and the Cloud: *VCAST* and the intersection of private copying and communication to the public' (2018) 13(9) *JIPLP* 711

M Radin, 'Property and Personhood' (1982) 34 *Stan L Rev* 957

G Raemello and F Silva, 'New Directions in Copyright Law and Economics' (2007) 3(3) *Rev L & Econ* 643

A Rahmatian, 'Originality in UK copyright law: the old "skill and labour" doctrine under pressure' (2013) 44(1) *IIC* 4

A Ramalho, 'Copyright law-making in the EU: what lies under the 'internal market' mask?' (2014) 9(3) *JIPLP* 208

W Reese, 'Dépeçage: A Common Phenomenon in Choice of Law' (1973) 73(1) *Colum L Rev* 58

J Reinbothe, 'The new WIPO treaties: a first resume' (1997) *EIPR* 171

A Reindl, 'Choosing Law in Cyberspace: Copyright Conflicts on Global Networks' (1998) 19 *Mich J Int'l L* 799

T Rendas, 'Copyright, technology and the CJEU: an empirical study' (2018) 49(2) *IIC* 153

D Reznik, 'A Pluralistic Account of Intellectual Property' (2003) 46(4) *Journal of Business Ethics* 319

F Rizzuto, 'The European Union law concept of communication to the public and the protection of copyright in electronic transmissions' (2012) *Computer and Telecommunications Law Review* 179

E Rosati, '*GS Media* and its Implications for the Construction of the Right of Communication to the Public within EU Copyright Architecture' (2017) 54(4) *CMLR* 1221

—— 'The CJEU Pirate Bay Judgment and its Impact on the Liability of Online Platforms' (2017) 39(12) *EIPR* 737

—— 'Towards an EU-wide copyright? (Judicial) pride and (legislative) prejudice' [2013] *IPQ* 47

A Ross and C Livingstone, 'Communication to the public: Part 1' (2012) *Entertainment Law Review* 169

—— 'Communication to the public: Part 2' (2012) *Entertainment Law Review* 209

W Rumphorst, 'Broadcasting of Films Via Satellite' (1990) 4 *EBU Review* 34

—— 'Cable distribution of broadcasts' (1983) 19 *Copyright* 301

P Samuelson, 'Aspects of Public Expenditure Theories' (1958) 40 *Rev Econ & Stat* 332

—— 'Should Economics Play a Role in Copyright Law and Policy?' (2004) 1 *U Ottawa L & Tech J* 1

—— 'The Pure Theory of Public Expenditure' (1954) 36 *Rev Econ & Stat* 387

P Savola, 'EU Copyright Liability for Internet Linking' (2017) 8 *JIPITEC* 139

—— 'The ultimate copyright shopping opportunity – jurisdiction and choice of law in website blocking injunctions' (2014) 45(3) *IIC* 287

P Schonning, 'Applicable Law in Transfrontier On-Line Transmissions' (1996) 170 *RIDA* 21

J Schroeder, 'Unnatural Rights: Hegel and Intellectual Property' (2006) 60 *U Miami L Rev* 453

C Semmelmann, 'General Principles of EU Law: The Ghost in the Platonic Heaven in Need of Conceptual Clarificaton' (2013) 2 *Pittsburgh Papers on the European Union* 1

H Sidgwick, 'Utilitarianism' (2000) 12 *Utilitas* 253

C Sieburgh, 'Principles in Private Law: From Luxury to Necessity – Multi-Layered Legal Systems and the Generative Force of Principles' (2012) 20(2) *European Review of Private Law* 295

J Smith and H Newton, 'Hyperlinking to material on the internet: the CJEU expands on the circumstances when it may amount to copyright infringement' (2016) 38(12) *EIPR* 768

H Spector, 'An outline of a theory justifying intellectual and industrial property rights' (1989) 11(8) *EIPR* 270

S Sterk, 'Rhetoric and Reality in Copyright Law' (1996) 94 *Mich L Rev* 1197

A Stojkov, G Naumovski and V Naumovski, 'Economics of Copyright: Challenges and Perspectives' (2013) 7(1) *Mizan Law Review* 126

A Strowel and N Ide, 'Liability with Regard to Hyperlinks' (2001) 24 *Colum VLA JL & Arts* 403

K Sykes, 'Towards a Public Justification of Copyright' (2003) 61 *U Toronto Fac L Rev* 1

T Synodinou, 'The lawful user and a balancing of interests in European copyright law' (2010) 41(7) *IIC* 819

CHY Tan, 'Technological "nudges" and copyright on social media sites' [2015] 1 *IPQ* 62

A Tsoutsanis, 'Why copyright and linking can tango' (2014) 9(6) *JIPLP* 495

R Van den Bergh, 'The role and social justification of copyright: a "law and economics" approach' [1998] *IPQ* 17

A Yen, 'Restoring the Natural Law: Copyright as Labor and Possession' (1990) 51 *Ohio St LJ* 517

CS Yoo, 'Copyright and Public Good Economics: A Misunderstood Relation' (2007) 155 *U Pa L Rev* 635

P Yu, 'Reconceptualizing Intellectual Property Interests in a Human Rights Framework' (2007) 40 *UC Davis L Rev* 1039

—— 'Ten Common Questions About Intellectual Property and Human Rights' (2007) 23 *Ga St U L Rev* 709

M Walter, 'Telediffusion and wired-distribution systems: Berne Convention and copyright legislation in Europe' (1974) 10 *Copyright* 302

G Westkamp, 'Transient Copying and Public Communications: The Creeping Evolution of Use and Access Rights in European Copyright Law' (2004) 36 *Geo Wash Int'l L Rev* 1057

Wittem Group, 'European Copyright Code' (2011) 33(2) *EIPR* 76

L Zemer, 'On the value of copyright theory' [2006] *IPQ* 55

Reports

ALAI, *Provisional Opinion of ALAI's Executive Committee On the Right of communication to the public; the Advocate General's Opinions in Filmspeler Case C-527/15 and Ziggo Case C-610/15* (2017)

ALAI, *Report and Opinion on the making available and communication to the public in the Internet environment – focus on linking techniques on the Internet* (2013)

ALAI, *Opinion Proposed to the Executive Committee and adopted at its meeting, 17 September 2014 on the criterion 'New Public', developed by the Court of Justice of the European Union (CJEU), put in the context of making available and communication to the public* (2014)

ALAI, *ALAI Report and Opinion on a Berne-compatible reconciliation of hyperlinking and the communication to the public right on the Internet* (2015)

American Law Institute, *Intellectual Property: Principles Governing Jurisdiction, Choice of Law, and Judgments in Transnational Disputes* (2008)

L Bently *et al*, 'Calls For Views: Modernising the European Copyright Framework' (2016)

European Copyright Society, 'Unification of copyright law' <http://www.ivir.nl/syscontent/pdfs/78.pdf>

European Copyright Society, *Opinion on The Reference to the CJEU in Case C-461/12 Svensson* (2013)

European Copyright Society, *General Opinion on the EU Copyright Reform Package* (2017) <https://europeancopyrightsociety.org/opinions/> accessed 6 August 2018

European Max Planck Group, *Principles on Conflict of Laws in Intellectual Property* (2011)

Institute for Information Law, *The Recasting of Copyright & Related Rights for the Knowledge Economy* (University of Amsterdam, 2006)

Institute for Information Law, *Study on the Implementation and Effect in Member States' Laws of Directive 2001/29/EC on the Harmonisation of Certain Aspects of Copyright and Related Rights in the Information Society* (University of Amsterdam, 2007)

Institute for Information Law, *Copyright and Electronic Document Delivery Services – Background document* (1993)

Legal Advisory Board (LAB), *Reply to the 1995 Green Paper on Copyright and Related Rights in the Information Society* (1995) <http://www.echo.lu/legal/en/ipr/reply/reply.html>

WIPO, *WIPO glossary of terms of the law of copyright and neighbouring rights* (1980)

WIPO, *Guide to the Copyright and Related Rights Treaties Administered by WIPO and Glossary of Copyright and Related Rights Terms* (2003)

Conference Papers

G Austin, 'Private International Law and Intellectual Property Rights: A Common Law Overview' at WIPO Forum on Private International Law and Intellectual Property (Geneva, 30 and 31 January 2001)

T Dreier, 'Copyright Digitized: Philosophical Impacts and Practical Implications for Information Exchange in Digital Networks' in WIPO Worldwide Symposium on the Impact of Digital Technology on Copyright and Neighbouring Rights (1993)

M Ficsor, 'Digital Technology and Copyright' in *Copyright in the Asia-Pacific Region: Reprography and digital Copying* (Australian Copyright Agency Limited, 1995)

M Ficsor, 'International Harmonization of Copyright and Neighboring Rights' in WIPO Worldwide Symposium on Copyright in the Global Information Infrastructure (1995)

Theses

P Hubkova, 'Economic Reasoning in the Court of Justice of the EU: A Study on the Use of Economics in Competition Case-Law' (LLM Thesis, European University Institute 2014)

Newspaper Articles

BBC, 'Illegal football streams are "dangerous", study says' (1 February 2016) <http://www.bbc.co.uk/news/technology-35434765> accessed 2 February 2016

Forbes, '"Game of Thrones" Sets Piracy World Record, But Does HBO Care?' at <http://www.forbes.com/sites/insertcoin/2014/04/15/game-of-thrones-sets-piracy-world-record-but-does-hbo-care/> accessed 12 March 2015

Websites

T Berners-Lee, 'Links and Law: Myths' (*Axioms of Web Architecture*, April 1997) <https://www.w3.org/DesignIssues/LinkMyths.html> accessed 1 August 2018

J Driver, 'The History of Utilitarianism', *The Stanford Encyclopedia of Philosophy*, E Zalta (ed) (Summer Edition, 2009) <http://plato.stanford.edu/archives/sum2009/entries/utilitarianism-history/> accessed 18 March 2014

'Applying EU law' <http://ec.europa.eu/info/law-making-process/applying-eu-law_en> accessed 10 August 2016

'Qualified majority voting and the ordinary legislative procedure' <http://eur-lex.europa.eu/legal-content/EN/TXT/?uri=URISERV:ai0015> accessed 10 August 2016

'Regulations, Directives and other acts' <https://europa.eu/european-union/law/legal-acts_en> accessed 10 August 2016

Stanford Copyright and Fair Use, 'Connecting to Other Websites' <http://fairuse.stanford.edu/overview/website-permissions/linking/> accessed 4 March 2015

INDEX